Modern Cruising Under Sail

Modern Cruising Under Sail

Don Dodds

The Lyons Press

Design by Joel Friedlander, Marin Bookworks

Printed in the United States of America

10 9 8 7 6 5 4 3 2 1

Library of Congress Cataloging-in-Publication Data

Dodds, Don.

      Modern cruising under sail / by Don Dodds.

               p.   cm.

      Includes index.

      ISBN 1-55821-626-X (pbk.)

      1. Sailing. 2. Sailboats. 3. Yachting. 4. Yachts. I. Title.

GV811.D63   1998

797.1'24—dc21   97-40749

                                                                  CIP

To

Susan, Margaret, Katie, Beryl, and Debby

CONTENTS

1

Introduction

This book—conceived as a natural outcome of my research into cruising—was intended to be published before I began bluewater cruising. Delays will be delays, however, and I didn't finish the book until I'd been cruising for three years.

A gracious soul could choose to look on this lack of discipline as fortuitous, for during our journey I became increasingly aware that most bluewater cruisers (including me) were unaware of and unprepared for the physical and emotional conditions that they encountered in their new lifestyle; in addition, many had left with the wrong equipment.

Those with the wrong equipment were victims of the technological explosion that hit cruising, as it has just about every sport. For example, I remember backpacking when there was no freeze-dried food and the Trapper Nelson packs weighed about 8 pounds empty. Then an influx of participants generated product improvements, so more people could participate, which generated a bigger market and still more improvements, and the process continues in a self-exciting cycle.

Cruising has reached a point in its development where changes in equipment are occurring rapidly. Books written even five years ago still extol the virtues of Trapper Nelson boats and equipment. But much of the modern equipment is far superior to that espoused by the old guard, and it allows a broader cross-section of the public to experience cruising.

Technology is advancing so rapidly that some of what is written in this book will be out-dated in a few years.

To prolong the usefulness of this book, then, I have tried to include enough technical background that you will understand the principles behind the equipment and so make satisfactory choices even as the market changes. One of the major premises of this book is that one size does not fit all. You are an individual whose boat should be tailored to fit your specific needs, not my needs or the needs of any other cruising-book author. Some of the convictions put forth in this book fly in the face of traditional beliefs. There is an old saying in the journalistic world: "If the truth conflicts with the legend, print the legend." I have endeavored to stay with the truth, regardless of the wisdom of that choice, both when dealing with equipment and with the mystique of cruising.

The lack of emotional preparedness I encountered among cruisers was almost epidemic. More surprising was that most of them had read considerable amounts of cruising literature. In my case that meant four or five monthly periodicals regularly, and several hundred books on sailing and cruising over a period of 20 years.

Figure 1.1   *Author Reflecting on Passage*

Reflecting while on passage—one of the few things you can do on passage—I realized that most of the books I had read on sailing and cruising were written to convince me that cruising is the ultimate lifestyle. Some of the authors were downright zealous in their presentation. I could recall only one article about someone who had quit cruising, and even that piece was not really critical of the cruising lifestyle. The people involved had simply grown tired of cruising. Further research showed a complete lack of any real opposing view; even a middle-of-the-road book with fair treatment pro and con was unavailable.

I had to wonder: What about the thousands of people who sail into the sunset on a long-awaited "dream passage" only to pitch it all when they reach the first port—sell the boat, maybe get a divorce, and figuratively buy a chicken ranch in Arizona? Where are their stories? Why did they quit?

There's no dark conspiracy here, I realized, only the workings of the marketplace. If cruising magazines published more negative articles, their readers and advertisers would have a fit. One prominent magazine, *Writers Market,* goes so far as to request only articles on the enjoyable aspects of cruising. And most marine books are produced by publishing houses specializing in boating subjects; they are not going to slap the hand that feeds them, either.

This has left a niche for a book that realistically presents the facts of cruising. A book that tells the dark as well as the bright side. Surprisingly, most cruisers I have met encouraged me to write about the negative aspects of cruising. So I have shifted the emphasis of this book to provide some of that missing information and partially fill the need for "the rest of the story."

Another major premise of this book is that the cruising lifestyle is not *the* lifestyle, nor even a very good lifestyle; it is *just* a lifestyle. Like any other, it has its good and bad parts. During the research stage of this project I was on occasion offended by the zealous approach of many authors. In fact, I blame zeal for many of the things that are wrong with the world today. If a zealot at all, I am a zealot for moderation, for the middle of the road, for both sides of the story—you could say a zealot against zealots. So with these windmills to tilt, infidels to scourge, fair maidens to rescue, and zealots to slay, fire was given to my pen, and motivation to my mission.

If this mission is accomplished, you will see all sides of cruising, and, more important, will make better decisions about it. This may reduce the number of boats for sale cheap in

Hawaii, and may reduce the sale of unwanted and unneeded cruising equipment as well. The industry will survive, however, and may become healthier for a little bright light shining in dark places.

The first of the dark places to explore might as well be the foundations on which I wrote this book: research of the presently available literature on cruising, oceanography, boat design, sailing, and related subjects, along with my own training and experience. The first three sections of this chapter will deal with the present state of boating literature, my qualifications and prejudices, and critical reading. The final section is on processing all the divergent data to make decisions.

The State of Present Boating Literature

An old joke in the mining business goes: Ask any two geologists the same question, and you will get two different answers. Well, if you ask two different cruising experts the same question, you will get three different answers. Further, the answers will be widely divergent and presented with equally strong conviction. I conclude from all this chaos and confusion that, first, there seems to be very little absolute truth in the science of boating; and, second, the people who write about boating are often closed minded, individualistic, and opinionated.

The science of boating is not really much of a science. Even though sailboats have been around for thousands of years, only recently has anyone begun to systematically gather data and develop defensible conclusions and rational design equations. These are steps in the right direction, but designing a boat using completely rational methods is still a long way in the future. Present design still relies on many rules of thumb, old folk tales, and the instincts of the designer.

This is fertile ground for confusion. Like the blind men describing the elephant, many boating experts have come in contact with only part of the creature. It is indeed difficult to see the whole of a subject as complex as boating. This volume tries to blend the opinions of different authors to form a useful picture of the entire elephant from the descriptions of its various parts.

Maybe because sailing small boats around the world attracts people who have strongly individualistic natures, books written by these people often exhibit opinionated and closed-minded points of view. Many authors have had extensive experience—but only on a few kinds of boats. Their conclusions, therefore, are based on insufficient data. That fact, of course, does not alter their zealous confidence in their beliefs.

In any event, it only seems fair to warn you that only a small amount of what is in this book is proven fact. Most is a consensus of opinions, at least as best I could interpret them. The remaining small percentage is my opinion. As much as I hate to admit it, I probably am as guilty of being opinionated and individualistic as any other author—but not, I hope, as closed minded. When I interject a personal opinion, I try to identify it as such.

To evaluate the opinions that you will encounter in your reading on cruising, you will need two things: a little knowledge about the authors and an ability to read critically.

About this Author

This book is based on my research and experience. The research was performed in the beginning by a curious neophyte, in much the way anyone new to sailing would approach the subject. Over the course of it, though, my knowledge and skills were increased by hands-on boating experience, and where applicable this experience was added to the general fund of knowledge contained in this book.

BASIC PHILOSOPHY

I believe in life. I believe you cannot have life without growth, and you cannot have growth without change. It follows that change is an important part of life. I have no quarrel with progress. The evil commonly laid at progress's door is not the fault of progress. I see the advancements of modern societies as basically positive. The science or art of boating, too, has advanced over the last 50 years, and many of these advances are important. Like changes in any other field, however, these advances are resisted by the traditionalist, who stubbornly believes that the old ways are best.

Tradition has its role, but it is not to stand in the way of progress. History is replete with doomsayers warning society to return to its old ways. Occasionally society listened. The last stopping of the wheels of progress was called the Dark Ages. Yes, history and tradition have a role: to learn from past mistakes.

PHILOSOPHY ON SAFETY

I believe that risk is an integral part of living and especially cruising. Did the pioneers require risk-free passage across the Plains? Did they buy ambush insurance?

More to the point, did Josh Slocum, author of *Sailing Around the World Alone,* have a bulletproof hull, radar, or even a life raft? No, J. Slocum relied on J. Slocum for his safety and accepted a lot of risk by today's standards.

Today, however, a growing number of people believe that life should be free of risk, that somehow such a risk-free life was decreed by God and guaranteed by the government. The result is a preoccupation with safety—a sort of safety overkill in the literature. Enormous anchors and chains designed for much larger boats are recommended for little cruising yachts. Hulls are made from ½-inch steel plate. Boats are equipped to the gunwales with life rafts, life vests, lifelines, safety harnesses, man-overboard poles, survival suits to prevent hypothermia, flares, dyes . . . the list is endless, and the truth is that there isn't an anchor Mother Nature can't drag or a boat she can't sink or otherwise destroy. And each of these safety items costs money, takes up valuable space on board, and imposes restrictions on the cruiser.

I have tried to point out multiple, overlapping, and unnecessary safety items—to eliminate the overkill wherever possible and so reduce the unnecessary costs and burdens to cruisers. I know this runs contrary to the current belief in the holiness of safety, but it is time for a voice to cry out, "Enough!" If you are going cruising, you had better be able to rely on yourself and accept some risk.

While it may be true that you can reduce some risks with very little cost, it is also true that eventually you'll get to the point where further reductions become extremely costly. The question is, which risks should you allow and which should you eliminate? Only risk analysis can bring rationality to selection of safety-related gear. This subject is complex and beyond the scope of my text, but risk analysis was used to form many of the conclusions in this book. If you're interested, you can find more information on the rudiments of risk analysis in the book *Analysis of Decisions under Uncertainty,* by Robert Schlaifer.

PHILOSOPHY ON HAPPINESS

I do not hold to the popular beliefs that dropping out and being laid back are prerequisites to happiness. Although many books equate cruising with the ultimate in dropping out and laying back, and although many cruising people have done just that, those are not the only reasons or even the best reasons for going cruising.

Happiness is a state of mind that can be found anywhere. Those who enjoy the rat race should do so with a clear conscience. Nothing is intrinsically wrong with progress, consumerism, and the like. There can be as much happiness in a good solution to a business problem or a Fourth of July picnic with the kids as there is in exotic ports of call.

I recall hearing a man exclaim over ham radio as he dropped anchor after sailing 4,000 miles to an atoll in the Pacific: "Now for the good life." Tropical islands are interesting, but I would not associate them with the good life. In fact, I have often wondered how they became known as paradise. The diet is limited, the climate is monotonous, recreational pursuits are minimal, and opportunity for growth, or opportunity for anything, is almost nonexistent. If your idea of having a good time is to do nothing, then a tropical island is your meat. I couldn't help wondering as I shut down the radio: If that man had needed to sail 4,000 miles to find the good life, would he find it there—and if not, would he find it anywhere?

EXPERIENCE

My sailing and cruising experience dates back to 1963. In that year I purchased a 17-foot sloop and learned to sail on the lakes of California and in San Francisco Bay. Then I bareboat chartered for 10 years, cruising in 12 different boats in the waters of Puget Sound and the Bahamas. I have chartered monohulls of light to heavy displacement, full and fin keels, sloops, cutters, and ketches for periods from two weeks to one month. Since 1987, I have cruised the North Pacific from the Kiribati Islands along the equator to Alaska in a light-displacement, modified-fin-keeled 43-foot cutter.

Finally, my professional background as an engineer and scientist has trained me in the scientific thought process. I believe that the scientific approach to understanding complex systems is essential. As a scientist I realize that in the physical world there is always more than one plausible answer for any given problem. To get the answer *closest* to the truth, *all* the variables must be identified and studied to determine how each is related to the problem and how each affects its outcome. In most cases the observed conditions can be produced by more than one plausible hypothesis. Although it is true that figures don't lie, it is also true that liars can figure.

Care needs to be taken to preserve scientific detachment, however, so that the facts are not forced to fit personal prejudices. This is not as easy to do as you would think; it is all too common to find an investigator with an ax to grind, manipulating facts to support a point of view. Most of the time the manipulation is an unconscious lack of vigilance rather than a malicious intent to defraud. If you catch me losing my scientific detachment, please count it as belonging in the former category. (There are those who would say I'm unconscious most of the time.) Read this book—or any nonfiction book, for that matter—in a critical manner.

Critical Reading

In many professional fields, all published literature is reviewed by peers and required to be defended or revised to include valid dissenting opinions. No such process is available for the popular press—including the boating press. More's the pity. The unsuspecting reader searching for simple truth is often led astray.

The only defense against such one-sided writing is critical reading, which can go a long way toward keeping you from pursuing too many wrong ideas. It is the simple process of asking the obvious questions that may have been skillfully ignored.

To illustrate this process, I have taken excerpts from *The Capable Cruiser*, written by Lin and Larry Pardey, on the reasons for some mishaps at Cabo San Lucas in December 1982.

> *The question of what to choose for an anchor rode in the ultimate conditions such as those found at Cabo San Lucas seemed to be answered with a single word by the people who survived that fateful night, chain.*

This is a strong statement leaving little room for doubt. Such statements should signal alert readers to look for a similarly strong proof statement. In my example, the authors' proof statement followed.

> *Over 20 sailboat owners complained that nylon anchor lines chafed through, yet in spite of initial reports to the contrary, not one anchor chain parted.*

This proof statement sounds strong but is actually weak. It does not answer the critical questions:

1. The authors lead you to believe that every sailboat with nylon line experienced chafe failure. How many sailboat owners had nylon lines that did not chafe through?

2. The authors let you infer that a chafed-through nylon line led to boat loss. However, a single chafed-through line does not necessarily lead to boat loss. How many of those complaining about chafing actually lost their boats?

3. The authors imply they are talking about bow anchors. How many of the lines that chafed through were stern anchor lines?

4. The authors lead you to believe that chafe is the only important criterion in rode selection. It is not. A rode without sufficient elasticity or a too-short rode can also cause the anchor system to fail by pulling the anchor out of the bottom or by destroying the bow roller, two common occurrences at Cabo San Lucas.

5. What about those initial reports (on chain) to the contrary?

The authors go on to say,

> One powerboater did break the chain on their Mexican-owned mooring but we were told this was poorly maintained and undersized.

Here they toss out evidence contrary to their own opinion by inferring that "Mexican-owned" is shoddy. A more scientific approach would have been to verify the size and quality of the chain in question and report these factually.

> Another boat owner told of losing the shackle that held his chain. On the other hand, chain presented special handling problems. On Wind Dancer, a Globe 46 ketch, there was no restraint on the bow roller, no way of securing the chain into its cathead on the windlass. At the height of the gale, Wind Dancer's chain leapt free and pulled the samson post right out of the deck. The boat was a total loss.

This speaks to the very failure that inelastic chain rode can cause in the shallow-water, short-scope conditions mentioned above. Yet the authors fail to consider that the use of chain may have led to the problem. How many boats were lost because of this kind of failure?

> The second problem with chain was getting rid of it when owners or skippers decided it was time to get out to sea. Since the boats were anchored so close together at the cape, most skippers who tried to leave found other boats were over their ground tackle. They then made the decision to leave their anchor and chain behind and come back to retrieve it when things were calmer. "You try cutting a damned piece of ⁵⁄₁₆-inch chain with a hacksaw when your boat is bucking like a wild horse and it's raining and dark as hell,"

one crewman told me when we were sitting at an outdoor cafe overlooking the wreckage-strewn beach.

Once again, how many boats were lost because they couldn't get rid of their chain quickly and sail free of the harbor? Would these two numbers equal the number of boat losses attributed to nylon rode and invalidate the claim made at the beginning of the section? Also, the authors do not point out the relative ease of cutting a nylon line in this situation. These questions indicate their relative lack of objectivity.

> *When I explained a trick we'd learned from a powerboater he headed back to his anchored boat saying, "I'll rig that right now." We rig a heavy length of nylon line as a safety release at the inboard end of our anchor chain. We secure it to a strong point inside the chain locker with two round turns and a half hitch so it can be released even if it is under pressure. When the time comes to get out quickly you can buoy the end of the chain then cut or untie the nylon safety line.*
>
> *We discussed this with Richard Spindler, editor of* Latitude 38, *a California yachting magazine, who'd come down to Cabo to rejoin his boat and accidentally found himself in the middle of a very important yachting story. When we compared notes he said, "Your solution's fine for getting rid of the chain quickly and it will work as a good snubber if there's room to let out all your chain. But here there just wasn't enough room. The lesson all this taught me is I'm going to carry two or three heavy-duty 30-foot nylon line snubbers just in case." The most successful way of attaching this line to your chain is to use a rolling hitch. To get the spring effect you need, let out ten feet of chain and ten feet of nylon line at the same time. Secure the line then let out another ten feet of chain to hang in a loop. Heavy vessels like* Elias Mann, *described in the previous chapter, may need several.*

These paragraphs on how the authors would have prevented the above occurrences from happening are at best supposition. Both solutions are rather involved and suspect. The authors point out that the editor of *Latitude 38* felt that the first solution may not have worked under the conditions at Cabo. It's always easy to be an armchair quarterback, but it is entirely probable that if the authors had been anchored at Cabo with this rode system, they would have lost their boat along with all the rest.

Finally, the authors could have written about protecting nylon anchor line from chafe, thereby solving the problems with nylon rode. Many of the methods for protecting nylon line from chafe are much simpler and more effective than the recommended system of using three heavy-duty 30-foot nylon snubbers to solve the problems generated by chain.

In conclusion, this book—although written by famous experts—is biased and, in many instances, without much basis in fact. Most is only the authors' opinion. Of course, they have a right to their opinion, and you may wish to take it because of their vast experience in cruising. However, if you wish to avoid following lemmings to the sea, develop your skills in critical reading. In any article, look for the lack of alternative solutions or alternative interpretations of the data that would indicate single-sided arguments. Look for incomplete data, such as not presenting facts that discount conclusions; look for lack of external references and other signs of half truths. None of these necessarily mean that the conclusions are faulty; they do mean that you may want to verify the facts and determine whether other conclusions are possible—or perhaps even more likely.

A Primer in Decision Making

THE NEED

Once you have obtained the pertinent facts, you must process them properly to arrive at a suitable decision. Much of the process involved in preparing for cruising requires decisions. These can be made in three ways: by the head, by the heart, or by somebody else. And the latter way is the easiest. It requires no thinking or effort, just trust in an expert and the expert's opinions. The successful outcome depends on how close the personality of the expert is to your own.

Decisions made by the heart are also relatively easy: Simply do what you feel or believe is best. These kinds of decisions are often necessary. The color of your boat's upholstery, for example, cannot be decided by "rational" methods.

Because the rational process requires considerable labor—determining facts, then sorting and evaluating those facts—many shun it. Most people can get the facts; the difficulty comes during the sorting and evaluating processes.

Our schooling has trained us in solving problems that have absolute answers. Problems in science or math most of the time have only one correct resolution. Two plus two always equals four, force always equals mass times acceleration, and so on. Even in courses outside the sciences we are trained to see only one correct answer—most often the opinion held by the instructor.

In the real world, however, many problems have no single "right" answer. The optimum answer can vary, depending upon the individual solving the problem. A good example of this is judging figure skating or gymnastics. Several judges watching the same performance can rate it differently; which judge was "right"? Other examples abound: Where should money be invested for the best overall return? Should a couple have a child? Such typical, complex, everyday problems are not easily answered.

Faced with such questions, many people seek counseling or guidance from an expert; more often they make the decision based on incomplete data or simply by feeling or whim. The latter methods can lead to unsatisfactory and sometimes disastrous results. Fortunately, there are some methods to help you reach rational decisions. Problems with many variables, for instance, can be controlled by using a rating matrix.

AN INTRODUCTION TO THE RATING MATRIX

A rating matrix is a table grouping the variables of a problem so that a numeric value is assigned to each. Rows or columns are then compared to locate the most advantageous combination of variables. The following table, taken from chapter 7, is an example of a rating matrix.

TABLE 1.1

Comparison of Common Hull Materials

Quality	Wood	Fiberglass	Steel	Aluminum
Cost	2	4	2	1
Warmth	4	2	2	2
Performance	2	3	1	4
Toughness	2	1	4	3
Maintenance	1	4	2	3
Ease of repair	3	3	1	1
Total	14	17	12	14

Each hull material has been given a value from 1 to 4. The rating is, of course, subjective, and dependent upon the judgment of the individual who assigns the values. Nonetheless, if you are doing the rating and you honestly represent your opinions, your results will fit your problem. For example, you may feel that fiberglass produces a warmer boat than steel or aluminum; therefore you should give it a value of 3 rather than 2, thus raising fiberglass's total to 18.

While this rating method allows multiple twos in the second row, another method is to arrange the variables in order of preference. An example of this is table 7.1, page 177. The choice of method depends upon how you wish to rate the variables and how each method applies to your problem.

THE CONCEPT OF FUZZY VARIABLES

In the table above a single variable—say, "Performance"—is assigned a value from 1 to 4. This implies that we can represent this variable with an exact value. In the real world, however, many problems have variables with properties that are inexact, vague, or ambiguous. An example might be "old." For a child of 5, anybody over 8 would be considered old; a woman of 40, on the other hand, may define only those over 65 as old. Further, some people possess more "old" than others. For the young child, 8 is old, but 25 is really old, and 65 is unbelievably old. It is necessary when analyzing problems of this kind to be able to represent the variables both by entrance requirements—that is, you are not old until you are eight—and by degree of belonging—for example, you are old or really old. This struggle with the concepts of uncertainty, and optimum solutions to problems with inexact values for variables, has led mathematicians to develop the Fuzzy Set Theory. I have just introduced you to the basics of that theory.

THE RIGHTNESS OF RELATIVE WRONGNESS

Another type of annoying problem that continues to crop up in daily life is the problem with no right answer—one for which all the available courses of action have negative consequences. In this case a clever trick is to (figuratively speaking) look through the telescope from the other end. Instead of looking for the best solution, that is, look for the one with the fewest disagreeable consequences.

For example, when you're approaching a difficult harbor in conditions of poor visibility after a long and bumpy passage, should you wait for better visibility or enter right away to avoid spending another night at sea? If you go into harbor you might damage or even lose the boat; if you stay at sea, you will be exhausted and uncomfortable. Neither alternative is desirable.

In this case the correct decision will become apparent quickly if you compare the two undesirable outcomes and choose the least odious. Most people will select another night of discomfort over damage to or loss of their boat. Still, it is also possible, even in this simple problem, to be so severely exhausted (exhaustion being a fuzzy variable) that further effort would produce a greater risk to life and property than attempting the passage into the harbor, thus reversing your decision.

This example has only two variables, and the correct action can be determined almost intuitively. The real value of this process will be more apparent when you apply it to more complex problems with more variables. As the number of variables increases, the rating matrix also takes on more value in solving problems.

A NEW LOOK AT THE COST-BENEFIT RATIO

Another concept that is useful in making decisions in everyday life is called the cost-benefit ratio. In an engineering system, this is the ratio between the cost of a facility and the amount of money it will return over the course of its useful life. Anything with a cost-benefit ratio of less than 1—that is, it costs less than it will return—could be considered as a possible solution. The solution with the smallest cost-benefit ratio may be considered optimum.

For the purposes of this book, I would like to broaden the definitions of both *cost* and *benefit* to include variables other than just dollars. Cost could include, for example, some fuzzy variables such as time, comfort, or pollution; benefits could include pleasure, peace, and so on. In this context everything has a cost and a benefit. It is, of course, difficult to quantify these values, but this kind of evaluation is necessary if you hope to make an informed decision. Although making the correct decisions for the problems discussed in this book is not as difficult as judging the cost-benefit ratio of, say, nuclear power, the problems are complex enough that you will find all these techniques useful.

2

What Is Cruising?

There are certain absolute truths in life. *Water runs downhill* is one. *Cruising is romantic* seems to be another. The fantasy of cruising kindles interest in and fires the imagination of many people. When reality gets too harsh, the thought of an apparently endless Saturday, or of the simpler days of childhood when we wandered happily along the beach without a care, becomes very alluring. But is cruising really that kind of activity?

Answering the question "What is cruising really like?" is as difficult as describing the universe and giving two examples. I am not sure how to answer it satisfactorily; however, I do know some ways not to. For example, the typical narrative accounts of cruising trips helped me very little before I went cruising myself. The narrative format is designed more to entertain than to inform, and depends on both the author and the reader for its meaning. Those same accounts took on a whole new meaning after my cruise.

After considerable thought, then, I have decided that what cruising is depends on who is doing it. Therefore, a discussion of the motivations and personalities of cruisers will help you understand their experiences. Also, it is often easier to describe a complex subject by discussing some of the things it is not. I have included such discussions here and they, along with later chapters, will I hope answer your questions.

Warning: Young children and impressionable starry-eyed skippers should not be allowed to read this chapter without supervision. Cruising does not take place in a mythical land but in the real world, which is sometimes cold and hard. Some of what is in this chapter may therefore be threatening and disconcerting.

Cruising Motivation

Cruising motivation is like a blended whiskey. Although the exact blend may be different for each person, the basic ingredients are similar. And while it may not be possible to describe a particular blend precisely, it is possible to describe the basic motivations that make up the blend.

Most people, it seems, choose to go cruising because they think that cruising will provide:

an economical way to travel,

adventure,

peace,

freedom,

a carefree life,

an uncomplicated lifestyle,

and the "Good Life."

Some of these motivations are similar—a carefree life and an uncomplicated lifestyle, for instance—but each has a slightly different emphasis, so I will discuss them separately. This should help you determine if cruising is likely to match your own desires and motivations.

AN ECONOMICAL WAY TO TRAVEL

First, let me establish the perspective from which I will be examining economics, because this perspective always radically affects the conclusions. For example, two people could cruise around the world on a luxury liner for about the purchase price of most used 33-foot boats. The fare would cover all their costs for travel, food, lodging, and some local transportation; for the bluewater cruiser, though, those are additional costs. Thus, as will be shown in chapter 4, the *absolute* cost of bluewater cruising is very high.

However, the *relative* cost of bluewater cruising—including travel, lodging, food, clothing, and local transportation, but not the cost of the boat or the cruiser's loss of income—is low. Cruising has thus long been considered the poor man's way of seeing the world—and rightly so, even though it is not really inexpensive and is becoming more costly every day. Seventy-five percent of the people I met cruising were on a low budget. They needed to take on odd jobs to supplement their budget, or to restrict their activities to stay within it.

Travel costs include getting to and from the destination, along with the cost of meals eaten and fuel used while on passage. Because air travel is the most common and economical way to travel long distances, the cost of an airline ticket provides a useful comparison. And air travel is about 25 percent more expensive than passage making.

Once the port of call is reached, the cost of lodging can be considerably lower for a cruiser than for an air traveler. For example, monthly moorage fees at the Ali Wai Marina in Honolulu are approximately the same as a single night's lodging in one of the hotels that overlook the marina and Waikiki Beach. The hotel residents may enjoy a few more amenities (air conditioning, for instance), but their view and beach access are essentially the same. In remote areas the cruiser's lodging costs are even less; many times, swinging on the anchor in an isolated bay is free. However, there is a tendency for beginning cruisers to overestimate the time they will spend in isolated anchorages. Many cruisers spend most of their time in marinas.

Figure 2.1 Background: Living, Expensive;
Foreground: Living, Cheap

Although it is possible to live in shorts and eat only crabs and coconuts while cruising, in my opinion this is only one step above, and not much more enjoyable than, living naked and eating grubs. I don't particularly recommend this sort of bare subsistence; I believe it spawns much of what is wrong with cruising today, and so will leave its treatment to other books on cruising, such as Don Casey and Lew Hackler's *Sensible Cruising*. However, there is no need to go to extreme measures to reduce the costs of food and clothing while cruising. Cooking and eating aboard is commonly cheaper than eating in restaurants. How much you can reduce your food budget depends on where you cruise, how satisfied you are with local foods—and, sometimes, your resourcefulness.

One cruising friend of ours prides himself on being able to locate restaurant food cheaper than home cooking. On occasion, we have accompanied him on his forays. The food was more filling than tasty, but our friend is fond of saying, "You couldn't even buy the food for this price." He may someday be revered as the father of a new discipline—if not as a gourmet or even a gourmand—a sort of *gour-a-peu-de-frais*. Because of his skills, he and his wife ate out far more often than the rest of the cruisers in the marina.

Finally, local transportation has a major effect on the economics—and the day-to-day enjoyment—of cruising. A lack of local transportation can reduce the range of access of the cruiser to a radius of 5 miles. Since many ports are a great distance from population centers and points of interest, such a cruiser may be forced to shop at more expensive local markets or miss important or interesting local features. Even if cheap public transportation is available, shopping in this manner requires extra effort and limits the amount of supplies handled in a single trip. And many rural places have no public transportation.

To avoid this inconvenience many cruisers bring along collapsible bicycles; we took the regular off-road, or mountain, variety. This increased our access to a radius of about 25 miles, but required more onboard storage space. And although bicycles proved better than walking, they were still not ideal. Their load-carrying capacity is low, and many points of interest lie beyond 25 miles. A few cruisers bring motor bikes to extend their range—but the storage space and maintenance these require produce mixed results. Surprisingly, most cruisers solve the transportation problem by spending more money and renting a car. Car rentals are available not only in major cities but also in such remote locations as Long Island in the Bahamas and Christmas Island in the Gilberts; I have rented vehicles in both spots. (I hesitate to call them automobiles, since the one in the Bahamas had no floorboards on the passenger's side.) Sometimes several boat crews pool their money and rent a single car with some sort of loose agreement as to its group usage. Others—such as those who intend to spend six months or so in an area—buy and later resell a used car. I would not consider this option unless I was a good mechanic and an excellent salesman.

In summation, all of the relative costs of cruising are lower than those of air travel—except local transportation, which is about the same. And although there are some destinations where you can't spend money, since there is nothing to buy, not even fuel or food, my experience is that nobody's cruising budget is too large, and almost everybody spends more money than they expected to. For a more detailed discussion of a cruising budget, refer to chapter 4.

ADVENTURE

Adventure was probably the primary motivation for early cruisers, and it's still important to almost all of us. Adventure is a fuzzy variable, however, which ranges in magnitude from small to large, so it may be wise to start by defining *adventure*. The dictionary generally uses such phrases as "an undertaking of hazardous or questionable nature," but I have always thought that a good definition is "something that is uncomfortable and frightening, and while you're in the middle of it you wish to be somewhere, anywhere, else."

Adventures make each life different and provide the stories told most often among a group of friends. These tales of life's adventures usually deal with situations that are uncomfortable or frightening. Certainly, cruising can provide these experiences. No, it's not one life-threatening event after another, but if you are going to sea to have adventures you will assuredly find them—rounding the Horn, riding out storms, exploring remote areas.

Be aware, though, that there are no shortcuts to adventure. It requires fitness, years of training to develop the necessary skills, and a willingness to deal with hardship. Cruising is different from the packaged "adventure" trips available today, on which experts guide you and protect you from any actually harmful events. On these trips the guides are having the adventure; the guests are merely watching it happen. When you are cruising, however, there will be nobody to insulate you from your own ineptitude or stupidity. All the dirty work is yours, the danger is real, and there is no platoon of highly trained specialists to bail you out of trouble (De Roos, *Northwest Passage).* It is just you, the boat, and the sea. If your tolerance for discomfort is low you will surely become miserable, and if your capabilities are low you may become dead. Although passage making sometimes includes at least one of the requirements for good adventure—it can be uncomfortable—it only becomes frightening and consequently, an adventure, if done without proper preparation.

At the same time, cruising can be downright boring on occasion. Sitting in the cockpit of a small boat, or on the beach of a hot, humid tropical island, can be far from stimulating on a month-in, month-out basis. Many of cruising's routines may seem from the outside to be exciting but in reality are quite commonplace. For example, in passage making, the scenery is the always the same—bumpy, sky-colored water day in and day out. On a well-planned trip, with a properly maintained ship, there is very little to do but watch the sea and the clouds and wait for time to pass in a very small space that is constantly in motion. One of the best-kept secrets of cruising is that 90 percent of cruisers I met hate passage making because of this tedium.

The few who enjoy passage making find that navigation, preparation of meals, watch keeping, and repairing the boat keep them from being bored (Vogt, *Altering Course)*. They get pleasure from the peace and simplicity provided by the rhythm of their days as they sail alone on their small life-support capsules. They enjoy the feeling of self-sufficiency, the isolation, and the opportunity for introspection and peace.

I must agree: If navigation, meal preparation, boat repairs, and watch keeping are not tedious, then you won't be bored on an ocean passage, for that is really all there is to do. However, consider that if your boat is in proper condition, repairs should be minimal; also, your GPS will be doing the navigation. Will preparing meals and keeping watch prevent you from being bored? As for introspection, passage making can most assuredly provide the necessary peace and isolation, and in larger quantities, than almost any other endeavor available to the average person.

PEACE

The pursuit of peace is a motive with which many of us can identify. As the pressures from the kids, the parents, the boss, the traffic, and chasing the dollar press in, who wouldn't dream of the peace and freedom of a warm surf gently washing on the shore of some distant sun-bathed lagoon? While the picture in the imagination may soothe our frazzled minds, though, the reality may be somewhat different.

Peace can be external, associated with isolation, or internal, associated with inner satisfaction. Often the two are related: Some seek the peace of isolation in hopes of finding the peace of inner satisfaction. Undoubtedly cruising can provide isolation. Whether it will bring internal peace is another matter.

ISOLATION

Nothing can be more isolated than a deserted island or a long passage at sea—and isolation alone can provide significant benefits.

If industries had any idea how efficiently an ocean cruise would return burned-out executives to vigor, they would all adopt cruising programs. And the length of cruise needed may be less than you think: For most people it would be measured in months, not years (Zuckerman, "Sensory Deprivation"). Six to nine months of cruising will refresh the most exhausted individual. Indeed, after a year that person may begin to have secret desires to once again yell a string of obscenities at someone on a crowded freeway.

I speak from experience. Before I took my extended cruise, I spent many vacation cruises heading my boat for an isolated anchorage as far from civilization as time permitted. Once there I lounged as long as I could, thoroughly enjoying the peace. So naturally I planned isolated anchorages into my extended cruise. However, about three months into my actual journey those isolated anchorages began to lose their attraction. Instead, we spent more time in smaller towns and villages. At the close of the trip a couple of years later, Debby and I sat on the terrace of the Illikai Hotel in Honolulu, toasting sundown with "*This* is cruising." We were both glad to get back to a big city.

In retrospect it seems to me that there is a relationship between time and attitude. Somewhere around two weeks asea and thoughts of the office and job go away. After a month you're sure that this could be an enjoyable permanent way of life. After three months healing is taking place and extreme isolation loses its importance. Somewhere between 9 and 18 months the repair is complete—and you begin to yearn for the satisfaction of the business world. The old saw about variety and spice has a strong basis in truth.

Too much of anything is not good, and isolation is no exception. Very few individuals are capable of dealing with prolonged periods of it (Lawick-Goodall, "My Friends the Wild Chimpanzees"). That is why banishment was historically such a feared punishment, and why solitary confinement is still used to threaten hardened criminals.

Even voluntary isolation is difficult to handle. The space program has provided a wealth of information on the effects of isolation on the human mind and body. Studies have shown that it produces serious consequences (Haythron, "Program of Isolation"). The problems start with the discomfort commonly called loneliness, at which point most people look for relief. If the isolation continues, the individual becomes disoriented and experiences hallucinations. Perception of the environment changes, and lethargy sets in. Finally, if there is no relief, the lethargy becomes so severe that the individual dies.

If this seems extreme, read some of the accounts that single-handed sailors have written. You can find examples of all of these stages in various stories. Donald Crowhurst's suicide in the *Times* Golden Globe race, for instance, can be attributed at least in part to isolation sickness (Tomalin and Hall, *The Strange Last Voyage of Donald Crowhurst*). The most commonly reported symptom is hallucination, probably because it is the most pronounced and interesting to both subject and reader. Other symptoms may or may not be reported directly, depending on the style of the writer, but some, such as lethargy, can be read into the narrative.

Be aware of the symptoms of severe isolation; if you recognize them in yourself, act immediately to end the isolation.

All this evidence indicates that human beings are social animals and require the presence of other humans to be healthy. The question is, how much presence? Too much contact seems to cause as much discomfort as isolation, as evidenced by the number of people seeking solitude.

To my knowledge there have been only a few studies of the phenomenon of social saturation among humans. There doesn't even seem to be an English word for the opposite of isolation; sociologists get by with the term *overcrowding* (Hamburg, *Society, Stress and Disease*). Their limited research has shown that overcrowding can cause death in tree shrews, and an increase in aggression in humans. Further, these studies show that crowding is a function of space as well as numbers of individuals. For example, six crew members on a 40-foot yacht can be termed crowded.

The combination of this crowding and the seclusion imposed by passage making can produce strange and sometimes catastrophic events. Normally likable and rational people can become neurotic and irrational and even commit murder at sea (Stadler, *Psychology of Sailing*). Although I have never witnessed murder, I have seen some extremely abnormal behavior among cruisers arriving from long passages. If you intend to make passage with more than three on board, consider the individuals and their personalities with care.

What can be concluded from these studies is that people seem to need a balance between isolation and social saturation to be healthy. Now I come to one of the clear advantages of cruising: It is a lifestyle that allows you to socialize until isolation is needed, and then allows you to get a little peace by heading for the open sea, returning once more to civilization when company is again desired.

You can do this with other lifestyles—backpacking, for instance—but cruising provides a sort of off-and-on isolation spigot. Turn it on and your isolation will be complete, relatively simple to attain, and experienced in the presence of familiar surroundings—your own boat. Turn it off and the social saturation you'll find will also be unique; interaction will be with strangers and new friends, rather than the old friends and relatives who close in on the average backpacker upon return to civilization.

Cruisers have another distinct advantage in that they can select both the level and the type of society to which they will be exposed. For example, you can choose to visit a large metropolitan area, a small local village, or a secluded bay—and with anything from a simple hunter-gatherer culture to a complex, high-tech industrial one.

Both extreme isolation and overcrowding can be part of cruising, and the two extremes are equally distasteful. Do not overestimate your need for isolation, then; be careful when selecting crew for long passages; and do provide relief valves in your program. These valves can be safe harbors to leave your vessel temporarily while you fly back to visit family and friends, or decision points where you can sail home relatively easily.

INNER PEACE

Inner peace is definitely harder to find in cruising than isolation—but then it's harder to find in general. The number of people searching for inner peace is testimony to its elusiveness. Many cruising books imply that it can be found while cruising. While it may be true that some of those who have written books about cruising have found a rewarding way of life and inner peace, it is also true that what satisfies a few does not necessarily satisfy everybody. If the simple process of changing lifestyle produced inner peace, there would not be so many people still looking for it.

I have met no greater number of inwardly satisfied people cruising than I have in any other walk of life. Cruisers have no lock on inner peace; there are certainly as many dairy farmers, stockbrokers, and social workers who have found it. And if you are one of those farmers, say, who has *not* found inner peace, probability says that you won't find it cruising, either. Yes, cruising can provide isolation, which in turn can furnish the opportunity for introspection. Whether or not this introspection will lead to inner peace, however, depends more on your character than your lifestyle. Inner peace is not so much what you do as what you think, and finding it means coming to terms with yourself.

In many instances you must make a radical personality change to achieve inner satisfaction. Studies have shown that such a personality change generally requires extreme stress levels—and cruising can and often does provide these. For example, surviving a storm at sea or completing a difficult passage are the types of strong emotional experiences necessary for dramatic changes in behavior. While not unique to cruising, these types of experiences are often part of it, and can act as catalysts for significant change. Some cruisers, like Clare Francis in her book *Woman Alone,* have reported finding such experiences gratifying. Whether they resulted in a feeling of inner peace, however, is not clear. I personally find them to be mostly physically uncomfortable.

In the end, it is possible to find inner peace while cruising, but the probability of doing so is not a whole lot greater than that of finding it while living any other life experience—gardening, for example.

FREEDOM

Cruising almost always conjures up images of freedom, of gulls soaring in the blue sky—free, free as a bird! I don't actually know how free a bird is, but if you consider *freedom* to be the ability to do what you want, when you want, then cruising is not it. The reality is that the average person loses freedom when cruising.

Cruisers are restricted by sea and weather. Winds, waves, and currents determine if, when, where, and how fast they go. Once asea, they are prisoners of the boat. Just try to get off your vessel 10 days out on a 20-day passage!

Sure, you can stay in one little bay until you feel the urge to move, and then sail off to the next little bay, but do not overestimate that freedom. It may be easy to change anchorages; not so to go skiing, visit the kids, get a cold drink, or go to a ballet.

If you define *freedom* as a hassle-free life, sorry, you will be disappointed again. Hassles are as much a part of cruising as they are of any other lifestyle. Consider the difficulty of maintaining your equipment in strange ports. You do not have to get very far from local waters to become infuriated with repair facilities or apathetic port officials. Many a cruiser has been victimized by shoddy repairs to his or her boat. I recall sending the entire "Attorneys" section of the Honolulu Yellow Pages to one overwrought cruiser who had left that city after having some repairs done to his boat—repairs that turned out later to be particularly shoddy. His frustration was anything but soothing.

Certainly the cruising lifestyle is not worry-free. In most instances the greater part of the cruiser's financial worth is embodied in the boat—which must be protected from wind, current, reefs or rocks, weather, and thieves. Cruisers in harbor worry about storms; at sea they worry about storms. If they leave the boat they worry that it will sink, or the wind will change and perhaps cause the anchor to drag.

The thought of through-hulls failing, heads overflowing, or any other of the many things that can sink your boat will never be far below your consciousness. Anytime I have left my boat for more than a few hours, I've returned to find my eyes subconsciously searching the harbor for the first visual clue, generally the mast, that the boat was still above water. The relief when I can verify that it's still floating is as much a part of cruising for me as watching sunsets. Surprisingly—or maybe not—I have discovered that this subconscious search is almost universal among cruisers.

If you look to cruising to give you freedom to do nothing, look again. Yes, cruising does attract an irresponsible element, and accepts this element better than most social structures. (Indeed, the attraction may be related to the acceptance.) However, change is blowing across the marinas, quays, and harbors. The sun-bleached teak that was once the badge of the "real" cruiser is being slowly replaced by well-maintained teak. The floating junkyards with their eye-irritating cabin tops and decks covered with cherished bits of personal trash are still there, but their numbers are diminishing.

There is much to do just to keep a boat in shape to face the open ocean, let alone keep it presentable. If social pressure kept your front yard looking respectable ashore, that same pressure will be there while cruising to keep your boat looking respectable. Cruising is not a license to be irresponsible, and being responsible has nothing to do with not being free.

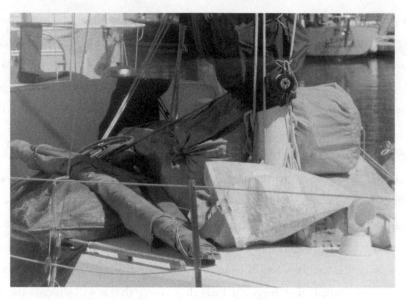

Figure 2.2 Freedom from Ambition and Common Decency

FREE FROM CARE

Cruising somehow evokes in almost everybody the image of an innocent, wandering, carefree existence; a Tom Sawyer–like life. Who among us has not secretly desired to drift through life without a worry, not knowing or caring what is around the next bend, confident that when hunger strikes there will somehow be a watermelon patch just waiting? In this fairy-tale life, all the events that arise are handled successfully and produce only happiness.

I sometimes believe that the almost universal appeal of cruising rests on this image. Even those who are not interested in going cruising themselves are interested in the fortunes of those who do. They want to know if the image really exists. What can I say? It does and it doesn't. The answer depends more on who is doing than on what is being done. For the overwhelming majority of people the image does not exist, because they cannot go back to that age of innocence. Such innocence requires a willingness to take risks without regard for consequences.

Going to sea without full knowledge of the consequences is foolhardy. Some try, but fate and probability are stacked against them. I have known few who perished at sea, but some who came very close. I wonder sometimes whether these people were motivated by a carefree life or just incredibly naive.

The probability of anyone over the age of 10 finding a life free of care is low and only decreases with age. Long life is filled with disappointments, which tend to make people wary of the risk taking necessary to a carefree life. The ability to assess risk is one of those capabilities responsible for the success of the human species. Two thumbs down on finding a carefree life.

AN UNCOMPLICATED LIFESTYLE

The search for the elusive and fabled uncomplicated life is not new; throughout history there have been those who cried, "Alas and repent, return to the simple life!" The hippies of the 1960s were more recent seekers. And cruising under sail appears to offer a return to the simple life. (Some rather notable cruisers have even gone to sea without an engine.) Only a very few people can find real simplicity at sea, however.

Unfortunately, viewing the simple life from the perspective of a complex one can distort it. You tend to focus on the joy rather than the inconvenience generated by simplicity. It turns out that complications are directly proportional to comfort. That is, the more comfort you need, the more complicated your life will be. When the pioneers were freed from splitting and storing wood for the winter through the introductions of oil and electric heat, they paid for it through the complications of producing and using these labor-saving devices. There is no free lunch. If you are going to simplify your life it will be at some cost in comfort and ease. If you cannot reduce your comfort level, it's unlikely you'll reduce the complications or frustrations of your life—you'll just change them for different ones.

On the other hand, getting away from it all is not the same as taking it all with you. If you are planning to have on board equipment such as self-steering, freezers, bread machines, microwave ovens, roller furling, electric anchor winches, GPS, radios, LORANs, radar, and weather-fax machines, then you are *not* going to have an uncomplicated lifestyle.

True, some of this stuff will improve your chances of survival, or make your life more enjoyable, but the price will be complication. Electronic and mechanical gadgets require power and maintenance. Getting either in a remote location is anything but uncomplicated, and certainly not cheap. For example, dealing with a local port official or a customs official in a third-world country, or trying to find replacement parts in a strange port, is often far from soothing or uncomplicated, as described by writer Steve Rubin in *Sail* magazine.

A salty, damp environment that gets tossed about is not the most conducive atmosphere for trouble-free operation of modern equipment, either; and when it's inoperable, you'll be out of tune with your environment. If the equipment is necessary for your safety because you lack the skill or strength to sail without it, that time will also be dangerous and filled with apprehension.

Many authors have noted that those who require considerable creature comforts on their boats rarely enjoy cruising. Most of the authors attribute this disenchantment to the above-discussed complications. I think it runs deeper, though. Cruising is just not compatible with a personality that requires the level of comfort supplied by bread machines, microwave ovens, and the like. Somehow the inconvenience of boat living rarely gets into the boating press (just as photographs of picturesque foreign markets don't portray the smells, confusion, filth, and flies). But the inconvenience, like the flies, is still there, and it does not diminish no matter how many gadgets are put aboard.

The conflict between the simple life and the comfortable one has been well described by author Annis Pepion Scott. During a 15-month cruise in the Caribbean her initial positive attitude was changed by reality: The remembered comforts of king-size beds, flush toilets, and air conditioning slowly overpowered her tolerance for small bunks and the constant regulation of hatches needed to provide ventilation. These and other similar cruising rituals convinced her and her husband to return to their former life in New England, where they are now living happily ever after.

To those who have never slept under an open hatch in the Tropics, its hassles may not seem like much. So let me provide a more detailed description. The hatch *must* be open, first of all, to provide those cool refreshing breezes to waft you off to sleep. At approximately the same time that you reach a state of deep, pleasant sleep, however, the next regularly scheduled tropical shower begins. This cold rain in the face has a disquieting effect on the above-mentioned peaceful slumber.

Now in this half-awake stupor there develops a little gamesmanship among you and your boatmates as to who will close the hatch. The luckless individual getting the largest volume of water generally loses and begins a semiconscious struggle to close the hatch before becoming entirely drenched or fully awake. Of course, semiconsciousness tends to increase the number of occurrences of head banging and finger smashing.

The ensuing verbal barrage and the occasional flying object does very little good for anyone sleeping anywhere in the immediate vicinity. Even someone who may have missed the cold splash of rain will be disturbed by the foot in the face and the sheer volume of profanity, much of which would stop a mother's heart. Still, once this short burst of violent energy has resulted in a closed hatch, the thrashing and mumbling slowly subside, and peaceful sleep returns.

Returns for about an hour, at which time stifling heat and suffocation change it from peaceful to fitful and rouse one of the sleepers again, this time to reopen the hatch. Now all the players are again in position to repeat the comedy, because the next shower is only about an hour away. The process continues until dawn or exhaustion.

Those who can enjoy this type of life are rare. If you and your crew have the dogged determination and dedication to do it the hard way, then returning to the simple life can be found in cruising.

THE GOOD LIFE

What is this good life, and can cruising provide it? It seems to me that we will have to answer the former before we can consider the latter.

One popular definition is succinctly put in the expression "The one who dies with the most toys wins." Somehow the good life has become just another product to acquire, like a video disk player, and preferably one your neighbors don't have, one uncommon and unfamiliar that will induce envy. Under this definition of the good life, what is important is that others desire what you have.

At some point in the 19th century, tropical islands, blue lagoons, and swaying palm trees came to symbolize paradise. How many TV commercials have you seen picturing happy, laughing people running along the beach of a tropical island? All those happy people must be living the good life. Because cruising allows you to reach these tropical paradises, obviously cruising is just one continuous good time. Right?

The truth is that while cruising can be both unfamiliar and uncommon, and can induce envy, for that matter, it provides a very poor outlet for this particular need—which relies on others knowing you have the good life. When you're in the middle of the ocean, no one knows what rich and rewarding events you're experiencing; and when you reach shore, whom can you tell, except other cruisers? Boring! They tell the same kind of stories!

Even when you can relate your experiences to your envious friends back home, it will take only hours to describe what took you months to live. Talk about a bad cost-benefit ratio. Those who try to buy the good life can reach the fabled tropical islands, but may find that their actual pleasure is not what they had imagined.

The cruising life provides subtle pleasures—more common and personal, perhaps, than those found elsewhere, but not much different from them. Whether it is good or not depends on your definition of *good*. Most of the flash and dash of cruising is media hype, not only TV, but books as well. A quiet talk with friends, a good book, or the beauty of nature are the major constituents of the cruising good life—not really too different from the good life anywhere else.

The Typical Cruising Personality

Some people like cruising and some do not. It follows that each group exhibits some common characteristics and values. Examining the common traits of those who do like cruising may help you determine if you have the "right stuff."

If you don't really care whether you fit into the psychological profile of *Cruiser domesticus,* you already have two of the qualities of successful bluewater cruisers—a closed mind and an inclination to take risks. Nevertheless, the following "naval" examination may still help prepare you for your new nautical lifestyle.

Bluewater cruisers seem like ordinary people, yet they are different even from liveaboards and summer cruisers. This difference is also evident across all the various subclasses of bluewater cruisers; sabbatical cruisers, for instance, are different from lifestyle cruisers. The length of time they will spend cruising can be correlated to that difference. The stronger the traits and the more closely you fit the profile given below, the longer you will enjoy cruising.

Common traits among bluewater cruisers, then, are independence, resourcefulness, self-sufficiency, optimism, curiosity, an outgoing nature, and an enjoyment of physical activity. These people also are generally risk takers; they are strong willed, have a high tolerance for failure, are internally motivated, and look forward to tomorrow rather than backward at yesterday.

INDEPENDENCE, RESOURCEFULNESS, AND SELF-SUFFICIENCY

Most people enjoy the feeling of doing what they want, when they want. However, the independence involved in cruising is of a particular kind. The lifestyle is such that it almost forces you to give up familiar and comforting help, such as police and fire protection, ambulance service, and the family doctor. Health insurance and personal property policies may no longer be readily available. Thus you must not only be independent enough to choose a lifestyle considerably different from what's accepted as "normal," but also rely on yourself for many of the things provided by others in that more normal life.

Well-known cruisers—for example, the Hiscocks, the Roths, and Donald Street—not only don't mind being different, they enjoy being different. They like the independence of weathering a storm at sea alone, or of swinging on the hook in some isolated harbor. They eschew complicated equipment, preferring to rely on their own abilities. This capacity for self-sufficiency by its very nature tends to foster the belief that simple is better.

To bluewater cruisers, life is a problem to be solved. They must be able to pull themselves off a reef, patch a hull, or fix a broken rig well enough to get out of trouble. Complete self-sufficiency requires you to be secure in your skills, because you cannot rely on others for direction or aid. When you are far out to sea or on a remote deserted island, help ain't comin', and you shouldn't require or expect it. The radio will not save your bacon. The most you can count on is that, if you do sink, the world will know what happened to "Old What's-His-Face."

Passage making over long distances is very hard on equipment. (One night while on a passage, I heard four of the five boats before me on the ham radio net roll call report failed equipment.) If your passage is to a remote location, a large amount of resourcefulness may be necessary to jury-rig your equipment with simple tools and inadequate supplies. As recalled in his book *Blue Water*, Bob Griffith once blasted a path through a coral reef with dynamite to free his trapped vessel—a rather uncommon solution, as most cruisers carry very little dynamite. Even after crude repairs are complete, you'll need to have a tolerance for many more months' sailing in a boat in less-than-prime condition. It is common for long-distance cruisers to voyage for tens of thousands of miles with equipment that is not working properly or is held together by wire or tape.

WHAT, ME WORRY?

Along with cruisers' independence, resourcefulness, and self-sufficiency often comes a disturbing overconfidence or a sort of Alfred E. Newman mind-set. The "What, me worry?" attitude of some cruisers is maybe one they could do without. These folks simply do not worry about lack of money, lack of proper equipment, lack of knowledge or skill, or what the future may bring. They eschew planning, advice (unless it supports their beliefs), and formal and informal training. Part of this attitude may be due to stubbornness and part to a desire to remain in the enchanted land of cruising. Perhaps they feel that the truth will somehow return them to the "real world." At any rate, they go on their way free of care with an almost childlike trust that nothing bad will happen to them.

I recall mentioning to several cruisers who had decided to enter a race from Hawaii to Tokyo that the course crossed the most prolific hurricane belt in the world at the peak of hurricane season. None of the captains seemed to be concerned. I was not so much amazed at their cavalierness about tempting the odds as I was shocked at their complete lack of interest in any data that indicated danger existed (such data can be found in Nathaniel Bowditch's *American Practical Navigation*). They seemed more afraid of discussing hurricanes than of encountering one. Perhaps they wanted to trust in providence, or believed that the race officials wouldn't expose them to danger.

As it turned out, all the boats made it to Tokyo without running afoul of a hurricane. Maybe the cruisers' trust was well founded and my fears groundless. Then again, could they have been just plain lucky?

I consider the concept of luck as perhaps our worst enemy. Believing in "bad luck" allows you to feel that any bad things that happen to you have nothing to do with your own actions. In reality, whether outcomes are good or bad depends a lot on planning and preparation. Far too many cruisers set to sea ill prepared, ill trained, and with inadequate equipment. Attempts to enlighten them are met with indignation and contempt. And it's not only the skippers; often the crew has a similar overconfidence. Too often the result is that within a few years, "luck" will produce an event or a series of events so objectionable that cruising is abandoned by all.

AN OUTGOING NATURE, AMIABILITY, CURIOSITY, AND CHEERFULNESS

Cruisers as a group are no more trustworthy, loyal, helpful, courteous, kind, obedient, brave, clean, or reverent than anybody else. Cheerful and friendly is another matter, however, along with having an outgoing nature and a sense of curiosity. The constant travel of cruising requires the ability to make friends quickly. And dealing with local populations or foreign dignitaries, real or imagined, can be much more pleasant if done on a friendly basis. Not all world cruisers have been outgoing, friendly folks, but taking pleasure in meeting new people and observing nature, history, and different cultures is important if you're to enjoy cruising.

Some notable exceptions are found in the ranks of single-handers. Either they are exceptionally good at making friends, it seems, or they couldn't care less. Some are single-handing because they have no choice, others because they enjoy being alone. The latter tend to be a little antisocial—even rude on occasion. Generally speaking, those who have single-handed for a long time tend to enjoy their privacy more than socializing.

For those cruising with a crew, a healthy dose of cheerfulness is necessary to keep up enthusiasm in the face of the hardships and discomfort of cruising compared to shore life. Griping may help you vent your internal frustrations, but looking on the bright side of things sure helps soothe the frustrations of those around you. I recall visiting a little store in a fishing village after a particularly bad fishing season. The proprietor had obviously been exposed to too many tales of woe and had finally lost patience, because pasted to the back of the cash register was a hastily hand-lettered sign: NO SNIVELING. A similar sign in needlepoint now graces our main cabin.

A healthy curiosity—to visit a foreign country, to see what is beyond the next wave—is another childlike attribute that helps keep the spirit and freshness of cruising alive. It is curiosity that finally casts off the mooring lines and drives you into the next passage.

PHYSICAL FITNESS

The physical health and strength of cruisers vary a great deal, but normally those who enjoy physical activity get more out of cruising—which is a very physical activity. Sails must be raised and tended; both operations require pulling and cranking. Setting an anchor can be a physically demanding operation with the safety of life or property in the balance. And cruisers must often do things the hard way. Shorthanded passage making is especially exhausting work. True, there are labor-saving devices, but these can break down—and often do so at very inopportune moments. Then, too, the cost of and constant maintenance required by such equipment often keeps it off cruising boats.

Even off the boat, the cruising life is physical. Shoreside transportation is limited to walking more often than is usual in Western countries. Carrying supplies and laundry over fairly long distances is common. If the loads are large it may mean several trips. Dealing with authorities or emergencies is often done on foot. Going out to dinner or exploring an area usually means walking. Bicycles or car rentals in some cases make the work easier.

A STRONG WILL AND TOLERANCE FOR FAILURE

I am not sure why cruisers are so immensely stubborn and obstinate as a group. I once watched a cruising skipper wrestle with chain, dinghy, and mooring buoy for 20 exhausting minutes rather than give up and accept the suggestion to slack the bow line offered by the dock watchers present. He evidently felt that once he was committed to an approach, any change would be tantamount to admitting he'd been wrong. It was not a pretty sight.

Many skippers seem to have fixed, inflexible opinions. I suspect it is because they have all had to overcome a continuous procession of obstacles. Adversity must be conquered from the very start of the planning stage to the final beating against the wind and current to make a landfall. If you're convinced that what you're doing is right, it's easier to continue. And tolerance for failure is necessary to keep trying until you succeed.

The difference between success and failure is slight. Success is achieved when the number of trials exceeds the number of failures—by only one. Think of the heavyweight champion who told himself between each round, "I'll fight just one more." Those who are out cruising, too, have had many setbacks, but they do not give up easily.

Unfortunately, along with tolerance for failure and strong will sometimes come a closed mind and a large ego. This combination can make an individual unwilling to accept advice and can lead to decisions that prevent skipper and crew from reaching their cruising goal; it can even place a vessel and its crew in peril.

For example, I watched a couple prepare for cruising for six years. The man was an excellent craftsman and gradually brought his boat into peak condition. During this process they refused to listen to opinions different from their own. They were fond of saying, "We will do it our way."

Well, they did it their way, and got less than 100 miles down the coast before she debarked and refused to continue. Their gadget-laden boat had not performed well in the open ocean. The sad part is that there were any number of warning signs; they might have had a good cruising experience if they had been willing to take advice.

THE SEARCH FOR APPROVAL

Every stable, happy individual wants approval; this desire is what motivates us to action. *External* approval comes from others, *internal* approval from within ourselves. Most of us seek both kinds—but the majority strongly favor external approval.

This may be why so many people dream of cruising but so few actually go. Those most likely to succeed at it are geared toward interior approval. Cruising can give you satisfaction from a job well done, but only as judged from within by your personal standards. There are very few people around to approve of your actions in the middle of the ocean; that approval *must* come from within.

Motivation by internal approval has a significant advantage over motivation by external approval. When a task is completed, the reward or punishment comes from within—immediately and consistently. Psychologists tell us that one of the best ways to cultivate positive behavior is with instantaneous and consistent reward or punishment. Thus, those motivated by internal approval learn very early how to succeed. Many become super-achievers.

Superachievers often enjoy the challenges of cruising at first—but realize that these challenges are not strong enough to satisfy for very long (see Jeffrey Briggs's article "Cruisers Talk Cruising"). It is not uncommon to meet people cruising who have made major achievements in the business world. Most of them are out there to repair burnout. Generally they find that the body recovers quickly and that cruising is not stimulating enough to hold their interest longer than 18 months.

The odds are definitely against superachievers becoming long-term cruisers for other reasons as well. Cruising is not life in the fast lane. It is more difficult to leave a fast-paced, exciting lifestyle than is commonly imagined. Like freeway driving, life can be a disaster if you slow down while you're still in the fast lane; better to change lanes gradually.

Second, the exposure to many different experiences affects the basic cost-benefit ratio of cruising by reducing the level of the benefit. For example, seeing the Taj Mahal is the same experience whether you get there by jet or by sailboat—and the satisfaction of sailing there might not be enough to counterbalance the hardships. True, there are places that you can only see by boat, but you need to assess the value of seeing your 26th blue lagoon. Will it be compensation for the time and effort you spent to get there? You really have to be a purist to greet this lagoon with as much enthusiasm as you greeted your first.

The longer you cruise, the more the benefits of going somewhere diminish while the costs remain, at best, the same. If the benefits diminish enough, of course, the cost could begin to outweigh them. For example, we know some cruisers who circled the world in 1960 and waited and planned for 25 years to do it again. However, they gave up their second voyage very early, because the experiences were just not the same. The benefits to them were reduced, while the costs were the same.

Further, the process of achieving success in a business or profession tends to bring with it benefits that, once enjoyed, are hard to relinquish. That is why there are so many farm boys in Paris. Once you've lived the high life it's difficult to enjoy life without those same comforts. Those who have enjoyed material comforts before cruising will tend to find life asea too harsh and uncomfortable. Cruising with air conditioning, fine china, and sterling silver is not normal bluewater cruising.

This may be the reason that most cruisers I've met were from the middle class or below. Before going cruising, most of these people had not gone far from home or seen much along the way. The few who were from above the middle class were predominantly on sabbaticals or trying to join that select group of people who have sailed around the world: In other words, they either cruised for short periods or were motivated to achieve another goal.

By the way, the idea that you can only benefit from cruising by staying in it long term is false. The average cruise lasts less than a year. Cruise just as long as it is important to you to cruise.

Qualities Unimportant to Cruisers

When describing complex things it is often easier to convey what they are not than what they are. Certainly much can be learned about the cruising life by examining what cruisers are not. What is most often unimportant to them is space, personal possessions, comfort, convenience, privacy, and contact with the world.

SPACE, THE IMPOSSIBLE FRONTIER

A survey of 23 live-aboards in the Pacific Northwest noted that their major complaint was living in cramped, dark, and damp quarters (*Northwest Sailor* editorial, "Living Aboard in the Northwest"). The same might be said by cruisers: Even large sailboats have very little space.

This lack of space demands exceptional neatness. It does not take long to trash a living space 12 feet by 20 feet. Every activity must be finished and put away before the next project is started. That is not easy on a boat, because every item you want is generally under several other unrelated items, all of which have to be shifted around to get what you want, then shifted back again to make room to work.

Each person has his or her own threshold for neatness. Those intending to spend considerable time aboard the same boat should have thresholds within a very few points of each other—otherwise, the neater one will slowly be driven mad.

A certain amount of slovenliness can be tolerated in port; at sea, however, it is not only unsightly but can also become costly and even dangerous. Equipment not stowed properly can be thrown about the boat, breaking or even injuring someone. Mix a sloppy cabin, a choppy sea, and a 40 degree angle of heel and you quickly get a hopeless squalor   and also a downright dangerous critical mass of sliding and flying equipment. It is difficult enough to move about on board an oceangoing yacht without also becoming entangled in loose gear.

ASSAULT AND BOATERY

Even given neatness next to godliness, the lack of space on board your boat will increase the amount of contact between various tender parts of your body and firm parts of the vessel. The two extremes of the body seem to take the majority of the beating: Heads and toes are constantly crashing into projections. It is wise to wear shoes, at least when working your boat, and always to move your head slowly. These precautions may not reduce the number of attacks, but can at least reduce their severity. I have given serious thought myself to dressing like a hockey goalie to get some respite from the assault.

A friend of mine, who had just reached Honolulu after a long passage, went shopping to resupply. She was wearing shorts and a halter top that exposed a large number of passage-acquired bruises. While in the checkout line, a woman ahead of her kept glancing at her. Finally this woman handed my friend a card with the simple comment, "If you need me, give me a call," and disappeared. My friend stared after her a minute and then read the card. The mystery lady ran a safe house for battered women.

LACK OF LIGHT AND AIR

For safety's sake, cruising boats have small portholes—which of course restrict the amount of light and air reaching the cabin, exacerbating the sense of being in a small area. The phenomenon can produce claustrophobic reactions in those even mildly susceptible to this kind of fear.

In the Tropics the lack of air circulation below decks can make the atmosphere in the cabin stifling; encourage the growth of mold and mildew; and promote the development of unpleasant boat odors—most often diesel, fiberglass, or mildew, but sometimes pet odors or cigarettes as well. These odors are usually stronger and more difficult to get rid of on the boat than on shore—because of that same lack of circulation.

You don't have to accept this discomfort, however. Chapter 9 explains many acceptable, safe ways to get both more air and more light into a boat. The result is certainly not like living in the great outdoors, but it is an improvement.

TOLERANCE OF CONFINEMENT

In cold, wet areas such as the Northwest Coast, life below decks can be intolerable. Being confined to the cabin for two weeks because of rain can bring on some nasty dispositions, to say nothing of the dampness. Everyone who comes below brings water, either blown down the hatch or on rain gear and boots. Cooking, taking showers, and even breathing create more moisture in the air. Within a short time everything is damp. If the dampness persists everything gets moldy: books, clothing, bedding, cushions, everything. It may even begin to "rain" down below as condensation on the overhead forms falling drops. (Actually, it can be worse than rain. Normally, gravity causes drops to fall straight down and hit the same spot repeatedly; not so on passage. Drops from a single source can strike an amazing number of places within the area of the base of a cone described by the erratic gyration of the boat under the action of wind and wave.)

LACK OF PRIVACY

Two people on a boat is tolerable; four people for more than a few weeks strains everyone's patience sooner or later. Sights, sounds, and odors easily travel from one end to the other of a small sailboat. There can be very few secrets, and there is no place to go to be truly alone.

Most cruisers travel in pairs; however, some take on extra passengers for passage making. This practice sounds good and certainly reduces the workload. It makes watch keeping much easier and can even shorten the passage: Sail changes can be made more often when there are many fresh hands for the task. The price of this assistance, however, is loss of privacy. Let me reemphasize that if you feel you need extra help, consider the crew candidates well, and specify a space on board to serve as a refuge. A good spot might be the foredeck. You might also declare that anyone who goes forward and sits with legs over the edge should be left alone. It's a good idea, too, to give a prospective crew member a written copy of the ship's rules before signing the person on. The ship's articles I use are in appendix B; you can modify them to suit your own needs.

LACK OF PERSONAL POSSESSIONS

Living in a small space requires reducing the number of possessions before setting sail and limiting the acquisition of new items while under way. New cruisers tend to jam everything possible on board. The result is that, with little room for airflow in the lockers below, all the treasures become moldy. Stowing things above deck is no solution; this practice breeds floating junkyards that are as dangerous and hard on the equipment as they are offensive. Recall figure 2.2. Personal treasures simply have no place aboard a small sailing ship, especially not if you care about their condition. Water and salt get everywhere. Very few things can take exposure to salt water without corroding, molding, or being otherwise corrupted. Nice things just cannot be kept nice on a boat. Some of my favorite books have been turned to glue by undetected small leaks.

So you must be prepared to make do with very few possessions—and even those must be practical and easily replaceable. Any treasures purchased along the way must be incorruptible or regularly shipped home.

ABSENCE OF CONVENIENCE

Convenience is in short supply on boats, because of the lack of so many other things: water and power, for example. Even if you spend all your time tied to a pier, the electricity available there is at best less than a quarter that of the average home, more often an eighth or less. This means reductions of all those shoreside, labor-saving conveniences such as toasters and microwaves. It also means budgeting what you do use at any given time so you don't overload the circuits. It is often not possible to operate a heater and an iron or hair dryer at the same time.

The lack of water on board changes even the simple act of taking a relaxing shower into a combination of a ballet and a lube job. Washing dishes requires rethinking, to minimize rinsewater use.

Washing clothes is another matter. This requires a trip to a shoreside laundromat, which by international treaty is always located at least a mile from any marina. Because few cruisers have access to a car, it is desirable to have spent several years as a journeyman Sherpa in Nepal before going cruising. Reprovisioning, too, requires logistical planning on a scale only slightly smaller than that required for Operation Overlord (in this instance, maybe Operation Overload).

Still, the lack of a car is small potatoes compared to the lack of a telephone. You may end up plugging $6 of quarters into a telephone to get things done, or even to reach out and touch someone for a few minutes. The more expensive alternative, calling collect, will show you who your real friends are. Imagine how you would feel if your mother refused your call.

DISREGARD FOR COMFORT

Sailing exposes you to the elements: sun, rain, and always the wind. Although bimini tops, dodgers, and, lately, pilothouses offer protection, you'll still need a tolerance for standing in the wind and rain in storm gear. To many cruisers, however, the beauty of the sea during the rain offsets the small trickle of cold water seeping down the back of the neck.

But weather is not the only element you are indecently exposed to while cruising. Various insidious insects, such as mosquitoes and their numerous biting relatives, gnaw away on you while you are trying to enjoy the outdoor living.

Indoor living in tropical climates, on the other hand, will increase your contact with spoon-size cockroaches and rats much larger than that. Vigilance and persistence can keep your rat exposure to a minimum, but you will have to develop a certain tolerance for cockroaches. You will encounter them not only on board but also ashore and in even the best stores, restaurants, and homes.

Much has been written about this subject, but as far as I am aware there is no known chemical, incantation, or patron saint that will protect you from eventual cockroach infestation. Indeed, one of the joys of trips into colder climates is knowing that while you are pulling on the long underwear, somewhere on board there are cockroaches freezing to death.

While on the subject of comfort—or rather lack thereof—a few words on *mal de mer.* It is usually caused by the unaccustomed motion of the boat, which affects the inner ear and stomach. Most, but not all, people are affected by it to some degree or other. The risk of being adversely affected is greater if you are cold, apprehensive, or hungry. Keep something in your stomach, then, if possible, and keep warm. Avoiding apprehension comes from confidence that the boat and, consequently, you, are in no danger, even in rough weather. For this reason, experience lessens the number of seasickness attacks.

If you find yourself getting queasy, go above deck, fix your eyes on the forward horizon, get the wind in your face, and try to find a comfortable position. The position of least motion is in the dynamic center of the boat. Some people find this spot close to the deck just forward of the mast, if it isn't too wet; others find that lying down in the cockpit works best.

For some reason steering the boat will often help you to overcome the queasies. It may be because at the helm, you often have the wind in your face and your eyes on the horizon, or it may be because you have some control over the boat's motion there. Concentrating on your course through the water may also allow you to adjust to the motion of the sea with more success. Many cruisers hand steer early in the passage, rotating duty among crew members to help them get their sea legs.

I have no personal experience with the various antiseasickness devices or medicines available. I understand that each has its own side effects, from mild to severe depending on the person. If you think you will need such devices or medicines, experiment with them before the trip.

If all else fails and you are reduced to throwing up, may I recommend the use of a plastic bucket? It is portable, easily cleaned, and takes little skill or concentration to hit. It does not require you to know which way the wind is blowing, nor does it expose you—at a time when your equilibrium is not the best—to falling overboard while hanging over the side.

Prolonged seasickness can be dangerous, especially if no liquids can be held down. The victim becomes dehydrated, and the constant throwing up depletes the body of necessary minerals and electrolytes. Either situation in the extreme can cause death. The vomiting must be controlled and liquids kept down within a few days if dire consequences are to be avoided. Drugs may have to be used. Trimethobenzamide suppositories are handy to reduce vomiting in an emergency. However, like any suppository, they need refrigeration in tropical climates. Once the vomiting has been controlled, a sports liquid supplement such as Gatorade can be used to replenish electrolytes and minerals.

SCARCITY OF CLOSE RELATIONSHIPS

One of the major drawbacks to cruising is the loss of contact with your family and old friends. You may go several years between visits with even the closest of shoreside friends and relatives. Even letter contact is restricted, as getting mail while cruising is at best a hit-or-miss, once-every-couple-of-months event.

Nor does the cruising lifestyle lend itself well to developing close relationships. It takes time to develop friendships, and generally speaking, the more time, the more valuable they become. But you do not have the time while cruising to spend on this process. Because you are constantly coming and going, the friendships that you establish will by necessity be casual. You will get to know many people but none really well. Cruising is a banquet with no main course—just an infinite variety of hors d'oeuvres.

The only lasting relationships that can be established are those with other cruisers. These can become quite strong while you're cruising, but they tend to die quickly once the trip is over. They can be compared to relationships with old army buddies: They are formed under difficult or stressful conditions with limited choices available, and they're extremely loyal while those conditions prevail. Once conditions return to normal, though, the friendships are often not maintained.

THE NEED TO KNOW

The need to know what is going on in the world has to be a low priority for cruising people. Magazine subscriptions are most often given up. Newspapers and television are available only in population centers. Shortwave radio news is the only steady source of information, but frankly, very few cruisers listen to these broadcasts. World events seem to lose their relevance on a cruise.

And that to the best of my knowledge is what cruising is like.

3

How to Get There

As long as they avoid strange taverns along the waterfront, most people do not wake up one day and mysteriously find themselves outward bound on a sailboat. Going cruising, unlike being shanghaied, is the result of a whole series of small decisions and events over time. The pathways are many, varied, and strewn with obstacles. Some we have control over, like preparation; others, like opportunity, we can effect only in a minor way.

Good preparation consists in part of good planning, proper training, and the right equipment—subjects covered in detail in the remaining chapters of this book. But good preparation also involves avoiding common mistakes and pitfalls, knowing how to go when the opportunity presents itself, and knowing what to expect in the critical first year.

Common Mistakes

Several case histories of people who have failed to make the transition from shore life to life afloat have been reported in such literature as Jan and Bill Moeller's *Living Aboard*. These failures generally resulted from lack of team effort, bad communication, or poor preparation.

TEAM EFFORT

One of the things I most enjoy about cruising is talking with dock walkers. I walked the dock for 15 years before I left to cruise, and such conversations are an important part of the dream. Dock walkers often come with partners in tow—some equally enthusiastic about the dream, but many more obviously less so. That latter partner generally has little to say. As I watch the silent person's reactions to the discussion, I can see that the two are not a team. It is a little sad to watch the enthusiasm of the talker and know that he or she will never realize the dream.

Anyone contemplating cruising should understand that the single most important item to a successful cruise is neither the boat nor the budget but a good cruising partner. Single-handed cruising appeals to very few people. Without a partner most people simply won't go.

If you look at successful world cruisers such as Eric Hiscock, Hal Roth, Maurice Cloughley, and Miles Smeeton, you will find one common element—a satisfied cruising companion. It is a safe bet that none of the above names would be familiar without Susan, Margaret, Katie, and Beryl beside them. The personalities and attitudes of these cruising companions are the single most important factor required for a successful cruise. I am constantly amazed at their grit. Katie Cloughley, for instance, apparently got seasick on every passage from the first to the last, five years later (Cloughley, *A World to the West*).

So if you want to go cruising, you must either develop, find, or have a companion. Developing companionship isn't always easy, but it is a whole lot simpler than finding one. If you are lucky enough to have a companion, do not destroy the relationship, lest you destroy your dream along with it.

DESTRUCTION OF THE CRUISING COMPANION

An example might be helpful—but first let me note that the following story may sound sexist, because I've placed a man in the role of cruiser, a woman in the role of partner. This is partly a literary convenience and partly a reflection of the reality I've seen: Men seem to offend most often. Of course, women may also be lead cruisers and make these same mistakes when dealing with their partners. (One woman I know would bring the boat into the slip then debark and conspicuously retie all the dock lines secured by her husband. They never went cruising.)

Take, then, the couple who have just bought a new boat. Neither knows much about sailing, but they have read books, and it sounds like an interesting and romantic thing to do. *He* gets the equipment he feels is necessary to outfit the boat, and off they go on a short cruise to a place *he* has picked out. Already the developing problem is apparent.

Once asea, what happens? *He* gets to play with his new toy, *he* ups the sails, pulls on various lines, twiddles knobs on electronic boxes—all of which will bring unpredictable results. But no matter. He looks jaunty in his captain's hat, and the spirit of adventure and learning is present. Exhilarating!

Meanwhile, *she* gets to cook and clean just as *she* did at home—except that not only does she have no new toys, she also has none of the conveniences or space of home. Further, the kitchen tips. Do you think she is exhilarated? Probably not, but she may tolerate matters because he is having a good time and there are interesting things to see and do ashore.

Does the man count his blessings? No, he is determined to self-destruct. They bring the boat back to the home pier with all the marina watching, and of course he brings it in too fast (slowly would show him up as a beginner), and also misjudges what the wind will do to its drift. As the edge of the pier is about to scrape a long gouge on the side of his new hull, he realizes his mistake.

The boat is by this time totally out of control. Helpless and confused, he turns to the only outlet left. He yells at his wife, giving her garbled instructions—something about making a superhuman jump to the dock, then pulling or pushing something to save the boat from disaster.

Of course none of what he has asked is possible or even sensible, and disaster strikes. The verbal tirade grows even more fevered. The poor woman is made the goat in front of the whole marina by a male ego trying to save face. Can you predict the result of this scene? Do you see yourself here? Does your partner see you here? I hope not, for in either case you can kiss cruising good-bye.

Now all of this has eroded the wife's confidence in her husband's ability to handle the boat safely. He decides that the best way to calm her fears is to show her how much he knows and how capable he is. What better way to do this than by going out sailing in a near gale? Right! While he sits back enjoying the waves and the wind, she spends the entire trip reciting the Lord's Prayer under her breath and promising anything if she is just delivered from the jaws of death. Is it any wonder so many wives dislike cruising? There are already enough things about cruising to create fear in your partner without your adding to them.

Fear is often the most serious objection to cruising. Sailing around a big ocean seems risky and unfamiliar, and can generate considerable concern in a companion. This is normal and healthy; fear is a basic human emotion. People fear what they do not understand but respect those dangers that they do.

For example, driving certainly has its dangers, probably many more than cruising. Yet most of us still drive, because we understand and are familiar with driving and its dangers. We know something about automobiles, freeways, and traffic laws. This allows us to deal with the dangers in a rational way. Even though survival at sea isn't all that difficult, crossing big oceans in little boats provides plenty of areas for concern: storms, becoming lost, being run down by a freighter or attacked by pirates. Learning about such fears may offer insight, aid communication, and help build a cruising team.

Violent weather strikes terror into the hearts of most people, whether they are in Kansas City or the Japan Sea. However, those in the Japan Sea may have a bit more anxiety, for they have no place to go to seek shelter from the violence. They are literally blown before the storm, tossed at its whim for as long as it lasts. The power and energy of a large weather disturbance are immense, the motion of a boat in a storm is violent, and the noise is almost unbearable. Add the smell of sulfur and you have all the ingredients of Hell.

Dealing safely with violent weather requires the combination of a proper boat, good seamanship, and judicious planning. A good boat and proper seamanship training are discussed in later chapters; as for planning, note that understanding weather and weather patterns may allow you to avoid violent weather altogether. Some cruisers have gone all the way around the world and never been in a violent storm at sea.

Although being lost at sea is not a real or significant problem, the fear of it can be considerable. This apprehension has two sources: an individual's lack of knowledge about the methods of navigation, and the fact that the human animal is basically a visual creature.

Over the centuries vision has been the single most important sense for supplying information to the brain about individual security. When we hear a noise we do not understand, we first look to see what caused the noise, and only then relax, run, or fight. Any of our senses may warn us of impending doom, but we always confirm it by sight. Deprive us of vision and we become very uneasy. The same effect can be produced more subtly by just removing the information provided by sight. Who, for example, has not felt anxious in the dark or fog? We can still see what is immediately in front of us, but we feel uneasy because of the things we can't see just beyond that blank gray wall of sameness; that's what troubles the mind.

The ocean is a very large place, and it all looks the same. Your eyes provide very little information to help your brain figure out where it is and what is in front of it. Whichever way you look is just bumpy blue water. The uneasiness generated by this situation is understandable. Learning the proper boat-handling and navigation skills will go a long way toward reducing it, though.

Being lost at sea on a boat doesn't even come close to being lost at sea without a boat. Getting lost overboard and watching the boat sail slowly off into the sunset is the ultimate in horror stories. For that matter, coming on deck after a good night's sleep to find the cockpit empty can also be very disconcerting. Can this happen? Yes. Can the chances of its occurring be minimized? Yes. The best bet is to stick with the ship at all costs, and fortunately that is not hard to do.

In the average cruising boat on passage most people work and live in the cockpit. Thus the cockpit is your first line of defense against falling overboard. It should be large enough to contain the crew comfortably while working and relaxing, and large enough that if you lose your footing you fall into the cockpit rather than out of the boat. The next lines of defense are adequate deck space and lifelines; for information on these subjects see chapter 7.

Collision at sea with whales and ships has received considerable press. Certainly ships, whales, or even large floating debris can cause severe damage to a small cruising vessel. Commercial ships travel in excess of 20 knots; warships can exceed 30 knots. At these speeds, a ship that is completely out of sight just over the horizon (hull down) can approach and cut you in half in less than 20 minutes.

All large ships, even those standing proper watch at sea, should be treated as if they cannot see you (regardless of the claims made by the manufacturer of your radar reflector). If you get hit by a large ship, the fault of the matter is of little importance to anyone except the survivors, among whom you probably will not be found. The larger ship won't even realize it hit you.

Malicious attack by whales is something I don't choose to believe in. Since 1819 there have been 13 reported attacks by whales; I feel that all have been cases of circumstantial evidence or bad press. The details on all but three of these attacks are sketchy, and it is difficult to tell if the whales attacked or if the boat ran into them. (Hitting a sleeping whale will do considerable damage to both vessel and whale.) In most cases a cruiser felt a heavy blow to the boat, rushed up on deck, and saw a whale in the area. In at least one of these "attacks," the whale had been wounded previously by a Japanese whaling vessel (Hollander and Mertes, "The Successful Castaways").

Guilty or not, whales are very large animals, and when they fix you with that unblinking eye at a close range, you know that they are in control of the situation. Fortunately, most whales I've met seemed to be decent fellows. I have seen humpback and killer whales go through some amazing gymnastics to miss my boat. If they come near yours, stay calm and disavow any knowledge of the Japanese whaling industry.

Certainly there are large pieces of barely floating garbage that, if hit, can do considerable damage to a small boat. In fact, most cruisers report having had close calls with such objects. It is always startling to find a large, silent, stationary object close to the boat in the middle of a fluid world. I would have struck a large, unseen tree once, except that my approach startled some roosting sea birds in time for me to take evasive action. The outcome might not have been so benign had I not been standing watch.

And therein lies the simple solution to collision at sea. Standing watch is not always one of the most pleasant tasks, but do it. It may be warm and cozy in your bunk, and most of the time nothing will happen requiring your attention, but stand watch anyway. If you don't you are taking a risk, and as with any other risk you will on occasion get caught. The consequences of getting caught on this one are severe. On our first long passage, we saw only four ships in 22 days—but we had to change course to avoid collision with two of them. The probability of that occurring was remote, which is a good example of what can happen if you rely completely on probability. Standing watch is lonely, sometimes cold, sometimes beautiful and peaceful, but always necessary to the life and safety of the boat. The key to workable watch schedules is rest. Each crew member must get sufficient rest to function properly.

If there are enough people on board to stand three distinct watch crews during the night, then the traditional watch hours (8 to 12, 12 to 4, 4 to 8) are okay because each crew member can get eight hours of sleep. However, when sailing shorthanded—with only two watch crews available—I prefer to change to longer stints so that the person off watch gets through rapid eye movement sleep and rises refreshed.

Because you have to allow 20 minutes on each end of a watch for such matters as changing clothes, using the head, or perhaps brewing a cup of tea, a four-hour watch schedule means you'll get only about three hours of sleep at best. Most people wake up groggy after only three hours of sleep. Arriving on deck in the middle of the night in this state is not one of the best ideas in the world, and several days of it can lead to exhaustion.

Six-hour evening watches, on the other hand, allow the off-watch person to get enough sleep (more than five hours) to awake feeling reasonably refreshed, and a catnap later in the day will bring him or her back up to feeling normal. Each cruiser can experiment and find what works best. We use a 2100 hrs to 0300 hrs, 0300 hrs to 0900 hrs evening schedule, with three-hour watches during the day.

On the other hand, six hours can be a long time to be alone and alert. This may be a good time to use the concept of the rightness of relative wrongness. We choose six-hour watches, but let the autopilot steer. Also, we've found that Debby can sleep better during daylight hours than I can, and so our system has evolved into a sort of day- and night-shift routine.

If you trust electronics, the newer radar units have built-in detectors that will sound an alarm if an echo is returned within any preset radius from the boat. The alarm can be triggered by another boat, a ship, or other hard substance. It may also malfunction, providing an electronic false alarm or failing to sound when it should. I consider radar to be an aid to rather than a substitute for watch standing.

If vigilance fails, be prepared to handle holes in the hull of the boat and, if necessary, abandon the vessel in a safe, orderly manner—both necessary seamanship skills beyond the scope of this text.

Avoiding ships that are trying not to hit you is easier than avoiding those ships that are. For example, the final chapter of Bill and Patty Kamerer's dream cruise will probably never be known: "Pipe Cay, Bahamas. The bloodstained sloop *Kalia III,* found drifting with its anchor line cut and a body half out of the dinghy . . ." (Dvorak, editorial in *Practical Sailor*). What is certain is that the couple encountered modern-day pirates. It is unfortunate that a dream so serene and peaceful can be punctuated by such violence. Fortunately, piracy, like the other dangers I've discussed, is a rare occurrence.

Pirate defense is somewhat similar to storm defense, in that both adversaries are generally confined to specific areas. Piracy is presently prevalent in areas where drug trafficking is common, such as the Bahamas and Colombia; areas where law enforcement is weak, such as the Philippines and Vietnam; and areas of political unrest, including the Near East. If possible, avoid these areas.

If you are determined to visit such places, though, try to do so with a group of boats. If you are forced to go alone, be wary of all boats, stay far offshore, and travel as quickly and as inconspicuously as possible. It may be best to travel at night with your radar reflector down and running lights off to minimize detection.

If you are anchored in "pirate areas," post an anchor watch. Use radar if available to detect any target within a preset distance from the boat. This, along with a loud-hailer used as a listening device, can give you early warning of the approach of suspicious vessels. The earlier the warning, the more distance between your vessel and theirs; the greater this distance, the greater your advantage. Once they get their hands on your gunwale someone is going to get hurt. The odds are that it will be you.

In any pirate contact your options are limited to running, negotiating, and fighting. Some people have outrun or outmaneuvered pirate vessels, but in most instances the pirate boat will be faster. Those who choose to negotiate will be doing so from a very weak position—which might be summarized as feed the lion your arm in hope that it won't eat all of you. "Take what you want but don't hurt me" is a tricky set of negotiations. You must determine who is in charge and the correct position to adopt instantly.

Some pirates are best approached by complete subjugation; others are excited to further violence by this. Sometimes a cavalier attitude and humor will win. Other times being firm is the best approach. You must be able to read personalities quickly and correctly.

In 1984, Herb Payson polled nine cruising boats to determine their crews' attitudes toward guns (Payson, "Guns on Yachts: Peril, Placebo, or Panacea"). Seven had or would take guns. Unfortunately, the decision to take a gun is easier than the decision to use it. The presence of a gun without the firm commitment to use it can be an invitation to disaster, because it can quickly escalate the level of hostilities. There is no place for hesitation; that split second while your conscience sorts things out is just long enough to allow the meanies to ventilate you.

If you have never killed anybody, it is not easy. Most people are not physiologically prepared to kill. Do not depend on fear to motivate you, either; fear tends to hope for other solutions first and only falls back on killing as a means of self-defense. This is not a defensive situation, though. Against superior numbers and weapons, surprise and offensive action are your only hopes. Anger can cause offensive action; the provocation it takes to arouse enough anger for you to kill, however, can be significant, and may get you killed in the process.

It takes a detached, businesslike efficiency to kill—as if you're passing the butter. Few people have that attitude. Before carrying a gun you should examine yourself carefully to see if you indeed have the personality to use it.

CREATING THE CRUISING COMPANION

Creating a cruising companion involves using common sense and showing consideration. Make your partner a real part of the project by involving him or her equally in the enjoyment of sailing; in sail handling and navigation; in boating decisions, duties, and planning. Make sure the team effort is reflected in the layout of the boat as well as the itinerary.

Men, in particular, can be very single minded and miss some very simple points. They tend to concentrate on the boat and the systems that run it. They reason that the boat and its systems play a major role in the occupants' safety; therefore, it should come first. But this logical argument can destroy your own dream. The days of tyrannical ship captains were over long ago.

The captain who doesn't include the first mate in the planning is in for a very short or lonely cruise. Of course the boat has to be sound, and the systems that run it in good order. But adding life's little amenities—hot water and refrigeration, for example—to a boat can improve performance more than a fully battened main. The captain who considers the first mate's comfort helps create a partner who shares her or his enthusiasm for cruising.

Quite often, though, the partner is not interested in thinking about cruising. The error in this case would be to go on making decisions without your partner's input. While this path certainly offers less resistance, it is a sure breeding ground for later trouble. Somehow interest must be generated in both partners or the probability of ever going cruising is small.

The partner whose dream it is to go cruising must determine any underlying problem, and search for a mutually acceptable solution. It helps to concentrate on the joys of cruising until interest is sparked.

Most people assume that their own feelings are normal, that everyone feels the way they do. The potential cruiser believes that cruising is so exciting that everybody wants to go. The noncruiser feels just as strongly that all this talk about boats is just a phase and will soon pass, because no right-thinking human being could want to give up all the comfort and security of shore life.

The persistence of either attitude will breed trouble. Without honest communication one of the parties will simply be waiting for the other to lose interest—and often will see to it that the loss of interest is realized, generally as quickly as possible. If you are into martyrdom this situation is ideal. Both during and after the cruise one of you will be a martyr. Remember the golden rule of martyrdom: Whosoever is sacrificed gets to demand payment for that sacrifice again and again.

Good communication from the outset is the best solution. Listen to your partner, and be sure the words you're speaking have the same meaning to each of you. I know a man who spent two years arguing with his wife about cruising because they understood the phrase "living on a boat" differently. They both had the same basic approach; they just misunderstood the words used by the other to describe that approach. Unfortunately the error was not detected until the opportunity to cruise had passed. They never went bluewater cruising.

PREPARATION

The laws of probability dictate that in any given normal life span both good and bad things happen, and in almost equal proportion. One of the surest ways to effect the laws of probability, though, and maximize the chance of good things happening, is proper preparation. Just as cold is the absence of heat, bad luck can be thought of as the absence of preparation. Or, in other words, good Boy Scouts never have bad luck. Ah, the wisdom of probability!

It is true that there are cruisers who used little planning, or made bad use of the planning tools. However, who can say that if these folks had better planned, they would not be enjoying their cruises more? And many of the people who have quit cruising may well have stayed with it if their planning had been better. It is impossible to lead parallel lives, of course, but the odds for success are definitely with good planning.

Although *selecting an itinerary* is often used synonymously with *planning*, I consider the itinerary just one part of a good plan. This good plan includes goals and strategy along with schedules, budgets, mileposts, and an itinerary. A good plan will help you get the right boat equipped properly; it will help you be at the right spot at the right time of the year with the necessary know-how. I have witnessed examples of bad planning in the larger sense as well as in the smaller context of just a bad itinerary.

WRONG EQUIPMENT

Many cruisers do not spend enough time and effort getting the right boat and equipment. Fortunately, some of these people end up with a more or less suitable boat simply by chance; however, I know of several people whose early purchase left them with a large investment sunk into a craft they later found unsuitable.

For example, an acquaintance spent 10 years constructing a boat in his backyard and finally launched it in the Columbia River, where he intended to learn to sail for a year before venturing offshore. He was in his late 60s and poor health. The boat was a heavy-displacement, traditional cruising boat with a bowsprit and heavy tiller—according to much of the literature, the ideal cruising boat.

Unfortunately, because it was so heavy, it required large sails and a bowsprit to drive it. My friend and his wife could not handle such a rig. Setting and dousing sails on a bowsprit is not a job for anyone who is not physically fit—even in good weather, let alone in a blow.

Since the boat would not sail in winds of much less than 10 knots, and certainly not without a sail on the bowsprit, the two were forced to sail only in moderately heavy conditions and had to motor the rest of the time. Learning to sail in winds of 14 knots is not a soothing experience.

Further, because the boat had a full keel, it was sluggish on the helm and a nightmare to bring into the slip. Each time the pair came back from a learning experience they had new fears, ranging from bouncing off docks to turning end around in locks and battling to get the sails down on a boat out of control. Each new fear helped to extinguish the dream. Finally, they were reduced to motoring only, and after several harrowing experiences they gave up their dream as impractical. Moral: *The wrong piece of equipment for the right couple.* Chapters 7 through 10 will help you avoid such problems.

POOR TRAINING

Another couple I know also spent 10 years building their boat before they were finally ready to go. When the great day arrived, they knew a lot about boatbuilding but very little about sailing or seamanship.

They chose to launch the vessel in a nearby river that emptied into the ocean, because it was the closest body of water to their building site. Unfortunately, such harbors are notorious for their treacherous bars. With no experience sailing, the couple did not realize their error in selecting this launch point, nor did they understand the channel-marking system.

They got their only boat-handling experience on the trip from the launch point to the slip, then immediately began loading up with supplies and gear for the long-awaited voyage to Hawaii. After a modest send-off by friends and relatives, they set out to cross the bar—at the wrong time. They misread a buoy and their boat was driven back onto the beach, where it was pounded to pieces by the surf. Happily, no one was killed or injured, but the boat was a complete loss within 72 hours of its launch. Moral: *Sailing skills are as important as the boat.* These skills are discussed in chapter 5.

POOR ITINERARY

Jan and Bill Moeller, in their book *Living Aboard,* told of encountering an individual who set a 50-mile-a-day schedule—no matter what. After only a short time he gave up cruising, because of the difficulties of holding to this schedule. The Moellers concluded that the schedule caused his failure.

This belief is not uncommon among the cruising gentry, many of whom consider scheduling the antithesis of cruising. They believe that to enjoy a cruise you need but a minimum of direction; true freedom is the complete escape from schedules.

I think this conclusion is too simplistic and thus invalid. If a board is cut too short, do we blame the saw? Improper use of a tool will generally produce unsatisfactory results. My experience has shown that the people with no plan to go anywhere generally go nowhere.

They tend to drift around a small area and become floating vagrants or, at best, victims of the environment.

For example, we met a couple in northern British Columbia who followed the philosophy that no plan is a good plan. We were both cruising north to Alaska and spent some time together in Klewnugget Inlet, 30 miles south of Prince Rupert. Forty-five days later we met up with the pair again, this time on our way back from points north. We had traveled as far north as Skagway and Glacier Bay; they had turned around much farther south, at Petersburg. What is of interest here is that it was north of Petersburg that we had been surrounded by humpback whales for several hours on two different occasions and had seen a tidewater glacier calve—just a few of the adventures that they did not experience, and that I would not have traded for any amount of carefree swinging on the hook in a warm, secluded, picturesque bay.

Not that we didn't sometimes swing on the hook in warm, picturesque bays longer than we'd planned. We did. But by using our target itinerary we knew what tradeoffs to expect. Had we continued to lay over in picturesque bays because we didn't know what to expect elsewhere, we would have missed those whales.

Proper planning, like the use of any tool, requires training and practice. Because we had an itinerary, when we added a few days' unscheduled layover in one area, we could assess what we were going to lose later somewhere else. This gave us a basis for value judgments and a certain amount of control over our destiny.

It is hard to say whether we or our friends had a more enjoyable cruise, but that of course is not the point. No matter what kind of adventure you enjoy, a good plan will improve your chances of enjoying it. Chapter 4 is dedicated to helping you sharpen your planning skills.

The Business of Going

Training, planning, and equipment are all easily recognized as parts of preparing to go cruising. What sneaks up on a lot of people, though, is the difficulty involved in just the business of going. Questions such as when to go, how to finally untie the mooring lines, and what happens during the critical first year to cause disenchantment need to be considered as well.

WHEN TO GO

Each cruiser will have a different *best* time. The choice depends on your own personal goals and priorities. Still, it may be helpful to reflect briefly on some of those who are presently out and about.

My own somewhat less-than-rigorous data-collection methods—conversations with those hundred or so boats I encountered while cruising—show that cruisers seem to fall into two distinct groups: those 24 to 36 years old, and those 52 to 68. There are very few cruisers younger than 24 (children of cruisers excluded), over 68, or in the middle group from 36 to 52. Since these groupings apparently exist, there must be some valid reasons for their existence.

EARLY CRUISERS

Early cruisers seem to have a window available before their lives are complicated by career or family. Lack of complications and this group's enthusiasm, vitality, and ability to tolerate discomfort all lend them to cruising. Youth's ability to adapt reduces the shock to the system from the radical change in lifestyle that cruising brings. Culture shock is also less, because these folks have had less time to establish living patterns and prejudices. If they are tolerant and open, they have an excellent opportunity for growth, by gathering wisdom from the interaction with other cultures. They also have long lives ahead in which to apply that wisdom.

The disadvantages for this group are the lack of funds, the disruption of working toward other goals, and the lack of general life experience. Early cruisers tend to go with smaller boats and smaller budgets than those who leave later. They generally spend proportionately more of their principal—but then they can afford to, because they still have years of strong earning power left.

Since the trip can be very disruptive to any career plans, these cruisers usually stay out for only 18 to 36 months. The longer they cruise, however, the greater the shock on returning to a more standard life.

Because they are so young and their education (and sometimes their schooling) is incomplete, the significance of much of what they see is lost on them. For example, the appreciation of art requires experiences gained from living. The *Mona Lisa* is simply an old painting of a girl with a funny smile unless you have experienced the same feelings the artist captured on the canvas.

A general and broad education improves the cruising experience. How many cruisers would pass right by a nondescript bay on the eastern side of the Athenian Peninsula exposed to the winds from the south? Probably quite a few, unless they knew that convenient depths existed under the lee of a small peninsula on the northern side of the bay—and that the Persian fleet anchored there before its battle with the Athenians (Markov and Helmert, *Battles of World History*). A broad education acquaints you with a battle fought here 2,500 years ago that affected much of the democratic world—not because it added the marathon race to the sporting world (although it did) but because here, just inland on the broad Plains of Marathon south of the river, the Greek phalanx propelled the Athenians to victory over the Persians, securing their place in history, popularizing their method of government, and laying the groundwork for the success of Alexander the Great.

LATE CRUISERS

Late cruisers seem to fall into two subclasses: people in their early 50s who are on a sabbatical cruise and those in their 60s who have retired. Most have adequate money, have reached most of their goals in life, and have the necessary experience and education to appreciate their experiences more fully. They generally try not to spend their principal, because they have little earning power left when they return.

The sabbatical cruiser is looking for a short break from the pressures of life. (Slocum may have been among the first cruisers of this type.) These people are looking for a place to recover from family and business pressures and heal their wounds. Cruising is an excellent resource for this. These cruises need to be between 18 and 36 months: Shorter cruises will not repair the damage, and longer ones make it difficult to reenter the business world. In most modern careers, if you are three years out of date you might as well be dead. Retired cruisers tend to cruise longer than either sabbatical or early cruisers.

An advantage of cruising late is that it does not disrupt your life as much. In addition, the properly prepared older cruiser has more time to get the necessary skills. Older cruisers also generally have larger, more comfortable boats (on the other hand, they require more comfort to be content). Also, the long-established habits of the older person may be difficult to modify.

The disadvantages to cruising late in life are often the low threshold of discomfort, along with the lack of vitality, strength, and time to assimilate what is experienced on the cruise. The cold, wet sea and its constant motion can take its toll on anyone's strength and vitality. If those reserves are low to begin with, the discomfort can easily go beyond an individual's personal threshold. The result is that it ain't fun, so why do it? And late cruisers don't—or, ideally, they alter their go-anywhere-anytime plans to better match their capabilities.

OTHER CRUISERS

There aren't many cruisers between 36 and 52 out there—I suspect because those years are critical to family and career. People in this age bracket who do go cruising suffer more disruption to their lives—they simply have less time to reach goals either before or after the trip. In addition, they often have teenage children who want and need exposure to other teenagers. The early 40s is also the time when most careers hit their steepest climb, and the loss of those years is disruptive to any career.

Some (small) numbers of people below 24 and above 68 are out there. The only ones I've met dropped out quickly: The young lacked money; the old, strength.

UNTYING DOCK LINES

Untying the dock lines may seem like a nonproblem to most prospective cruisers, and it is—until the actual moment arrives. Watching your dream become reality is not as free of stress as you may think. My own final check of the weather, and of our decision to head into the Pacific, was made near the edge of panic.

I looked up from that weather chart and said to Debby, "Okay, we go now." My feelings are easy to remember but hard to explain. There was a strange unreal air in the boat, as if I were no longer a part of the world but somehow watching the scene from afar. My words didn't sound as if they had come from me. The pit of my stomach was hard. I had a crazy notion that I was Eisenhower making the decision to launch the attack on D Day.

These feelings fell away only sluggishly as the coastline slowly shrank behind us. It is hard to say how you will feel, but it may very well be similar.

Nevertheless, there comes a time when the engine must be started, the lines untied, and the horizon crossed. As with getting into cold water, there are many different techniques. Some take a deep breath, run headlong to the edge, and plunge over; some stand on the edge and vacillate, with alternate feelings of anxiety and anticipation; others wade slowly in, dying by inches.

Who can say which is the best way? To each his own. I will ignore the first type of individual, however, who needs no help to get into cruising (even though he or she may need help getting out). Instead, let me address the second and third types.

Many times the conscious mind says *Jump now* and the subconscious mind paralyzes the body into inaction. Leaving a shoreside life with all its familiarity and security can bring waves of paralyzing anxiety—maybe rightly so. I know cruisers who treat it by installing another radar or GPS so they will be "fully prepared." Of course, everyone who has ever gone cruising has gone unprepared (some more than others). You have to realize that you will never be 100 percent ready. But if you have the basic training, the necessary equipment, and the budget, you should have a safe and, if not comfortable, at least successful voyage.

Anxiety probably can't be eliminated, but it can be lessened by learning as much as you can about the conditions you are plunging into, what you are going to do when you are there, and how you are going to get out again. A good plan will reduce anxiety by providing a sense of being in control. Reading about cruising and talking to cruisers will help, too. Unfortunately, both sources tend to focus more on the positive than the negative. Try to gather both. Knowing the necessary skills and having proper equipment to cruise safely will reduce worry and distress.

Finally, the best way to avoid anxiety is not to concern yourself with the whole plunge; turn instead to each small intermediate step. If you take each step as it comes along, the last step will be there before you are aware of it. This step will be just another small step, like all the others, and with confidence born of experience you will take it. With anxiety, but controllable anxiety, you will find yourself floating free, going where you think you intend to go.

THE CRITICAL FIRST YEAR

Surprisingly, perhaps, most cruises are abandoned in the first year. Some unhappy cruisers adapt to "just another lousy day in paradise," but the majority quit prematurely.

Like any change in lifestyle, cruising requires an emotional adjustment. This can be more severe than other life transitions, though, because you will be subjected to two different kinds of emotional shock—that encountered when you change lifestyles, and that of interacting with different cultures.

All this can cause considerable discomfort, and the reasons for it are not always self-evident. Understanding and preparing for these changes can reduce the shock to an acceptable limit and help you to adjust during the critical first-year period.

Stress caused by a change in lifestyle is subtle and will occur even if you do not leave your neighborhood. This kind of shock is relatively common; for example, it occurs when we graduate from high school, enter or leave military service (especially if there was combat involved), get married (where there is always combat involved), experience a death in the family, get a divorce, or even have a change in employment pattern (changing jobs, getting downsized, or retiring). Any of the "thousand natural shocks that flesh is heir to" can cause stress.

Stress manifests itself as uncomfortable feelings, insecurity, or a general lack of enjoyment. All of these feelings may be very real, but they may also be more a part of the transition than of the cruising life. The negative effects of the transition can be minimized by being aware of some of the changes that will occur, though, and by waiting until the shock subsides to make any drastic or pivotal decisions.

The most common problem in adjusting to cruising is failing to realize that the basic rules of living will change when you shift from shore to sea. Three big differences come to mind immediately: You will have more time, less money, and no fixed residence.

Time will become at once more available and harder to control. Money there will definitely be less of, but there will also be less use for it, so it will have less value. Mobile living requires limited personal possessions and constantly making and leaving friends.

THE REDEFINITION OF TIME

This involves slowing down and adjusting to the loss of external controls on your time. *Slowing down!* Many people say that is what they want to happen when they go cruising. What does it mean? Let me give you a personal example. When my shiny new yacht was delivered, I took a week off to outfit and commission it. I had already had several months to contemplate its arrival, which I passed by dreaming and planning.

I appeared on the dock that spring morning with a complete complement of tools and parts and a schedule of things to be done. Full of my usual shoreside vigor, I attacked the first item on the schedule. It happened to be a task on deck. I had not worked more than 10 minutes before I was interrupted.

"A new boat?"

"Yes."

"Nice looking."

"Thank-you."

"What kind is she?"

One thing about having a new toy: You cannot resist talking about it. More than an hour passed as I proudly showed off the new vessel and we discussed the merits of its features. Eventually my new friend moved off to his own tasks and I set about starting mine up again.

Ten minutes later I was again interrupted.

" 'Morning. New boat?"

Another hour and a half went by as I talked to the second individual, likewise the third and fourth. When the sun went down I discovered I had accomplished about 45 minutes of work.

On the second day much the same thing happened, except that along about 11 A.M. I realized I had worked 10 minutes without being interrupted. By this time I had begun to enjoy the interruptions. I looked around for the next but I saw nobody coming, only another fellow working on his boat down the dock.

So I did the only thing I could do. I put down my tools and walked down the dock.

"Working on your brightwork?"

"Yep."

"Looks nice."

"Thanks."

"What you using?"

It took a little ingenuity, but at the close of the day I had worked only another 45 minutes. As I sat in my cockpit, toasted the sundown, and surveyed my accomplishments of the last couple of days, I realized that although I had finished very few items on my list I had accomplished a great deal. I had found out what *slowing down* was.

I shifted gears regularly for the next several years: down when I walked onto the dock, up when I went back to the office. It works great as soon as you find the shift lever. By the way, I didn't throw out my schedules; I just made them more realistic. In fact, I became quite good at hitting them, especially if I got ahead.

However, learning to slow down is only part of the problem; the other part is learning to like it. That may not sound like much of a problem from your present hectic, overstressed vantage point, but it is. Somewhere in the 1960s someone sold Western culture a large dose of snake oil, and much of the hyping is still going on today. Lay back, drop out, and you will enjoy life. This seems to make sense to millions of people, then and now, struggling with overstressed lives.

In truth, though, laying back, dropping out, and simplifying have nothing to do with enjoying life. A life that is exciting and challenging can be very enjoyable—and let's face it, the rat race can sometimes be exciting and challenging. Indeed, the more excitement and challenge in your life, the more difficult it will be for you to gear down and enjoy cruising. Many people have found that the simple life is a boring life.

The thrill of victory is as powerful a motivator in the business world as it is in sports. The stimulation of an active career can even have an almost narcotic effect that is difficult to overcome. If you have been involved in a high-powered career, you may find that cruising doesn't hold your interest. A young cruiser I met who holds several of the patents on color xerography is already looking past cruising to developing other patents. It is ironic that some of the very things we seek in cruising threatens to destroy our enjoyment of it.

And unlike lightning, irony can strike twice: Many people caught in a structured life controlled by their jobs, children, and other external demands look longingly at the unstructured life of cruising. In truth, however, managing your own time is more difficult than you can imagine. The removal of external controls on your time can be disorienting—even devastating.

Substituting new controls for those that no longer exist is difficult. Look, for instance, at the number of new retirees who return to the old time controls by starting a new career or, worse, die shortly after retirement because they cannot make the transition. Such emotional upheaval can be laid at the doorstep of the loss of external controls in their lives.

Another good illustration of this was the situation of three men just beginning the cruising life in the Pacific Northwest. One was providing the boat and most of the cruising kitty; he, of course, was the captain. The other two had apparently contributed but little money, so they did 90 percent of the work. They cleaned and fixed the boat and prepared the meals while the captain relaxed and did as he pleased. He was living a life of leisure just as he imagined it should be lived.

The outcome was as predictable as it was difficult for the captain to understand: The two crew members had a great time, while he was miserable and about to chuck it all in. The difference was control points to organize life around. The crew members had a routine. They had a reason to get up—an engine to tune or even just a deck to scrub—whereas the captain had nothing to make today look any different from yesterday. Life would go on regardless of whether he got up or not. He didn't understand why he longed for his previous job; didn't realize that while he was working, he had to perform, make decisions, solve problems; didn't know that he had structured his cruising life so that all of that was missing. He had turned from a highly structured life to a life of no structure at all.

Worse, he had fallen into a trap common among people who find themselves suddenly without structure: He turned to a life of constant enjoyment. It's pleasant to sleep in on Saturday, because it's the only day you can. Sunday you have to get up to go to church, Monday through Friday to go to work. Saturday you sleep in because there is no reason to get up.

But if every day is Saturday, Saturday is not a joy, it's a bore. The average life is structured around external controls. These begin at an early age and quietly continue throughout our lives. As children our lives are controlled by our parents, relatives, teachers, and some generally accepted guidelines. Parents tell us when to eat, sleep, and play. Teachers tell us when to be at school, what and when to study, when to eat lunch and go home. As we grow older, the control shifts to spouses, children, and supervisors. Individuals moving into adulthood may believe they are taking control over their lives, but generally all they are doing is modifying the controls imposed by family, organized religion, or work.

As a beginning cruiser you have just given up your work and most of your family and social contacts; possibly you have also severely altered your commitment to organized religion. In short, you have rid yourself of all external direction in your life. Although it is a major shock, this loss of external controls is not felt immediately. It comes several months after the controls have been removed, and it will be felt as a loss, as something missing from your life, and of course something is.

The human animal seems to need the order generated by external controls—which simply are not compatible with the cruising way of life. True, you could show Junior the world on the back of a boat, be a floating missionary, or dedicate your life to finding the truth about the blue-footed booby. However, these solutions will not work for most cruisers; they will have to deal with becoming responsible for the day-to-day direction of their own lives.

Unfortunately, I cannot give you much guidance here. Those people I am aware of who have cruised for a significant number of years belong predominantly in one of two groups. Both have successfully transferred the work ethic to cruising. The first group are those who make their living from cruising. Some, such as the Hiscocks and Pardeys, are famous; others, not so famous, include Dennis and Lynn Trudeau of the *Dreammaker,* who worked their way around the world by fixing engines and mending sails. In these cases the need to work provides the necessary money—as well as the not so obviously necessary structure to life.

For the second group attaining a specific goal—usually sailing around the world—provides structure. Cruising is just what happens on the way to the goal.

Other successful structures for cruising may exist; I just haven't encountered them.

What I have encountered that doesn't seem to work, despite its obvious attraction and the number of times it is repeated in the cruising literature, is the idea that cruising should have no structure, that you should just drift. If cruising is defined as the long-term process of getting to destinations far from home, however, then in my experience those who simply wander are not cruising, for they seem either to forsake cruising quickly or never get very far afield.

Another common idea that doesn't often work is that of the extended vacation. Travel for travel's sake is rarely enjoyable for longer than a year. The cruising pace is too slow. Long before you pass through the Pacific you tire of the endless string of blue lagoons (in Greece it is icons; in the Pacific Northwest, totem poles). Eventually any thinking person gets around to "There has to be more to life than this." Most often the answer is to return to the life the cruiser left—generally, with renewed enthusiasm. This is why cruising works so well as a sabbatical leave.

MOBILE LIVING

Many cruises are short lived or never even start because of the difficulty of leaving friends and relatives. Thoughts of loved ones are usually not in the forefront of your mind while you prepare to go cruising, but I guarantee that they will fill it as you look back at the distant shore dipping below the horizon. You will have been at sea for five or six hours, the hustle of leaving will be over, it will be quiet, and the routine of the passage will begin to settle over the boat. At times like this only an insensitive person would not look back with some regret, remembering the smiling faces on the dock.

One way to solve this problem is to take them along. This can be done in several different ways. You can share your trip with friends and relatives by planning regular visits. Most boats can accommodate four people for a couple of weeks; plan your itinerary to allow hosting friends for a week or two. You will be glad to see them come and glad to see them go. Some of our most enjoyable times on our cruise were those shared with friends.

Another way to take friends along is by correspondence. Here the modern boater with a portable computer has an edge. Regular or irregular newsletters can keep those you love up to date on your adventure, help you plan personal visits, and bring a flood of return mail. Reaching the next mail port and finding a full bag of correspondence brought us real orgies of enjoyment.

Or you might take a vacation from your vacation: Leave the boat in a safe port and fly home for visits. Two weeks or a month back on the old homestead can do wonders to renew your spirit for adventure. You may find that life has reversed poles, and those short trips away from the boat have become like short vacations from work—you're not really ready to return when they're over. If so, lengthen the stays at home.

Finally, you can deal with absent friends by making new friends. Cruising provides exceptional opportunities for this, because as a cruiser you belong to two special groups. First, you are a member of the cruising fraternity, and there is a tendency to greet old cruising buddies like old army buddies. Boaters you have never seen before will treat you as a trusted friend. Second, in many ports you have a pseudocelebrity status. The locals along the dock will seek you out to chat, and invite you to shoreside parties as the special guest. Consequently, as you travel, your number of friends will grow considerably.

CULTURE SHOCK

One reason people cruise is to experience a different lifestyle; few expect this to be the reason they are uncomfortable with cruising. The difficulty lies in the difference between observing a culture and living within that culture. Like going to the zoo, how much you enjoy your trip depends on which side of the bars you are on. As a cruiser you are often inside the bars, living like the natives, rather than just observing them.

There is much in cruising that is new. In some cases it may be a new boat or new skills, but in all cases it is new places, people, and customs. And you must deal with these new conditions while removed from old and familiar surroundings. To set an old saying aside, "Familiarity breeds content." In times of great stress most people instinctively want to return home to the familiar; back where they know the neighborhood, the neighborhood knows them, and they know what to expect.

Each person has a different capacity for dealing with change. Some are only happy living in the old neighborhood and doing what their parents or friends are doing. Those who get satisfaction from learning to do a new job will tolerate the changes that come with going cruising better than those satisfied by knowing they can do an old job well. Those who fall between the two extremes can overcome uneasiness by recognizing what is causing it, and realizing that it will go away as the cruising routine becomes familiar.

The severity of the culture shock you experience depends on how much change you encounter. Moving from a modern Western culture with its Christian, consumer orientation to an island culture with a pagan, subsistence focus, for example, might produce a severe emotional reaction.

Even insignificant differences in acceptable behavior can be irritating or disconcerting. On one remote Pacific island where we were the only cruising boat in the harbor, anytime I walked through the village young and old alike asked me, "Where are you going?"

I always felt like telling them, "It's none of your damn business!" Instead I smiled and gave them a straight answer. They were asking out of curiosity—the question may even have been considered a courtesy, to show they cared about me—but I always felt uncomfortable.

On another occasion we accepted an invitation to visit a native family. It was an uncomfortable evening for them and us as we tried to bridge the cultural gap and reach some ground for conversation. Even in areas of common knowledge our divergent points of view produced a potential for misunderstanding and conflict. We also found it difficult to remain relaxed and casual in a cloud of flies and spent most of the time praying under our breaths that they would not offer us anything to eat or drink. The highlight of the evening—for everybody—was our graceful, early exit.

The shock of the transition can be minimized by reducing the degree of cultural change. Plan your itinerary so that the countries you visit in your first year have familiar cultures; better yet, deal first with the shock due to change in lifestyle by spending the first 6 to 12 months cruising in domestic waters. Then, when you're comfortable with your new lifestyle, leave for foreign ports to deal with new cultures.

Remember that culture shock comes not just from different foods, living conditions, and social attitudes but also from different moral codes and social structures. The Western concept of basic human rights does not necessarily travel with you. For example, in many countries you are not innocent until proven guilty; you are guilty until proven innocent. You may be at considerable risk if you count too heavily on your rights.

Dealing with foreign dignitaries and bureaucrats requires patience, tolerance, patience, good humor, and patience. One method is simply to smile and wait, repeatedly proclaiming your inability to comprehend anything. Eventually this approach will produce someone who will solve your problem—if just to clear the floor space.

Herb Payson's method is to fight fire with fire by keeping the convoluted bureaucratic process going with numerous appeals, written by hand, with key words illegible and misspelled (Payson, *Blown Away*). These are purposely sent to wrong addresses and wrong officials to lengthen the delay. He points out that eventually one of four things happens: Your excuse is believed and your request granted; the officials lose patience and grant your request to get rid of you; you have taken up so much time that you are ready to leave anyway; or you are threatened with imprisonment. As he says, "Three out of four chances for success isn't bad."

If your adjustment to "foreign" ways is difficult, remember that people are, after all, everywhere the same and everywhere different. It is this dichotomy that makes cruising interesting. We all laugh, cry, love, feel pain, show courage and vanity, and so on, but our expressions of these human emotions are shaped by our culture. A healthy interest in observing such differences may help stabilize the neophyte during the transition period.

Even though much of the world has been affected by Western culture, Westernization is far from complete. In a few hundred years, perhaps, the world will enjoy a single basic culture. Meanwhile, however, understanding and respect are necessary to ease the transition period and make your visit more enjoyable for you and your hosts. As the guest, the responsibility is on you to conform. Your hosts have as sound a reason for their behavior as you have for your own strange Western ways. Accepting different viewpoints and values can be one of the most rewarding experiences of cruising.

The ability to understand and accept new cultures requires several special characteristics, including an awareness of the ways in which cultures can differ and the emotional security to accept that your personal views do not constitute worldwide standards. That is not to say that you have to give up your values; just refrain from criticizing others'.

IGNORANCE OF LOCAL CUSTOMS

Such simple acts as touching someone's hair, touching someone with your left hand, or stepping over someone can be grave insults in other cultures. Most of the time, insensitivity to native customs just adds to the lore that Americans are ignorant. Once in a while, however, it may result in you being the main course at a state banquet. Cook and Magellan both were felled by their ignorance of native customs. They may have had valid excuses, since no guidebooks had been written at the time; but in this age of rapid communication and transportation, ignorance is not an excuse for travelers.

Do a little research at the local library before your visit. Conversations with fellow cruisers who have been in the area you are going to visit are another source of information. The better informed you are, the more easily you can be accepted by the new culture—and the more you will benefit from your exposure to it. You can be featured as the entrée du jour, tolerated as a rude outsider, accepted as a respected outsider, or inducted into the culture as a fellow member.

Most cruisers spend little time—a few days to a few months—in areas where the culture is truly "foreign." On such short visits all you can hope for is to leave a positive impression.

In any small closed group, outsiders pose a certain amount of threat.

Western culture can be both disruptive and threatening, so it is normally not your presence but the culture you bring with you that is the threat to these groups. This is particularly threatening to the older natives. But this threat can at least be reduced to a tolerable level by showing respect for the native customs and refraining from engaging in some of the more annoying Western customs.

What you are wearing often colors natives' first impression of you. In some places skin is in, but in others it is definitely out. In the Marshall Islands, for example, women do not wear any clothing that shows even the outline of the hip or thigh. They do not often swim, and when they do, they wear full skirts. Casual clothing there can thus be interpreted as a lack of respect. It is safer to assume that modesty prevails. Do not wear shorts for visits ashore in an unknown area. You will not offend if you are overdressed.

When in doubt, the best course is to be quiet, modest, and firm. Strength without aggression is admired almost universally. Good manners are often just plain common sense and as such are good manners in any culture. See how others are behaving and pattern your actions and dress after theirs. If you do not know what fork to use to eat your boiled wombat, watch your host and eat your wombat after he eats his and in the same manner.

The cost of your boat is more than most natives could make in a lifetime. This places you, like it or not, in the aristocracy (Ward, *Living Overseas*). Thus the natives will often treat you with a certain amount of respect and expect you to act in a manner worthy of their respect.

Most people respond well to others who appear to approve of them. The advice given to beauty contestants is relevant here as well. Smile, smile, smile! Be a person you would like to be around yourself. Move with enthusiasm for life, with a quick step and an erect posture, and have a positive outlook.

Giving and receiving gifts is an important part of the social patterns of many cultures. Giving implies that the giver is kind, generous, and affluent; receiving, that you respect the giver and value that person's goodwill and friendship. You will be expected both to give and to receive gifts graciously. In many places the people are extremely poor; the only thing they have is food. They will freely give this to you. Accept it graciously and return a gift in kind and of equal value.

Remember, though, that accepting a gift of food is different from taking food without asking. Even on deserted islands the coconuts belong to somebody. One or two coconuts may seem like small potatoes to you, but it is a significant part of the personal wealth of many Pacific Islanders. If you take these coconuts without permission you are stealing. What is more, you are stealing from the very poor and giving to the relatively rich. Leave the coconuts alone.

4

Planning

M ost people just let life happen to them. I don't know whether there is any correlation between this and a failure to fulfill the cruising dream. I do know, however, that if you have a plan you can minimize wasted effort, time, and money, and increase your odds of success. One tool that can help is called program management.

Perhaps to you, nothing seems farther from the essence of cruising than program-management techniques. However, don't be too hasty. Let me point out that getting there is not the same as being there.

If your goal is to go cruising, there is no doubt that good program-management techniques will improve your chances of attaining it. Not so apparent is that many of the tools used to *reach* your goal of cruising can be modified to improve your enjoyment *while* cruising as well. And if the term *program management* upsets your stomach, call it cruising management.

The Basics

Most cruisers already use cruising-management techniques, even if unconsciously. For example, the proverbial task list, which never gets completed before you leave, is a form of planning. In fact, just by saying "I am planning to go cruising someday," you are planning.

Who is to say that 40 years ago, when I bought my first book on sailing, I wasn't planning someday to sail away? Or, for that matter, that if at that time I'd had a good 15-year plan, I would have started cruising 20 years earlier?

To explain cruising management, let me break it down into its component parts and look briefly at each. A plan consists of an objective (a goal and some guidelines), the process by which the objective will be reached (a strategy), a process that defines each step (a work breakdown structure), a schedule (ordering the steps according to time), and a budget (planning the flow of money in and out). For example:

Goal and Guidelines:	Get something to eat for dinner. Don't bring home okra.
Strategy:	Get in the car and go to the store.
Work Breakdown Structure:	Get meat, vegetable, and dessert.
Schedule:	Leave now so that you will be back in time to cook dinner.
Budget:	Take $30 from wife's purse.

These five steps take you logically from the beginning to the end of a project. For the simple goal above you hardly have to think about the plan. The more complex the goal, however, the more important good planning will be. Complicated goals require considerably more thought, and it becomes easier to get confused and forget important points. In these cases, writing down the various steps may help you keep them straight. A large portion of cruising management is just this process of writing down key elements. It then becomes easier to visualize the relationships among them and manipulate them to increase the probability of a successful adventure.

Visualizing these relationships provides two benefits: It focuses your effort on the most important tasks, and, more important, it allows you to determine the best course of action to take when things *do not* go according to plan. The strength of good formal planning is that it can tell you how a six-month delay or a $10,000 change in the budget can be handled with minimum effect on your goal.

I cannot emphasize enough, however, that *plans should not be rigid.* The single most common mistake made in cruising management is trying to conform to an unworkable plan. This almost guarantees that things will not go according to any plan, even a relatively informal one. Both Slocum and Bligh planned to go one way around the world and ended up going the opposite. No matter how formal or informal, plans will change.

One way to respond to changes is to shoot from the hip. With a good plan, however, all your options will be apparent, and you can make a reasoned response—which is more likely to have a favorable result. You can't predict the future, but you can set up the present to maximize the probability that a given event will occur. For example, if you stay out of the jungles of India, the probability that you will be eaten by tigers is low.

You may find that as the variables become more numerous and your goals move farther into the future, your plan becomes more complex, and its outcome harder to define or accurately predict. One response to this difficulty is to try to predict the future with too much detail—becoming progressively more frustrated in the process.

Such frustration can be relieved by simply not trying to do the impossible. Leave your plan general in the long term, where things are fuzzy, and get more detailed only as you approach the present. For long-term planning, move back and look at the big picture; group items together and use values that err on the side of safety. This approach produces at least three layers of planning: strategic planning (those general plans that are concerned with actions more than five years away); tactical planning (for actions between one and five years in the future); and operational planning (for those activities to be performed this year).

For example, writing "Purchase boat" on your plan is all you need do to cover this strategic task when it's 10 years down the road. When that task is two months away, though, it should find its way into your operational plan in much more detailed form: "Call Mike Smith at Last National 555-5544 and arrange for loan." Better yet, if your strategic plan functions properly, the operational plan might read, "On April 4 transfer cash from investment account to checking account."

Good planning is simply good common sense written down. This is where a good personal computer can help. The ease with which you can correct or rearrange things on your computer will greatly facilitate your planning process. Project-management software is available, but a good word processor with outlining and spreadsheet capacities can be used to manage a cruise as well.

Once you understand the concepts, planning can be fun—which brings us to a negative aspect of good planning. Eventually you have to deal with the trip. During the planning phase the trip sometimes becomes so idealized that the real adventure cannot match it, thus adding to the depression created by the cultural and lifestyle changes.

Goal and Strategy

If you've resolved to go cruising someday, a plan is already under way. The question now is whether it helps or hinders you. Do you have a good plan, no plan, or a bad plan? Certainly no plan is better than a bad plan, but let's shape this into a good one.

To start with, the decision to go is in reality the second step in the definition of a goal; the first is the determination if this goal is realistic. Most people make this judgment solely from the financial viewpoint: Can I get enough money to go? A few may also consider whether they possess the necessary skills for cruising. Both are certainly important, but they are not the only considerations. Maybe the most crucial—and certainly the least-considered—factor is whether cruising will provide the anticipated enjoyment and whether it conflicts with any other of your life goals.

Everybody sets priorities and goals, most often unconsciously. Planning is an attempt to bring this process to the conscious level, thereby gaining much better control over the outcome of your life. Sometimes conscious priorities conflict with subconscious ones, though—and the subconscious ones are stronger. For example, the conscious goal to lose weight may conflict with the subconscious one to eat ice cream. This conflict causes a certain dissatisfaction. A way out of this dilemma is to align the conscious priorities with the subconscious.

One way to do this is to rid yourself of all conscious priorities, which was essentially the philosophy of the 1960s. I think it is better to go the other way—to identify the subconscious priorities and then make them conscious, or delete them from the subconscious.

To begin, write down your priorities and goals. The act of writing down the words will help force these thoughts to the conscious level, revealing what matters in your life. *All* parties involved in the cruise should make this list individually. The lists may grow or shrink as the parties get a better understanding of what is important to them. Sometimes a close friend or cruising partner can offer insight into whether your listed priorities are real or imagined. See if your friend or partner agrees with your self-evaluation.

When your list is complete, order your goals from most important to least. Then examine your lists to determine whether all your goals can be met either before, during, or after cruising. Chapter 2 might help you determine if the cruising lifestyle will meet these goals. If not, one of two things may be wrong: The listed goals might not be your true ones, or maybe cruising will not answer your needs.

Once work on all individual lists is completed, cruising partners should compare their lists. Conflicting priorities or goals are bound to arise. The degree to which cruising changes lifestyle can affect two completely compatible people quite differently—and depends to some extent on their goals. The number of dream cruises ending in divorce attests to this difference. The earlier conflicts are resolved by honest communication, the better. Ideally, this process will allow both parties to adjust their lives to minimize the negative effects of conflict.

Now it is time to develop a general strategy to accomplish your mutual goals. The strategy is a long-range plan on which short-range decisions and plans can be made. Its aim is not to predict or make future decisions, but to make present choices that will optimize the chances of reaching future goals.

In a few sentences, describe how you intend to get from where you are now to your goal while accomplishing your priorities. If you don't have enough information to answer all the questions, you need to get it. If finding the time to accomplish your goal seems impossible, then the importance of the goal should be questioned. Some iterations between goal and strategy should be expected; the iterations will help optimize both parts of the plan.

Don't forget that a good plan includes a way to get back home when you are through cruising and a way to abort the trip partway through. For example, what happens to your household furnishings? If you store them while you're gone for five years, you'll probably spend enough to buy them twice over on your return. If you sell them, however, they'll likely bring you only 10 cents on the dollar; if you then abort your trip early, you'll have to buy all new goods.

Aborting the trip can be time consuming and expensive. Without careful planning you might find yourself with $150,000 of equipment in some far-flung port—which is generally downwind and downcurrent from home. To make matters worse, the weather probably won't be right for return, either. Cutting short a cruise and returning home is not like getting off a merry-go-round; there is usually a delay of at least a year and some rather difficult sailing.

The Work Breakdown

Your next step is to break down the work of achieving your goals so that all the major and minor activities are listed. Essentially, you will be outlining your overall program. Starting with your major program elements, break down each one layer at a time. For example, the major elements might be each of your individual and group goals. Breaking cruising down into its component parts might go as follows:

1. Preparation
2. Equipment
3. Financing

That was fairly simple and elemental—and by taking your entire program one step at a time, breaking it down into its components will remain very simple and elemental. Let's break down our sample program another level, into subcomponents:

2. Equipment
   2.1　Boat
   2.2　Outfit

Yet another level might produce the following work packages:

2. Equipment
   2.1　Boat
      (Work packages)
      2.1.1　Determine whether to build or buy
      2.1.2　Determine kind of boat
      2.1.3　Acquire boat

And yet another level breaks each work package into tasks:

2. Equipment
   2.1　Boat
      2.1.2　Determine kind of boat

(Tasks)

2.1.2.1   Assess comfort requirements

2.1.2.2   Assess safety requirements

2.1.2.3   Assess cost requirements

2.1.2.4   Assess individual needs

A task may be broken down even farther, into subtasks:

2. Equipment

  2.1   Boat

    2.1.2   Determine kind of boat

      2.1.2.2   Assess safety requirements

      (Subtasks)

      2.1.2.2.1   Seaworthiness

      2.1.2.2.2   Stability

      2.1.2.2.3   Strength of hull

      2.1.2.2.4   Cockpit

      2.1.2.2.5   Performance

The more detailed your breakdown, the better you'll understand the task ahead, and the less chance that you'll leave out an important point. More detail will also greatly increase your accuracy when you get to the scheduling portion of the management package. If a work package can not be broken down adequately it may indicate that you need to add a task to your plan: Research the subject of that work package.

At the subtask level you can begin to see how individual activities contribute to an eventual decision. For example, determining how the length of the boat affects cost, or how displacement affects safety—along with defining the relative importance of cost, comfort, and safety—produces a description of your optimum boat and completes the work package "Determine kind of boat." This information then can be fed into the task "Acquire boat." The interdependence of the various tasks begins to become apparent to you now, as well.

For a complete look at a sample work breakdown process, turn to appendix B.

After your goals, strategy, and work breakdown have been developed, you can try your hand at either scheduling or budget. The two are closely related; what you do in one area will affect the other. This may require you to redo both several times until they match. As a matter of personal preference, I will begin with the schedule.

Scheduling

For all of you who feel that scheduling has no place in cruising, hold your fire. I have chosen to make a division of terms here: I call *scheduling* what is done before cruising, and *itinerary planning* what is done while cruising. It is on itinerary planning that you really want to vent your spleen. So save your ire for a few more pages; you will get your chance.

Scheduling has been used in industry for years—that's probably where it picked up its bad connotations. Those who are trying to break away from the confines of the working world usually also wish to shun its trappings.

Now, I'm in favor of shunning as many trappings as the next fellow, maybe more; however, I am also interested in reaching goals. Scheduling has helped industry to reach goals for years. And remember, in industry time is money; in cruising time is life. Scheduling clearly can help you reach personal goals as well.

SCHEDULING AS A TOOL

To use the scheduling tool properly you must understand the basic principles behind scheduling:

- » Schedules can be changed.
- » Schedules must be flexible.
- » Schedules are layered.

Schedules are written to be changed. Too many people have been trapped into thinking that once they're on paper, they can't change. This image of a dictatorial schedule driving its human slaves toward inflexible goals is responsible for most of the bad press schedules have received. There is no need for this, though. Keep control over that schedule; change it to make it fit the latest facts.

A schedule is intended not to force you to get things done on a specific timetable but to show you how activities are related in time, so that when things go wrong you can assess the effect of each component. With a little manipulation of the schedule, you can then select the option with the least undesirable effect on your project. And the definition of *undesir-*

able effect is up to you: It may be stress, harassment, delay, or whatever is important to you to avoid.

The first and second principles are almost the same, but there is an important subtle difference. Flexibility in a schedule is a factor of the number of options available to correct a problem when it occurs. For example, if it will take two weeks longer to finish installing the water tank than originally scheduled, flexibility will allow you the choice of (a) working overtime to complete it, (b) slipping the schedule two weeks, or (c) rearranging the schedule so that the delay in the task is not critical to the goal.

When schedules that need to be changed are not, it is most often because they lack flexibility. If too much is scheduled for completion in too short a time, the schedule will fail. The man who intends to build a boat in his backyard in his spare time within three years is generating a rigid, overly optimistic schedule. The result is almost guaranteed failure as the builder tries to meet the schedule and instead meets the inevitable anxiety, frustration, or worse. Experience has shown that this effort will take from 5 to 10 years; very few finish in less than 7.

A good schedule would have allowed more time for this task. If this man had better understood the task of building a boat, he would have known that three years was too short a time span. If he did not understand the task, but knew good scheduling procedure, he would have allowed more time because of his ignorance. Whenever a task is unfamiliar or complicated, it's better to allow too much time than too little. If the resulting schedule doesn't give you an acceptable end date for your goal, then you must explore alternative methods or reduce the scope of your project. If neither option is available, seriously consider scrapping the project before you waste time and money.

Schedule flexibility is achieved in two basic ways: by providing ample time and by minimizing related tasks—the ones that cannot be started until other tasks are finished. Allowing more time for boatbuilding would substantially increase the flexibility of our builder's schedule. If he had given himself 12 years to complete the work, for instance, he could handle a delay caused by late equipment delivery or unexpected sickness. And task independence would allow him to work on an unrelated task earlier than anticipated, helping him make up at least some of his lost time.

Schedules should also have several layers or levels; each covers the same time period but in increasing detail. The amount of detail you should go into is directly related to the amount of information you need to complete your schedule satisfactorily. Not all tasks require all levels of scheduling, but if one is complex or important, it will demand a higher-level schedule.

Level-one schedules cover the entire period of the plan. They should be general in nature and broad in scope, simply showing how the major components of the plan interrelate. They generally show time increments of half or quarter years. A level-one schedule can come directly from a list or from the first couple of levels of your work breakdown. Figure 4.1 is an example of a partial level-one schedule.

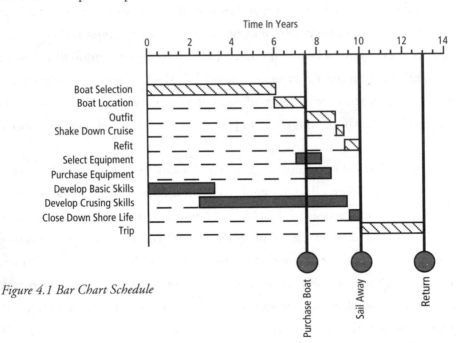

Figure 4.1 Bar Chart Schedule

Level-two schedules are more detailed; they show the actions necessary for the successful completion of midterm goals. These goals may consist of only one work package of your work breakdown—for example, "Outfit the boat." Level-two schedules are broken down into weeks and may show one or two years of activity.

Level-three schedules show the day-to-day activities for the near term. It is best to create these schedules very close to the fact. They deal with individual tasks or subtasks of your work breakdown—for example, "install galley stove." However, trying to use a level-three schedule for the purposes of reaching a cruising goal seems to me a little like using a

12-pound hammer on thumbtacks. I seldom use this level of schedule; but then, I also make an inordinate number of trips to local marine hardware stores.

FORMS OF SCHEDULES

The form you use for your schedule should depend on what it's meant to show. If its primary purpose is to depict the duration of tasks and goals, then a bar chart—a visual representation of the entire project—can be used. One step above a job list, a bar chart is simply a list of activities along a vertical axis shown in relation to time, along the horizontal axis. The time required for each activity is then indicated by the length of the line drawn opposite that activity (again, see figure 4.1). The interrelation of the tasks is shown by overlapping bars, or by where bars begin and end. The first thing that becomes apparent from figure 4.1 is that getting ready to cruise takes time, especially if you are going to have to extend this schedule to allow 10 years for building a boat.

The effect of changing the length of any task can easily be seen on a bar chart. However, this type of schedule does not easily show how tasks are dependent on one another—that is, which must be finished before others can be started. It also is difficult to differentiate between items on the schedule that are tasks, which take time to complete, and events, which occur instantaneously. For example, selecting a boat is a task, whereas purchasing a boat is an event. To resolve these problems a network schedule can be used. The events are shown as nodes or circles, the activities as arrows connecting the events. Figure 4.2 is an example of this kind of schedule.

On a network schedule each activity begins and ends with a node. Some nodes are related to a major milestone such as purchasing the boat; others just indicate the beginning or ending of the task. With this format it is easy to show which tasks must be completed before others are started; thus it can be very helpful in keeping carts and horses in the right perspective. Some nodes may initiate more than one activity; for example, node 6 in figure 4.2 initiates the shakedown cruise and also the closing down of shore life. Likewise, more than one activity may end on a node; following events then cannot be started until *all* the activities ending on that node are completed. For example, node 5 shows that the boat and the equipment must be purchased before outfitting can begin.

Another form of scheduling that can on occasion be helpful is the resource/time-line schedule. This, a marrying of budget and schedule, shows cash flow in and out. It can tell

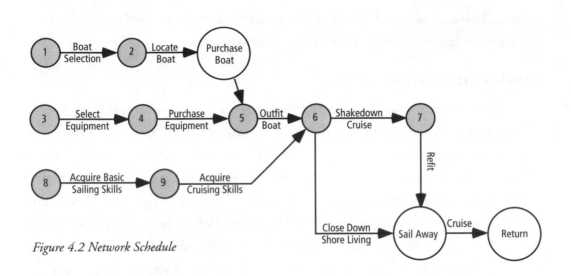

Figure 4.2 Network Schedule

you the best time for purchasing that expensive piece of gear, or when and how much help you are going to need from your friendly banker when cash inflow and outflow do not match. Providing a well-thought-out resource schedule to your banker certainly won't hurt your chances of getting that loan, either.

MAKING A SCHEDULE

Start with the task breakdown you made earlier. Take each of the work packages and estimate the time required to complete it. Starting at the work-package level generates the upper levels of your schedule. On some occasions it may be necessary to dip down into the task or subtask level to get the detailed information necessary to schedule the work package accurately. With a little practice this will become the easiest way to generate accurate schedules.

A workable schedule can also be generated from the ever-present job list and an inquiring mind. For example, if you make a list of the activities needed before going cruising, it might look like this:

Purchase boat

Outfit

Sail away

Return

Notice that all these activities are events except "Outfit," which is a task. Now, to outfit the boat, you need to buy equipment. So that leads to:

Purchase equipment

What about determining what equipment and, for that matter, what boat you want to buy? That adds:

Select boat

Select equipment

What about finding the right boat after you have determined which kind?

Find boat

Getting the boat and equipment is only part of the problem; how about getting the necessary skills?

Develop basic skills

Develop cruising skills

That about completes the list, except for maybe a shakedown cruise. Of course, not everything will work properly, so plan for some time for refit. All that's left are closing down shore life and sailing away:

Take shakedown cruise

Refit

Close down shore life

These items can now be rearranged in a more logical manner by grouping similar ones together. If the duration of each of these tasks is added (as shown in table 4.1), you have all the information you need for a first cut at a level-one bar chart.

TABLE 4.1

Typical Work Packages

Work-Package Item	Duration (in months)
1. Select boat	72
2. Find boat	18
3. Purchase boat	1–30
4. Select equipment	12
5. Purchase equipment	15
6. Outfit	18
7. Develop basic skills	36
8. Develop cruising skills	78

(continued)

Work-Package Item	Duration (in months)
9. Take shakedown cruise	4
10. Refit	8
11. Close down shore life	6
12. Sail away	1–400,000
13. Return	?

This table was used as the basis for the bar chart presented earlier. To create such a chart, select a scale and draw a line, called a bar, equal to the length of the task opposite that task on the chart. A good scale might be 1 inch equals 16 months; that way 1 month would equal ¹⁄₁₆ inch. The line opposite boat selection would be 4½ inches long (72 ÷ 16 = 4.5), and since it is the first task to be started, it begins at the left edge of your schedule. The task of finding a boat cannot begin until the boat has been selected, of course, so the line for this must begin where the boat selection line ends. The bar for boat location then is drawn oppo-

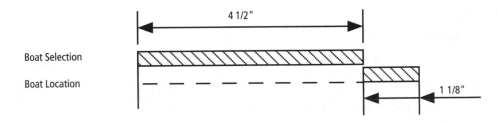

Figure 4.3   Construction of a Bar Chart

site the boat location entry on the chart, starting 4½ inches from the left edge and extending 1⅛ inches (18 ÷ 16 = 1.25) farther (as shown in figure 4.3).

Repeat this process for each task. Not all items need to begin where another item ends. For example, some equipment can be purchased while you are still selecting other equipment, and outfitting can begin as soon as some equipment is purchased (see figure 4.4).

The duration numbers used in this table are just first guesses. Get something down on paper, then modify it as more detailed information becomes available. One way to get this is to break a task into its component parts. For example, the time allotted for the boat selection process might seem adequate, until you analyze the parts of that task. Then you

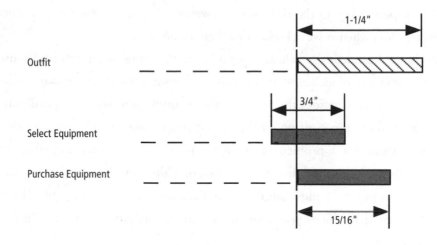

Figure 4.4 Detail of a Bar Chart Showing Overlapping Tasks

may realize that the work package for selecting a boat is comprised of three separate tasks: reading, talking to owners, and bareboat chartering. You can now see that six years isn't all that much time for boat selection, since you'll be chartering only a few weeks each year. In those six years you can charter only about seven different vessels.

This lower-level schedule also shows the interrelationship between boat selection and sailing skills. If sailing skills are weak, boat selection will be further lengthened; it may even be replaced as the leadoff task by "Get basic skills," which you'll need before you can charter.

It is easy to see that schedules are not drawn, they are redrawn. Less evident is another truth about schedules: They never get shorter, only longer.

Finally, the relationship between time and money will become apparent as you deal with schedules. Generally speaking, you can save money by taking more time on a task; conversely, if you need to complete a task faster, throw money at it.

Itinerary

Itinerary planning has a bad name among many cruisers. Many people can abide the rudiments of planning—making lists of things to take along or do—but balk at making a detailed itinerary.

A fundamental argument against such planning is that good cruising cannot be scheduled; you must be free to go wherever you want, whenever you want. One of cruising's major attractions, in fact, is this perception that it is a simple wandering without fear of consequences or responsibility. In the real world, however, most of us have time, weather, and budget constraints whether we acknowledge them or not.

The basic argument for itinerary planning is that time is an absolute constraint, because the time any of us has to cruise is limited even if we do it for our entire lives. Nobody lives forever. Consider the young cruising couple who want to spend only three or four years of their lives cruising, or the retired couple who are 65 and can only cruise for 10 years before health problems force them ashore. It makes no difference whether cruise time is limited by health, finances, weather, or whim: It will be limited. It only seems reasonable, then, to get the most out of that limited time. The world is a big place, especially if there are many things you want to see and you are going at a speed just slightly faster than walking.

Those who ignore time are in for disappointment. Those who ignore the weather are in for much worse. Only the foolish don't give in to control by weather patterns. For example, it is wise to get to paradise after the typhoon season is over and get out again before the next typhoon season starts. A friend who once crossed the world's most prolific belt of hurricanes at the peak of hurricane season had to delay his cruise for two years while he repaired and replaced broken and lost equipment.

Even some who accept that time and weather do limit cruising, however, still argue against an itinerary, because "a cruise is too full of surprises and things that don't fit into a schedule"—bad weather, say, or unexpected mechanical breakdowns, or spots you want to stay in longer than you'd planned. True, those things happen, but they don't have to invalidate your itinerary. My own solution to such problems is something I call time banking, and I'll get to it in a moment.

To use the scheduling tool properly we must change its traditional objectives slightly to emphasize the importance of time—not just any time, but quality time. The definition of this term depends on the individual, so you must exactly fit your itinerary to your individual cruise, to the goals that you shaped during your planning process. The itinerary schedule provides the link between the planning and the actual execution of the trip. Use it to see that, as much as possible, all the effort and money you've spent to go cruising provide the result you desire.

The secret of good itinerary planning is simple: Take your time. Take the time to do the necessary research on the areas you'll visit. The more information you gather about each place, the better your itinerary will fit your needs. Take your time while you are making your trip, too. Allowing plenty of time for each event will keep your itinerary flexible.

Then you can take an extra couple of days in a beautiful area, or an unscheduled lay-over day when the weather turns bad or equipment fails. But what happens if you get to Lovealot Port and it stinks, or the weather is fine during the week you expected storms? Not to worry: time banking!

THE CONCEPT OF TIME BANKING

The idea is simple. If you reach a place where you had planned to stay for several days and it doesn't meet your expectations, you don't stay; you move on and put those days into the time bank. Now you are effectively one or two days ahead of schedule; as the trip progresses you may eventually get a couple of weeks in your time bank. Then when you get bad weather or find Really-Hot-Spot Harbor and want to spend some extra days, you just draw them out the bank.

As you can see, being ahead of your itinerary is not nearly as traumatic as getting behind it. If you are ahead of schedule you can dillydally in a favorite spot until all your surplus days are gone. On the other hand, being behind schedule may mean you get hit in the behind with a typhoon. Hence the first rule of good itinerary planning: Don't get behind schedule.

An easy way to do so is to throw in some contingency days early in your trip. The number of days depends on your knowledge of the area. The less you know, the more contingency days you need.

But suppose you somehow get a large negative balance in your time bank. Say, your harbor is hit with a nuclear strike or something. Cleaning the radioactivity out of the sails will clearly put you behind your schedule. Not to worry! Good itinerary planning can still save the day.

You can't manufacture time, so you must omit something from your schedule to make up the deficit. Scan your written itinerary, find what you consider the least-interesting place, and cut it. You're back on schedule, and all you've lost is the part of the trip with the least promise.

I have rarely cruised with a plan for more than a month without changing my itinerary; on occasion I have rewritten it more than once. (I use a computer and a spreadsheet, so

I can make the changes quickly and easily.) Some people wonder why I make them at all if I change them so much, but that is the point. The value of an itinerary is its ability to allow optimum change in a dynamic situation.

However, there are certain spots in your itinerary that must be met. These are called hold points. At these spots your time bank balance is zeroed out. Some are more important to meet than others. The two most common hold points are a scheduled rendezvous and a predictable weather event. If you are meeting Dick and Jane at Topu for a two-week cruise and are a week late, Dick and Jane will not speak very highly of you. Such hold points are called hard points, because you must meet them exactly. Winter weather, hurricane season, and things of like ilk impose hold points that are a little more flexible, called soft points. Still, the consequences of missing a soft point may be more severe than just ruining Dick and Jane's holiday.

TOOLS OF THE TRADE

The tools of the itinerary scheduling trade are charts, cruising guides, sailing directions, maps, pilot charts, travel books, geography books, and atlases. Use navigational charts of various scales: Those that cover large areas are useful for basic planning, while charts showing small areas show the details of individual anchorages, such as depth, location of rocks, and protection from wind and waves. These detailed charts also indicate some of each spot's character, from which you can infer for example, whether there might be interesting sites to explore, or interesting reefs to dive.

The costs of the charts necessary for a trip are no longer trivial. When I first began cruising the charts for the Pacific Northwest ran to about $400; now they cost about $5,200. This increase has forced many a cruiser to set sail with inadequate charts—and cruising unfamiliar areas without the proper charts is a prelude to disaster. While we were moored in Everett, Washington, on our way north, a boat that was 60 miles into a world cruise was brought into the marina lashed to a tug because it had struck a large, well-charted, local shoal area. The rescue and repair probably cost more than $6,000. Unfortunately, this is not an isolated event; the scene was played out much too often throughout our cruise.

Your next most important tool is an accurate cruising guide. These unfortunately are only available for the more popular cruising areas. A good one will describe not only the best anchorages, points of interest, and things to do and see ashore, but the local hazards as well. Most large governments print sailing instructions for their coastal waters. The United States and the United Kingdom publish them for the entire world. Although these volumes are intended for large commercial vessels, they still provide a wealth of information for the small-boat owner. Because they are not meant for tourists, though, they lack information on points of interest.

This deficiency can be filled by books on the area written for land tourists. Their maps will be useful for planning inland tours and sight-seeing. If the area is so remote that no general travel books exist, you can still glean some information from books on the geography and history of the area.

Pilot charts are a specialty item compiling wind, weather, and oceanographic information useful to the navigator selecting ocean routes. They are very helpful for routing your voyages and passages. They do for the open ocean what navigational charts do for inland waters. They cover five areas: the North and South Pacific, the Indian Ocean, and the North and South Atlantic. They provide a graphic representation of the prevailing winds in 5-degree squares over a specific time period, usually a month. The wind percentages are concentrated on eight points of the compass. Also given is the percentage of calms or light and variable winds. The number of gales is listed for each 5-degree square, along with expected tracks for all tropical and extratropical storms. The direction and velocity of the ocean currents are shown, along with the frequency of wave heights above 12 feet. But as the pitchman says, that's not all you get: You get contours showing the percentage of days with visibility of less than 2 miles; contours of atmospheric pressure, air and sea temperatures, and the minimum, mean, and maximum limits of sea ice. You can see that pilot charts will fill many a winter evening for armchair cruisers. The more you know about where you intend to go, the more you'll enjoy your cruise.

LEVELS OF ITINERARIES

The guidelines for developing an itinerary are the same I discussed earlier for planning work packages and schedules: general in the long term and specific in the near. And as with scheduling, different levels of itineraries can be made, each with its own purpose and use. A level-one itinerary should be part of every plan. A level two will help friends and relatives follow your travels. A level three is the mainstay of good itinerary planning. It should be quite detailed and accurate for the upcoming three months, and roughed out for the rest of the year. A level four will only be necessary on special occasions, such as when you're off your normal watch schedules or are sailing where tidal streams pose hazards for crew and vessel.

LEVEL ONE

A level-one itinerary should be laid out in months or quarter years, and should be made for the entire trip. This itinerary should show the general area or country where you intend to cruise—for example, New Guinea, January and February; Solomon Islands, March to May. The idea of this schedule is to show the whole period from the present to the end on one sheet of paper.

All that you need for a level-one itinerary is an estimate of time and the general route you intend to take. As a guide, the average trip around the world requires about five years if you don't do much mucking about. To go around in three years is unrealistic if you intend to see anything at all. If you really want to see a country, it takes several months, and your trip could stretch out to more than 20 years. It will become readily apparent just how big the world is during the construction of your itinerary.

A good way to start your long-term planning is to list where you would like to go. Start with a world map or globe and list all the places that interest you. Rearrange the list into the most efficient order of travel, using pilot charts to establish your route. Next, identify the areas where weather will enforce hold points, such as the location and seasons of hurricanes, gales, fog, ice, and generally inclement winter weather. These can be found in pilot charts or a comprehensive book on the weather.

Now you can calculate the time necessary for your trip, using table 4.2 as a guide. This table breaks cruising into two different types: point-to-point and linear.

Linear cruising involves almost daily sailing between anchorages, exploring as you go, such as cruising the Great Barrier Reef, the Pacific Northwest, or the Atlantic Intracoastal Waterway. Point-to-point cruising is like cruising the South Pacific, where you make relatively long passages between islands and anchor the boat for longer periods of time, exploring the area from your anchorage before moving on the next long passage.

TABLE 4.2

Planning Guidelines

Type of Cruising	Value	Units
Linear	20	Miles / Day
	100	Miles / Week
	300	Miles / Month
Point-to-point	1	Point / Week
	2½	Points / Month

Notice that the units for linear cruising in table 4.2 are in miles per unit of time, whereas for point-to-point cruising they are given as points per unit of time. The longer time spans are used for less detailed schedules—that is, level one. Notice also that the table is inconsistent in that sailing 20 miles a day would seem to equal 140 miles a week, not the 100 miles shown in the table. The value given in the table accounts for the time banking necessary to cover the unscheduled contingencies that will inevitably occur over longer periods of time. These numbers can sometimes be altered during detailed short-term planning but should be held to religiously for general, long-term strategy. They are designed to keep your time balance positive.

It is also a good idea to schedule in a base stop every year or so, where you can spend two to three months in one location to make any major repairs, return home for a visit, and the like.

LEVEL THREE

Once your level-one itinerary is completed, it is best to skip to the meat of itinerary planning, level three. (The only real use for a level-two schedule is as a convenient way to summarize several level-three schedules.) Here you will attempt to make the time available and the time required agree. Since weather patterns are relatively fixed, you must subtract or add distance or stopping points until you find a match. If your available time varies a great deal from your required, chances are the trip will be rushed and out of control.

The level-three itinerary is broken down to the day, shows the ports and towns being visited, and covers one to two years. A convenient way to make one is on a computer spreadsheet, changes, even major ones, can be made instantaneously. It is of course also possible to write out your itinerary in longhand. In either case the form shown in figure 4.5 is a good place to start.

Date	Port	Distance (Miles)	Remarks	City, Country
Saturday 6/26/99	Kodiak	240		Alaska, U.S.
Sunday 6/27/99			Sailing	Alaska, U.S.
Monday 6/28/99	Seward			Alaska, U.S.
Tuesday 6/29/99				Alaska, U.S.
Wednesday 6/30/99	Anchorage		Land travel	Alaska, U.S.
Thursday 7/1/99			Land travel	Alaska, U.S.
Friday 7/2/99	Fairbanks		North by land to see the midnight sun	Alaska, U.S.
Saturday 7/3/99			Land travel	Alaska, U.S.
Sunday 7/4/99	Seward	45	Food, fuel, and laundry	Alaska, U.S.
Monday 7/5/99	Puget Bay	18		Alaska, U.S.
Tuesday 7/6/99	Port San Juan	20		Alaska, U.S.

Figure 4.5 Typical Level-Three Itinerary Form

The form has five columns: the day and date, the port where the ship is anchored for the evening, the distance between ports, a remarks column, and a country column, which is sometimes of value to plan customs entries and exits. This form is a convenient way to show when and where you will be, how long you intend to stay, what you are going to do when you get there, where you are going next, and how far you have to go to get there.

To fill out this form it is best to use a detailed chart with a scale of about 1:100,000. Using a divider or compass, measure off the required daily mileage and search that area on the chart for a nearby harbor or anchorage. If there is more than one choice in the area, refer to the guidebooks for information to choose the one most suitable.

The schedule in figure 4.5 indicates Saturday night in Kodiak, Sunday and Monday spent sailing on passage the 240 miles to Seward (mainland Alaska), then Monday and Tuesday nights in Seward. Wednesday's plan is travel to Anchorage by land, and so on. Notice that the first day's run out of Seward is 45 miles long, which is considerably lengthier than the guidelines. Obviously, suitable anchorages and harbors are not found every 20 miles, so you will have days with longer runs. This is one of those days. The 45 miles is a long day's sail and will require good winds from the right direction or the use of the engine to cover it in less than 9 or 10 hours.

Sometimes after a long day it's nice to schedule a layover day. However, here your next day's sail will be only 18 miles. This can be covered quite comfortably in five or six hours, even into a headwind. Still, while it doesn't show in figure 4.5, a two-day layover is due in Port San Juan.

Continue this scheduling process until you reach your next hold point. Then rework times and distances until you reach an acceptable match. Your level-three schedule is now finished and ready for modification as your trip unfolds.

THE EVEN-NUMBERED LEVELS

The level-two and level-four itinerary schedules are specialty items. The level two can be used to provide a one-page synopsis of several level-three schedules. Give this to friends and relatives for those moments when they wonder where in the world you are. It will show your general location on a week-by-week basis, and may cover several years on a single page.

Level-four schedules may also be needed on occasion for passing through tidal rapids or over a bar—anywhere that exact timing is important. These schedules are prepared only for the period of two days to a week and are broken down into hours. They can show duties—who's on watch, or who's cooking dinner—and when the boat has to be at the tidal rapid or bar to get through safely. Posted in a conspicuous place, they can be referred to at will. Figure 4.6 is an example of such a schedule.

Day/Date	Place	Time	Duty	Crew	Remarks
Monday, August 4	Hole in the Wall	0700 hrs	Cook	D. J., Libby	
		0800 hrs			Breakfast
		0830 hrs	1st watch	Jen, Julie	
	Dent Rapids	0852 hrs			Slack tide
		0900 hrs	K.P.	Paul, Kathy	
		1130 hrs	Cook	Libby, Paul	
		1200 hrs			Lunch
		1200 hrs	2nd watch	D. J., Kathy	
		1300 hrs	K.P.	Jen, Julie	

(continued)

Day/Date	Place	Time	Duty	Crew	Remarks
	Green Pt. Rapids	1308 hrs			Slack tide
		1600 hrs	3rd watch	Paul, Libby	
		1800 hrs	Cook	D. J., Julie	
	Whirlpool				Slack tide
	Forward Harbor	1830 hrs			Drop anchor
		1900 hrs			Dinner
		2000 hrs	K.P.	Jen, Kathy	

Figure 4.6 Typical Level-Four Itinerary

I have also used level-four itineraries to maintain a fair distribution of labor when we have guests aboard a boat. Many people are intuitively repulsed by the sight of a level four, with its implied regimentation. However, guests of ours who have sailed both with and without such itineraries generally request that we use them. They enjoy the control a schedule gives them over their own destinies. When the duties are complete their time is their own, without interruption from a whining captain, or internal guilt that they are not doing their fair share and should get up from their book to do the dishes.

Budgets

The reason that money is called the root of all evil is that money is the root of everything. Eventually the question of cruising, too, comes down to a dollar value. A few books have been written on low-budget cruising, and there seems to be a common belief that it's an inexpensive way to travel around the world. However, I believe that low-budget cruising is a myth that should be discounted for many reasons, not least of which is that adversity can change "low-budget" into "inadequately funded." Calamity seems to strike these vessels more often, perhaps because their owners are more likely to skimp on safety equipment or postpone the replacement of faulty gear.

Unexpected costs are the rule during cruising. They can break a bare-bones budget and result in shattered dreams, petty thievery, and minor con games. The poorer you become, the more difficult it is to remain honest. On more than one occasion I've seen the arrival of a ragtag ship send the rest of the cruisers in the port to quietly stowing all the loose equipment on deck that might be tempted to walk away.

Cruisers on inadequate budgets are generally accepted by the cruising community, and generally treat that community reasonably honestly—they can expect to meet some of the same boats in other ports. It is instead the indigenous population that bears the brunt of their pillage-and-burn, "What-the-hell-I'll-never-come-this-way-again" attitude.

Certainly one of the most pleasurable experiences of cruising is to be welcomed warmly by the local population and fêted as a semicelebrity. This happens most often in remote areas where cruising vessels seldom call; it rarely happens anymore in the popular cruising areas. Ever wonder why? The answer is a simple result of the laws of supply and demand.

I have known remote communities that have almost adopted a cruising vessel. In one instance an inadequately budgeted cruiser was towed into a small fishing port with a broken mast. The cost of repairing the mast was well beyond the means of the crew—so the townspeople rallied around the damaged boat. A prime piece of seasoned timber was donated to a woodworking shop, which turned out a new wooden mast. The fittings from the old mast were refurbished and the mast was restepped by a local crane company, free of charge. After several months of repairs the boat sailed out of the harbor to horns tooting and flags waving, once again on its voyage around the world.

But such heartwarming experiences are rarer and rarer as more and more inadequately budgeted cruisers flood the scene. You must consider that the cost of an effort like this to a small community was considerable. Their compensation was to see an unfortunate individual overcome the odds and continue his dream. However, the more unfortunate individuals who show up on remote doorsteps with tales of woe, the more they will be looked on not as unfortunate heroes but as ignorant bums. The supply quickly outstrips the demand. Eventually all the cruisers who visit will be considered bums.

You can go either high budget or low budget but please go adequately. How much money is required to go cruising depends on individual tastes and circumstances, but it is definitely not a cheap activity. On the other hand, do not get the idea that it is necessarily beyond your means; remember that the majority of cruisers come from the middle class and below. Let me try to give you a realistic idea of how much cruising will cost, and to suggest ways to gather the necessary money.

ESTIMATING COSTS

One of the questions most often asked of cruising couples is how much it costs. Numbers ranging from $300 to $1,500 per month have been bandied about; unfortunately it is sometimes hard to tell what these estimates include and what they don't. Costs can vary depending on how long you intend to cruise, the condition of your boat, and the amount of spare parts and food you put on board before you leave. The first year is always the cheapest, and the years get more expensive as they go along, especially if the cruise is long enough that you need to replace major equipment, such as rigging or sails. Another variable is your tastes. Where on the hog do you like to dine?

One way to approach this taste factor is to assess how much you are spending today and then judge how much you want to change your lifestyle when you cruise. Table 4.3 is a sample budget that you can use, with a little individual adjustment, to estimate how much you might spend while cruising.

TABLE 4.3 COMPARATIVE BUDGETING

Item	Cruising Cost as a Percentage of Current Shore Expenses
Rent/House Payment/Slip Rental	20
Food	120
Utilities	15
Medical Expenses	250
Clothing	15
Maintenance	50
Fuel	65
Transportation	200
Insurance:	
Life	0
Health	0
House	0
Car	10
Boat	150
Liability	0
Entertainment	50
Miscellaneous	50

Your rental expense while cruising will relate directly to the number of times you will swing on the hook or lie tied up to a dock. Some places charge fees even if you do swing on the hook. If you're making boat payments they should show up in this category as well and will increase it beyond the 20 percent.

Food is more expensive away from home, unless you eat native foods or eat a large quantity of seafood. So what you spend now is probably a little less than what you'll spend under way.

Your utility expenses could go down, though, because your power consumption will go down, and its cost is generally included in a slip fee anyway. However, some of your utility costs will transfer over to diesel fuel to generate electricity or heat your boat. Also, remember that telephone calls will now have to be *very* long distance and on pay phones, which are more expensive than home phones.

Medical costs might increase as your health insurance lapses and you are required to pay in full. Clothing costs will come down, especially in the Tropics. Also, neither fancy nor large wardrobes can be used or even stored aboard a boat, so yours will be reduced to basic and fundamental items.

Maintaining a boat costs about the same as maintaining a home and a car, but if you're currently maintaining all three, that cost will be cut only in half. You'll have day-to-day costs such as oil and filters, and longer-term expenses like new sails or rigging (although if your trip is short and the boat in good condition when you leave, you'll probably avoid these larger expenses).

Fuel cost can be controlled some asea, but to do so requires patience, a long schedule, or a boat that can sail upwind in light breezes. Even then you'll find it surprisingly difficult to average less than two hours a day on the motor, whether you're coastal cruising or passage making, especially given the time you'll spend getting the anchor up and down and motoring between calms. Depending on the size of your boat, that could mean 60 gallons a month. However, if you are willing to ride out calms on passage, you can reduce your fuel use. As a target, consider the 70 gallons of diesel fuel used by Joanne Clarendon on a two-year cruise from California to New Zealand (Clarendon, "The Cost of Cruising"). I should emphasize that such frugality takes a special ability to relax and go nowhere in the middle of the ocean. I know few cruisers who possess that.

Insurance costs vary. If you'll be getting rid of your house and car, your auto and home insurance costs of course go down to zero.

It might appear that you can save money by canceling your car insurance. This will provide only short-term financial relief, however. If you remain uninsured for two years, when you return to shore life you will be unable to purchase preferred insurance, regardless of your previous safety record. Regular insurance can cost twice as much as preferred. One way around this is to keep in force only the comprehensive insurance on an inexpensive automobile while you are cruising. This may cost you $10 or $20 a year—but saves $600 or $700 when you return.

Health insurance has very little use on a world cruise. Hal Roth only had medical insurance when he spent time in the United States; we keep only a high-level deductible policy in case of catastrophic disease (Roth, "After 25,000 Miles"). The importance of life insurance should also be reevaluated. If you're embarking on just a short midlife cruise, then keep it. If you are retiring, however, and have enough money for two of you to live out your lives, you certainly have enough for one person to do the same, so life insurance is probably unnecessary.

It's presently expensive to insure a boat for overseas use, and the policies are very restrictive. Many cruisers go without insurance; we did not. We were insured in the waters of the United States and Canada by Allstate, which offered a very reasonable policy. Many people put extra money into anchor systems in place of boat insurance; I suggest you also consider putting extra money into adequate charts and navigational guides if you skimp on the insurance budget.

Liability insurance seems to be needed only in the United States, where the legal and insurance businesses have created a market for themselves. Most people cruise unprotected against liability.

Entertainment budgets can vary as widely as you wish. How many times will you want to eat out, rent a car, go to the theater, or fly home? The miscellaneous budget covers haircuts, taxes, visa fees, bribes, gifts, souvenirs, and the like. It is best to make this budget as fat as you can.

Another approach to budgeting is to study what other people spend while cruising. The difficulties here are that few cruisers keep good records, and that it is difficult to establish a consistent baseline for comparison. For example, everyone starts a cruise with extra food and supplies stored in every available space aboard the boat; the monthly expenses depend directly on how much this reserve is drawn on. But because each boat has a different amount of available space, this reserve varies widely from cruiser to cruiser. Also, most other cruisers' budgets need to be adjusted for inflation.

With this in mind, let's look at some published budgets.

In the late 1960s Hal Roth was spending about $2,100 per year, which he felt was slightly below the average. In 1981, Bill and Alma Russell were spending $6,700 per year (Russell, "What It Costs to Cruise Away"). The same year Sue Moesly reported a budget of about $7,500, counting what they spent and what they took from ship's stores (Moesly, "Tips for Long-Range Cruising"). That makes for an inflation rate of about 10 percent per year, which would result in a budget of about $13,000 for 1987. In fact, that is about what it cost us to cruise the Pacific between 1987 and 1989. Figure 4.7 shows a curve based on a 1984 survey by Vicki Carkhuff on the distribution of annual expenses for 19 cruising boats in Papeete adjusted for inflation to 1987 dollars (because that is when I went cruising). The average monthly cruising budget was about $810, the median about $670. Assuming 5% inflation over the last 11 years, that relates to about $1,400 per month and $1,100 per month respectively in 1998 dollars (Carkhuff, "Seeing New Places but Always at Home").

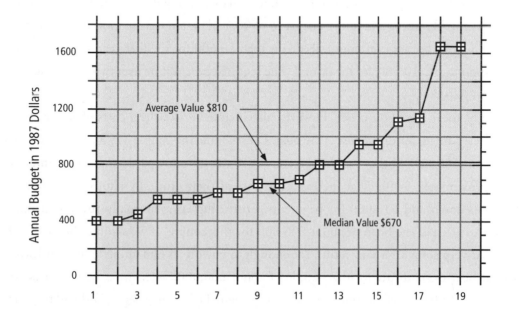

Figure 4.7   *Survey of Cruising Budgets in Papeete*

Budgets are affected not only by inflation but by the strength of the dollar as well; with a weak dollar, budget figures need to go up. By the end of my cruise I was spending close to $1,500 per month. I don't know if my taste for luxury increased or things just got more expensive—maybe a little of both.

Clearly, it's difficult to predict what costs will be a few years into the future. The only thing you can do is err on the side of safety by estimating on the high side. Like a surplus time budget, you can always get rid of a surplus money budget, maybe even more easily.

Now that you have a rough monthly budget figure, determine how much money you will need for the entire cruise. This will depend on several factors, such as the length and timing of your trip. To explain how this estimate is made, let me give you two different examples, one on each extreme. You will have to modify them to suit your conditions.

Example one assumes a young couple who intend to cruise for only a couple of years; they have minimum cash assets, but considerable earning power ahead of them when they return. Example two is an older couple who have maximum cash assets and no earning potential on return; they intend to cruise for five years.

The younger couple can spend their entire cruising kitty; they can earn it back when they return. Also, since these people are younger, they can most likely take more hardship, and will be physically able to get along with fewer labor-saving devices and a smaller boat. Therefore we'll assume a monthly budget of $800, and an annual inflation rate of 10 percent. The total amount of money needed is then $9,600 for the first year, plus 1.1 times that amount, or $10,560, for the second. The required expenditure over two years amounts to about $20,000.

The total cost of the cruise, however, also includes other direct costs plus some hidden ones. The major direct cost is the boat. Let's assume the couple buy a used boat costing about $80,000. If they put 20 percent down, the monthly payments would amount to approximately $750. That increases the cost of their cruise by another $34,000—$16,000 down and $18,000 for payments. Outfitting costs normally run about one-third the price of the boat, or about $26,000 for this couple. If we assume they will sell the boat very soon after they return for enough to pay off its remaining loan, that leaves a total boat expenditure for this couple of about $60,000. Their total visible costs are now about $80,000, all of which must be in the bank before they begin, and will be gone when they return.

In addition, there are hidden costs. Assuming the combined annual income of the cruising couple is about $70,000 (which is consistent with being able to bank $80,000 in a reasonable time), and further assuming a normal sequence of raises over the two-year cruise period, they will forfeit about $150,000 in wages. The complete cost, then (summarized in table 4.4), of a two-year fling cruising the Pacific will be about $230,000 in expenditures and lost revenue.

TABLE 4.4 BUDGET SUMMARY FOR YOUNG COUPLE

Item	Cost
Living	$20,000
Boat payments	$18,000
Down payment	$16,000
Outfitting	$26,000
Hidden costs	$150,000
Total cost	$230,000

The second couple, with no earning power, elect to maintain all their principal to live on when they return. Because they are older, we can assume they'll want more comfort than the younger pair, so their monthly cruising budget will be $1,200 instead of $800. If we assume a rate of return of 10 percent on their invested principal (a number that is easy to work with and as good as any) they will need $144,000 in principal to get their necessary $14,400 annual return—before inflation.

However, since inflation is often a factor that cannot be ignored, this picture needs to change considerably. Assuming a 5 percent inflation rate, the second year will require 1.05 times $14,400, or a return of about $15,120. This is an increase over the first year's takeout of $720. To get that extra $720, at a 10 percent return rate, they will need another $7,200 in principal. That means they'll need not only $14,400 their first year, but an additional $7,200 to add to the principal, or $21,600 total return on investment to keep from attacking the principal. To get $21,600 at 10 percent they'll thus need $216,000 in principal to start: This will allow a draw of $14,400 but still leave $223,200 to begin the second year. The increase in principal will allow the use of $15,100 the next year, plus an additional $7,200 to add to the principal to increase the payout for the next year due to inflation, and so on. These calculations depend more on the difference between the rate of return on investments and the actual inflation rate than on the actual rates themselves. We assumed a 5 percent inflation rate and a 10 percent return on investment. The 5 percent difference between these rates turns out to be not too bad an assumption. The results of the calculations would be essentially the same if the inflation rate was 10 percent and the percentage of return was 15.

The other direct costs for this second couple are a little greater because of their assumed greater needs. The boat will cost about $135,000 and require about $45,000 in outfitting. Since this couple probably have more assets, they can afford to pay cash for the boat. There is no hidden cost of lost wages for the older couple, though; just the loss due to the devaluation of the boat and equipment over the five-year period. With luck that may be around $50,000, or only $10,000 per year. Their cruise does require, however, an initial cash outlay of $400,000 just to get into the game.

Four hundred thousand dollars is a staggering number. Even $80,000 is a staggering number for a young couple. Maybe this is why so many people talk about going cruising but never make it. Still, although these amounts of money may seem enormous, they are not impossible for the average person to acquire. Remember that current cruisers have had middle-class incomes or less. How did they come up with this sort of capital? Win the lottery? Inherit it from a rich relative? A few have turned a windfall into a cruise, but there are more dependable ways to be successful—along with some that are not. Let's examine a few of each.

GETTING THE MONEY

First, look at how those people who are out cruising now made it. Among the older cruising crowd are many retirees who have turned good retirement funds into a cruising kitty. To purchase and outfit their boats, they sell the family home and other investments.

By talking with other cruisers, we have found that the two methods most often tried by those wishing to go cruising—building a boat and upgrading from a small boat before sailing away—are noticeably unused. I think it is worthwhile to discuss why these two obvious methods fail so often. Then I will turn to other routes open to those who do not have a lucrative retirement program.

UPGRADE PATH

The typical upgrader—let's call him Bob—gets involved in boating very early, buying a small boat and through the years upgrading it until he has one suitable for cruising. Bob really has no long-term plan, just a general slant. To understand what happens here, I'll give you some more details. At age 30 Bob buys a $10,000 small boat, putting half down and paying off the balance at $120 per month. Now he can enjoy sailing, but along with that enjoyment come additional expenses for equipment and maintenance—say, $55 per month. After five years Bob sells his first boat for what it originally cost and uses the money as a down payment on a $15,000 boat; the outflow of $175 per month for payments and maintenance continues.

Five years later Bob owns outright a $15,000 boat. Again he sells it for cost, purchases another for $30,000. The monthly payment increases to $300. Since this boat is bigger, the maintenance and other expenses also go up, to $80 per month. At the end of 15 years Bob sells the boat and puts $30,000 on a $50,000 boat—again increasing his payments, now to $500 per month. The maintenance and moorage also rise again, to $150 per month. Table 4.5 summarizes these calculations.

TABLE 4.5

			Upgrade Method		
Time	Income	Savings	Investment	Monthly Payment	Equipment/ Maintenance
0 yrs	$175	$5,000	$5,000	$120	$55
5 yrs	$175	0	$10,000	$120	$55
10 yrs	$380	0	$15,000	$300	$80
15 yrs	$650	0	$30,000	$500	$150
20 yrs		0	$50,000		

At the end of 20 years Bob is the owner of a five-year-old $50,000 boat, considerable boating knowledge and sailing skills, and some cruising skills. He can now sell his home for a $120,000 cruising kitty.

THE BUILD-A-BOAT PATH

People who take the build-a-boat path have usually read about cruising and become enchanted with its romance—but don't generally know much about boats or sailing. Building a cruising boat thus seems like a good way to save money.

But because the typical builder—say, Cathy—knows so little about boats and cruising, she's unaware that the boat itself is only a third to a sixth of the cost of a cruise. Further, all she'll save by building the boat is the labor costs; the costs for the materials are essentially the same. A high estimate of labor costs is about a quarter the cost of the boat. That means that building saves only about $20,000 to $30,000—for several years' effort.

Let's give Cathy the same funding as Bob and then compare the results: Cathy can invest the entire initial kitty of $5,000 at 10 percent interest, and add to it the same $175 per month for 10 years. At the end of the 10 years she can draw out what's now nearly $50,000 and begin construction. Cathy uses the additional $205 a month to buy $25,000 worth of additional material over the next 10 years. At the beginning of year 15, she invests the additional $270 a month to create a cruising kitty. Table 4.6 summarizes these calculations.

TABLE 4.6
Build-a-Boat Method

Time	Income	Savings	Investment	Expense	Equipment
0 yrs	$175	$5,000	$175		
5 yrs	$175	$22,000	$175		
10 yrs	$380	0	0	$380	$50,000
15 yrs	$650	0	$270	$380	$75,000
20 yrs		$20,000		$100,000	

At the end of 20 years Cathy has a new $100,000 boat and $20,000 for a cruising kitty and outfitting. The sale of a $120,000 home will leave her with $140,000 for cruising. She has intimate knowledge of her boat, but probably limited sailing and cruising skills.

THE LIVE-ABOARD PATH

Like the builder, the person taking the live-aboard path—say, Dave—invests his $5,000 at 10 percent interest and adds to it the $175 per month for 10 years. However, at the end of the 10 years Dave sells his family home for $90,000, and invests the $50,000 profit and the $50,000 savings in a $100,000 boat. He moves aboard the boat, investing the $380 a month plus the $175 house payment. The expenses for maintaining his boat are assumed to be offset by those expenses Bob and Cathy incur in maintaining their homes. Dave takes a cruising vacation every year for the next 10 years. After 15 years his monthly savings are increased by $270 per month to a total of $825 per month. Table 4.7 summarizes these calculations.

TABLE 4.7
Live-Aboard Method

Time	Income	Savings	Investment	Expense	Equipment
0 yrs	$175	$5,000	$175		
5 yrs	$175	$22,000	$175		
10 yrs	$380	0	$555		$100,000
15 yrs	$650	$33,000	$825		$100,000
20 yrs		$82,000			$100,000

After 20 years Dave has $82,000 in the bank, a $100,000 boat, and six months' cruising experience. He has an intimate knowledge of a 10-year-old boat, and no home to sell.

Note that the boat does not appreciate in value, as a house does.

THE THRIFT PATH

Edna uses a straight-ahead thrift approach. She invests the $5,000 and the $175 monthly payments in a 10 percent account. After 10 years she adds the extra $205 dollars to her investment account. After 15 years she spends the $2,400 annually on bareboat chartering and adds the extra $70 to her investments. Table 4.8 summarizes Edna's transactions.

TABLE 4.8
Thrift Method

Time	Income	Savings	Expense	Equipment
0 yrs	$175	$5,000	$175	
5 yrs	$175	$22,000	$175	
10 yrs	$380	$50,000	$380	
15 yrs	$650	$110,000	$450	$200
20 yrs		$220,000		

After 20 years Edna has $220,000 in the bank and six months' cruising experience. She can now buy a $100,000 boat and still have $120,000 in her cruising kitty; sale of the $120,000 family home will yield the $240,000 she needs to cruise without touching her principal. The problem with this system is the tendency to spend the accumulating savings.

SUMMARY

Figure 4.8 summarizes the results. Now, you can fiddle with the numbers one way or the other, but—this may surprise you—the thrift system is the clear winner. The exercise shows that owning boats is expensive, that live-aboards pay a premium for getting the boat early, and that building your boat can save you some money but may deprive you of sailing and cruising experience. It also shows that if you really want to go cruising, just pay attention to your business and save your money—good common sense even if you do not want to go cruising!

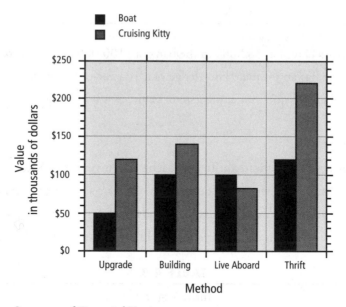

Figure 4.8   *Summary of Financial Tactics*

This is all good for those who want to take off in their 50s, but what if you want to cruise for two years, with a reasonable budget, in your late 20s or early 30s? Remember, we determined that the budget for this would be about $80,000, which would require placing $750 a month into an investment of 12 percent for six years, or $975 for five years. This is quite a bit to put away if your combined gross income is $70,000. For most people, it would mean a lowered standard of living. If you are willing to forgo some comforts and conveniences, however, there are ways to reduce the time you'll have to live in reduced circumstances.

Consider two people taking a job in a remote and difficult area, such as working on the Alaska pipeline. Such jobs generally offer room and board plus a high salary. Further, there is little opportunity to spend the salary, so it can all go into savings. This is precisely the scheme Maurice and Katie Cloughley used as outlined in *A World to the West*. They both taught school in the Canadian Arctic—not a particularly comfortable spot. Because there were minimum expenses, however, they were able to salt away the necessary cash to go cruising in their late 20s and early 30s.

SAVING AND INVESTING

Just a quick note about the magic of compound interest. Table 4.9 shows the value of an IRA at different interest rates in 10, 20, and 30 years given a $2,000-per-year deposit. The numbers in this table are astounding, especially in the lower right-hand corner—but remember that it is practically impossible to make 20 percent interest consistently over 30 years.

TABLE 4.9

Return on IRA Investments

(profits reinvested, interest compounded)

Return Rate	Future Value per $2,000-per-Year Deposit		
	10 yr	20 yr	30 yr
6% (savings acc)	$27,900	$78,000	$167,600
8% (money mkt)	$31,300	$98,800	$244,700
10% (bonds)	$35,000	$126,000	$361,900
12% (mutual fnd)	$39,300	$161,400	$540,600
14% (mutual fnd)	$44,100	$207,500	$813,500
16% (stocks)	$49,500	$267,700	$1,230,300
20% (high-risk stock)	$62,300	$448,000	$12,836,500
Total investment	$12,000	$24,000	$36,000

Nevertheless, a couple of conclusions are readily apparent. Saving $2,000 per year for 10 years isn't going to solve your problem of financing, even at high-risk returns; however, you must save for the first 10 years if you're going to have the second 10. It is in these second 10 years that the numbers begin to get interesting. The mutual fund accounts outlined above could easily finance a cruise. After 30 years these mutual funds could finance both my cruise and yours. Moral: *Start early.*

Over longer terms the rate of return becomes more important. Over 10 years the difference between 6 and 20 percent return is only a factor of 3. Over 20 years it jumps to a factor of 6, and by 30 years it is almost 17. In the long run, then, the rate of return is more important than what you put in yearly. For example, if you doubled your investment to $4,000 per year but kept it at 6 percent, you'd make $335,000 in 30 years—as compared to the $540,000 you'd earn by investing $2,000 at 12 percent.

Now, investing in mutual funds and stocks takes a little more work on your part than putting money into savings and money market accounts. Risk is involved—you can suffer major losses, for instance, if you need to take the money when the market is down—but you can protect your money by diversification, knowledge, and common sense. You need to read, pay a little closer attention to the world financial markets, and get a good broker. Still, the difference between 6 and 20 percent return is worth a little extra effort.

Arranging Financial Matters while Cruising

Handling financial matters while cruising has been greatly simplified with the introduction of money management accounts by several large brokerage houses. These accounts allow you to continue drawing reasonable interest on your cruising kitty while making its money available to you almost anywhere in the world. We kept a small envelope of cash on board the *Bird of Time* for emergencies—some in U.S. dollars, some in the coin of the realm. This cache should be kept to a minimum because it is susceptible to robbery, and also because it is earning no interest.

Using a credit card (one with no yearly fee) was also convenient for us—and in effect gave us an interest-free 30-day "float." Using the card whenever possible also meant we didn't need to carry large sums of cash. The card aided us in our record keeping, too: Even though we did not get mail regularly, it was a simple matter to call an 800 number once a month to learn the balance of our account. We then mailed a check for the entire amount from our money management account. Paying off the entire balance meant that we avoided any finance charges; paying only once a month meant that the money was in the management account earning interest as long as possible. Large organizations call this working off the float. The method is, of course, only possible when traveling in a country with reliable mail and telephone services.

Earning while on the Cruise

CHARTERING AND PAYING CREWS

During our travels we occasionally met people who had decided to make up a short-fall in their cruising kitties by chartering or taking on paying crew. In two cases the results were satisfactory; in one, questionable; in three, disastrous.

The most successful venture was run out of the Queen Charlotte Islands in Canada. The couple had a large 70-foot-plus vessel and a good gimmick: They ran theme cruises to the abandoned Haida Native American villages, with lectures and tours ashore by professional educators. Their success came because they had a good product; ran the venture in a businesslike, efficient way; and had built up a reputation over several years chartering in a single area. Their long-term goal was to cruise farther afield after reducing their debt load.

The odds of their successfully cruising other waters, however, were reduced because of the size of their boat. Seventy-plus-foot boats are not easy for two people to operate; they require crew. The problems involved in dealing with crew can be illustrated by the experiences of another vessel we met in tropical waters. The skipper-owner was an easygoing New Zealander who wasn't much for rules or organization and had just completed a long and apparently happy passage. All but one of his crew had left when the boat reached port. The skipper and this crew member seemed to get along quite well as they worked to get the boat back into shape for the next passage—north to Alaska. Since we had just cruised Alaska we became acquainted, swapping lies and advice.

The skipper needed to pick up three or four more crew members for his trip north. I recall his discussing with me ways to defend against the Coast Guard's zero drug tolerance policy and the possibility that it might seize his boat if a new crew member carelessly brought drugs aboard without his knowledge. He balked at my suggestion of subjecting prospective crew to a urine analysis and finally settled for a stern talk.

He had a rather loose policy of supplying room and board to the crew in exchange for work. This policy may have been his undoing, since the value of the work and the value of the room and board were left undefined. Anyhow, he left for Alaska with a crew of five of which one, a surly individual, seemed to me to be risky.

In Alaska everything went fine for a few weeks; then an argument developed between this surly individual and the skipper. The argument rapidly escalated, and the skipper ordered him off the boat in a place called Fruit of the Loom, Alaska. The surly crew member promptly went below, returned with a knife, and threatened to remove parts of the skipper's body. The skipper fetched the police. The police threw the surly fellow in jail. When the skipper pressed charges, the rest of the crew objected and abandoned ship, including the individual who had sailed with him for more than a year.

All of this upset almost everybody, including the U.S. immigration people, who do not like foreign nationals being abandoned on our shores with no visible means of support. After considerable hassle, the skipper finally took the boat south alone and has now spent more than a year in a little port on Vancouver Island. It is unclear how much this episode has affected his desire to continue cruising.

Trouble with unpaid and semipaid crew is common. Another friend on a British boat lost several crew members, some in rather out-of-the-way places. We also once saw a boat coming in from a three-week passage. The man who came ashore with the mooring lines had his duffel bag in one hand. He tied up the boat, stomped off down the pier without looking back, and was never seen again. The muttering of the remaining crew on board gave us the strong opinion that he was not sorely missed.

Those who pay for their passage can be even more trouble. The exchange of money seems to imply certain privileges. I know of three boat owners who thought that cruising with paying passengers would be a great way to finance their dwindling cruising budgets. One departed Washington State after selling three round-the-world passages for about $10,000 each. At the time I remember thinking that all parties should have realized that a three-year trip around the world would cost more than $40,000. As it turned out, the boat only got from the mouth of the Columbia River to San Diego before the financial system fell apart. The crew became disenchanted and demanded their money back, and the Coast Guard impounded the vessel. The skipper got into trouble for transporting passengers without a license. Furthermore, he had spent so much money getting to San Diego he had very little of the $40,000 left to return to the unhappy passengers, who did their best to see that he was as unhappy as they were. All in all they succeeded. His boat never left San Diego, at least not belonging to him.

Some other cruising friends did a little better at planning; they sold passages in one- to two-month lots for their trip down the Pacific Coast from Mexico to Panama. I believe they got around the legal aspects of carrying paying passengers by not getting caught. The first couple of legs of the trip went well; then they picked up the crew for the trip to Costa Rica. A personality clash developed between the captain and one of the crew on the first major passage. Major passages have a way of bringing out conflicts that would remain hidden in normal circumstances (Stadler, *Psychology of Sailing*). By the time the boat reached port, a truce, let alone any lasting peace, was out of the question. The boat had split into two muttering groups that kept as much to themselves as possible. When the time came to move on to the next port of call, the rebellious crew failed to meet the captain's sailing deadline. Fed up with the situation and seeing their failure to appear in time as a way to solve the problem, he sailed without them. The crew, returning and finding the boat gone, went to the Costa Rican Coast Guard and claimed that the captain had stolen their personal belongings. The Coast Guard ran my friend down before he reached the next port and confiscated his boat.

A long legal battle ensued, with claims and counterclaims; it lasted well over a year. All the while the boat was under the jurisdiction of the Costa Rican Coast Guard. With the prospect of another six months of red tape to free the vessel, the skipper slipped his mooring lines late one evening and headed for international waters. He made it, but not without some harrowing experiences. Certainly not a recommended practice.

To end on a positive note, another skipper we know did increase his cruising coffers on occasion by selling passage. However, he is a no-nonsense sort of a guy who spelled out exactly what was expected and included in the package. Essentially, he sold passage only: The crew embarked on the day the boat left port and disembarked when it reached the next port. This was billed as a fun-filled tropical vacation but as cheap transportation. The skipper and his wife didn't get rich, but they did manage to turn a small profit without much hassle. Once more the legal issues were ignored.

BOAT REPAIR

Depending on your skills, you might be able to make some money while cruising. The two most popular ways we encountered were providing boat repair services and writing. Those people we met who worked in boat repair were generally in their early 30s and cruising on a very low budget; in fact, almost half the cruisers I met in this category were doing boat repair. Young, low-budget cruisers often sail from place to place, working at odd jobs among the boating population when their money runs out. Some specialize in woodworking or diesel mechanics; others do general repairs and maintenance; a few do electronic repairs.

You can usually find one of these cruisers in any major port. In many instances you're better off patronizing them than local repair services, because their reputation follows them in the cruising community. Once you sail away from a port you rarely return, but it is not uncommon to cross and recross the path of companion cruising boats. If the repairs a fellow cruiser made were unsatisfactory, the problem thus can be and generally is rectified. A negative grapevine report is more devastating than a positive one is helpful. The amount of money made from this effort is generally small; the major advantage, as explained in chapter 3, may be the structure it gives to the cruising life.

JOURNALISM

If you're considering financing your cruise by writing articles for cruising magazines, you should know that writing such articles is more common on the circuit than selling them. A simple market analysis shows the reason. *Cruising World* magazine, for example, buys about 140 manuscripts each year for an average payment of $500. That produces about $70,000 a year, spread among maybe 30 authors. How many major magazines are there? Maybe five! That means that the total pool for paying cruising writers is about $350,000; if there are 350 authors competing, each can logically expect about $1,000 annually (realistically much less because well-known authors take the lion's share). There are of course many minor magazines, but they pay considerably less (under $200) for their articles.

Unless you have published a lot, the income from writing is best considered windfall money. Look to writing for other than monetary rewards, especially early in your career as a cruising journalist.

COMPATIBLE PROFESSIONS

There are other ways to make a buck while cruising. Certain professions are in such demand that they can be used to support a semicruising lifestyle. These professions require some training and skills easily marketable on a short-term basis. They also generally require stopping in large population centers, where these skills are in demand, getting necessary work permits, and staying for a while. Nursing is a good example: We met a couple of nurses who cruised the Hawaiian Islands for six months, then took a job in Kauai for a year and a half before leaving for Mexico. Another couple from New Zealand spent two years in Anchorage, Alaska, working in the hotel business before heading south again.

Temporary employment agencies are another good source of easy employment. If you sign up with a large national chain, your reputation will follow you from place to place. In many locations my wife and I found work through the winter months quickly and easily through this network.

5

Training

W|hy so many people feel that the safe operation of a sailing vessel is a simple task that requires no experience is beyond me. No amount of good planning or good equipment will help if you find yourself in a life-threatening situation without the necessary skills to handle it. If you're considering cruising you should also consider spending many months working your boat and its equipment in gradually more complex steps until you have the necessary skills—before you go cruising. Setting sails is not just pulling them up. Navigation, ship handling, anchoring, maintenance, and myriad other tasks require study and practice if you are to become proficient. We do not have to fear the sea, but we need to respect it. Those who do not should not go to sea, because eventually it will destroy them.

Stupidity, the Mother of Disaster

The consequences of neglecting your cruising skills could be disastrous. For example, one man and his children left California to sail to Hawaii, a trip he thought would take but a few days. This was a drastic underestimation, and a short way into the trip they ran out of food and water. However, they had extremely good luck and chanced on another sailboat making the same passage. The other cruisers shared some of their food and water. Two weeks later, more good luck: A night watchman on a passing freighter noticed a rhythmic white flash on the horizon. The rhythm of the flash fascinated him until he realized that its pattern was *SOS*. The captain of the ship altered course and found the drifting vessel, now out of not only food and water but fuel and battery power as well.

Its passengers were weak and could no longer sail their vessel. One of the children was already in a coma and near death. They had been reduced to getting moisture by licking the dew that condensed on the boat. The vessel was abandoned at sea and the victims flown to Hawaii for treatment.

Was this an accident? I think not. It would have been an accident if they'd have made it. Lacking knowledge of cruising, the father had made numerous bad choices. If he had planned better, provisioned better, sailed better, realized there was still 10 gallons of fresh water aboard in the hot water heater, understood that the range of his VHF was only 20 miles, or any number of other things, he could have saved health, happiness, and taxpayers' money.

Unfortunately, there is no limit to these kinds of tragic stories of sailors' inability to cope with the complexities of the environment. They are sobering demonstrations of how unaware most people are of potentially dangerous situations and how cavalierly they make decisions. Many do not even recognize that their own ineptitude led them to disaster, and therefore are doomed to repeat their mistakes and lament that their luck always seems to be bad.

Certainly sailing can be very pleasant and relaxing on those warm summer days in sheltered waters where gentle winds and calm seas prevail. Nonetheless, these same forces of wind and wave can become overpowering very quickly. The sea is large and its weather is unpredictable and powerful. You can only hope to overcome this disparity in force by skill and cunning.

Few people would go cruising without safety equipment aboard, but things are not going to save you; only you are going to save you. Safety does not come from things, it comes from using your head. The most important piece of safety gear is a competent sailor.

Certainly advances in equipment technology have reduced the training time and strength required to cruise successfully, but they have not eliminated them. Sailing skills can be best gathered by reading, taking classes and seminars, and practicing. The best way to get practical experience is by day sailing, crewing on friends' boats during local cruises and races, and bareboat chartering.

Start with small boats and short sails, and gradually move up to bigger boats and longer, more difficult cruises. Using this system, when the opportunity arrives to go cruising you will be in a much better position to take advantage of it. If it never arrives you will still have had years of enjoyment just in the learning process.

It is not possible to cover all the skills you will need in this book. Only the minimum of knowledge and proficiency required will be outlined here, along with some reasons you need them. You must look to other sources to get a complete education. The information this involves can be broken down into two general categories: need to know and nice to know. Sailing and seamanship skills fall into the first category; geography, history, and languages into the second.

Sailing

Inasmuch as the whole cruising process requires the sailing of a small vessel, you might think it unnecessary for me to insist that some knowledge of sailing is important to the successful completion of your adventure. However, I have already noted many instances of people setting to sea with no or very little sailing experience or knowledge. Countless other such misadventures have occurred. It is certainly general knowledge in boating circles that many cruisers lack sailing skills.

This lack is due partly to the large amounts of self-confidence and assurance found in many cruisers, and partly to the old notion that cruising boats have to be heavy and ponderous to be safe. Such traditional cruising boats sail so poorly, however, that any attempt to get them to perform properly is fruitless and frustrating.

The idea that cruisers do not need to go anywhere quickly and therefore don't really need to know how to sail has served to move a lot of old, outdated boats to the used boat market and has ruined many cruising dreams. While it's true that sailing is very slow compared to traveling by jet, there is a great difference between very slow at 3 knots and very slow at 7 knots.

Almost all experienced long-distance cruisers list "better boat performance" as one of the things they would look for in a future cruiser explains Jimmy Cornell in *World Cruising Survey*. Getting good performance from any boat will increase the enjoyment and safety of any trip—and while this can certainly be accomplished by using good equipment, it can also come from simply improving your sailing skills. Adequate training includes not only the basics of sailing but some of its theory and advanced techniques as well.

Please do not let bad planning rush you aboard and under way. The "learn-as-you-go" plan is the least-efficient method of learning to sail, and adds unnecessarily to the stress of the critical first year. High stress leads in turn to short trips. Unless based on knowledge and skill, self-confidence and assurance indicate a careless fool. They are no substitute for good preparation.

THEORY OF SAILING

Although you can improve your basic sailing skills through experimentation, everybody benefits from knowing elementary theory on how sails work. You and your crew should understand how to shape each sail for optimum performance in all wind strengths and how to adjust the running rigging to change each of the parameters; you should also be familiar with the terms *camber, draft,* and *critical angle of attack.*

Also crucial is knowing the difference between true and apparent wind so that you can better comprehend sail force and its components. Breaking the wind into its various components (driving and heeling) will make it easier for you to understand how each affects the movement of your boat, as well as what the running and standing rigging do. This in turn will assist you in tuning your rig.

Finally, information about the rudiments of sail making and sail materials will help you make decisions on when to fly or strike a sail and how to fold and store sails properly. Understanding the effects of the strength of the materials used, the lay direction, and the thread types used will help you get more performance from your boat in the form of speed, and from your sails in the form of longevity.

In short, knowledge of all these elements of the fundamental theory behind sailing will enhance and substantially increase the efficiency of your learning process.

BASIC SAILING

Both the skipper and the crew need to know the basics of sailing. Too often the crew responsibilities are divided strictly along gender lines, with the crew knowing little more than how to act as a substitute autopilot and steer the boat on a given course. The prudent skipper, however, insists that the entire crew have the basic sailing skills necessary for safe operation of the vessel, if for no other reason than to recover his body if he falls overboard.

Although you can learn to sail in any size boat, the best way to begin is by sailing a dinghy. The skills you need to sail one of these small boats are the same as those needed for larger. A larger boat has larger winches and more momentum; a small boat, though, has the advantage of responding immediately and much more markedly to changes. The consequences of your actions will thus be immediately apparent to you. The adjustment from sailing a dinghy to sailing a bigger boat is easy.

Basic sailing skills include knowing how to set the sails and steer on all points of sail. You and your crew should understand apparent wind and know the differences between running, reaching, and sailing close hauled. You should know the location and understand the basic function of each piece of running rigging aboard. You should know how to attach and raise as well as how to douse, furl, flake, fold, and bag all sails. You should know how to tack and jibe, reef a sail, heave to, recover a person who has fallen overboard, put the boat into irons, and get it moving again.

ADVANCED SAILING

One of the things that makes sailing intriguing is that advanced skills are never quite mastered; there is always something new to learn. Advanced skills are sometimes boat dependent, but still worth acquiring to make your cruising safer and more enjoyable.

You should be able to balance your boat, and should understand the defensive tactics used in heavy-weather sailing as well as the finer nuances of light-air sailing. If your boat has some of the presently exotic racing equipment, such as adjustable backstay tensioning, you should know how it operates and affects your boat.

BALANCING THE BOAT

Balancing the boat is the process of setting the sails in such a manner that the boat will hold a given course without the use of any auxiliary self-steering gear. A balanced boat, then, reduces the workload of the self-steering equipment.

A balanced boat is also easier to hand sail, and sails faster, than one poorly balanced. Optimum boat speed, however, is attained when the boat is just slightly out of balance, producing a small amount of weather helm.

Balancing the boat was the means of self-steering used by many of the first bluewater cruisers. Since the advent of vane steering, balancing skills have declined; still, self-steering gear is not a substitute for good sail handling. Your gear could fail, and you'll then need to be able to fall back on basic boat handling to help you steer.

LIGHT AIR

You may not think of sailing in light air as an advanced technique—but think again. Good light-air skills will keep your boat sailing at faster speeds in light breezes. Since patience is a variable, each skipper has a threshold below which she or he will not sail. But if you're a skipper with good light-air skills you'll keep your boat under sail longer, providing longer periods of the peace and joy that sailors seek, and you'll use less of that expensive, polluting fossil fuel in its noisy engine. Much cruising is done in 7-knot winds, and keeping your boat going 3 to 5 knots in such a wind will be worth the extra training to you.

Handling a spinnaker shorthanded is not as difficult as it's often made to appear. However, you and your crew should understand the difference between a reaching and a running spinnaker, along with what causes and how to prevent spinnaker knockdowns and the self-exciting roll, sometimes called the death roll. Both of these troublesome occurrences are a symptom of a heavily overcanvassed boat and are commonly seen in races, when it's important to get the spinnaker up in all kinds of winds. Cruising skippers, however, have the luxury of using the spinnaker only in light air, where it is much better behaved and more easily handled. The only problems are keeping track of the true wind speed when running downwind, and dousing the spinnaker before the winds get too high.

HEAVY WEATHER

Heavy-weather sailing begins when the wind exceeds by 5 knots anything you've previously experienced under sail. Unlike light-air sailing skills, most of sailing's heavy-weather techniques, other than reefing, are not practiced. Very few would feel it prudent to put to sea in a full gale just to practice heavy-weather sailing techniques.

Reefing can be practiced in light air, and it is a good idea to do so. Also, if heavy air is expected it's better to reef at the dock or in protected water than somewhere exposed to the full force of the elements. When the wind is up is no time to iron out small glitches in procedure. Small blunders on a bucking boat with a belly full of wind have a way of getting out of hand.

The other techniques are better learned by reading about how others managed to survive a storm at sea and applying their strategies when you're in similar conditions, modifying or adapting as necessary. Unfortunately, the "best" procedure for weathering a storm is a much-disputed subject (Coles, *Heavy Weather Sailing*). Some, all, or none of the few available tactics may work at any given time, depending on the boat, the crew, and the situation.

What is not disputed is that to understand and choose the correct evasive action, you need a basic knowledge of the wind and the effects of its force on your boat and the water. Dealing with extreme weather comes down to preparing your boat and crew to take what comes and, again, selecting the proper defensive tactic. There are many good books on the subject, including Adlard K. Coles's *Heavy Weather Sailing* and Errol Bruce's *This Is Rough Weather Cruising*. In addition, any good general text on sailing should include a chapter on heavy-weather sailing.

RACING EQUIPMENT

Many pieces of racing equipment are now finding places on modern cruising boats, and many are very helpful. To use this equipment properly, though, you must understand how it operates. Besides reading about both sailing theory and advanced sailing, a good way to do so is to crew on a local racing boat for a few summers. If you choose a knowledgeable skipper who rotates the crew from job to job, you can learn more about the proper setting of sails in two summers of racing than 10 years of cruising.

Seamanship

However, racing does not usually help you learn seamanship skills. Racing sailors often have no need for many of these skills. (For example, except in open-ocean races, the only navigation involved is getting to the course and from one buoy to the next.) Seamanship skills are essential to your survival while cruising, though.

Seamanship is a composite of many skills, including boat handling, navigation and piloting, anchoring, dealing with emergencies, working with rope, handling communications, and interpreting weather information.

BOAT HANDLING

All boats react to the loads applied to their hulls in a similar manner, but each behaves slightly differently depending on its hull shape, trim, speed, and weight; the shape and position of its rudder; and the conditions in which it is operating. Thus you must become familiar both with the forces that affect your boat and with basic boat handling—for example, stopping, turning, and backing.

Once you've mastered these skills, you'll need to learn the principles of advanced boat handling—for example, docking, avoiding collisions, and handling your boat in currents and in limited visibility.

Finally, because the life of a cruising skipper seems too simple, obstacles that require special maneuvers to get under, over, or through have been purposely placed in waterways. These are called bridges, bars, and locks.

DOCKING AND MOORING PROCEDURES

Docking is not only approaching and leaving docks under various wind and current conditions, but also choosing and fastening the proper docking lines, placing fenders correctly, and protecting boat and lines from chafe. Picking up and leaving a mooring, mooring Med style, rafting, and docking without an engine are all skills that will be required of you while cruising.

AVOIDING COLLISIONS

Avoiding a collision requires identifying when a collision is imminent, and then taking the appropriate actions to avoid contact. You must know the rules of the road—and when to use them. Since there are no licensing requirements for recreational boaters, there is no guarantee that a burdened boat will know you're the privileged boat. Further, many commercial boats are unable to yield, so in many cases pushing your supposed right-of-way may be foolhardy. It is best to use common sense and vigilance, rather than just "the rules," to avoid collision.

It is necessary to understand the operation of commercial vessels, large ships, tugs, and fishing boats; all can present risks, some of them unseen. For example, the tow wire on a tug can be under water one moment then instantly snap to the surface the next, where it can entrap a foolhardy boat and force it under the blunt bow of an oncoming barge.

IN CURRENTS

Maneuvering a boat requires general knowledge of how ocean, river, and tidal currents behave. Ocean currents are generally less than 2 knots, but because of the considerable time your boat remains under their influence, they play a major role in its course and performance. Going with or against a 1-knot current can result in a 50-mile-per-day difference in the distance you cover—significant, given the 100- to 150-mile daily run of most cruising vessels.

Currents in rivers may reach velocities great enough to impede the upstream travel of small boats. In any case, upstream travel will be easier if you understand the basics of stream erosion and deposition. Using this information, you can predict where the current will be slower or where shoals will form.

Tidal currents—the flow of water generated by the periodic rise and fall of the ocean's surface due to the gravitational pull of celestial bodies and the rotation of the earth—have a considerable effect on cruisers. Tidal rapids occur in numerous places throughout the world and present considerable danger.

William Van Doren, in *Oceanography and Seamanship,* has reported that on Takaroa Atoll, brightly colored reef fish were once seen spinning around in a tidal vortex 10 to 15 feet deep, apparently unconcerned. It is highly unlikely that the term *unconcerned* would be used to describe an unsuspecting cruiser caught in the same predicament.

Any restricted channels can cause a tidal current to reach extreme velocities. Successful maneuvering through tidal rapids, then, requires you to have specific information concerning the force of tidal currents and the times and duration of slack water. You can find this information from tidal current tables, diagrams, and charts, sailing directions (published by government agencies), and coast pilots. But the proper use of these resources requires some practice.

It will also be necessary to know how to handle your boat in poor visibility. Darkness and fog produce similar conditions, yet they have some major differences. For example, in fog the helmsperson can see relatively well close to the boat, but distant vision is severely limited. In night sailing the situation is reversed, though: Long-range vision is enhanced by the lights on buoys, which make them easier to find than during daylight. Radar can, of course, aid your navigation under conditions of low visibility, but it is not a replacement for crucial basic skills.

Running without radar in times of bad visibility is nothing to fear. It requires knowledge of currents, piloting skills, and the use of the compass. The key to not getting lost is to stay found. Move from one known position to the next, like building a row of dominoes that twists and turns. The location of each domino depends on the ones immediately ahead and behind it.

BRIDGES, LOCKS, AND BARS

Bridges are of concern only in areas with little commercial traffic. The protocol used to open a bridge and pass underneath is simple, and all sailors should know it.

Passing through a dam takes a little longer than passing under a bridge, however, and involves a process called locking through. Locks, which vary in size and complexity, are also used on artificial waterways such as canals to raise or lower boats. If the locks are designed to handle large commercial traffic, their size is generally no obstacle to a single cruising vessel. But wind and current can still be tricky in these structures, and both you and your crew need to know what to expect, as well as how to handle the boat in and out of the lock.

Bars across the entrances to harbors and estuaries can be extremely dangerous to small boats. Crossing a bar is a matter of timing; the best time is during a calm with no sea running, at or just before high-water slack. The worst time is mid-ebb-tide with storm wind and wave conditions. Unfortunately, it is in these extreme conditions that your thoughts will turn to the inviting serenity and safety of a nearby but unfamiliar harbor.

It is practically impossible to judge bar conditions from the deck of a small boat on the bar's seaward side, because the breaking action of the wave is on its shore side. By the time your boat gets close enough to judge the extent of the breaking action, you are many times beyond the point of no return and caught in the rush of the breaking wave. Because the flow of water in the breaking wave and your boat are going in the same direction, the boat's maneuverability is reduced. Once you're into this water, any turn to escape will place your boat parallel to the waves, vulnerable to being rolled.

NAVIGATION AND PILOTING

Guiding the boat safely from one spot to another is called navigation or piloting. Piloting means guiding the boat when the boat is in sight of land, using landforms and navigational aids; navigation covers the skills required to guide the boat in open water when land is not in sight.

PILOTING

More specifically, piloting is the art of safely moving a vessel along a desired course by frequent positioning with respect to land features given on navigational charts and in sailing directions. It is the most ancient of navigational arts. About 300 B.C. Pytheas of Massalia sailed from a Mediterranean port along already established trade routes to England, Scotland, and Norway (Romola and R. C. Anderson, *The Sailing Ship*). There is no record of the navigational methods he used, but because most of the voyage was within sight of land, he undoubtedly used his piloting skills.

These skills involve reading charts and transferring their information to the real world. You must be able to locate your boat both on the chart and in the real world and understand such terms as *range* and *bearing*. You must understand how to use a magnetic compass, and be able to plot a course using basic piloting tools: dividers, parallel ruler, and drawing compass. You must understand the meanings of channel markers, range markers, buoys, and the other aids to navigation, as well as terms like *line of position,* a *fix,* and *danger bearing.*

No other form of navigation requires the continuous alertness, experience, and judgment needed in piloting. The easiest way to find your position is not to lose it in the first place. Every trip starts from a known location. It is a simple matter to move that known position ahead when the boat changes course; passes a landmark such as an island, bay, or point; or enters a new channel.

Updating your boat's position can be done electronically or manually. If you do it entirely electronically, your equipment needs to be of sufficient accuracy that all dangers can be avoided. This accuracy depends on the proximity of the danger, the size of the waterway, and the detail of the chart. Electronic piloting is no replacement for standard piloting practices, however.

COMPASS

The compass is probably the one navigation instrument most commonly found aboard modern yachts. You and your crew should understand the differences among compass, magnetic, and true bearings, and should know how to read and use both handheld and fixed compasses. You should be able to take a magnetic bearing on a fixed object, and have the steering skills necessary to run a compass course accurately. As skipper, you should understand the cause and magnitude of errors generated by magnetic variation and by deviation, leeway, magnetic anomalies, and human capabilities. A good skipper should also know when the compass is out of adjustment and needs calibration.

CHARTS

Given the choice between a compass and a chart at sea, I would pick the compass, but along coastal areas I think the chart is the more important. And because a lot of cruising is done in sheltered coastal areas—which contain the real dangers to navigation—it's mandatory that you have considerable skill at chart reading.

Never is the old saw about pictures and their worth in words more true than when it comes to explaining how to get from place to place. We have no record, of course, but there is a good possibility that the first three ways humans used the stick were to get food, as a weapon, and to diagram navigational directions in the dirt.

Graphic representations of the earth's surface are an excellent way to convey large amounts of information. With a little practice, looking at a map or chart is the next best thing to being there. It lets you "see" in your mind the location of rocks, shoals, and various structures, along with the shapes of the bay and surrounding hills.

There is no better or cheaper boat insurance than a good set of charts for the waters you'll be sailing—and the skill to use them properly. You can buy 40 charts for the cost of a year's boat insurance or a 45-pound CQR anchor.

Everyone aboard should know whether the chart soundings are in fathoms, feet, or meters, and when the chart was published. This information is especially important to the navigator, because natural and artificial changes are occurring constantly, and some may be critical to the safety of the vessel.

Everyone should also be aware of the vertical datums, which vary and depend on the tides of the area charted. In spots where vertical clearance is restricted either above or below the water and these restrictions are close to the height or draft of your vessel, understanding these chart datums and the difference between them and actual water levels becomes critical.

The large amounts of information shown on a chart and the detail with which many items are shown require the extensive use of graphic marks, symbols, and abbreviations. You and your crew should be familiar with those most commonly used and be aware of chart 1, which contains a standard set of symbols and abbreviations used by the National Oceanographic and Atmospheric Administration (NOAA).

Finally, everyone aboard should understand contour lines and be able to identify islands, bays, and other physical features from their chart representations. You should also be able to identify and use natural range markers.

NAVIGATION

Navigation beyond the range of land used to be synonymous with celestial navigation. That is no longer the case. Electronic navigation is slowly replacing celestial, because it is much more reliable, more accurate (200 times), more consistent, and simpler to use. And since satellite navigation gives accurate and immediate information on the course, speed, and distance you've traveled, it also reduces your dependence on the compass and distance log.

No one should put to sea in a small boat without GPS navigation equipment on board, if for no other reason than that it allows you to transfer the exact position of your boat at any given moment to permanent memory by touching a single button. Thus if a person is lost overboard, the problem of returning and finding the victim is simplified. The boat can return to within as little as 10 meters of where the button was pushed. Both you and your crew should be familiar with the operation of the GPS system.

The only benefit celestial navigation provides that electronic lacks is the feeling of accomplishment from successfully navigating a boat across a large open body of water. That may not seem important, but the major part of the enjoyment of passage making probably originates from this feeling.

LIFEBOAT NAVIGATION

Navigation implies that the boat can be steered and that it has some form of power to move it in the direction in which it's being steered. Life rafts are not boats; they are little more than large flotation devices. If you have to abandon ship and take to your life raft, the form of navigation you use will depend on the equipment available—anything from a handheld GPS and compass to your wits alone. Thus it is necessary that someone aboard understand simple celestial navigation using a sextant and almanac, and progress in steps to navigation with less and less equipment. Knowledge of star courses and bird or cloud navigation techniques may make the difference between survival and other less palatable options.

Having "a star to steer her by" may not apply to tall ships anymore, but it still applies to emergency navigation. In fact, almost every form of emergency navigation depends on signposts in the sky. Given the recent demise of celestial navigation astronomy is not as important now as it once was to the cruiser, but a general knowledge of the subject is both helpful and rewarding. Watching the stars whirl overhead is as much a part of a night passage as the motion of the sea.

Further, this knowledge is also a hedge against emergencies. All you need for emergency navigation is the ability to identify some constellations, all first-, and some second-magnitude stars. This may sound like a tall order, but remember that only about 30 of the 88 constellations and about 40 stars in the entire sky are useful for navigation.

ANCHORING

During a typical cruise your vessel is likely to spend more time in port than under way. A good portion of that time in port will be spent at anchor. Anchoring certainly seems easier than entering a slip. There are no hard docks to hit when anchoring; you just move into a big open area and throw something heavy overboard. Why, then, does the process generate apprehension?

It's because, once your anchor is dropped, questions surface: "Will it hold? Isn't that rock/reef/shore getting closer?" As more boats enter the harbor more questions are added to the list: "Is that turkey going to drop his anchor on mine? Swing into me? Drag his anchor back onto me?" These and similar gnawing questions are what cause heads to pop off the pillow all night long and eyes to peer into the darkness wondering if doom, real or imagined, is about to strike. When dawn finally arrives, the apprehension can be detected in almost any skipper's red eyes.

Life will be much simpler if you know some of the basic principles and techniques of anchoring, and have the proper equipment. Still, although much has been written about anchoring, it is probably the least understood of the cruising techniques. More misinformation, half-truths, and outright bull are spread about anchoring than about any other subject I know.

What holds your boat to the bottom is not the anchor but a system of which the anchor is only a part—and maybe not even the primary part, because a great many incidents of dragging anchors can be attributed to the wrong rode. For example, the Cabo San Lucas debacle I mentioned in chapter 1 can be attributed directly to the use of chain rode in shallow water (Van Doren, *Oceanography and Seamanship*). Modern anchor systems are composed of the anchor, rode, boat, and composition of the bottom. Any one component can cause failure.

To choose the proper anchor system for a particular condition you should understand the general theory, understand how each of the various parts of the system works, and be able to calculate (or at least estimate) the loads on your system. Evaluating the wind and current loads can make setting and retrieving your anchor considerably easier. Ninety percent of the time a 45-foot cruising sailboat can be held quite satisfactorily on an anchor of 20 pounds or less. Why bother struggling with one weighing 45 pounds or more?

If you poll cruising people on anchor weight, the overwhelming majority will tell you they have very large, heavy anchors, and all will swear by them. This is a case where two wrongs make a right. The overwhelming majority of cruisers do not know how to anchor properly, and their lack of proper technique is hidden, most of the time, by their use of an extra-large anchor.

Anchors are not dropped—they are placed, using simple but specific procedures. You and your crew should be aware of how to prepare, approach, deploy, and retrieve an anchor. You should be familiar with single and double anchoring methods, and have the skills required to set and retrieve anchors with the dinghy. As skipper, you should be familiar with the techniques needed to anchor in heavy weather; you should know how to select a suitable anchorage, and a suitable anchoring spot in that anchorage. You should also know anchoring etiquette, how other boats in the anchorage will affect your anchoring process, and how to retrieve a fouled anchor. Such knowledge will make for pleasant dreams and restful sleep.

HANDLING COMMON EMERGENCIES

Emergencies are often brought on by bad judgment, bad planning, or stupidity—and since none of us are immune to stupidity, even properly trained cruisers need to know how to extricate themselves when they get in a fix. Some of the most common emergencies are grounding, hull leaks, loss of steering, fire, loss of engine power, and person overboard. And while I'm about to discuss some techniques for dealing with each, it is also prudent for you to know a little about abandoning ship and helicopter rescue.

GROUNDING

Unintentional grounding can be a nuisance or an emergency depending on such circumstances as boat speed, firmness of the bottom, sea state, and state of the tide. There are four techniques commonly used to get off the bottom: Use engine power to back off, be pulled off by another boat, kedge off, or float off on an incoming tide. The easiest is backing off and the surest is kedging. The most embarrassing is floating free, while being towed off is a close second. A competent skipper will be familiar with all four methods.

LEAKS

If a leak occurs it is helpful for you to know a little about the physics of the process, have a system to quickly locate the leak, and be familiar with various methods to control the inflow. These methods depend on what caused the leak, the number of crew present, and the size of your boat. Only the foolhardy skipper relies on pumps. A 3-inch-diameter hole—certainly not the largest hole you can punch in your hull—can let in a whopping 350 gallons of water per minute. It is therefore imperative that you and your crew understand the deployment and use of collision mats.

LOSS OF STEERING

Steering failures can be broken into two broad classes: those stemming from the failure of the rudder and its attachment and those stemming from the failure of another part of the steering system. Common causes include loss or failure of rudder, rudder stock, or pintel; failed tiller; and broken cables or hydraulic lines on wheel-steered boats. Some problems can be repaired at sea. If yours can't, you will need to jury-rig some kind of emergency steering to get your boat to a repair facility.

Jury-rigging depends on the boat, the problem, and the materials at hand. But a good skipper should be familiar with rigging sweeps to use in place of the rudder, and with steering via the sails or via dragging objects.

FIRE AT SEA

Any extensive fire on a small vessel is terminal (Zadig, *The Complete Book of Boating*). Those that start with an explosion get too large too quickly to fight on a small boat. Take what little time you have to signal *mayday* and then abandon ship. Once you're over the side get well clear of the boat; many fuels commonly kept aboard are likely to cause multiple explosions.

Obviously, the best policy is to prevent fire from occurring in the first place. The major sources of fires on board are the galley, the engine room, the fuel lines, the electrical circuits, oil lamps, heaters, and cigarettes. Handle and stow all fuels properly, then; use proper ventilation; inspect and maintain fuel lines; keep the bilge clean and free of fuel or vapor; and keep flammable material away from open flames (curtains over cooking stoves, for example). Any condition that might contribute to a fire should be corrected at once.

Small fires can sometimes be controlled by prompt action. Turn off any fuel-supply lines and jettison any burning material over the side, if possible. Do not waste your fire suppressant; aim the flow at the base of the fire. Most onboard extinguishers will last for only 8 to 20 seconds; this means that on the typical recreational vessel with three or four extinguishers, you have only about a minute to control the blaze.

TOWING AND BEING TOWED

Many people instinctively think that towing is the primary solution to all emergencies. Not so; requesting a tow should always be your last resort. The consultant syndrome—the guy from out of town must know more than the locals—seems to be operating here. You should know, however, that the feeling of security you get when your disabled boat is under the control of another vessel may be misplaced. First, two boats tied together are much less maneuverable; second, your boat is now under the control of a foreign crew with questionable skills. Even the U.S. Coast Guard occasionally makes errors.

The safest course is to relinquish control only after all other measures fail. Many boaters, even those with single engines, forget that they may have auxiliary power at hand in the form of a dinghy and outboard. I have on several occasions used my dinghy and a 6-horsepower outboard to push my 43-foot sailboat—once when fully loaded for cruising, weighing more than 40,000 pounds. Being towed at sea is not as simple as having your car towed on land, however: Each boat has specific duties and responsibilities. As skipper, you should be familiar with each as well as with how the dinghy can be used as a towboat.

PERSON OVERBOARD

In any but the most moderate conditions retrieving a person lost overboard is difficult, and the chances for success are uncertain. As in the case of fire, prevention is your best defense: toe rails; adequate handholds and grab rails; nonslip, uncluttered deck surfaces; and lifelines and pulpits strong and high enough to contain a possible victim are crucial. Just as important is having a good safety harness, one that can be slipped into quickly in rough conditions—and using it.

When moving about on deck, keep your body weight low and follow the age-old rule of the sea—one hand for yourself and one for the ship. Be aware of special risks such as filling a bucket, landing a fish. (Also, the number of men recovered with their flies open is reported to be disproportionately large.) Keep the decks clean. Cluttered decks tend to snag safety lines and restrict movement to such an extent that the lines become difficult to work in; you and your crew might avoid using them when you most need them.

If someone does go over, his or her chance of survival depends on (in order of importance) the number of people in the crew; visibility; wind strength and sea conditions; point of sail; temperature of the water; flotation of the victim; lack of predators; and, finally, ability to haul the victim out of the water. If the boat loses contact with the victim, survival depends on you and your crew's knowledge of search and retrieval methods.

ABANDONING SHIP

Abandoning ship is a last resort. Even though the life raft is called a *life* raft, you are always better off on the boat itself; stay with it as long as possible. When the boat is abandoned, so is a great deal of control over what happens to yourself and your crew. In a life raft you must depend on chance, wind, and others for survival. There are many documented cases of people abandoning ship only to be found dead in a raft—with their abandoned boat still floating.

There are only a few reasons to abandon ship (Knox-Johnston, *Seamanship*). An out-of-control fire or a hole that is letting water in faster than it can be pumped out are two already discussed. Another might be a boat driven so hard on a lee shore that it cannot be salvaged. Because land is nearby this is not quite as serious a situation. Before trying to make it to shore unaided, however, keep in mind that distance over water is often grossly under-estimated.

Some books recommend that survivors stay near the boat, because it is more easily seen than the raft (Chapman, *Piloting, Seamanship, and Small Boat Handling*). But this advice makes no sense: The only common reasons to leave the boat in the first place are fire and a large hole in the hull. In either case the boat is going to leave the area before you do. And if your boat is not about to sink then it should *not* be abandoned.

HELICOPTER RESCUE

Helicopters are becoming the vehicle of choice for rescue missions, especially if one or all of the crew require evacuation. Being successfully rescued by helicopter requires that you have some understanding of the operation, though, as well as preparation by you and your crew. Will the transfer be effected from the deck or from the water? What is the best course for the boat? What type of hoisting equipment will be used? These are some of the questions that you must be able to answer. Remember that communication between the boat and the helicopter by radio will be practically impossible with the noisy craft overhead.

WORKING WITH ROPE

It is difficult to say anything exciting about rope, especially after talking about such exciting things as sinking boats and helicopter rescue. The truth is that rope is mundane and uninteresting. When was the last time your dinner conversation revolved around it? Nevertheless, selecting, handling, and working with rope are fundamental skills in good seamanship.

Once a piece of rope has been assigned a task, it loses the label *rope* and becomes known by its use—*halyard, docking line, sheet,* or just the generic term, *line.* You must be familiar with the various kinds of rope to select the proper one for each specific task. Although there are approximately 1,500 knots, splices, and hitches, the well-educated sailor needs to know only how to coil and put up a line, how to whip a line, how to tie 10 or 12 knots, and how to make a few splices (Lane, *The Boatman's Manual*).

RADIO COMMUNICATION

You and your crew should know something about radio—the basic principles, the types, a little about antennas and grounding, and a lot about proper procedure, especially that for emergency calls, which is legally binding. Morse code may become part of your life because of the usefulness of ham radio to cruisers.

WEATHER

Watching the sky will tell you much about impending weather changes. Nowhere—except maybe the polar regions—is weather knowledge so important as in the middle of the ocean. Certainly you can listen to weather broadcasts and scan weather-fax charts, but if you don't understand the basics of weather, you'll find it difficult to make use of this information. Weather reports cover large areas and can be wrong; even correctly reported conditions can change unexpectedly. Sometimes the change can affect your safety.

Sometimes it affects only your enjoyment—no small matter. Those who look to the sky for safety alone miss a great deal of life. Skywatching can be a spiritual, ethereal, entertaining, and even healthful experience. Looking up reportedly expedites the delivery of oxygen to the lungs (Roth, *The Sky Observer's Guidebook*). Certainly the ever-changing sky can be a beautiful thing to watch, particularly on a passage, where cloudwatching takes on a whole new meaning.

Those who have seen the unbroken horizon filled with only three elements—sea, sky, and a small boat—will forever perceive the sky differently. The sight of small white cumulus clouds scudding through a blue sky will always draw them back to those warm trade winds and sunny decks.

As skipper, you should know about storms, weather prediction, and weather elements—solar radiation, atmospheric pressure, and temperature gradients. Changes in these elements influence weather, and the interplay among them forms such things as wind, fog, and storms—all of great interest to cruisers.

Although storms get considerable press they are relatively uncommon. Even though strong winds can cause considerable damage, you will rarely encounter any above force 8—and avoiding these encounters is easier than you may think. The chance of properly trained cruisers ever encountering a hurricane at sea is remote.

On the other hand, it has been calculated that if a boat was to cross the world's most prolific hurricane system (near the Philippines) during the worst possible time at a mean speed of 6 knots, its odds of encountering winds at gale force or above would be about 12 to 1 (Van Doren, *Oceanography and Seamanship*). This is about the same as the odds of being dealt two pairs in a game of draw poker. Now, I have been dealt two pairs considerably more often than I would like to face hurricanes. Further, the consequences of being dealt two pairs are considerably less than those of being hit with a hurricane.

Eighty years ago most cruisers got their weather information from looking at the sky. Today, the same information comes from almost every form of communication: radio, television, newspapers, and telephone. You may even think that the only skill you need to predict the weather is the ability to punch the correct button and listen to a professional report.

And certainly there's truth in that statement. If a weather report is available, it is not in your best interests to try to predict the weather yourself. Weather prediction is for professionals who are trained in this complicated and difficult task. Even these professionals are right only about 60 percent of the time. If they, with all their equipment and training, make mistakes, what hope is there for the amateur?

If you said "slim to none," you're only half right. Even limited knowledge of weather will help you assess the believability of the available professional reports, and to adapt area-wide forecasts to your local and changing conditions. In addition, sometimes accurate professional weather reports are unavailable or nonexistent.

At a minimum, you should know where to go to get good weather reports, what information is available on weather fax, and how to make the best use of weather-map information. To increase the value of weather reports, you should also understand the use of some simple weather instruments and develop a "weather eye" capable of interpreting nature's warning signals—clouds, wind shifts, and wave action.

LEGAL MATTERS

As it turns out, Adam was not sent out of paradise; lawyers were just sent in. No matter how idyllic a pastime may be, as it becomes more popular the law will eventually raise its ugly head. Such is the case in boating and, more specifically, cruising. There are more and more domestic and foreign laws—formal and informal—that must be observed or eschewed.

The formal laws can be broken down into five distinct areas: laws that cover the operation of the vessel, laws that cover the vessel and its equipment, laws that require registration, regulations that concern the environment, and laws dealing with entry into foreign countries. The informal laws are known collectively as common boating etiquette and courtesy.

Many of the formal regulations are in constant flux. It requires continuous effort to keep abreast of what it is that you are not supposed to do.

VESSEL OPERATION

Sometimes called the rules of the road, vessel-operation regulations include the rules for passing, overtaking, and crossing the path of other vessels to prevent collision. They also specify the proper location, color, and visibility of the lights that must be carried on each type of vessel, and the type, frequency, and duration of the audible signals. Unfortunately, the laws governing vessel operation vary slightly depending on where the vessel is being operated—international or inland. Unless you are *sure* you will stick to one or the other general areas, you should be familiar with both sets of laws.

Another type of vessel-operation law concerns gross negligence—the operation of a boat in a way that endangers life, limb, or property. Reckless operation of a boat is forbidden by both local and federal laws that are enforced by the U.S. Coast Guard, as well as local sheriff and police departments. Breaking these laws is a criminal offense and can subject you to large fines or imprisonment. Offenses generally considered to be negligent operation include:

Overloading the vessel, with either persons or freight

Speeding in confined areas

Speeding in a posted or swimming area

Operating under the influence of alcohol or drugs

Creating excessive wake

Operating without proper lights at night

Employing unsafe waterskiing practices

Riding in exposed positions at high speed

Refusing to correct hazardous conditions (Lane, *Boatman's Manual*).

Besides the obligation to operate your boat in a safe manner, you're also required by law to provide assistance to any person in danger at sea. The failure to meet this obligation could subject you to a fine, imprisonment, or both (U.S. Department of Transportation, "Federal Requirements and Safe Tips for Recreational Boaters").

THE VESSEL AND ITS EQUIPMENT

The laws dealing with the vessel and its equipment are equivalent to the seat-belt and helmet laws, which are designed to protect people from doing stupid things and harming themselves. They require that certain equipment be present on a boat. This varies according to the size of the boat, but in general includes personal flotation devices, visual distress signals, fire extinguishers, explosion- and flame-control devices, and sound-producing devices. The regulations also govern marine electrical systems, ventilation requirements, and the processes of taking on and storing fuel.

REGISTRATION

In the United States, all undocumented vessels equipped with propulsion machinery must be registered in the state of principal use. (The Coast Guard still documents pleasure vessels.) Procedures and fees vary tremendously among the 50 states. Coast Guard documentation does not protect you from all of these fees, but if you plan to visit countries other than Canada and Mexico, you will find that foreign governments prefer Coast Guard documentation to state registration.

Registration laws specify the size and location of the registration numbers and the fee to be paid, which all depend on the size and type of boat. Failure to register a boat properly can lead to large fines. You're also required to notify the registration agency of any changes in the address or ownership of the vessel, or if the vessel or the certificate is lost, damaged, destroyed, or stolen.

ENVIRONMENTAL REGULATIONS

Environmental regulations governing boaters are multiplying rapidly. Pollution of the water by oil or fuel, bottom paints, solid waste, and sewage are all covered by these laws. Discharge of any oil or fuel that causes a film or sheen on the water, discoloration of its surface, or a sludge or emulsion beneath its surface is prohibited. Violators are subject to a penalty of $5,000. This is a rather stringent requirement considering that it takes less than ⅛ teaspoon of oil to cause a sheen or discoloration on the surface of the water.

FOREIGN COUNTRIES

Regulations for pleasure craft sailing in foreign waters are relatively simple and consist of entrance and clearance procedures. As the skipper, you should be aware of how and where to obtain permission, and what documents, records, and papers you must carry on your boat. Although it is not necessary for a documented U.S. vessel to clear customs when leaving the United States or its territories, it is a good idea to secure clearance papers and a Bill of Health from the U.S. Department of Health if you will be entering any foreign country other than Mexico or Canada. Foreign customs officials are used to seeing papers that clear your vessel from its last port of call; entry will be considerably easier if these papers are in proper order.

Because regulations vary from country to country, it is also prudent for you to carry several extra copies of all passport photos, as well as photocopies of the ship's documents, that can be surrendered, if requested, to inspection officials.

On reaching foreign port, you must raise the yellow Q flag on your starboard spreader or yardarm. The captain is the only person who is legally able to leave the boat until it and its crew have been inspected and cleared by customs and immigration. This restriction includes any crew member stepping off the boat onto the dock for any reason, even to fasten mooring lines. The captain is allowed off the vessel only to secure clearance and must proceed directly with this mission and only this mission.

When your boat and crew have cleared customs and immigration, the Q flag is replaced by the national ensign or flag of the country you're visiting. Failure to fly the flag of the host nation properly is not only considered discourteous, but in some nations is punishable by fine or imprisonment (Lane, *Boatman's Manual*). Knowing when, where, and how to fly the U.S. and other flags also reflects your knowledge and experience.

ETIQUETTE AND COMMON BOATING CUSTOMS

Of all these laws the most worthwhile for cruisers are the unwritten laws concerning etiquette and common courtesy. Boats are small, private spaces and should not be boarded unless you are granted permission to do so. If no one is on deck, a sharp rap on the hull will generally attract the attention of someone on board. The simple question, "Permission to come aboard?" is all you need ask. Above and below decks is almost one contiguous space aboard small boats, and entry into one is entry into the other. You would not consider entering someone's home without knocking and being invited in; extend the same courtesy to someone's boat.

When you must raft against another boat, permission to raft should be secured before you do so. This permission implies that the people on the outside boat will have to cross over the inside boat or boats to reach the dock. The crossing should be done quietly, by way of the foredeck, as few times as possible, and at reasonable hours. Parents with children should see that their children respect the adjoining yacht.

Boats under power—especially speeding dinghies—should be constantly aware of their wake. This can play havoc with and even damage other vessels. On narrow and sensitive channels it may erode the shoreline.

Improper passing is almost epidemic these days; the proper procedure is to reduce as much as possible the discomfort to the boat you're passing. This can be done by passing well astern or to the leeward of the boat, or slowing down so that the boats' relative speeds are only a few knots different. This is especially important when powerboats pass small craft.

Many people go boating to find peace. Consideration for this peace is an important element of boating etiquette. Secure your halyards before you leave your boat. They may not be flapping when you leave, but let a little wind arise and they'll hammer out a cacophony of clatter, which is worse than dripping water on the forehead. Consider your neighbors, and remember that sound travels better over water. Keep your level of conversation and music low, and shut down your generators after dark.

6

The Right Boat

There are many people out there with the wrong boat—and some who are not out there, for the same reason. I would schedule a minimum of 5 years for learning about boats; ideally, it should be 10 or 12 years. You will find that during the process your opinions about the "right boat" will change. For example, I was enamored of a ketch until I chartered one for a month.

Selecting the proper boat requires an inordinate amount of information. The better the information, the better the boat will fit your needs.

There are three ways to obtain this information: Get it free, buy it, or acquire it with your own sweat. If you get free advice from your friendly boat salesman, it will be worth every penny you paid for it. It's not that boat salesmen are dishonest—just that their aim is to sell boats, not educate you. Their negative advice is often more useful than their positive. When they tell you what's wrong with a competitor's boat they are more apt to be candid.

Increasing what you pay for information may increase its value. If you decide to go this route, find a reputable naval architect, one who has designed all types of cruising boats and is open minded, and pay that person to talk with you about what will suit you and your cruising plans. The advice you get will only be as good as your ability to express, and the architect's ability to discern, your personality and cruising needs. Also be aware that the professional's advice will err on the side of moderation.

Acquiring the information on your own takes time and effort, but it is probably the surest way to get a boat that matches your needs. As for any purchase of like importance and expense, high-quality research is necessary for a high-quality outcome. The amount of research varies from person to person, and so does the level of satisfaction with the final choice. In fact, you could probably find some rough correlation between the level of research and the level of satisfaction.

How to Gather the Necessary Information

You will be talking to and reading information produced by "boaters." In dealing with this subspecies the boater, you must keep in mind three facts:

1. Almost all boaters are strongly individualistic.

2. Most boaters are opinionated.

3. Many boaters are closed minded.

EXPERTS CAN MAKE ERRORS

Therein lies the rub. All the information you gather will come from opinionated, closed-minded individuals, and some of it will be erroneous. Many an innocent, well-meaning cruiser has spent considerable money and time chasing the right dream in the wrong boat.

Here is one example of an erroneous statement from an expert:

> *Heavy displacement provides motion comfort. If two boats have the same waterline area and one has twice the displacement of the other, the former will receive only half the motion of its lighter sister in a rough sea* (Ted Brewer, *Ted Brewer Explains Sailboat Design*).

This is such a common misconception that many authors quote it without thinking. Common sense tells us that a light-displacement boat in a 12-foot sea will rise at least 12 feet as the wave passes under it. If the heavy-displacement boat has only half that motion, however, it is going to be extremely wet, with 6 feet of seawater washing its deck, since the above statement predicts that the heavy-displacement boat will rise only 6 feet. Really?

In another instance,

> In addition to providing an indication of stability, [the ballast-displacement ratio] identifies that portion of the total displacement that is available for food, water, fuel, equipment and so forth. This is simply calculated by subtracting the weight of the ballast from the total displacement (Gufstafson, *How to Buy the Best Sailboat*).

Although this sounds logical, it supports Dodds's First Law: Any idiot can write a book. The cited author apparently does not know the meaning of *displacement* or *ballast*, let alone the use of the ratio. Unfortunately, the error here is obvious only to a knowledgeable individual; common sense is not much help.

The displacement of a boat is equal to the total weight of the boat. The ballast is that portion of the boat's total weight that is added to provide stability. The indicated calculation, subtracting the ballast from the displacement, will provide the weight of the hull, rig, and basic internal furnishings, such as cabinets, berths, and so on, and has nothing to do with the ability to carry additional stores. There is no fixed rule for additional stores that can be carried, but the pounds per inch of immersion will indicate how much a boat will sink with added weight.

As for the amount of additional stores, you could conceivably add them until your gunwales are just above the waterline. While that certainly is not practical, most cruising boats do go out with every existing space filled and the boat sitting several inches below its designed waterline. These additional stores affect many factors—including performance, especially if the boat's gunwales get slightly below the waterline. This and subsequent chapters will provide more information on these subjects.

Uninitiated cruisers can protect themselves from bad advice by listening and reading critically and using common sense.

TOO MUCH INFORMATION TOO FAST

Time is an important factor in information gathering. Information can only be fed to the mind at the rate that it can be processed—a rate that varies from person to person. Once saturated, the mind goes into sort of an overload mode and shuts down. Symptoms are confusion, then mild panic.

It is important for you to gather data below your critical rate, because an overloaded mind can blindly plunge into a bad decision. This plunge very often results in choosing whatever option is currently being presented.

This is what makes high-pressure sales so successful. The salesperson simply feeds information, any information, to you as fast as he or she can, until your mind can no longer process it; you get confused and go into overload. The result is a sale.

If you find yourself in this situation, just remember that your confusion and panic are normal human behaviors. Stop; literally take a deep breath, which will fight the panic; then just walk away. Let your brain rest and don't think about the problem for a few days. You will save yourself much money and grief.

Be forewarned that it is extremely easy to reach overload when you're researching cruising vessels and equipment, because of the extreme number of variables and the wide range of opinions you'll be processing.

COMMON PATHS TO LEARNING

Since most of your information will be gathered from cruisers, who are opinionated and individualistic, use common sense and remember that you too are one of those boaters—an individual, and different from all those other individuals with whom you're dealing.

So, first know yourself. Almost any boat designed by a reputable architect and built by a reputable yard will suffice. Pick the boat and its equipment to suit your personality, not that of the author of a book, or the 10-year cruiser two slips over, or any other experienced sailor.

Get all sides of the story. If you want to know what's good about roller furling, ask someone who has roller-furling sails. If you want to know what's bad about that system, ask someone who doesn't. I've heard people loudly extol wind vanes and others, just as experienced, say they wouldn't have one on board. How can this be? Simple! There are very few completely wrong answers in boating. Almost anything, well built, will work as long as it fits you.

BAREBOAT CHARTERING

Nothing is as valuable as direct experience with cruising equipment, and the bareboat charter industry is an excellent source of this experience. Living aboard and using a boat for two weeks will show you many of the strengths and weaknesses of its design, as well as those of any alterations made by its owner.

Over the course of 5 to 10 years, too, chartering for a couple of weeks each year will sharpen your cruising skills and keep your spirit alive. As we saw in chapter 4, owning a boat is considerably more expensive in the long run than chartering. Further analysis would also show that unless a boat is used for more than six weeks a year, it is cheaper in the short haul to charter.

Chartering gives you all the advantages of owning a boat—except pride of ownership—and none of the maintenance or worry. You can get a clean, well-equipped boat of your choice, in the location of your choice. When you're finished with the boat you clean it up, take off your gear, and leave. The maintenance of the brightwork, bottom paint, engine, refrigerator, and a hundred other balky items is the responsibility of the owner. During the off season, when high-wind warnings or subarctic temperatures strike, you sleep soundly.

Your only worries will be how well a boat is equipped and whether it's in good mechanical condition when you take it away from the pier. The first problem can be handled by assembling a boat bag and taking it with you on all your charters. The bag should contain all the various parts and pieces most often left off charter boats—a hand-bearing compass, field glasses, a handybilly, dividers and a parallel ruler, extra charts and guidebooks, and so on. The second problem is handled by patronizing only reputable charter organizations with good maintenance programs and fast chase boats.

What Information to Gather

A cruising vessel should provide a safe, comfortable journey within a specified budget. Therefore, selecting the right boat means finding a workable balance among these factors as well as your individual needs. Unfortunately, these criteria are not always compatible; increasing one may decrease the other. For example, increasing safety can increase cost, and what good is an ultrasafe boat that costs so much you can't afford to sail it? The key here is to find the right mix of safety, cost, and comfort that still answers your basic needs.

This is not an easy thing to do, especially if you have never been cruising and are not totally sure of your needs. Ted Brewer proposes that the proper ocean cruiser should be 30 percent seaworthiness, 30 percent comfort, 20 percent performance, and 20 percent economy (Brewer, *Sailboat Design*). These are all tough concepts to quantify, though, and I'm not sure I agree with his cuts of the pie.

I tend to value performance and seaworthiness as highly as comfort at the expense of economy—say 30, 30, 30, and 10 percent. If you're on a tight budget, you may want to rate economy higher—30, 20, 20, and 30, perhaps—but what is important here is that *you* make the ratings. They serve as a place to start your evaluation. Remember that this formula is just a guide that may, and probably should, be changed as you gather information. You may even wish to add other factors that are important to you, or remove factors that are not. For the purposes of the following discussion, though, I have reduced the number of factors to three: safety, comfort, and cost. These seem to be the most basic, since all other points can be related to them. (For example, I view performance as being a part of both safety and comfort.)

SAFETY

The components of safety for you to consider are seaworthiness, performance, and strength of hull. Seaworthiness is the vessel's ability to remain on top of the water in all kinds of conditions. How well it moves through the water in these conditions makes up performance. Strength of hull is self-evident.

Certainly, water pouring into the boat through a hole in the hull can be very disquieting. Concern about that problem can grow severe enough that a person develops BPH, or bulletproof hull syndrome. This disease is manifest by a strong desire to construct a boat out of ¾-inch-thick steel plate, with watertight compartments that can be sealed to provide positive flotation, and to install on board pumps with enough capacity to empty any single lock in the Panama Canal in under three minutes.

My advice is to forget it. The *Titanic* has already been built, and you know where it is. You cannot depend on hull strength and pumps alone for protection against sinking. The premium in performance that you'll pay for these heavy hulls is way out of proportion to the probability of a terrible event occurring.* As weight goes up, so does cost—but more

_____

* I had one boat owner assure me that they didn't need detailed charts or have to worry about rocks because their

important, down comes performance, which in turn affects safety. For example, more weight requires more sail area, making sail handling more difficult and dangerous. Weight also slows the boat down, making passages longer, which results in more exposure to risk.

No one should go to sea without a sound, strong hull, but a satisfactory hull can be made from wood or fiberglass as well as aluminum or steel. (See chapter 7 for more on the properties of these individual materials.) How much strength is enough cannot be expressed definitively by a number; it depends on whether the job is to hold the yolk and white together or protect a missile site from a nuclear strike.

For most cruisers, the job of a hull is to provide a watertight membrane against the normal forces of the sea. The hull should be strong enough to withstand minor collisions with debris without springing a leak. The hull is not your main defense against collision; you protect yourself from hitting things by competent navigational skills, good judgment, and vigilance.

PERFORMANCE

Don't let anybody tell you that cruisers don't need a boat that performs well. Performance is more important in cruising than in racing. In racing, good performance means you win the race; in cruising, it means you live to sail another day.

Performance can be measured by a boat's abilities to sail close to the wind and to move through the water. Judging performance will be covered more thoroughly in chapter 7, but for now you should note that there are three times when it is particularly important: when clawing off a lee shore, when caught in heavy weather, and when sailing in light air.

The ability to claw off a lee shore is related to a boat's ability to point into the wind, especially a heavy wind. A boat that can do this can sail away from danger without relying on a motor or anchor for safety.

The main propulsion of a sailboat is its sails. It is difficult for the new cruiser to trust this system, however, and a common mistake is to believe that your auxiliary engine will save your boat in an emergency. In truth, this engine has considerably less power than your sails; that's why it's called an "auxiliary." It will not push your boat against strong headwinds and seas. And it might not work in an emergency; its cooling-water intakes can become

hull was made of aluminum. It seems they navigate by going in one direction until they hear a noise, then they try going in another direction.

clogged with debris, or a prop become fouled (Pardey, "The Ultimate Gear Test"). The number of cruising boats that have been lost because they could not go to windward under shortened sail is alarming and is directly related to poor performance.

In heavy weather every boat eventually has to fall away from its desired course and take up defensive courses to protect itself from foundering. However, some boats need to take this defensive action before others. Good performance will delay the need for defensive tactics and allow the crew to remain in control of their destiny, rather than running before the storm or heaving to and passively relying on providence for preservation.

On the other side of the wind-velocity scale good performance is less spectacular; still, it will have much more effect on your enjoyment of cruising, because you will face light winds much more often than heavy. Going 2 to 3 knots as opposed to 1 in a 5-knot zephyr will both reduce the amount of diesel you burn and increase your safety. Passage safety depends on accurately predicting future weather: It is much easier to predict three days of good weather than six. If a four-day passage can be cut to three, the resulting reduction in risk will be greater than just one-quarter.

On longer passages, regardless of how stout your boat, open water is always a hazard— and a boat averaging 3½ knots is exposed to open water for twice as long as a boat averaging 7 knots. Since winds on passage are ordinarily less than 12 knots 50 percent of the time, and since boat performance degrades as wind speed decreases, light-air efficiency significantly reduces your overall time in passage.

SEAWORTHINESS

Contrary to a popular notion, seaworthiness is not a function of displacement. Instead, it has to do with your boat's ability to remain floating on the surface right-side up. To do this, the water normally found on the outside of your boat must remain there. Only part of accomplishing that aim depends on the hull strength discussed above. The rest has to do with your boat's inherent stability and the openings purposely put into its hull to let in light, air, and people.

STABILITY

The dynamics of a sailboat in a seaway and under heavy winds are not yet clearly understood. The history of small (32 feet or less), ultralight, fin-keeled racing boats has not been too impressive relative to seaworthiness. However, full-keeled traditional cruisers don't do well, either. Miles Smeeton's yacht the *Tzu Hang*, a 45-foot classic heavy-displacement boat, has been rolled twice through 360 degrees and pitchpoled once (Smeeton, *Once Is Enough*). The *Pandora*, a copy of Josh Slocum's *Spray*, was rolled and dismasted.

The Tahiti ketch is often described as the ideal heavy-displacement, full-keeled cruising boat. But two Tahiti ketches, the *Atom* and the *Adios*, have reported 360-degree rolls and dismasting. Colin Archer–designed boats are also often used as examples of seaworthiness. Still, the *Legh II*, an Archer design, capsized and rolled 360 degrees (Vito, *Alone through the Roaring Forties*). Full keel and heavy displacement are not necessarily related to seaworthiness.

Recent studies seem to contradict traditional arguments for the safety of long keels. One such study showed that these keels apparently drag when a boat slides sideways down a wave face, and trip the boat. The more keel, the more easily the boat is tripped. On the other hand, in his book *Seaworthiness: The Forgotten Factor*, C. A. Marchaj seems to favor the older, full-keeled designs. However, many of his arguments do not apply to modern fast cruisers; his book compares traditional full-keeled yachts to modern, ultra-extreme racing hulls.

These racing vessels have hull, keel, and rudder shapes designed to take advantage of rating rules rather than provide good all-around performance. Therefore, their instability may not be a function of just keel shape. Indeed, a growing amount of evidence shows that extreme features play an important role in hull instability. A full keel could be considered an extreme feature. The best advice may be from Adlard Coles's *Heavy Weather Sailing*: "My own preference, if building again, would be towards moderate displacement and a well-proportioned hull with no extreme features."

A close look at stability will reveal that it is controlled by the beam, draft, ballast-displacement ratio, windage, and locations of the centers of gravity and buoyancy. The first four variables will be discussed in chapter 7, where the effects of each of the individual hull parameters are examined. The remaining two—the centers of gravity and buoyancy—along with the distance between them, called the righting lever arm, also play an important role in stability, however.

Calculating the stability of a boat requires dealing with weight, but rather than dealing with hundreds of individual weights in a complex object like a boat, the concept of the center of gravity allows the total weight of the boat to be considered concentrated at a single point. The center of gravity for any regular symmetrical object composed of a single material always lies on that object's symmetrical axis. For example, the center of gravity of a sphere is at the center of the sphere.

Unfortunately, the center of gravity for most boats cannot be easily determined mathematically, because they are not composed of a uniform material; nor are they of uniform thickness. However, if the boat is balanced and sits on its lines properly, then its center of gravity must lie on its axis. If the mast is not vertical, the center of gravity lies on the same

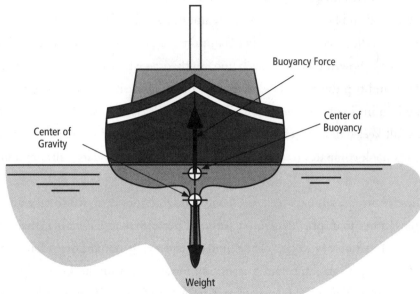

Figure 6.1   At-Rest Location of Forces

side of the boat's centerline toward which the boat is leaning. An unbalanced boat will be less stable on the side that contains its center of gravity.

The location of stores and equipment on your boat materially affects the location of its center of gravity—and thus its stability. Any weight positioned higher than the center of gravity will move that center upward and reduce stability.

The center of buoyancy of a boat is a concept similar to that of the center of gravity. It is defined as the center of gravity of the water that the boat displaces. Since water is a uniform material and has a uniform weight, the center of buoyancy can be determined more easily than the center of gravity.

When a properly balanced boat is not acted on by external forces, its centers of gravity and buoyancy lie on the same vertical axis. When external forces act on the boat, its center of gravity is unchanged, but the boat tips, causing the shape of the displaced water to change. The result is that the buoyancy force moves outward on the side toward which the boat is heeling (see figure 6.2). This movement generates a resisting couple, or moment, called the righting moment that balances the disturbing forces. For heeling angles of less than about 30 degrees, the farther the boat tips, the more the buoyancy force moves outward.

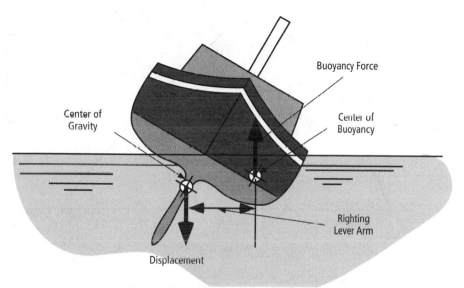

Figure 6.2   Location of Forces When Heeled 30°

Since the buoyancy and weight forces are always equal, the value of the righting moment is found by multiplying one of these forces, usually the displacement, by the distance between the forces. This distance is called the righting lever arm (L).

M = D x L   where: *Equation 6.1*

  M is the righting moment in foot-pounds,

  D is the displacement in pounds, and

  L is the righting arm in feet.

Since the displacement of a given boat will remain constant through any given instance of instability, the length of the righting arm will be the only variable. The righting arm starts at 0 when the boat is at rest in the water and increases to a maximum value, then returns to 0 and eventually goes negative as the heeling angle increases. The value of the maximum righting arm depends on parameters that I'll discuss below. When the righting arm is negative, the righting moment goes negative and assists the external forces in upsetting the boat. In other words, the boat will turn turtle. Figure 6.3 shows some typical stability curves for three different types of hulls.

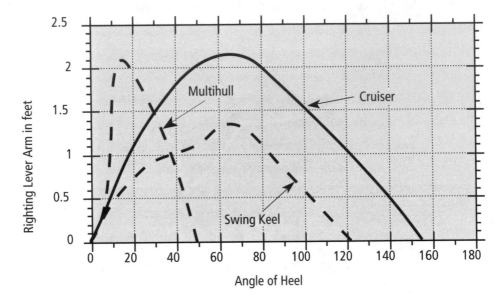

Figure 6.3   *Typical Stability Curves*

A boat can obtain stability from two sources: its form or the location of its weight. Form stability is significant early in heeling and increases rapidly for the first few degrees of that heeling. Most of the stability of a multihull is form stability. Note that the righting arm of a multihull increases rapidly and reaches its maximum at about 10 or 12 degrees. Thereafter the righting arm decreases rapidly to 0 at about 50 degrees. This is why multihulls do not heel much, and why once they reach 50 degrees they turn over and remain over.

The typical monohull cruiser gets most of its stability from the location of weight deep in its keel. The swing-keeled boat uses more form stability and less weight stability. However, both reach their maximum righting arm at about 80 degrees; thereafter the righting arm decreases, down to about 155 degrees for the typical monohull cruiser, and 120 degrees for the swing-keeled boat. Obviously, the larger the angle at which the righting arm remains positive, the better. Once upside down, the properly ballasted keel cruiser is relatively unstable. If the inverted cruiser rotates through a 25-degree angle, it will right itself. The swing-keeled boat, however, requires a major angle change to right itself.

To assist a boat in righting itself, the mast can be filled with foam, which displaces water and provides an additional buoyant force when the boat is inverted. This force will break the stability curve sharply once the mast enters the water at about 90 degrees. The curve will then flatten out and not turn negative for several tens of degrees.

As a practical matter you may never know the actual righting moment for your vessel; you should be aware, however, that several factors tend to produce higher righting moments and so contribute to better stability. Two have already been mentioned: a deep keel and high ballast ratio. A couple that I have not yet mentioned are the height of the deck and cabin top, and the weight of the hull material. Boats with high freeboard and center cockpits provide considerable room and light below, but they also decrease stability. A heavy hull material such as steel helps prevent hull rupture, but it also increases the tendency for the boat to turn upside down and remain in that position.

If you are lucky enough to have gotten your boat's stability curves from its architect, remember that these values are its upper limit. The actual righting moment once your boat is in service will be lowered by any modifications you make and stowage of gear, because most of these take place above the center of gravity. The more modifications, the greater the chance that you've degraded your boat's righting moment.

Placing equipment aloft—roller furling, mast steps, and radar antennas, for example—has an adverse effect on lateral stability, because it increases the weight and windage aloft. Increased windage intensifies the effect of the driving or unbalancing force, and increased weight decreases the righting moment lever arm by moving the center of gravity upward. Because we are dealing with moments, the weight aloft is not as important as the distance. Five pounds at the top of a 50-foot mast can produce almost 300 foot-pounds of reduction in righting moment.

If your boat has enough stability to remain upright on the water, only the size and location of its ports and hatches remain as factors affecting its seaworthiness. Very large ports are a hazard for a bluewater cruising vessel. They represent a weak spot in the superstructure that can be ruptured during heavy weather. Under such conditions—when your vessel is constantly being washed with waves—considerable water can get below through a broken port in a surprisingly short time.

Some cruisers carry pieces of plywood specially cut so that they can be quickly put into place to plug a porthole. However, in an emergency any piece of wood will do; the plywood locker covers under the settees are about the right size and generally handy. While these may not fit exactly, they will reduce the torrent to a trickle that can be handled by your pumps.

But please remember that I said *very* large ports are a problem. Although rupturing happens, it doesn't happen often. Don't let fear cause you to live in a gloomy world surrounded by just a few 5-inch by 10-inch ports. This tradition got started when ports were made from glass. With the arrival of Lexan plastic, safe ports of 2 or even 3 square feet in area can be installed.

Hatches at sea can also be a threat, but only if they are poorly constructed or carelessly left open. As a matter of routine all hatches should be closed and dogged at sea once the waves start running larger than 6 feet, or in any conditions where a knockdown can occur.

I see no reason why hatches must remain on a boat's centerline. I have four off-centerline hatches on my own boat that have given me absolutely no trouble. If conditions

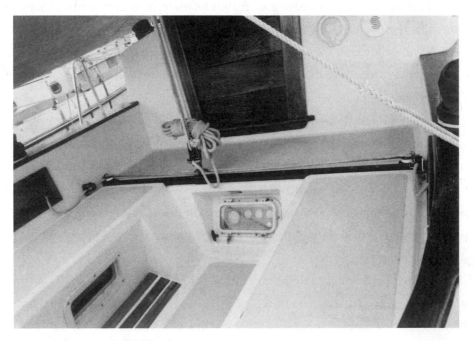

Figure 6.4   Bridge Deck

are such that water is reaching the off-center hatches, it's probably also reaching those on the centerline. In a violent storm, a difference in hatch location of 1 or 2 feet is not going to make any appreciable difference.

Louvered hatch boards or companionway doors can leak considerable water and should be removed and replaced with solid boards when at sea. Your companionway also needs to be protected from the cockpit sole by a bridge deck (a solid bulkhead between the cockpit and the cabin; see figure 6.4). This requires anyone moving between the cockpit and the quarters below to step up and over the deck. This small impediment to the crew is a major impediment to water's getting below. Without the bridge deck, a flooded cockpit means flooding below deck even if proper hatch boards are in place. A cockpit full of water is an unpleasant experience; a cabin full of water generally means a lost ship.

COMFORT

Many would consider *cruising comfort* an oxymoron. It depends, of course, on how you define *comfort* and what kind of cruising you are doing. The traditional cruiser defines comfort as the seakindliness of the boat—meaning that its motion under way is on the one hand free of excessive rolling or hobby-horsing, and on the other not so stiff that motion is quick. If that seems a little subjective or even contradictory to you, you're not alone. The idea that a stiff boat is uncomfortable at sea is common, yet I know of no controlled experiments verifying this conclusion and see no physical reason why it should be true. Certainly when heeled, a stiff boat returns to upright more quickly. However, it is just as true that a stiff boat will not heel as much under the same disturbing force as would a similar but less stiff boat; thus the distance traveled would be less, and the overall motion less. It is not clear to me that a 30-degree roll in 1.5 seconds is any more or less comfortable than a 5-degree roll in 0.3 second.

Further, if stiff boats are uncomfortable, then all multihull boats are uncomfortable, because they're all stiff. Yet very few multihull owners consider their boats uncomfortable; in fact, most include "comfort" among their top reasons for choosing a multihull. I am aware of at least one reported case in which two monohulls of exactly the same lines were constructed with two different stiffnesses. Both boats had the same owner and captain, but the two did not agree on which was the more comfortable (Marchaj, *Seaworthiness*).

What all this says to me is that seakindliness is too subjective to be useful as a guide to comfort in a cruising boat. Further, most cruising boats are at sea only a very small portion of the time, and the truth is that no boat smaller than the *Nimitz* is really comfortable at sea. Whether or not a design is "comfortable" depends on how the boat is used. Figure 6.5 shows a time-and-motion study of the distribution of activities in an average year of cruising.

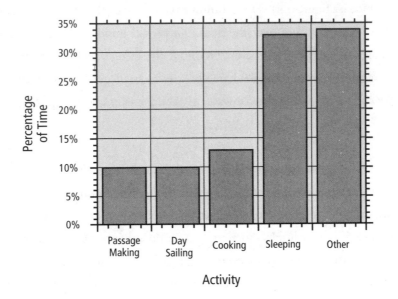

Figure 6.5   *Distribution of Activity aboard a Cruising Sailboat*

As you can see, the boat is used much more for living (80 percent) than for sailing (20 percent). In other words, the boat is first a home, and only second an attack vehicle to assault Mother Nature. Therefore its interior design should be directed at providing livable space.

LIVING

Passage making is a small, almost unimportant part of modern-day cruising. The single fore-and-aft sea berths traditionally deemed necessary for passage making are cramped and not very functional during the 80 percent of the time spent in port (Cloughley, *World to the West*). And the fiddles that the nautical hard-liners say are so important for passage making just get in the way while at anchor. I know of several experienced cruisers who removed them from the eating areas of their boats.

Athwartships bunks, another pet peeve of "real cruisers," are only a problem while on passage—and then only when you're sailing into the wind on the tack with the head down. In some passage situations they can be more comfortable than fore-and-aft bunks if the feet are down. Small portholes and hatches keep out a raging sea, but the light and air coming from larger openings are more important in a tropical port.

Several years ago, ice and cold drinks were considered too complicated for real cruisers. A few cruisers still snort when you show them your refrigerator, but the truth is that there are several reliable refrigeration units on the market that use very little energy. We ran ours for more than eight years without a failure, and in the Tropics it ran tirelessly on the power provided by three solar panels—with current to spare. The list of shoreside comforts making their way successfully to sea gets longer with each passing year.

Cramped, dark, poorly laid-out cabins turn day-to-day living into day-to-day existing. The boat must have enough space for you to comfortably bathe, cook, eat, sleep, relax, read, write, and entertain. It must have room to store all the things you need and can't do without, as well as all those things you must buy on your way. It must have enough water, power, and space to be self-contained. (I'll discuss all of these factors more fully in chapter 9.)

Onboard space is directly related to comfort. Again, this requirement varies with each individual. Our boat, the *Bird of Time,* is 43 feet long; it was designed for two people full time, four people for a couple of weeks of coastal cruising, and larger groups for only a matter of hours. We even choose not to use a crew on passages, primarily because of our lack of space. Some would say our comfort level is too high; maybe for them, but not for us.

SAILING PERFORMANCE

Whether you spend 20 percent of your time sailing your boat is to some extent dependent on your itinerary. How many passages do you intend to make and how long will they be? How much of the time will you be day sailing? How much time do you plan to power? How much windward work may be necessary? A reasonably accurate itinerary can supply the first cut at answers to these questions.

Your intended cruising grounds will determine such things as your keel depth, the relative importance of ventilation and heat, and the need for a dodger or a bimini. For example, if you are planing to spend a lot of time in the Bahamas, then a shoal-draft vessel is a great advantage. If you are cruising England, with its shallow bays and large tides, a twin-keeled boat may be the answer. Cabin heat increases the enjoyment of cruises in cold, wet climates; a bimini top or sunshade is necessary in tropical heat. Dodgers that add comfort in colder climates block the flow of air in the Tropics and actually reduce comfort there. If your cruise is to cover all seasons and conditions, you must have a little of everything and make sensible compromises.

In any case, the sailing characteristics of your boat should be such that you can enjoy sailing. And remember that 50 percent of your sailing on passages will be in winds less than 12 knots, while virtually all your day sailing, or coastal cruising, will be in winds of 12 knots or less (Dodds, *Modern Seamanship*). A boat that sails well in light to medium air is therefore the boat to have.

Regardless of what you may have heard, all winds do not come from the stern. A boat going into a headwind that tacks in greater than 90 degrees will soon be powering during day sailing, and off course when passage making. The British have a saying with which I heartily agree: "Gentlemen simply do not go to the windward." Mother Nature doesn't, either, and we spent an inordinate amount of time sailing in the prevailing noserlies.

The beginning of a windward passage is boat dependent rather than wind dependent. Some boats are hard on the wind within 50 degrees of the true wind, whereas others don't get there until 42 degrees. If you can sail 1 knot faster and 5 degrees closer to the wind on a 600-mile passage, you can shorten your uncomfortable windward passage period by almost 48 hours—a significant savings, believe me.

Under certain conditions, some boats lack pointing ability, tack in 180 degrees, and cannot go to windward at all. If this situation occurs off a lee shore, it's bye-bye, cruising. Pointing is degraded by heavy seas, high winds, leeway, and adverse currents. The boat you choose should be able to point high into the wind.

COMFORT AT SEA

Only about 10 percent of most cruising trips will be spent passage making. (That percentage was calculated using an average four-year trip around the world through the Suez and Panama Canals. If your trip is longer, it may be less.) In general, the experience of past cruisers has been that 30 percent of their passages were in winds of less than 10 knots, and that you can expect winds of over 35 knots about 5 percent of the time (Roth, *After 50,000*

Miles). Do a little arithmetic and you'll see that less than 1 percent of the time—2 or 3 days a year—will your boat experience storm conditions.

Now, it is true that that 1 percent is the most dangerous, and that your boat should be safe during it, but there is a tendency for the uninitiated to overreact. Insisting on a boat that could safely sail through the eye of a hurricane and not pick up a drop of water, or crash into a reef and bounce over the top of it for two days and still sail away, is overkill. Any well-designed sailboat will probably get you safely through the eye of a hurricane. No sailboat will do it comfortably, and the difference between the comfort levels of any two similar-size boats is unrecognizable by the inner ear of any sailor. In other words, the question again boils down to whether you choose to be uncomfortable for 3 days or 362 days a year.

For that 10 percent of the time you are at sea there are a couple of old rules of thumb on comfort—one true, the other false. The first is that a larger boat is more comfortable. This one is true. For example, being at sea in the *Queen Mary* is considerably more comfortable than being at sea in a dinghy.

The second rule of thumb, that heavy-displacement boats are more comfortable than light-displacement, is false. The old saw sounds logical at first; that is, something heavy moves more slowly because it has greater momentum. As we have seen, however, the motion of a boat in a seaway is a complicated, dynamic problem that depends on many factors, some wave related and some boat related. The most important of the boat-related factors are the shape of the hull and the locations of the centers of buoyancy and gravity—*not* the displacement.

To understand the role of displacement relative to motion let's look at two boats, identical except for displacement, as they are acted on by a simple wave pattern in which both vessels reach equilibrium with the wave. As the wave rises temporarily above the design waterline of each boat, buoyancy is increased. In turn the water applies an upward force to the hulls, raising the boats. Because the heavier boat requires more force to lift it, it will sink deeper into the wave before enough force is generated to cause it to overcome its greater momentum and rise as fast as the water surface in the wave. Eventually both vessels will return to their design waterlines and rise as fast as the wave surface. As the wave reaches its peak and the water starts to fall, the heavy boat still has more momentum and will continue upward farther than the light boat. Eventually it, too, will begin to fall, and again reach equilibrium on the backside of the wave, traveling at its design waterline down with the wave.

When the boats hit the trough, momentum again rears its head, and the heavy-displacement boat sinks deeper into the trough than its lighter companion. The result is that under the influence of a steady wave train the heavier boat will be rising and falling farther than the light boat during the same period. Thus the lighter boat has less motion. Score 1 for light displacement.

As far as the speed of the motion, both boats will stay essentially in step with the period of the wave train, rising and falling according to the wave period. Since that period is fixed, the lighter boat travels through less distance than the heavier boat in the same time, so its vertical velocity is slower and it will have a much easier motion. Score 2 for light displacement.

However, the onset of motion and the acceleration, or the rate of change in motion, will be slower for the heavier boat. Score 1 for the heavy-displacement boat. Finally, when the wave motion ceases, the heavier vessel, because of its greater momentum, will continue its motion longer than the lighter. Score 3 for the lighter vessel.

If we now consider a different system in which equilibrium is not reached, then neither boat will reach its design waterline on passage of the wave. Any differences between the height the boat can rise and the height of the wave will result in the wave rising up on the hull. Once the height of the wave reaches the height of the freeboard, any remaining portion of the wave will pass over the top of the vessel. The heavier boat, being slower to respond, will rise less than the lighter boat. It is thus the more likely to be swept by a wave—which is not only uncomfortable but also unsafe. Score 1 more for light displacement.

Final score: light displacement 4, heavy displacement 1. That score does not sit well with the traditionalists' belief in heavy-displacement comfort. When it comes to choosing between trusting tradition and trusting physics, I prefer physics. Before we leave boat motion, however, let's look briefly at the human mind and body. The human mind is easily swayed by the power of suggestion, and the human body is very insensitive to differences in motion changes of the magnitudes I've been discussing. Who can tell the difference between a velocity of 1 and 1.1 feet per second, let alone an acceleration difference of 0.01 foot per second? It would be interesting to place motion sensors in several boats of different displacement, subject them to the same wave patterns, and compare the curves. It would also be interesting to replay those motion patterns through a motor-controlled chair in a laboratory and find out if any individual could discern the displacement of the vessel from the motion of the chair. What might well be shown is the ability of the mind to generate whatever feelings it wants the body to have.

In the real world, where waves are transitory conditions coming from different directions and with different periods, the motion of any vessel is difficult to analyze. If it's of concern to you, though, concentrate on your boat's shape, and keep heavy equipment low and away from its ends. (And turn to chapter 7 for more information on how each of your boat's parameters affects its stability.)

COST

When you're choosing a boat, almost everything eventually comes down to cost. I discussed budgets in general in chapter 4; here my emphasis will be on the cost of the boat as a part of that budget.

Remember Goldilocks? Boats, too, come in three sizes: too small, too large, and just right. People have successfully circumnavigated the globe in boats ranging in length from 20 to 70 feet. The average boat presently circumnavigating is 35 to 39 feet long—although this average seems to be increasing each year.

Numerous sailors and writers stump for the small cruising boat; however, I have generally found that their evangelism runs only as deep as their pockets. Anyone who can physically handle a larger boat and who also has the money to purchase and maintain it suddenly has a larger boat, regardless of all that nonsense about the friendly little boat. Arthur Beiser, in *The Proper Yacht*, states that "the size of a boat is more important for cruising than any other aspect. . . . Within sensible limits, more is more."

Money is certainly not everything, and cruisers as a whole are not money oriented, but each has an individual threshold of poverty beneath which it is difficult to be content. It is wise to determine that threshold as closely as possible. The key is to find the largest boat that honestly fits your budget, all things considered.

You can cruise in boats under 30 and over 50 feet quite successfully. However, the lack of storage space below in boats under 36 feet will limit the number and size of possessions you can bring without using on-deck storage, which is unsafe, unwise, and unsightly. Once you reach a length over the mid-40s, though, you will probably need extra crew, especially on passage; in addition, your boat will require more maintenance and be more difficult to berth. The most practical range for a cruising boat for most people is thus about 38 to 44 feet.

As a rough rule of thumb the initial cost of a boat goes up as the square of its length: A 50-foot boat costs four times as much as a 25-foot. The initial cost is not a boat's only cost, though. Bigger and more expensive equipment is necessary to outfit the bigger boat. Maintenance costs are higher and repair facilities less common; more bottom paint is required, and insurance, moorage, and harbor fees are all more expensive.

Inexpensive used boats sometimes end up being the most expensive. They are generally in poor condition; many are home built. An inexperienced boat buyer can be drained of considerable cash by the hidden costs involved in putting a neglected boat back into seaworthy condition. And home-built boats are always of questionable quality: Safety, performance, seaworthiness, and comfort can all be adversely affected if a boat is innocently modified by the home builder—even if its original design is a proven one.

The temptation is to spend more money on your boat than you can really afford and plan to make up the shortfall later. Unfortunately, "later" may never arrive. There is a great deal of wisdom in choosing to cruise in style on a 20-foot, used pocket cruiser if your alternative is not to cruise at all.

Your budget for boat costs should include money for outfitting and for modifications or repairs to get the boat ready to go. Outfitting a boat can cost as much as 30 percent of its purchase price. For used boats the cost of outfitting goes down but the cost of repairs goes up; in either case, your overall budget should be about 130 percent of your boat's initial cost.

Maintenance costs will depend on the type of boat you select and how long you intend to cruise. If you are planning to cruise for 5 or 10 years, you had better figure about 5 percent of the boat's initial cost for annual maintenance. If your cruise will be only two years and the boat is in prime shape when you leave, maintenance can be less.

Physical Fitness

The physical condition of you and your crew will affect many of your decisions—from the size and type of boat you buy to the type of cruising you do. If you're fit and strong, for example, you can safely handle larger sails. Large winches can help multiply your strength for controlling the set of the genoa, but the pivotal factor is your ability to strike the sail when the wind gets too high to carry it safely.

For a large genoa this may only be 10 knots of wind, compared to 35 for a small spitfire jib. The strength needed to strike both of these sails is about the same—what you gain by striking the genoa in light winds you lose by the large amount of sail available to flog. In this instance you must rely on your crew's brute strength. Do not deceive yourself during cruising: No matter how many labor-saving devices you have aboard, eventually your survival may depend on the brute strength and endurance of your crew. It is true that self-furling jibs and mains have progressed to the point where they are reliable and can allow you to handle much larger sails than you could manually. If this system fails, however (which it may, and at a most inopportune moment), you will need to be able to manhandle the sail under control.

If you are planning offshore passages to remote locations, it may be more prudent for you to reduce the size of your sails to something comfortable to handle. The best way to determine correct sail size is by direct experience; there are, however, some rough rules of thumb. Those with good strength can reef a 600-square-foot main, and those without should look more toward a 400-square-foot main (Beiser, *Proper Yacht*). The size of the headsails is related to the size of the main. If you are considering using smaller sails because your strength is limited, you should consider a lighter, more easily driven boat before you consider a split rig.

While we're on the subject, remember that strength is a "use-it-or-lose-it" commodity. Labor-saving devices may make life easy, but they also sap your strength. It doesn't take long after the age of 40 to get out of shape.

I am not completely against labor-saving devices, because they can extend your cruising life for many years. I would just advise resisting them for as long as possible. Most 50- or 60-year-old people in reasonable shape can do a surprising amount of work. It may be painful for a while, but hang in there. The extra work will improve your health, increase your enjoyment, and add years to your life. And when the time comes that you need labor-saving devices, remember that although their use increases the time you can continue to cruise, it also increases your risk. Remember, too, that equipment failure is a given; 80 percent of boats on a passage experience some sort of equipment failure. If you cannot perform the task without the aid of a labor-saving device—handle your anchor rode, for example, without your electric windlass—you are taking another risk in an already risky business.

What Path to Glory?

Before you can acquire a boat you must of course have some idea how you intend to get it. There are two commonly accepted ways: buying and building.

BUILDING A BOAT

A common misconception is that the least-expensive way to cruise is to spend 5 to 15 years building your boat, then sail away (Gufstafson, *Best Sailboat*). I've shown in chapter 4 that this is not necessarily true. Further, because this path demands such a single-minded dedication to boatbuilding at the expense of all other tasks, it is often a highway to disaster.

I related two stories of how the time demands of boatbuilding destroyed cruising dreams in chapter 3; one concerned lack of training, the other lack of time.

Still another man I know spent seven years constructing a large boat, which he, too, launched in the Columbia River. Rather than just spare time, though, he had put much of his own working time into the boat, along with considerable money—by his account close to $400,000 from two different inheritances. When he finished he had no money to cruise with and a boat worth about $100,000. He never went cruising.

I recommend building a boat only if you are skilled with your hands and enjoy making things. That is to say, if enjoyment comes for you from the making, then build a boat—and sell it to someone and build another. Just don't go cruising. In most people's lives, there is not enough time to both build a boat and learn the skills needed to cruise.

BUYING A BOAT

If you are thinking about buying a boat you only have two options to worry about: new or used. If you want a new boat, then you only have two options to worry about: production or one-off. If you choose a production boat you only have two options—and so on. In selecting a cruising boat your decisions often just seem to keep forking. Each selection you make has its advantages and its disadvantages. I have tried to summarize the major points in table 6.1.

TABLE 6.1

Boat Choices: Advantages and Disadvantages

Choice	Disadvantages	Advantages
New boat		
One-off	Most expensive; unproven handling characteristics; resale value dependent on the yard and architect; outfitting costs high.	Fits your specific needs the closest; greatest pride of ownership.
Production model	Expensive; you must tailor your needs to the boat's design; outfitting costs high.	Known resale value; known handling characteristics; minimum surprise problems.
Used boat		
One-off	Greatest potential for nasty surprises; lowest resale value; you must tailor your needs to the boat.	Cheapest initial cost; often low outfitting costs.
Production model	You must tailor your needs to the boat.	Known handling characteristics and resale value; often low outfitting costs.

Use this table as a guide to direct your search. If money is a problem you will want to look at the used boat market. If it is *really* a problem, spend your time on the used one-off market, and be prepared to spend a lot of it.

How long it takes you to find a suitable used boat depends on your knowledge of boats and determination to satisfy your desires. Once you know what you're looking for, you'll generally need from one year for a production boat to two or three years for a one-off model.

Function, while important, is not the only consideration in selecting a cruising boat. A large part of cruising is enjoying the beauty of this world. Jan and Bill Moeller in their book *Living Aboard* state that beauty should never be the prime consideration when choosing a boat. I can agree with them only on the word *prime;* beauty has its place, and certainly some things done for beauty's sake are worth doing.

As much as we rally against judging a book by its cover or a person by attractiveness, human beings are, to a large degree, what their external trappings say they are. As a cruiser, the appearance of your boat will be your opening statement to the world about who you are and what you believe. Far too many cruising boats sport decks covered with lashed-on dinghies, bicycles, gas cans, windsurfers, and various other rusting treasures. Is it any wonder these people are treated as bums? There is a difference between *low budget* and *slovenly.*

The boat you cruise in can add to the beauty and enjoyment of your trip. An all-white, completely plastic hull is certainly easy to maintain, but then so is an asphalt "lawn." Just as well-maintained grass and bright flowers add to the beauty of a home and the enjoyment of the neighborhood, so also can the sight of a well-maintained boat trimmed with teak and color bring pleasure to a remote anchorage.

When I bought the *Bird of Time* its beauty was only a small consideration. I wondered about the wisdom of its high-maintenance black hull. However, the hundreds of strangers who have since admired the boat, shouting their approval across open water, slowly changed my mind. The joy *The Bird* has given to others, and in doing so, to me, cannot be measured.

Still, don't let an artist choose your boat. Many of the boats seen in paintings and photographs are neither seaworthy nor practical; they were chosen to convey a desired emotional effect. Be careful not to select a boat that performs poorly or is difficult to handle simply because it looks like a "seagoing vessel" you once saw in a picture you admired somewhere.

7

The Hull

Individual hull components (material; size and shape; and such parameters as beam, draft, and waterline shape) and the hull's appendages (keel, rudder, bowsprit, cockpit) all interact to define how a boat behaves. Knowing how each affects your boat's performance, safety, comfort, and cost will allow you to select a hull suitable for your needs.

Material

A perfect hull material would be weightless, infinitely strong and rigid, and astoundingly beautiful. Unfortunately, for the present we will have to deal with imperfect materials. The most common of these are wood, fiberglass, steel, aluminum, and ferrocement. Each has advantages and disadvantages, proponents and opponents. But before we can appraise the merits of each we need to define some basic terms: *strength, stiffness,* and *toughness.*

STRENGTH

The strength of a material cannot be expressed by a single number. It depends on how the material's strength is measured—for example, in tension, shear, or compression. For some materials, such as steel, these strengths are similar. Cement, in contrast, has a compressive strength an order of magnitude greater than its tensile strength.

To complicate matters further, there are different definitions of *strength* within any single type of measurement method—for example, ultimate strength, yield strength, and design strength. In sorting out this morass of numbers, we must take care to compare apples with apples, and be sure that the apples under consideration have some significance in boat construction.

Not surprisingly, steel has the highest ultimate tensile strength of the common hull materials; this number, however, has little significance in the design of boats. This is because boats must float, and to do so they must be lighter than water. For boatbuilding purposes, the most desirable material is both strong *and* light, so that the boat will float easily. To find the best material for boatbuilding, then, we need to compare each material's strength relative to its weight.

Figure 7.1 shows these ratios (strength divided by weight) for the common hull materials. The higher the number on this chart, the better the material is for hull construction. Some surprises emerge as we look at these data.

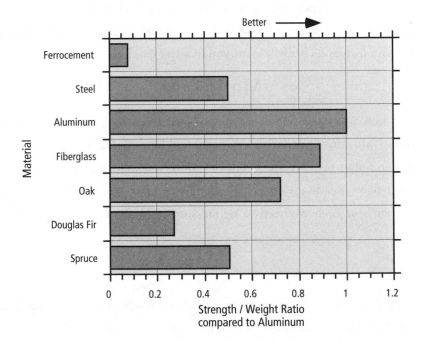

Figure 7.1   *Strength Properties of Common Hull Materials*

Aluminum, fiberglass, and oak all are stronger than steel per pound; those strong steel boats are also very heavy boats. Aluminum is the best material with respect to strength-to-weight ratio; fiberglass is a close second, and spruce and steel are essentially even. (Wooden cruising boats are generally made from a combination of woods. Their actual strength-to-weight ratios are therefore some combination of the individual ratios of the woods used.) Ferrocement is revealed as a very poor material in this comparison.

STIFFNESS

If a hull material is too flexible, the hull will pop in and out like an oil can as it moves through the water. Such a lack of rigidity is not only annoying but inefficient as well. The number of variables involved makes comparing rigidity of different material difficult, however. The comparison shown in figure 7.2 is based on Young's modulus (a ratio of stress to strain), strength, and weight.

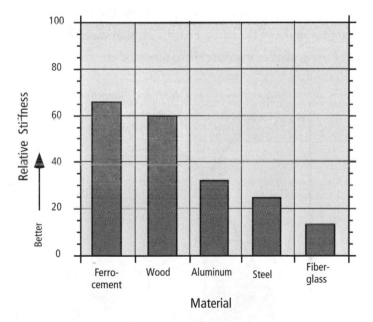

Figure 7.2   *Bending Properties of Common Hull Materials*

Material stiffness is a measure of the typical hull thickness, which varies from ¾ inch for ferrocement to ⅙₆ inch for steel. To keep a solid fiberglass or steel hull from flexing, it is necessary to use considerably more material than required simply for strength—or to add stringers and stiffeners to keep the unsupported span to an acceptable level. These data are for solid materials only. Both fiberglass and wood are commonly constructed using various laminates, which alter their weight and flexibility considerably.

TOUGHNESS AND RESILIENCE

The ability of a material to absorb impact is also of interest in hull design. Two terms describe a material's ability to absorb dynamic energy: modulus of resilience and modulus of toughness. The modulus of resilience is a measure of the material's ability to take an impact without denting or, as the material engineers say, without permanent deformation. This modulus is therefore defined only for elastic materials such as steel, aluminum, and fiberglass. Wood and ferrocement are not considered elastic materials; they do not really dent but chip or gouge when struck a light blow. The modulus of toughness is a measure of a material's ability to absorb energy without rupturing. Both of these moduli are defined as the energy stored under a typical stress-strain curve up to the elastic limit for the former and up to the ultimate strength for the latter. Figure 7.3 is an example of a typical stress-strain curve showing the areas used to calculate these two moduli.

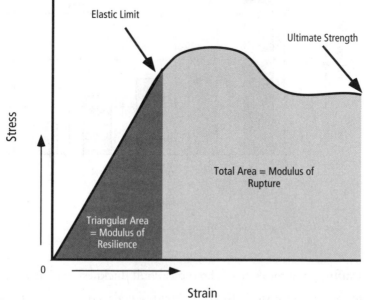

Figure 7.3   Typical Stress-Strain Curve

Since the modulus of resilience is the area of the triangle shown in figure 7.3, it can be found by multiplying the height times the base and dividing by two. The height is the stress at the elastic limit (S_{el}). Using the modulus of elasticity ($E=S/e$), the strain (e) or base of the triangle is the stress at the elastic limit (S_{el}) divided by E. Therefore, the modulus of resilience (u) is the stress at the elastic limit (S_{el}) squared divided by twice the modulus of elasticity (E):

$$u = (S_{el})^2 \div 2E$$ *Equation 7.1*

What this equation says is that all the elastic materials have roughly the same elastic limit, but because steel has such a high modulus compared to fiberglass, steel dents and fiberglass doesn't. Aluminum is slightly better than steel in the nondenting category. So much for cosmetic considerations. How about punching holes in the hull? Well, the modulus of toughness is not as simply a derived property as the modulus of resilience. As you can see from figure 7.3, the total area under the stress-strain curve is a more complicated shape than a triangle. Still, it's clear that the modulus of toughness for steel is the highest; aluminum is second; fiberglass, wood, and concrete follow, in that order.

The only surprise may be that fiberglass withstands impact better than concrete or wood does. This conclusion may seem contrary to the anecdotal evidence of damage sustained by various types of boats that end up on reefs. Here, fiberglass seems to sustain more damage than either wood or concrete. Much of the damage resulting from such a grounding, however, is due to abrasion caused by the waves working the vessel against the reef, and fiberglass is not very abrasion resistant.

Now that you have a general understanding of some of the terms used in discussing material properties, let me discuss each of the materials specifically.

WOOD

Wood has been used for thousands of years to build boats. Each type has a different strength, therefore various woods can be used for assorted functions aboard ship. White oak is used where high strength is needed, such as the stem, keel, and frames. Planking must be stiff, and spruce is a common choice. Using teak for the deck material is well known, while fir can be used for stringers. Ash's resilience makes it a good choice for a rudder. Cedar, holly, and cherry can find their place in the interior of the cabin.

Several years ago wood fell out of use, partly because of the lack of good wood and partly because of the growing popularity of modern materials. However, recent advances in construction methods are producing a resurgence of good wooden hulls. The major improvements to traditional design are laminated frames, strip planking, and lamination of the hull itself. To a large degree these can be attributed to the use of modern glues to fasten wood properly—reducing weight and increasing stiffness and strength. However, the lamination techniques also increase the difficulty and cost of construction.

Some advantages of wood are its beauty and the ease with which it can be worked with simple tools. The cost of a new, one-off wooden boat is comparable to that of a one-off made from other materials, although wood does not lend itself well to mass production. Because of its ease of working, wood is still chosen for some home-built hulls.

The disadvantages of wood include the amount of maintenance it requires; its susceptibility to swelling, shrinking, and dry rot; and the many organisms that enjoy eating it. Also, unless modern hull lamination is used, wooden boats lose interior room because of the hull thickness necessary to get the proper strength.

FIBERGLASS

Fiberglass is a polyester plastic reinforced with glass fibers. The reinforcing material is placed in several layers in the form of mats, fabric, or roving—which require hand placing—or short pieces called chop that are placed with the use of a gun. The introduction of the chop gun allows placement of the reinforcement and the plastic in a single pass. This reduces the cost of fiberglass hulls.

Both matting and chop place the fibers randomly. The matting, however, provides a more consistent distribution of random fibers. Since the fibers are aligned at random in both methods, fiberglass reinforced in this manner has more uniform directional strength properties but is not quite as strong as fiberglass reinforced with fabric or roving.

In the fabric and roving methods, the direction of the fibers corresponds to the direction of greatest strength. In fabric, the fibers are twisted into yarn and then woven into cloth; in roving, they are much coarser and not twisted into yarn before the weaving process. Fabric is the most expensive method of construction but produces a material with decidedly better resistance to impact. Fabric also provides a more uniform thickness and contributes to higher glass densities, which help to reduce blistering. The best boats are made with a combination of the different reinforcement methods, as shown in figure 7.4.

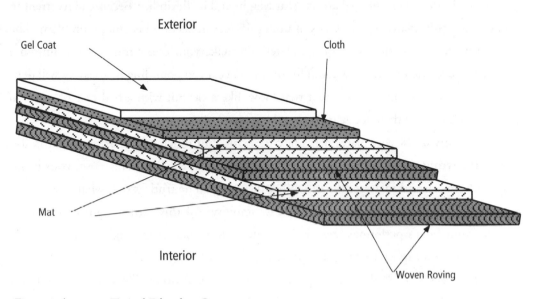

Figure 7.4   Typical Fiberglass Construction

Fiberglass is popular because it's cheap and it's cheap. It can be mass-produced with unskilled labor, it doesn't rot, nothing eats it, and it doesn't rust or corrode. It requires less maintenance than other materials and is therefore less costly in both time and dollars. And while major repairs to the hull are not as easily made to fiberglass as to wood, the material is certainly easier to work than steel or aluminum.

A major disadvantage of fiberglass is that it is difficult to tell from looking at a finished boat how well that boat was built. More so than with other boats (except ferrocement), then, be sure you deal with a reputable builder. The real scourge of plastic boats—gel-coat blistering—appears to be more prevalent in yards that use sloppy techniques and cheaper materials.

STEEL

Steel is very popular as a do-it-yourself hull material. Its big advantage is, of course, its great strength and toughness. Steel is also fireproof. If your scale is tipped toward safety, then steel may be your material. People who want to take on whales, coral atolls, supertankers, and torpedoes and come away dented but pretty much whole prefer steel hulls.

The disadvantages of steel are its great weight and its flexibility. Because of its strength you can use thin plates, but in boats of under 45 feet deflection becomes a problem. The noise from the constant flexing of the plates will make your cruise much like sailing in a drum; and because of steel's low modulus of resilience, even pounding in a seaway will dent those plates. Few people want a boat that looks like a peanut with a bad case of acne, so plates much thicker than necessary are used to prevent flexing.

Not only do heavier plates make heavier boats, but much of this extra weight is also put in the wrong places—up high in the sides and top of the hull. This raises your boat's center of gravity and increases the instability of its hull. The truth is that what you gain in ramming proficiency you more than lose in stability. All this extra weight carried high reduces your boat's performance as well. I believe steel boats are thought of as safer only because it is easier to understand the threat of puncture than that of capsize.

Maintenance of steel is as big a pain as maintenance of wood. What you give up in rot and wood borers will be replaced by corrosion and galvanic action. The only answers are to use paint as a protective coating, and constant vigilance. Rusting is especially troublesome on sharp corners and edges, where paint doesn't adhere well.

ALUMINUM

Aluminum is superior to all other materials in its strength-to-weight ratio, and is more rigid than steel or fiberglass as well. It resists puncture almost as well as steel. Given more money than I could ever spend cruising, I would select a boat built from aluminum, for it offers the best in both performance and strength.

The major disadvantage—and it is considerable, or all boats would be made of this material—is cost. Aluminum is suitable neither for do-it-yourself building nor for mass production; working it requires skill and equipment that few yards possess. Although corrosion is a minor problem, aluminum is very susceptible to galvanic action. You must maintain vigilance to prevent stray currents and dissimilar metals from eating away an aluminum hull—as much vigilance as you'd need to defend against wood worms or rust.

FERROCEMENT

We have moved from the high to the low end of the hull-material scale. The basic advantage of a ferrocement hull is that it can be built in the backyard by amateurs—usually, however, not built very well. Buying a used ferrocement hull can be a disastrous experience (albeit a cheap one). Reselling a ferrocement hull is practically impossible. Ferrocement has the worst strength-to-weight ratio and the least impact resistance. From a structural standpoint, it is the worst of all materials. Finally, although I have seen nice-looking hulls, many ferrocement boats are rather ugly.

SUMMATION

The matrix in table 7.1 may help you make a reasonable decision about hull material. In this matrix, qualities have been ranked from 1 (least desirable) to 5 (most desirable).

This table may generate considerable flak from boat owners and designers. However, in its defense, let me say that two conclusions apparent from it seem to be backed up by experience: First, when all qualities are considered, fiberglass comes out slightly ahead of other materials, primarily because of low construction and maintenance costs. The preponderance of fiberglass boats being constructed in commercial yards today validates this conclusion. Second, the table shows that where cost and ease of repair are no object, aluminum edges out the other materials. This is demonstrated by the large number of racing hulls currently made from aluminum.

TABLE 7.1

Comparison of Common Hull Materials					
Quality	Wood	Fiberglass	Cement	Steel	Aluminum
Cost	2	4	5	3	1
Beauty	5	4	1	2	3
Resale value	3	4	1	2	5
Performance	3	4	1	2	5
Toughness	2	1	3	5	4
Maintenance	1	5	3	2	4
Ease of repair	5	4	2	3	1
Total	21	26	16	19	23

If the rankings on this table don't match yours, make your own. Put down those qualities that are important to you and rate them as honestly as you can. Your own comparison will help you deal with the many variables involved in selecting a satisfactory hull material.

Hull Parameters and Performance

The hull has many parameters that control its behavior. The most important of these are:

length overall (LOA),

waterline length (LWL),

draft (D),

maximum beam at the waterline (B),

freeboard (FB),

area of amidships section (MS),

waterline shape,

displacement (D),

and the locations of the centers of buoyancy and gravity.

Let's examine each of these—first individually, and then in various groupings that will help predict performance.

LENGTH OVERALL

LOA is usually the first feature to be mentioned when people talk about a boat. It's defined as the distance from the tip of the bowsprit to the sternmost appendage, or as the length of a box that could contain the entire boat. The length over deck (LOD) measurement excludes any bowsprit. For practical purposes, these two lengths are roughly equivalent: Both give a general impression of the size of the boat, its rig, and its accommodations. They are also useful for bragging rights. As far as performance is concerned, both terms are fairly superficial, the equivalent of how many people the boat sleeps. When you are paying for anything, however—moorage, haul out, and the like—merchants are likely to use your LOA in figuring your bill.

WATERLINE LENGTH

LWL is the length of your boat at the waterline. The measurement is generally taken with the boat upright. On boats with long overhangs, the waterline length increases somewhat when the boat heels. These long overhangs were developed to get around a racing rule by producing a boat with a long LWL while sailing but a short one when measured for handicap. Waterline length affects the speed of a displacement-type hull, and since most cruising monohulls are displacement hulls, the longer the LWL, the faster the boat, generally speaking.

I say "generally speaking" because the equation for boat speed depends on frictional resistance, wave-making resistance, induced drag, eddy-making resistance, air resistance, and power available to drive the boat. While waterline length has a major effect on all of these resistances, the most important are frictional, wave-making, and air resistance. These three are roughly equal for an average yacht on the wind, but downwind the wind resistance is essentially zero, so frictional and wave-making become the major resistances (Baader, *The Sailing Yacht*).

Frictional resistance, which is the major resistance for sailboats at low speeds, is a function of the wetted surface of the boat. Therefore, the length of the boat and the lateral cross-section of the immersed portion of the hull control the magnitude of this resistance. This is why in very light winds a small boat will sometimes outsail a larger one. (Frictional resistance will be discussed more fully later under "Lateral Section.")

Whereas frictional resistance is essentially constant for a given hull, wave-making resistance starts at zero when the boat is not moving and increases gradually as its speed increases. At higher speeds this resistance makes up more than 90 percent of the total resistance, and forms a barrier for displacement-type hulls similar to the sonic barrier for airplanes.

Wave resistance is generated because, as the boat moves through the water, it pushes (displaces) the water out of its way, creating a bow wave. Once a single wave is created it creates a second, third, and so on, which trail out behind the boat and are called its wake. Since wave height is related to wave speed and length, the second wave peak is created some distance behind the bow. The faster the boat moves, the more water is piled up at the bow, and the higher the wave as well as the greater the distance between the first two waves. (See figure 7.5.)

The distance between these troughs (L_t) in feet can be found by using the fact that wave length (L_t) is equal to the speed of a wave (V_w) multiplied by the period (T):

$$L_t = V_w \times T$$

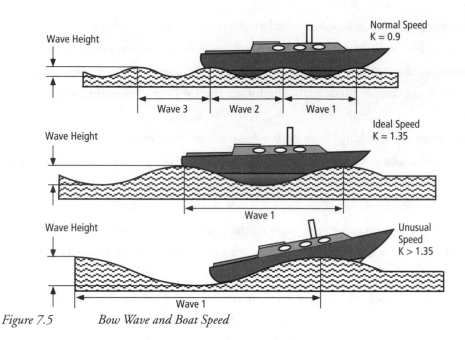

Figure 7.5   *Bow Wave and Boat Speed*

In a deep-water wave, the wave speed is 5 times the period, therefore:

$V_w = 5 \times T$ or

$T = V_w \div 5$ and

$L_t = (V_w)^2 \div 5 = 0.2(V_w)^2$

When wave speed is equal to boat speed (V_b), then $V_w = V_b$, and:

$L_t = 0.2(V_b)^2$

By converting units to velocity in knots while leaving length in feet:

$L_t = 0.56(V_b)^2$ *Equation 7.2*

The number of waves (N) occurring along the boat waterline (LWL) can be expressed as:

$N = LWL \div L_t$ *Equation 7.3*

From figure 7.5 it can be seen that once the wave length equals the waterline length, or N equals 1, the boat is just supported at the bow and stern by the wave crests with a deep trough at the center of the boat. Any increase in speed will increase the wave length and make the stern of the boat drop down into the trough, where it must literally sail up the back of the bow wave. The velocity at which this condition occurs can be calculated from equations 7.3 and 7.4, by letting N = 1:

$$N = LWL \div 0.56(V_b)^2$$
$$(V_b)^2 = LWL \div 0.56N = 1.78LWL \div N$$
$$V_b = (1.78LWL \div 1)^{1/2}$$
$$= 1.34 \, (LWL)^{1/2}$$

Equation 7.4

Behold the legendary 1.34 times the square root of waterline length to figure boat speed: A boat with a waterline length of 36 feet would have a theoretical speed of 6 x 1.34 or 8.04 knots. It is possible for this boat to reach higher speeds for short periods of time if it is surfing down a wave front. If your own boat seems to be going faster than this limit when you're not surfing, you had better recalibrate your speedometer. In truth, these optimum speeds are only *rarely* reached, and then only in ideal conditions with good winds and relatively no wind-generated waves. Next time you're sitting around the cockpit swapping lies about how fast your boat can sail, remember this equation; it may bring a few of those fast skippers back to reality.

However, lest you get too enthralled with theory, a duck has a waterline length of about a foot; according to the above theory, its top speed should be about 1.34 knots. I would estimate that most ducks can swim about twice that fast. The obvious conclusion is that you should put feathers on your hull   or take a closer look at the theory. To do this we will generalize equation 7.4 into:

$$V = k \, (LWL)^{1/2}$$

If this equation is solved for k and plotted against resistance of displacement hulls, a curve similar to the one in figure 7.6 is developed.

Notice that the energy required to move the boat through the water increases more or less linearly until k is equal to 1. At that point the power required increases rapidly until the boat is supported by only two waves (k = 1.34). Now the energy curve turns upward at an ever-increasing rate, and climbing out of this self-imposed trough requires adding large amounts of energy to the system. To go from 1.34 to 1.5 requires roughly a 100 percent increase in power. Few sailboats can generate that much power, so you are stuck behind the

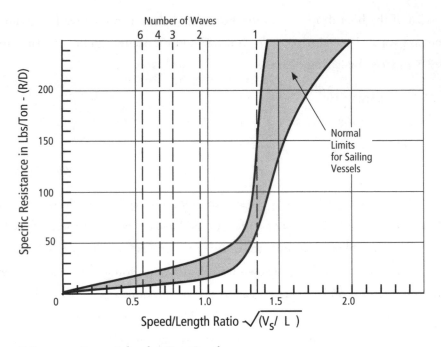

Figure 7.6   *Power Related to Boat Speed*

wave. In fact, transcending this barrier would require thrust approaching 5 percent of displacement (Van Doren, *Oceanography and Seamanship*).

Even though the commonly accepted upper limit for boat speed based on generalizations is 1.34, the actual upper limit of your boat speed may be quite different. For example, this upper limit of k can vary between 1.0, for full keeled, heavy-displacement hulls that are underpowered, and 1.5, for ultralight-displacement fin-keeled boats with maximum power. Its true value depends on hull shape and available power. One measure of a sailboat's power is the ratio of sail area to displacement (I'll discuss this later). If you have sufficient power you may leave the second wave peak and move up the forward wave slightly.

If more energy is added, the boat moves progressively up the bow wave until its center of gravity passes the peak of the forward wave. At this point the boat tips and begins to sail down the wave front. With gravity now assisting the boat, its speed can be maintained with reduced power. This is called planing.

For cruisers, planing is most often experienced in a dinghy. Tucked away in this discussion are the reasons why moving the weight forward in a dinghy helps in getting it to plane, and why a sudden throttle reduction can cause the onrushing stern wave to swamp a dinghy. I will leave the proof of that statement as an exercise for the reader.

DRAFT

The draft of a boat is the minimum depth of water in which a boat will float. It affects the boat's stability and its ability to go upwind and into shallow water.

The science of hydrodynamics is very similar to that of aerodynamics. A sailboat essentially flies through the water upwind, just as an airplane flies against gravity. Both do it by developing lift with a wing; the sailboat's wing is its keel. A deep keel, like a long wing, helps the boat fly upwind. However, it is not just the depth of the keel that is important, but the ratio of that depth to the length of the keel (called aspect ratio) as well. (This will be discussed more fully later under "Keels.")

Since ballast is often placed in the lowest part of the boat, a deep draft allows the ballast to be placed lower, which increases stability by lowering the center of gravity, and also improves upwind performance. As you can see in figure 7.7, when the boat heels, its center of buoyancy remains in the same place; lowering the center of gravity has the effect of increasing the righting arm and thus the righting moment as well. A 6-inch change in the

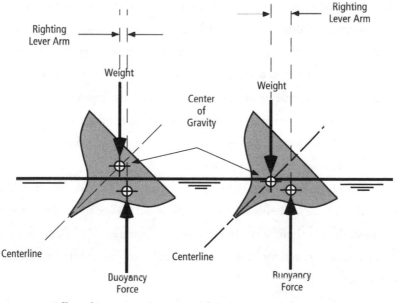

Figure 7.7   *Effect of Lowering the Center of Gravity*

position of the center of gravity can change the boat's stability by about 20 percent, and its ability to stand to its sails by 12 percent.

There is some evidence that indicates a deep draft also improves downwind performance. A study carried out by the Stevens Institute showed that the deep keel increased a boat's speed by increasing its stability and allowing it to stand up to its sails (Marchaj, *Sailing Theory and Practice*). This increase in speed was most noticeable in wind velocities from 13 to 20 knots. Unfortunately, in light breezes the additional stability was offset by the added wetted surface from the longer keel.

Recall that 50 percent of the winds encountered while cruising are of 12 knots or less; thus 50 percent of the time a deep draft will hinder downwind performance. This has led to the development of boats with adjustable drafts—now you have it, now you don't. (These modifications will be discussed later under "Keels.")

The major problem with a deep draft is that it is almost always the bottom of the boat that goes aground first. This reduces your ability to explore shallow water, areas such as the Florida Keys or Bahamas. Most often this exploration is done under auxiliary power, when the draft is maximum and provides no assistance in sailing.

BEAM

The beam—generally defined as the greatest width of the boat—affects its stability, livability, and performance (although it is not by itself a good indication of performance). On occasion there is an appreciable difference between a boat's maximum width and its waterline beam; if this is your case, use the waterline beam for estimating performance.

Stability gained from a wide beam is called form stability. Figure 7.8 shows two hulls with different beams. The difference in stability comes from the difference in righting lever arms. A wide hull tends to move the buoyant force farther to the side of the boat when it heels, thus rapidly increasing the righting lever arm.

Because of this rapid increase in righting lever arm, wide boats are initially stiff and can stand up to their sails well. Their ability to handle wind power allows them to sail faster; their stiffness allows them a slightly larger value of k in equation 7.6. Boats with a narrow beam, on the other hand, are tender, easy to heel initially, and must rely on weight stability for power to carry sails.

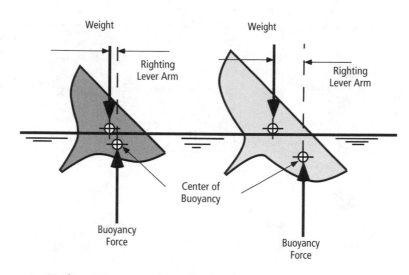

Figure 7.8   *Righting Moment Compared to Beam*

At lower speeds a large beam can also add to a boat's wetted surface, thereby increasing its frictional resistance and making it sluggish in light air. If a heavy-displacement boat has a significant wetted surface, it is essential that the beam be reduced to improve light-air performance.

Claughton and Handley reported in the *Southampton University Report* that as a beam increases, a boat's tendency to capsize also increases in large breaking seas. However, it should be noted that the major evidence for their conclusion was the number of wide-beam racing hulls that have capsized in the last few years. As we have already seen, however, boat stability can be attained in two ways—form stability or weight stability. In racing, weight slows a boat down, so many designers opt for beam in its stead. Thus it is entirely possible that these boats' reported instability could be due as much to their lack of ballast as to their extra-wide beams. Claughton and Handley also failed to indicate what constitutes "extremely wide." The beams of most cruising boats are not nearly as wide as those of boats built exclusively for racing. (Typical beams for the cruising sailboats listed in appendix C are shown in figure 7.9.) To ensure that your beam is not extreme, pick one within a foot or so of the best fit line. The equation for the best fit line is:

Beam = 18.4Log(LWL) - 15.5   *Equation 7.5*

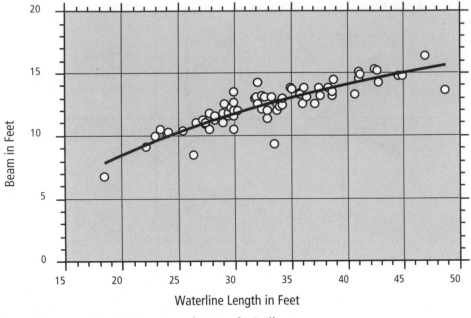

Figure 7.9   *Typical Beam-Length Ratios for Sailboats*

Beam is also an important factor in determining the load on an anchor system. Since a boat generally lies head to the wind, the wider its beam—all else being equal—the greater its wind resistance, and the higher load on its anchor. (This is discussed more fully in my own book *Modern Seamanship*.)

A wider beam can make your boat considerably more livable by increasing the space for accommodations, comfort, and storage below. A wide boat has more load-carrying capacity than a narrow boat of the same waterline length, because it displaces more water per inch of settlement. The wide boat also allows more weight of stores per inch of lost freeboard, and therefore sails closer to its design waterline when cruising loaded. The immersion of a hull can be calculated by using this common rule of thumb:

L = 15 x B x LWL ÷ 4   where: *Equation 7.6*

    L is the weight in pounds sufficient to cause 1 inch of immersion,

    B is the beam at the waterline in feet, and

    LWL is the waterline length in feet.

Finally, beam is a consideration if the boat is to be trucked or shipped any distance. Beams of more than 12 feet become increasingly difficult and expensive to haul, and may require special handling and escorts.

FREEBOARD

FB is the distance between the outboard edge of the deck, or gunwale, and the water level. A high freeboard can lower the water resistance of your boat when it is heeling by keeping the lee rail clear of the water; it can keep your boat drier and give you more headroom below deck.

Freeboard also affects form stability by adding weight and displacing additional water. Figure 7.10 shows two hulls that have the same cross-section; the second hull, however, has more freeboard.

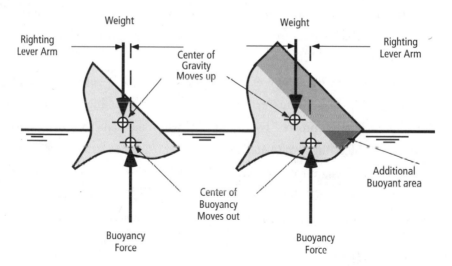

Figure 7.10   *Freeboard and Increase of Righting Moment*

The additional weight, atop the boat, moves the center of gravity upward along the centerline of the cross-section. As I mentioned earlier, such upward movement of the center of gravity decreases the righting arm. The amount of decrease depends on the weight of the hull material. This is a good example of why a hull material should be selected with reference to its weight-to-strength ratio.

The additional prism of water displaced by the extra freeboard is shown in figure 7.10 as a small dark triangle. This extra prism adds buoyancy and moves the center of buoyancy outward, increasing the righting arm. Whether the increased freeboard has improved or damaged stability depends on the net change in righting arm.

If the freeboard is initially very low, stability will increase with added FB, but only so far; then additions will reduce stability again. From a stability standpoint, then, moderation of freeboard is a good rule. Avoid boats with either an extremely high or an extremely low FB.

The disadvantages of more freeboard are increases in both windage and the difficulty of getting a lost crew member back aboard. The large surface presented to the wind can generate significant force. For example, 1 foot of extra freeboard on a 40-foot boat will generate the same amount of force in a 45-knot wind that the average mainsail will generate in a 15-knot wind. This can be significant under storm conditions at sea, because the hull cannot be reefed.

Coming into port with a high-freeboard boat under even moderate winds can be a nightmare. In tight quarters and at slow speeds, the boat is at the mercy of the wind. Also, because at anchor the large loads from the high freeboard are transferred to the anchor system, you'll need stronger and heavier tackle.

A great fear of many ocean cruisers is a person overboard. If you are lucky enough to find the person again, you still must retrieve him or her, and the higher your gunwale the more difficult your retrieval process. For example, a man 6 feet tall can usually reach a gunwale approximately 3 feet out of the water, maybe 3½ feet if he has a strong kick. At that point he still must have the strength to hoist himself aboard—no easy chore, even using any of the devices specially developed to aid in just such a retrieval. A permanently attached swim ladder is a great asset in such a retrieval, and is a must for any boat with high freeboard.

WATERLINE SHAPE

The outlines of the shape of the boat in the horizontal plane are called waterlines. The particular waterline of interest here is that taken exactly at the waterline: Its shape affects the shape of the wave generated when the boat is forced through the water, and to some extent affects how the boat behaves in a seaway as well. There are three basic shapes, as shown in figure 7.11.

Typical of designs from the 1800s is the cod's head–mackerel tail shape typified by Colin Archer boats. People noted the actual shape of those fish, and reasoned that since God designed them to go through the water, their shape must be optimum. There are several

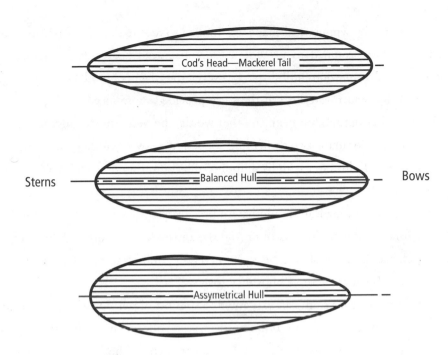

Cod's Head—Mackerel Tail

Balanced Hull

Bows

Assymetrical Hull

Figure 7.11   *Typical Waterline Shapes*

things wrong with that conclusion, of course, not the least of which is that fish swim completely submerged.

Boats with the cod's head–mackerel tail shape, such as the Westsail 32, have unnecessarily full bows, which add resistance when the boats are going to windward or when any kind of sea is running. The full bow rises quickly to an oncoming wave and the fine stern lacks adequate buoyancy to dampen the effect of that rising bow pushing the stern down. The result is excessive pitching in a seaway and a slow boat. This shape also produces excessive weather helm; the more the boat heels, the greater its weather helm. To keep the boat going forward under these conditions, the rudder must create large amounts of drag, which further slows the boat. Ted Brewer has pointed out that this shape of boat would sail backward better than it does forward.*

---

*Brewer, *Sailboat Design*, 37. Numerous dedicated owners of this type of boat disagree with me and believe that it is the ultimate in cruising design. If these owners are happy, good, but I have noticed in talking to many of them that this kind of boat is the *only*, or the *first*, that they have owned. Of course it is only fair to add that the fault does not lie with Colin Archer, whose much-copied design was originally intended as an oceangoing sailing tugboat, not a bluewater cruiser. It fulfilled its original function quite well.

In the 1930s the symmetrical shape was refined to reduce the weather-helm problem. Balanced ends were assumed to provide a more balanced boat. This certainly was an improvement over the previous hull shape. However, the advent of model testing in the mid-1960s showed that wider waterlines at the stern provided more speed on all points of sail, along with less pitching and less heel. In other words, the modern asymmetrical hull form is in every way superior to the two earlier hull shapes. Moreover, another look at figure 7.11 will show you that Ted Brewer is right: Flipping the cod's head hull 180 degrees produces the modern hull.

This modern cruising hull should have a fine entry with a bow half angle of 20 to 24 degrees, the forward waterlines straight or slightly convex, and smooth, full lines aft. As the lines approach the deck they should be given increasing fullness to provide increased working space, a drier boat, and reserve buoyancy forward.

The half angle at the stern can vary much more. A full stern provides both buoyancy aft and lift for planing off the wind. If the stern gets too wide it can create turbulence; it also adds wetted surface when hard on the wind at larger angles of heel. As I discussed earlier, stability problems have been blamed on excessive width in the stern.

LATERAL SECTION

The shapes of the boat in the two planes perpendicular to the water are called the lateral section if cut longitudinally, and the midsection if cut athwartships. The shapes of these sections affect the performance of the boat, particularly in light winds. As I explained earlier, waterline length controls the performance of the boat at higher speeds, where the major resistance is due to wave generation. Under light-wind conditions, however, the major resistance is the friction of the water along the boat's submerged surface. This frictional resistance is due to a change in the velocity of the water across a thin layer of it attached to the boat. That is, the water directly next to the skin of the boat is traveling at the same speed as the boat; but the water a small distance away has a velocity of essentially zero. And since water is not a solid, there is a transition layer between these two points in which the water changes its velocity. This transition layer of water is essentially attached to the boat. The faster the boat goes, the larger this transition layer becomes, and the more water the boat must drag—therefore, the more resistance. This increased resistance reduces the performance of the boat, especially in light conditions, where friction can provide as much as 90 percent of all resistance.

To improve performance, then, the volume of water being dragged must be reduced. The easiest way to do this is to reduce the amount of wetted surface to which the water layer can be attached. If you examine figure 7.12, you'll see that the modern cruising hull has much less wetted area than the traditional design.

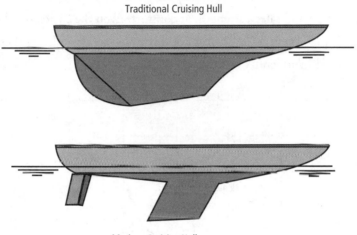

Traditional Cruising Hull

Modern Cruising Hull

Figure 7.12   Typical Lateral Sections

At one time it was thought that the massive keel of the traditional cruising hull was necessary to prevent leeway and provide good steering qualities. It has subsequently been proven, as noted in Marchaj's *Aero-Hydrodynamics of Sailing*, that the lateral area of the fin need be only about 4 percent of the sail area to provide adequate handling in all conditions. (Other features of the keel will be discussed later under "Keels.")

DISPLACEMENT

The term *displacement* is something of a misnomer—and just the first of many misunderstandings about the subject. The term refers to the amount of water a boat will displace according to Archimedes' principle. If it were truly displacement—a volume function— it would be measured in cubic feet. However, in this case, displacement would change depending on whether the boat was in fresh water or salt water. (Since fresh water is less dense than salt, a boat does not float as high in it, and thereby displaces more water.) It was decided, somewhat illogically, to measure displacement in pounds rather than use the more accurate term, *weight.* Displacement, then, refers not to the boat's actual displacement but to its weight.

The rest of the misunderstandings about displacement involve the notion that it alone says something about a boat's basic characteristics. There is, however, no direct correlation between displacement and safety, strength, or comfort. Even the correlation between water-line length and displacement is indistinct at best. Figure 7.13 is a plot of these values taken from the boats listed in appendix D.

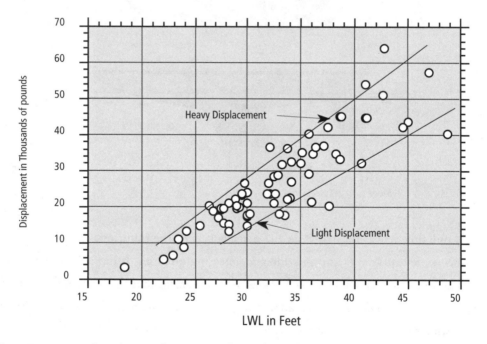

Figure 7.13   Common Displacements and Waterline Lengths

One thing we can say about displacement is that if cross-sectional areas on two boats are the same, then the greater the volume of displacement, the larger the wetted surface will be. The heavier boat will thus require more energy to drive it through the water. In other words, both sails and engines need to be larger on the heavier boat. All other things being equal, then, increasing displacement decreases performance.

The often-cited advantage of heavy-displacement hulls—that more gear and provisions can be stowed aboard without bringing the boat much below its design waterline—has already been shown (see "Comfort at Sea," chapter 6) to be false (Moeller, *Living Aboard*).

Whereas it is true that a light- and a heavy-displacement boat with the same waterline cross-sectional area will both sink the same amount under 3 tons of cruising gear, rarely do they have the same waterline cross-sections. Adding 6,000 pounds to a 24,000-pound boat does produce a greater percentage increase in displacement than adding the same amount to a 48,000-pound boat. But although the larger percentage increase in weight may have a more noticeable effect on the lighter boat's sailing ability, the heavier boat's sailing performance was originally lower. Therefore it is extremely likely that the heavily loaded light-displacement boat will still outsail the heavy boat.

Remember that sailing ability depends on the amount of wetted surface, the sail area, and many other parameters. To compare the actual performance of a well-designed light-displacement, wide-bodied, modified-fin-keeled boat with a well-designed heavy-displacement, narrow-full-keeled boat, we need to look at combinations of all the basic parameters (called performance ratios), not just displacement.

Performance Ratios

Several ratios can be formed from the basic hull parameters and used to compare sailboat performances. Most of these ratios were developed to handicap racing boats. The advent of such handicapping rules gave us two things: a better understanding of how boats perform, and rule-beater designs.

A classic example of the latter is the long overhang found on many boats designed in the 1930s. This long overhang was not included in the measurement of waterline length, but when the boat heeled its LWL was instantly increased by the amount of overhang—increasing its speed without increasing its handicap penalty. And, since sailboats heel when they sail to windward, these boats proved considerably faster upwind than their nonoverhang competitors.

The overhang did little for the interior room and other seagoing qualities of a boat; its only function was to beat the rule. So the rule was changed, and long overhangs have all but disappeared from modern hulls. Presently, however, beam is not penalized severely, and the rule beaters have gone to ultrawide boats. I suppose that this rule will be changed soon and beams will return to normal—opening the way for a new parameter to be exploited.

In the meantime we sensible, modest, right-thinking cruisers can profit from the mistakes of our impulsive, witless racing siblings. They have supplied us with many usable ratios by which to judge the performance of our vessels. The most helpful of these are displacement:waterline length; sail area:displacement; ballast:displacement; and the prismatic coefficient.

DISPLACEMENT:WATERLINE LENGTH

This was probably the first of the ratios to be recognized—and was also probably the most responsible for the long overhangs I mentioned above. It is sometimes referred to as just the displacement:length ratio. This often-used ratio is equal to the displacement (D) of the boat in tons divided by the cube of the waterline length (LWL) in *hundreds* of feet:

$$\text{displacement:waterline length} = D \div (LWL)^3 \qquad\qquad \textit{Equation 7.7}$$

It is a little confusing because of the strange dimensional units. Worse, some people use long tons while others use the U.S. 2,000-pound ton. To compare two displacement ratios, both should of course be calculated with the same set of units. Presently, most people use the 2,000-pound ton. For example, given a LWL of 39 and D equal to 24,000 pounds, then the ratio is:

$$12 \div (0.39)^3 = 202 \text{ tons/ft}^3$$

This ratio is important because it relates the weight of the boat to the speed-controlling waterline length. It assumes that if two boats have the same waterline length, the lighter boat will be faster.

TABLE 7.2

Comparison of Displacement:Waterline Length Ratios

Boat	LOA	LWL	Disp	D:LWL
Cuchulainn	55.9	48.8	40,170	154
Bird of Time	43.1	37.6	20,200	190
Ron Glas	47.0	36.0	21,440	205
Castle 48	48.7	40.7	31,900	211

(continued)

Boat	LOA	LWL	Disp	D:LWL
Bowman 57	57.4	44.6	42,000	211
Manatee	51.8	45.0	43,400	213
Gazelle	42.2	33.0	18,000	224
Sunshine	40.9	33.8	22,000	255
Muav	37.6	28.3	13,050	256
Valiant 40	39.9	34.0	22,500	256
Gudrun	52.5	38.6	33,000	256
Campanella	50.5	38.3	34,500	274
Bristol 29.9	29.9	24.0	8,650	279
Morin 45	45.2	35.8	29,000	282
Ericson 36	36.0	30.0	17,200	284
Swan 41	41.0	30.2	17,860	288
Brise 40	40.0	30.0	17,600	291
Pearson 365	36.4	30.0	17,700	293
Endurance 57	56.2	42.7	51,070	293
Whitby 42	42.0	32.7	23,500	300
Alden 44	44.2	34.2	23,500	300
Zeewind	41.1	32.1	23,370	315
Departure	35.0	27.8	15,300	317
Bowman 46	45.7	31.9	23,500	323
Vai Maris	51.0	37.1	37,000	323
NYYC 48	47.8	36.2	34,600	326
Souwester 50	50.7	36.4	36,600	338
Palisander	50.5	38.8	45,000	344
Wellington 47	46.9	38.7	45,000	344
Landfall 42	41.7	30.0	21,000	347
Isle	49.8	37.5	45,000	347
Downeaster 38	38.0	29.0	19,500	357
Rev d'Antilles	38.5	29.2	19,840	357
Victoria	45.1	32.9	28,500	357
Durbeck 46	46.8	35.1	35,000	361
Mischief 3	42.6	32.0	26,600	362
Moonbeam	46.5	34.2	32,400	362
Minots Light	58.1	42.8	64,000	364

(continued)

Boat	LOA	LWL	Disp	D:LWL
Jason	34.5	27.3	16,800	367
Bellatrix	44.2	32.5	28,450	370
Santa Maria	45.5	29.0	20,200	370
Benford 30	30.0	23.5	10,975	378
Westsail 42	42.9	33.3	31,500	380
Mercedes	35.0	30.0	23,700	392
Seawind II	31.6	25.5	14,600	393
Bermuda 40	40.8	27.8	19,500	404
Orca	37.2	29.5	23,520	409
Ann Caroline 3	38.0	29.5	23,520	409
Nicholson 39	39.0	28.3	20,854	409
Nicholson 31	30.6	24.2	13,000	411
Treasure	46.3	33.8	36,000	418
Westsail 32	32.0	27.5	19,500	419
Endurance 35	35.3	26.7	18,550	437
Erna	40.2	29.8	26,500	446

Although not ideal, displacement:waterline length is a fair indicator of performance. Its values generally range from 450 to 150; the lower values indicate the potentially faster boat, especially in light air.

The boats in this table range in size from 30 to almost 60 feet. As you saw under "Waterline Length," the speed of a boat depends on its LWL: Boats with short waterlines are slower than those with long ones. And under "Displacement" you learned that heavy boats require considerable effort to move. The combination of short waterline and heavy weight most often results in a very slow boat, as well as a very high displacement:waterline length ratio. Boats with these large ratios also produce deep wave systems; the rolling quarter wave of the heavy yacht is well known (Phillips-Britt, *Sailing Yacht Design*).

Someone who speaks of "heavy" or "light" displacement is often referring to this displacement:waterline length ratio. Those boats with a ratio of less than 250 would be considered light displacement; those above 350, heavy. Performance, however, does not depend solely on this ratio.

SAIL AREA:DISPLACEMENT

The sail area:displacement ratio is also useful in estimating all-around performance. It is calculated by dividing the sail area by the displacement of the boat in cubic feet to the ⅔ power. This is a more modern ratio; it is dimensionless, and displacement is expressed in cubic feet as it should be. Ratios without dimensions are easier to use and often more meaningful.

sail area:displacement ratio $(S_a:D) = S_a \div (D)^{\frac{2}{3}}$ *Equation 7.8*

For example, given a boat with a sail area of 960 square feet and a displacement of 32,770 pounds, the sail area:displacement ratio would be calculated as follows:

Displacement = 30,000 lbs ÷ 64 lbs/ft³ = 469 ft³
where 64 lbs/ft³ is the unit weight of seawater.

Note that if the boat is in fresh water the displacement goes up, because the unit weight of fresh water is 62.4 lbs/ft³ and the S_a:D ratio goes down. This would indicate that boats sail more slowly in fresh water—not too bad a conclusion, since they also have more wetted surface in fresh water.

S_a:D = 960 ft² ÷ (469 ft³)^⅔ = 960 ft² ÷ 60.4 ft² = 15.9

This ratio is a good indicator of performance, because it relates the power available to drive the load to the load being driven. However, it does not consider such important factors as rig type and keel configuration. Ketches, schooners, and yawls need higher ratios, because these rigs are less efficient and need more sail to drive them than single-mast rigs. Boats with full keels will need a higher ratio than those with a fin keel to get equal performance. A value of 15.9—adequate for a fin-keeled, high-aspect-ratio sloop—would likely be very low for a full-keeled ketch.

Further, these criteria were derived for bare boats and as such are valid only for comparison of design performance. Simply adding the weight of equipment and stores and then recalculating any of the performance criteria, however, is invalid and will lead to invalid conclusions. Unfortunately, this mistake is commonly made in cruising literature, like in Gufstafson's *Best Sailboat*. For example: "As a result, heavily loading a boat with a low displacement-length ratio will quickly lower the sail area–displacement ratio." This statement may be technically true, but it leads to a whole lot of wrong conclusions. It implies that a heavily loaded boat with a high displacement:length ratio will not be similarly affected. And while it might make sense intuitively that a light-displacement boat would be more adversely affected by loading than a heavy-displacement, intuition can sometimes lead to bad science. In truth, the heavy-displacement boat can be more seriously affected.

For instance, compare a Bedford 30, with a D:LWL ratio of 378, to the Mull-designed sloop *Sunshine,* with a D:LWL ratio of 255. A few quick calculations reveal a S_a:D of 16.2 for the Bedford and 15.6 for the *Sunshine.* Adding 10,000 pounds to each boat changes the S_a:D of the former to 10.5 and the latter to only 12.1. The heavy boat now has a lower S_a:D than the light boat and has changed 54 percent, while the light boat changed only 28 percent.

Ted Brewer, in *Sailboat Design,* makes the same mistake:

> *If we take two 33 foot WL yachts, one with a d/l ratio of 270, the other with 150, and add a modest 3,500 pounds of cruising gear to each, the d/l ratios increase to 313.5 and 193.5 respectively, a jump of 16 percent for the heavier yacht and 29 percent for the lightweight. Assuming both start life with a sail area/displacement ratio of 16.5, the ratio on the loaded boats will drop to 14.9 on the heavier yacht and 13.9 on the lightweight. It is obvious which will suffer the greatest performance loss.*

What is not so obvious is that the lighter boat has been set up to fail: Starting out with a sail area:displacement ratio of only 16.5 would provide only 543 square feet of sail for the light boat, compared to the heavier boat's 803 square feet. It is artificial to consider that a boat of this size would have so little sail area. If we give both boats the same sail area, then the light boat, even after being weighted down, has a S_a:D ratio of 20.6, which is considerably better than the heavier boat's 14.9. Is it still obvious which boat will suffer the greatest loss of performance?

Calculations of this type are essentially playing with numbers; it should be emphasized that they have nothing to do with either boat's performance under load, because the ratios were not determined for cruise-loaded boats. Table 7.3 lists the sail area:displacement ratios for the same yachts that appeared in table 7.2. The values for this ratio can range from 12 to 20; the lower the number, the poorer the performance.

TABLE 7.3

Comparison of Sail Area:Displacement Ratios

Boat	LOA	Sail Area	Disp	S_a:b
Gazelle	42.2	854	18,000	19.9
Campanella	50.5	1,261	34,500	19.0
Brise 40	40.0	775	17,600	18.3
Cuchulainn	55.9	1,324	40,170	18.1
Gudrun	52.5	1,131	33,000	17.6
Bowman 57	57.4	1,314	42,000	17.4
Swan 41	41.0	740	17,860	17.3
Muav	37.6	593	13,050	17.1
Whitby 42	42.0	875	23,500	17.1
Mischief 3	42.6	949	26,600	17.0
Bird of Time	43.1	895	24,700	16.9
Santa Maria	45.5	782	20,200	16.9
Valiant 40	39.9	840	22,500	16.9
Ron Glas	47.0	810	21,440	16.8
Ann Caroline 3	38.0	855	23,520	16.7
Moonbeam	46.5	1,056	32,400	16.6
Bermuda 40	40.7	741	19,500	16.4
Manatee	51.8	1,261	43,400	16.3
NYYC 48	47.8	1,077	34,600	16.2
Benford 30	30.0	500	10,975	16.2
Treasure	46.2	1,087	36,000	15.7
Durbeck 46	46.8	1,051	35,000	15.7
Castle 48	48.7	981	31,900	15.6
Endurance 35	35.3	683	18,550	15.6
Sunshine	40.9	765	22,000	15.6
Departure	35.0	600	15,300	15.6
Palisander	50.5	1,230	45,000	15.6
Westsail 42	42.9	968	31,500	15.5
Endurance 57	56.2	1,334	51,070	15.5
Rev d'Antilles	38.5	710	19,840	15.5
Vai Maris	51.0	1,074	37,000	15.5
Jason	34.5	634	16,800	15.5

(continued)

Boat	LOA	Sail Area	Disp	S$_a$:b
Souwester 50	50.7	1,060	36,600	15.4
Zeewind	41.1	785	23,370	15.4
Bellatrix	44.2	887	28,450	15.2
Bowman 46	45.7	779	23,500	15.2
Minots Light	58.1	1,518	64,000	15.2
Isle	49.8	1,123	41,850	14.9
Landfall 42	41.7	708	21,000	14.9
Seawind II	31.6	555	14,600	14.9
Bristol 29.9	29.9	391	8,650	14.8
Downeaster 38	38.0	665	19,500	14.7
Alden 44	44.2	825	27,000	14.7
Westsail 32	32.0	663	19,500	14.6
Victoria	45.1	847	28,500	14.5
Nicholson 39	39.0	687	20,854	14.5
Wellington 47	46.9	1,146	45,000	14.5
Pearson 365	36.4	615	17,700	14.5
Morin 45	45.2	854	29,000	14.5
Orca	37.2	705	23,150	13.9
Nicholson 31	30.6	475	13,000	13.7
Erna	40.2	754	26,500	13.6
Ericson 36	36.0	558	17,200	13.4
Mercedes	35.0	640	23,700	12.4

BALLAST:DISPLACEMENT

This ratio can help you judge the stability of a boat's hull, and how well that boat will stand up to its sails. Again, both form and weight affect stability; I discussed form stability under "Beam" and "Freeboard," weight stability under "Draft." Since ballast is always placed well below the center of gravity of the boat, it is a more effective way to add stability than placing weight elsewhere. The ballast:displacement ratio indicates how much of the weight of a boat is placed for maximum stability against capsizing.

Unlike form stability, weight stability increases as the boat heels (up to 90 degrees), thus giving the boat more stability at high angles of heel. The higher the ratio and the deeper the draft, the more stable the boat and the less likely it is to turn turtle. This ratio is calculated by dividing the weight of the ballast by the displacement. As such, it is simply the percentage of the total displacement that is ballast:

ballast:displacement ratio = B ÷ D   *Equation 7.10*

For example, if a 20,000-pound boat has 10,000 pounds of ballast, then:

ballast:displacement ratio = 10,000 ÷ 20,000 = 0.5

Although a high ballast ratio makes a more stable boat, one that is very high is said to make a boat extremely stiff, resulting in a supposedly uncomfortable "quick motion." As you saw in chapter 6, though, how quick is "quick" and how uncomfortable that is is measured by the seat of the pants, a singularly not-too-accurate sensor.

Table 7.4 compares the ballast ratios for most of the yachts in tables 7.3 and 7.2. (Some did not have ballast figures, so their B:D ratio could not be calculated; these were deleted from the table.) The ratios vary from about 0.2 to 0.55. The lower this value, the greater the tendency toward instability, the more tender the boat, and the less sail it can carry. It is interesting that many of the same designs make a poor showing on all three tables.

TABLE 7.4

Comparison of Ballast:Displacement Ratios

Boat	LOA	Ballast	Disp	B:D
Mercedes	35.0	5,500	23,700	0.23
Endurance 35	35.3	4,410	18,550	0.24
Wellington 47	46.9	11,000	45,000	0.24
Palisander	50.5	12,800	45,000	0.28
Souwester 50	50.7	10,500	36,600	0.29
Benford 30	30.0	3,300	10,975	0.30
Rev d'Antilles	38.5	5,950	19,840	0.30
Minots Light	58.1	19,050	64,000	0.30
Bermuda 40	40.8	6,000	19,500	0.31
Landfall 42	41.7	6,780	21,000	0.32
Ann Caroline 3	38.0	7,840	23,520	0.33
Brise 40	40.0	5,730	17,600	0.33
Ericson 36	36.0	5,800	17,200	0.34

(continued)

Boat	LOA	Sail Area	Disp	$S_a{:}b$
Orca	37.3	7,940	23,150	0.34
Whitby 42	42.0	8,000	23,500	0.34
Durbeck 46	46.8	12,000	35,000	0.34
Valiant 40	39.9	7,800	22,500	0.34
Westsail 42	42.9	11,000	31,500	0.35
Alden 44	44.2	11,000	31,500	0.35
Bowman 46	45.7	8,250	23,500	0.35
Moonbeam	46.5	11,400	32,400	0.35
Westsail 32	32.0	7,000	19,500	0.36
Nicholson 31	30.6	4,800	13,000	0.37
Jason	34.5	6,200	16,800	0.37
Victoria	45.1	10,650	28,500	0.37
Manatee	51.8	16,000	43,400	0.37
Mischief 3	42.6	10,000	26,600	0.37
Cuchulainn	55.9	15,430	40,170	0.38
Departure	35.0	6,000	15,300	0.39
Sunshine	41.0	8,570	22,000	0.39
Vai Maris	51.0	14,600	37,000	0.39
Seawind II	31.6	5,800	14,600	0.40
Zeewind	41.1	9,260	23,370	0.40
Pearson 365	36.4	7,300	17,700	0.41
Downeaster 38	38.0	8,000	19,500	0.41
Castle 48	48.7	13,200	31,900	0.41
Campanella	50.5	14,200	34,500	0.41
Bowman 57	57.4	17,170	42,000	0.41
Bristol 29.9	29.9	3,600	8,650	0.42
Gazelle	42.2	7,500	18,000	0.42
Santa Maria	45.5	8,400	20,200	0.42
Isle	49.8	18,000	41,850	0.43
Bellatrix	44.3	12,700	28,450	0.45
Endurance 57	56.2	23,520	51,070	0.46
Bird of Time	43.1	9,267	20,200	0.46
Muav	37.6	6,100	13,050	0.47
NYYC 48	47.8	17,600	34,600	0.51
Swan 41	41.0	9,700	17,860	0.54

PRISMATIC COEFFICIENT

The prismatic coefficient is another nondimensional number that equates the fullness of the ends of a hull to the amidships area. In other words, it measures how finely the ends taper to a point. It is calculated by dividing the displacement, again in cubic feet, by the product of the maximum submerged cross-sectional area (A_{max}) times the LWL.

prismatic coefficient (PC) = D ÷ A_{max}(LWL)   *Equation 7.11*

This is not as easy to calculate as the other ratios, because you must have access to the cross-sections of the hull in order to calculate the maximum submerged cross-sectional area. If the hull ends have no taper and the maximum section is held uniformly for the full length of the waterline (a rectangle), the PC would be 1.0. More commonly the PC will vary from 0.7 to about 0.45.

The higher numbers are important only for powerboats. In *Skene's Elements of Yacht Design,* Francis Kinney states that sailboats with a PC greater than 0.55 will be pretty much tubs, and those with less than 0.49 will be so fine as to suck up horrible quarter waves. Note that many double-ended yachts have a PC below 0.49—so if you want a yacht that pitches and goes nowhere, get a high-D:LWL, low-S_a:D, low-B:D double-ender with a PC below 0.50.

The value of this coefficient in predicting performance is limited, however, because most sailboats are designed for a PC between 0.55 and 0.50; and since the PC is reported to only two decimal places, there are only six different PC categories in which to place all sailboats. In other words, this coefficient is very insensitive to actual hull design. In general, however, hulls with high PC values perform better in heavy winds; the lower values perform better in light. When in doubt it is better to have too much PC than not enough, for the consequences of too much in low winds are not as serious as those of too little in heavy.

Another problem with the PC is that it does not distinguish between fullness in the bow and fullness in the stern. I already listed evidence under "Waterline Length" that it is better to obtain the PC from a full stern than a full bow. The latter would cause excessive pitching and have an adverse effect on windward performance.

SUMMATION

Granted, all this performance data is technical and perhaps confusing. Understanding it will still give you a better chance of finding a boat you will enjoy. Use these tables to compare the boat you're interested in to other boats. Although performance under sail depends on many factors besides these ratios, taken together they will give you a good indication of the relative performance of most vessels. Equation 7.12 reduces these numbers to a single value for performance comparison:

$$S = (B{:}D - 0.2) \div 0.4 + (S_a{:}D - 10) \div 10 + (1{-}(D{:}LWL - 150) \div 300) \qquad \textit{Equation 7.12}$$

Keel

Hull performance is strongly affected by hull appendages. Of these, the keel is the major; normally, it improves the boat's upwind performance, decreases its downwind performance, and improves its stability. The size and shape of keel best suited for cruising can generate considerable discussion.

FULL KEEL

Full-keeled boats have long been admired for their directional stability. Donald Street expresses this admiration well in *The Ocean Sailing Yacht*: "But on a cruising boat, helm watches often last for four hours, and having to concentrate on steering for all of that time can be most exhausting. If one can lash the helm for only a short while, take a stretch, drink a cup of coffee, life is much more pleasant."

Although the sentiment is apt—life is indeed more pleasant if you can take a break from steering—that break has nothing to do with a full keel. True, the full-keeled boat will keep going in the direction it is headed. Do not, however, mistake a sluggish helm for directional stability, which has to do with the center of balance, center of effort, and placement of the rudder. It has little to do with keel length.

The helm can be left unattended for hours on most modern modified-fin-keeled boats by the process of balancing the boat. This can generally be done by manipulating the center of effort and does not require lashing the helm. First let the rudder seek its own equilibrium position, then change the center of effort by changing the shape of the sails: Move it forward by flattening the sail, aft by giving the sail more fullness. The former will tend to turn the boat away from the wind, while moving the center aft will turn the boat into the wind. (For more information on this subject see Street's *The Best of Sail Trim*.)

One of the advantages of a cutter rig is that the main and jib can be set up for maximum performance on the desired course, and then the staysail can be fine-tuned to balance the boat. A boat that has its sails set for maximum performance will have a slight weather helm. Too much helm acts like a brake, and indicates it is time to reef, change headsails, or make some other major adjustment to sail configuration. When the boat is balanced properly, all weather helm is lost. While such a course is not optimum for speed, it is close enough to optimum to provide good speed and, more important, requires considerably less power from any automatic steering system.

A sluggish helm is responsible for what I consider the most serious disadvantage of boats with a full keel: They are difficult to maneuver in close quarters, and this inability to turn quickly makes them hard to tack. The capacity to move from the sails drawing full on one side through the eye of the wind until they are drawing full on the other has to do with how quickly the boat can be turned. If this sounds like racing nonsense, wait until you find yourself trying to claw your way off a lee shore in high winds. The difference may very well be your ability to get from tack to tack quickly while maintaining your speed.

The ability to turn quickly is also important in the open ocean in heavy weather. While William Van Doren said in *Oceanography and Seamanship* that "smaller vessels, being more susceptible to wave forces, will do better to lay a sinuous course on oblique headings, meeting the larger seas head-on or stern-to, and veering off crosswind in the troughs," I have found a slight modification of this course to be the best. Watching to the windward and slightly to the quarter, you can with a little practice turn, dodge, and slip through the constantly changing oncoming seas, thereby avoiding much of their destructive power and strain on the crew and ship. In this type of maneuver the full keel, with its inability to turn quickly, is a detriment.

Another false rumor concerning full keels is that they reduce broaching. In my view, their lack of steering sensitivity increases the probability of broaching, because once the process starts the insensitive helm makes it difficult to recover. The result is that long-keeled boats are more likely to broach than moderately short-keeled boats.

The seaworthiness of the full keel is being questioned as well. Studies have shown that the full keel of traditional cruising boats can contribute to capsizing: It seems that the full keel offers more resistance to the motion of the boat as it slides sideways down a wave and "trips" the boat, as it were. Douglas Phillips-Britt, in *Sailing Yacht Design,* is one of many designers finally speaking out on the problem: "The excessive length of keel and depth of forefoot once regarded as an essential of seaworthiness may be treated as a confusion of cause and effect in the analysis of seaworthiness."

The two advantages of full-keeled boats that seem to have some merit are related to what they may do best: Go nowhere. Going nowhere is important in heaving to and grounding. When a boat is heaved to, the effectiveness of the keel in the stalled position depends on the area of the keel, not its aspect ratio. Since the full keel has a much larger area, the boat will look after itself better with the helm locked; it won't fall off and gather way. The full keel also offers better support when the boat goes aground, because the larger volume of keel absorbs more energy from the impact. Thus the keel and the boat will sustain less damage than a similar boat with a smaller keel.

PERFORMANCE COMPARISON

There are very few data on the performance of full keels under way. Table 7.5 shows the proportion of skin friction and wave-making friction for various speed ratios of a full-keeled, wineglass-shaped hull. The table stops at a velocity ratio of 1 because full-keeled boats seldom get above that figure; the total resistance for the full-keeled boat gets so high at that point that the percentage data lose practical meaning.

TABLE 7.5

Resistance on Traditional Full-Keeled Hulls

Velocity divided by (LWL)$^{1/2}$	Skin Friction as a Percent	Wave-Making Friction as a Percent
0.6	84	16
0.7	69	31
0.8	60	40
0.9	53	47
1.0	41	59
1.1	——	——

FIN KEEL

Keel design has come full circle. The first yachts were of Dutch design and had leeboards to provide upwind performance. These narrow boards gave way to full keels due to the seemingly intuitive premise that if a short board prevents leeway in headwinds, the long, full keel will prevent it better. Within the last century, however, science has drastically influenced keel design, and short, efficient keels are returning.

The fin keel improves sailing performance by reducing a boat's wetted area and improving the aerodynamic shape of its underbody. The fin is essentially a short, swept-back wing that literally flies the hull through the water. Interestingly enough, if the hull of a modern design is mirror-imaged along the waterline, it greatly resembles a jet airplane (see figure 7.14).

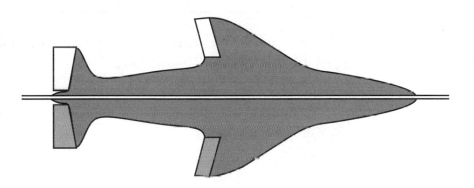

Figure 7.14   Reflected Hull Shape

You can see immediately that there is less wetted surface to produce skin friction, and since there is also less hull body to drag through the water, the fin keel's wave-making resistance is also less than that of a full keel. The distribution of resistance on a fin-keeled boat is shown in table 7.6, which reveals that the total resistance of a fin keel increases approximately five times before it hits the practical limit. This means that a boat with a fin keel has a higher top speed, is more responsive, and will reach any intermediate speed more quickly than a full-keeled boat.

TABLE 7.6

Resistance on Fin-Keeled Hulls

Velocity divided by (LWL)½	Skin Friction as a Percent	Wave-Making Friction as a Percent
0.6	83	17
0.7	79	21
0.8	75	25
0.9	70	30
1.0	65	35
1.1	51	69
1.2	37	63
1.3	26	74
1.4	17	83
1.5	——	——

The area of the fin, the aspect ratio, and the sweepback angle dictate the performance of a fin keel. The area of the fin should be about 4 percent of the sail area for the proper balance between water resistance and driving force on all points and conditions of sail (Marchaj, *Aero-Hydrodynamics*). The aspect ratio is the effective depth (d_e) of the fin divided by the average fore-and-aft length (l_a) of the fin:

$$AR = d_e \div l_a \qquad\qquad\qquad \textit{Equation 7.13}$$

The effective depth of the fin is essentially the depth of the leading edge measured from the hull bottom. The sweepback angle is the angle the forward edge makes aft of vertical. To work properly, the correct sweepback angle must be related to the aspect ratio. Tank testing has established the data in table 7.7, which shows the proper relationship between aspect ratio and sweepback angle. Fixing the center of lateral resistance and locating the ballast properly to balance the boat often requires the use of sweepback angles other than optimum. The base of the fin should be parallel to the waterline.

TABLE 7.7

Relationship between Aspect Ratio and Sweepback Angle

Aspect Ratio	Sweepback Angle in Degrees
0.5	58
0.6	47
0.7	37
0.8	29
0.9	22
1.0	16.5
1.1	11.5
1.2	7
1.3	4.5
1.4	2
1.5	0.5

The aspect ratios in this table stop at 0.5; those keels with aspect ratios below this are classified as modified-fin-keeled boats and may have an aspect ratio as low as 0.25.

Fin keels provide a quick and responsive helm. Some of these helms, particularly on craft with high aspect ratios, are so responsive that they require constant attention to sail. A proper cruising boat should be less responsive but still maneuverable. A boat with an aspect ratio of greater than 0.7 is most likely too responsive for cruising.

A well-designed low-aspect-ratio fin or modified-fin keel, together with a skeg-hung rudder, can provide excellent directional stability and superior maneuverability. It also contributes to cruising safety in several ways. Because a boat with such a keel is faster than a full-keeled, it is exposed to the perils of the open water for less time. What the fin keel loses in tracking ability it wins back by being able to return to the proper heading rapidly. Finally, the boat's smaller underbody is less likely to trip on a heavy sea, thereby reducing the possibility of broaching.

SHOAL OR FULL DEPTH

The only real question in my mind when selecting a type of keel is whether to go with a shoal or full-depth modified-fin keel. Deep keels offer stability and performance. Shallow keels allow participation in that favorite cruising pastime, gunkholing. Part of the answer for you depends on where you intend to cruise—in principally shoal areas such as the Bahamas, or deep areas like the Pacific Northwest. A 7-foot draft on your boat will be a minor problem in Alaska but severely restrictive in the Bahamas, where much of the water is less than 6 feet deep and a 4-foot draft is more appropriate. If you intend to cruise in a variety of areas, then you may need to compromise.

The most common compromises are shoal-draft keels, centerboards, swing keels, wing-shaped keels, and twin keels. The shallower, longer, shoal-draft keel has an aspect ratio of below 0.3—a considerable loss—and likewise gives up keel efficiency. My experience with these very shoal-drafted keels is that they make amazing amounts of leeway when sailed on the wind.

Twin keels protrude from the hull, on each side of the hull, at an angle of approximately 25 degrees off the vertical. This configuration provides the most efficient keel when the boat goes into the wind and is heeled at about 25 degrees. The keel is then vertical and deepest in the water. When the boat is upright, it loses about 10 percent of its keel depth, or 6 inches from a 5-foot keel—not a major gain in shoal drafting. The penalty for this extra keel is extra wetted surface and the accompanying loss in performance in light winds.

Twin keels are common in England, where harbors are shallow and tides large. This combination frequently leaves a boat grounded. Twin keels support the boat upright, however—a positive feature during grounding.

Wing keels have a little horizontal wing on the bottom. When a boat with a normal keel heels, the keel bottom moves upward through the water. If this keel is a 6-footer, its bottom would then be at a depth of about 5½ feet. With a 2-foot wing on the same keel, however, heeling would leave the keel bottom at a depth of 6½ feet, a gain in effective depth of about 1 foot. The addition of the wing adds a little extra wetted surface, but not nearly as much as the twin-keel system. Similar to the twin keels, the amount of shoal draft obtained from the wing keel is limited to about 10 percent.

Centerboards and swing keels are two possible and traditional answers when you want both performance and shoal draft. The efficiency of a centerboard is dependent on its aspect ratio and a streamlined shape. High-aspect-ratio centerboards are more common than those with streamlined shapes. Most boards are flat plates; they are less efficient as keels, but also less costly.

Windward efficiency can be recaptured by making the board deep and using an efficient high aspect ratio. The centerboard craft is probably a better performer downwind than a conventionally keeled model, because the unneeded appendage can be retracted, thereby reducing the frictional resistance. With a centerboard or swing keel, the draft of the boat can also be drastically reduced—from 7 or 8 feet at sea to 4 feet when gunkholing. A properly designed centerboard also performs very well in heavy air (Carleton in Street's *The Ocean Sailing Yacht*).

If centerboards are so good, then, why doesn't everybody have one? Because they also have many drawbacks. Stability is reduced, because the ballast cannot be placed as low in a centerboard boat as in a normal keel. Centerboards also have more mechanical parts, which are a source of potential failure. The centerboard trunk presents a weak point in the hull: This joint sometimes works apart and begins to leak. The pendant used to position the centerboard can also fail. If it does, the centerboard needs to have a device to keep it in place, preventing it from swinging wildly in a seaway and doing massive amounts of damage. Thought should be given to how to replace a broken pendant or remove the entire board without major structural modifications or digging a large hole under the boat.

At the bottom of the list, the centerboard trunk is difficult to maintain. Because the inside of this trunk is almost impossible to paint, crustaceans can grow in great profusion there. If the boat sits for a considerable time in warm water, the colony can grow so large that the board becomes inoperable.

Rudder

SPADE RUDDER

Spade rudders are by far the most efficient; they give the best combination of minimum resistance and maximum turning moment. They also improve the windward performance of the hull by providing a second leading edge, following the keel. This additional leading edge significantly increases the amount of lift over the keel alone and, hence, better windward performance.

The efficiency of a spade rudder is sensitive to the gap between the hull and the top of the rudder. A gap of ½ inch will reduce efficiency by 10 percent and increase drag by 4 percent, because of crossflow over the top of the rudder. This is particularly noticeable on deep V-hulls.

Unfortunately, spade rudders are not suitable for cruisers, as they are particularly vulnerable in a serious grounding or collision. Even a minor impact can damage one beyond use. The loss of steering at sea is neither a pleasant experience nor one conducive to long life.

By protecting the vulnerable spade rudder with a short, stout projection called a skeg, however, most of its undesirable traits are lost, while its advantages are retained. This configuration is called a skeg-hung rudder.

SKEG-HUNG RUDDER

Besides offering protection to the rudder, the skeg provides a few advantages of its own. It increases the stall angle (the angle at which the rudder will lose its lift), improves the lift of the rudder when the boat is heeled, and adds control area, thereby improving directional stability. Also, because the skeg is rigidly attached to the hull, you can add a second bearing to your rudder. If you place this lower bearing a short way up the skeg, the skeg and rudder can be subjected to considerable damage in a grounding but still have a chance of coming away operational.

Because the added area of the skeg adds wetted surface, it is not popular with most serious racing sailors; for cruisers, however, the skeg-hung rudder is the best of all worlds. In *Sailboat Design,* Ted Brewer states, "In this regard, I must add that a fin keel yacht with a skeg hung rudder of adequate size can have all the directional stability of a full keel cruiser and yet be more quickly tacked or maneuvered when the necessity arises."

A skeg with fore-and-aft width amounting to about 10 percent of the rudder's fore-and-aft width will add lift to the rudder. Any increase in width beyond that will reduce helm responsiveness and add wetted surface.

Like the spade rudder, the skeg-hung rudder should have a square profile at the bottom but be close to the hull at the top to prevent crossflow, which will reduce the lift. The shape should be streamlined, with its maximum thickness 30 to 35 percent of the skeg's width aft of its leading edge.

KEEL-HUNG RUDDER

There are two basic types of keel-hung rudders: one hung inboard, the other outboard. The inboard rudder has a stock that emerges through the hull; the outboard type is mounted on the transom or stern of the hull. Both are large and heavy.

The inboard type is slightly more efficient than the outboard if put hard over, and is considerably less likely to ventilate and lose lift when the boat is heeled at steep angles. However, it is also more likely to have a propeller aperture cut in it, which will lower its efficiency considerably.

The outboard-hung rudder is easier to inspect and repair if it has been damaged, and fitting wind-vane steering gear is simpler. As far as steering goes, though, it is the least efficient of all methods. The number of outboard rudders on traditional cruising boats is another example of how the uninformed cruiser can be sold an idea that was useful in the 1920s but not today.

If you are unlucky enough to own a boat with this type of rudder, at least make sure that this rudder, again, has a squared-off bottom and fits closely to the hull and keel to prevent turbulence and crossflow. It will be more efficient when without fore-and-aft rake. When the angle of heel gets to be greater than about 30 degrees, then a rudder with an aft rake of about 30 degrees at the top is more efficient. However, cruising boats are most often sailed with heel angles of less than 30 degrees; therefore, any rake to the rudder is a disadvantage. Top-raked forward rudders are less efficient than all other types of rudders.

Overhangs, Lifelines, Deck Space, and Bowsprits

If you're looking to get the most bang for your buck, note that hulls without long overhangs or bowsprits provide the most interior room, perform better, and are more seaworthy and seakindly. Their added waterline length improves their performance, while the full stern reduces pitching and the probability of being pooped with a breaking wave. Long overhangs are necessary only on heavy-displacement hulls.

The large rig required to drive a heavy hull itself requires a long deck length. Long overhangs are a method of lengthening the deck without adding weight or wetted surface underneath. This length can also be obtained—with less weight—through boomkins and bowsprits; however, these frames provide no extra buoyancy, and a heavy hull requires lots of buoyancy. The solution is to fill in these overhangs with hull that isn't normally submerged but provides what is commonly called reserve buoyancy when struck by a wave. Without this reserve buoyancy, heavy-displacement hulls are very wet and even dangerous.

Overhangs of from one-quarter to one-third of the boat's overall length have been recommended for a properly designed heavy-displacement hull. The longer bow may eliminate the need for a bowsprit, thereby keeping the rig inboard.

Reserve buoyancy is an often-cited and easily misunderstood term; it depends on waterline length, displacement, and overall length. These relationships can be seen from examining figure 7.15.

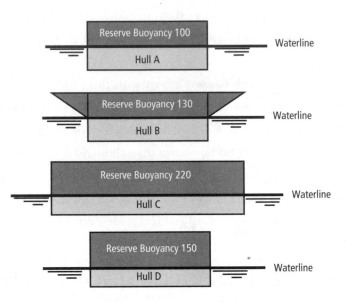

Figure 7.15   *Reserve Buoyancy*

Hulls A, B, and D all have the same waterline length. Hulls A, B, and C have the same displacement, while D has half their displacement. The heavy hull with the long waterline, hull C, has the most reserve buoyancy. The light-displacement hull without the overhangs, hull D, has the next smaller amount of reserve buoyancy; the heavy-displacement hull without overhangs, hull A, the least. Therefore, the only boat that benefits from overhang is the short-waterline, heavy-displacement hull.

I was once caught on passage in very steep, short waves. Without warning one broke right on the stern. Instead of being submerged in the breaking wave, though, the stern rose and the wall of boiling water passed under and around us. Our boat's light displacement and full stern had provided enough buoyancy to allow it to ride over the oncoming, breaking wave. We splashed through the surf and slid down the wave front, and hardly a drop of water came aboard. I am sure that wasn't the ultimate wave; I am also sure that a heavier boat without a full stern would have taken water.

LIFELINES

Most cruising boats are equipped with grab rails and lifelines, the latter sometimes raised to a height of 2 feet or more. This added height improves security. There is, of course, nothing wrong with going forward on hands and knees or in a crouched position; lifelines should be used as handholds to steady yourself, however, not relied on to prevent a falling body from going over the side. The loads placed on equipment when stopping a flying 200-pound weight are enormous and beyond the capacity of most lifeline systems.

DECK SPACE

When you go forward on your boat, the single most important safety feature the boat can have is enough deck width to give you secure footing. Keep these decks clear of equipment and use good sense. When you're out of the cockpit, good sense requires hanging onto the boat with one hand, especially in vulnerable positions such as while passing the spreaders. Good sense also means wearing a safety harness in marginal or unsafe conditions.

Figure 7.16   Poor Deck Storage

Unfortunately, it's common to see a cruising boat with all its deck space loaded up: extra fuel and water tanks, a dinghy, a couple of bicycles, a windsurfer, and various other equipment the occupants obviously can't live without (see figure 7.16). Using a safety harness to go forward on a boat like this while at sea must be a real mess; you'd snag on every piece of gear going forward and back. It is not hard to imagine this process becoming such a problem that eventually you start avoiding the safety harness when conditions are borderline. One day you may slip over the border and find out that you could've lived without all that equipment after all.

Having adequate work space and equipment forward is also important. A clean foredeck with bulwarks to brace your feet against provides safety. If you need winches forward, forget those cute little stainless-steel butt rails at the mast; move the winches off the mast and put them on the cabin top, where you can work them from a sitting position. It's okay to be macho in sheltered waters, but at sea you should do as much of your out-of-the-cockpit work as possible from a low-profile position—sitting or crouched. Finally, the worst place to work forward is on a bowsprit.

Bowsprits came into existence because they enlarge a rig, providing enough extra power to drive a heavy boat without adding the weight of a larger hull. Just about every-

Figure 7.17   *Bowsprit as a Launching Platform*

thing that can be said about bowsprits is bad. They are extremely dangerous. They are small, with very little to hang onto or brace against; the easiest place from which to be launched overboard is a pitching bowsprit in a heavy seaway.

Besides being unsafe, bowsprits make it difficult to tune the rig properly. There is too much play in the system, and it is difficult to get the forestay tension needed for good windward ability.

And contrary to popular belief, the bowsprit is a terrible place to hang an anchor. The weight is too far forward and is not supported by any hull buoyancy. When the boat is swinging on the hook, the dolphin striker is forever fouling the anchor rode and playing a nighttime tune that is far from soothing. A chain rode is just noisy; a nylon rode can chafe through under such conditions.

The arrival of roller-furling headsails has eased the problem of working the sails on the bowsprit somewhat. If I had to sail a boat with a bowsprit, I would insist on roller furling and pray a lot that it wouldn't fail. Roller furling changes the bowsprit from a nagging, day-to-day worry to a single worry over the mother of all catastrophes. If the furling did fail, it would probably do so in bad weather, and unscrambling a mess of sail and roller-furling gear on such a small platform would most likely be unpleasant.

Cockpits

The cockpit is the center of activity, whether the cruising boat is under way or in a harbor. Under way, the cockpit is the center of most of the shipboard operations—steering, sail trimming, eating, and relaxing. In port, it's where everyone relaxes and guests are entertained. A great deal has been made of the danger of large cockpits in cruising boats. However, I have never seen a single cruising boat with a cockpit so large that it was unsafe; on the other hand, I have seen many with cockpits too small to be safe, and certainly too small to be useful.

COCKPIT SIZE

Many authors recommend small cockpits for seagoing boats; their concern is that a large cockpit, if washed by a wave, will hold considerable water. The weight of this water will make the boat difficult to steer and increase its susceptibility to being swept with additional waves—possibly causing a broach.

Figure 7.18　　　*Grab Rails in the Cockpit*

Hal Roth had an 8½-foot-long cockpit, which was filled by a breaking sea several times during various passages (Roth, *After 50,000 Miles*). When he shipped a sea, however, he reported neither trouble steering nor any additional waves sweeping his submerged cockpit. Apparently, half the water would roll out with the next wave; what remained required 15 minutes to seep through the cockpit drains. This large cockpit was ridiculed by an experienced cruiser Roth met on his first trip, and he was persuaded to reduce its length by 3 feet. This still left him with what he felt was an ample cockpit, and although it did not stop the shipping of seas, he apparently felt better.

This and other accounts of the perils of large cockpits at one time provided a deadly fascination for me, because my own cockpit is almost as wide as Roth's original cockpit was long and is 9½ feet in length, producing a volume almost twice the size of his. After considerable research, however, I found the source of the often-cited apprehension. It seems that in the 1950s, large cockpits were installed in ocean racing vessels to allow the many racing-crew members to work from a position offering minimum air resistance. These cockpits comfortably held 10 to 12 crew members at work. The need to reduce air resistance pushed the sole of these cockpits to only inches above the waterline to keep the crew as much as possible below the deck line. When such cockpits were flooded by a wave, the weight of the water lowered the stern a few inches, pushing the cockpit deck below the waterline and reversing the flow of water in the cockpit drains: Water flowed into rather than out of the cockpit. That would certainly be a disquieting occurrence.

It should be noted, however, that people who warn of the dangers of a large cockpit are talking about a *large* cockpit, one several times larger than found on any cruising boat, including mine. Also, because the sole of these racing cockpits was only a few inches above the waterline, the stern did not have to be submerged very far to reverse the flow in the scuppers.

The tragedy of allowing this misunderstanding to spread unchecked is that it has produced some cruising boats with only footwells for cockpits. As I discussed in chapter 2, the cockpit is your first line of defense against the sea. It is where you live, work, and play while on passage. Thus the unsuspecting owners of boats with small cockpits have, in the name of protecting themselves against the (imagined) perils of wallowing in a cockpit full of water, exposed themselves to a much greater danger, that of being lost overboard.

The maximum volume of a safe cockpit is in reality related to the buoyancy and freeboard of the boat. The International Offshore Racing Rules provide the following rule for cockpit volume:

Figure 7.19   *The Cockpit on the* Bird of Time

maximum cockpit volume = 0.06 x LWL x B x F_b where: *Equation 7.14*

   B is the beam in feet, and

   F_b is the minimum freeboard in feet.

This equation limits the submergence of the stern of the vessel to about 20 percent of the freeboard. For a boat with 3 feet of freeboard, this amounts to about 7 inches of submergence. Using this equation would produce a huge cockpit, one much larger than found on any cruising boat. The cockpit found on the *Bird of Time* is very large (see figure 7.19). However, its volume could be increased almost 20 percent before it reached the maximum defined by the IORR. The term *large cockpit* is relative to the volume of your boat, not to that of your neighbor's cockpit.

The bottom line, then, is: Would you rather be in your cockpit for 15 minutes with wet feet, or over the side and facing a 1,200-mile swim?

A well-designed large cockpit should allow you to operate from a secure position with your feet 48 inches below the top of your lifelines. If you fall, you then fall into the boat. It also provides enough space for all the winches and equipment necessary to operate the boat almost entirely from within its confines—and enough for the crew to work these winches side by side without getting into each other's way or leaving the sole of the cockpit.

Figure 7.20   Snug Center Cockpit

Debby and I can work together in our cockpit on the three winches necessary to reef the main (see figure 7.19). While it is true that we can use this cockpit as a social center when in port (we can seat 8 to 10 in comfort), the folding cockpit table is stowed while at sea. Also, notice that in figure 7.18 the cockpit awning frame provides secure handholds, both overhead and around the cockpit sides, to steady the crew when moving about.

The location of the cockpit has some subtle effects on the safety, comfort, performance, and utility of the boat. Center cockpits can provide more living space below deck. They usually provide a larger engine room and, of course, the privacy of a large aft cabin. The added living space comes partly at the expense of lost storage space, though.

A center cockpit situated in the widest part of the boat can be a safe place to operate the boat during passages. Figure 7.20 shows a snug little center cockpit of this type. Since the cockpit is farther forward it sometimes gets a little wetter, although the forward cabin offers some protection. However, not much can be put under this kind of cockpit except the engine. As it turns out, this is not a bad place for the engine—low and near the center of the ship, where its weight contributes most favorably to dynamic stability.

Unfortunately, there is a tendency to overimprove this engine location by turning it into something all cruising skippers desire—a real engine room. To do this it is necessary to provide more space, to make it easier to work on the

Figure 7.21   Top-Heavy Center Cockpit

engine. Then just a little more space, to regain some of that lost storage; and how about space for a generator? And so on, until the cockpit sole gets raised—often to above the deck line (see figure 7.21). This high location now decreases the boat's stability and, instead of providing a safe, secure working area, increases the occupants' chances of being lost over-board, especially if the cockpit is small. Lose your balance and fall in this type of cockpit and you fall overboard.

TESTING YOUR OWN COCKPIT

If you are interested in finding out how far your boat will sink when its cockpit is filled, mark the water level at its stern, bow, and approximately in the middle on both of its sides with tape. Then plug the cockpit drains with flat rubber sink stoppers and fill the cockpit with a hose or 5-gallon bucket. If you're at all scientific, count the bucketfuls. When you're finished you will graphically see both how much your boat will sink with a full cockpit and—if you counted bucketfuls—how much water it will hold. My own boat, with its very large cockpit (540 gallons), sank only a little more than 5 inches.

To gain more information from this exercise, measure the differences between the tape you placed previously and the new waterline at all four points. Your bow has probably risen; if so, treat that measurement as a negative submergence. Average the four measurements; multiply this average submergence (S_a) in inches by 1,000; and divide the result by the num-ber of gallons (V) multiplied first by 0.1337, and then by 62.4. The result is the carrying capacity of your boat in inches per 1,000 pounds. This figure is handy for determining how much waterline you will lose when loading your boat with supplies; it's more accurate than equation 7.8. (A couple of notes: 62.4 is the weight of fresh water in pounds per cubic foot; if you used salt water, multiply by 64. Also, 0.1337 converts the gallons of water to cubic feet of water and the weight to 1,000 pounds.)

carrying capacity = S_a x 1,000 ÷ (V x 0.1337 x 62.4)   *Equation 7.15*

8

Cruising Rigs

T he 20 percent of time that a cruiser spends sailing is also the time when that cruiser is most vulnerable to accidents. And when danger presents itself, many cruisers instinctively try to motor out of its way. This is often the worst possible decision. In a crowded harbor the water may be full of debris and abandoned lines that can clog engine intakes and tangle propellers, rendering the engine inoperable. Or the engine might not have enough power to push the boat into the wind and waves. On the other hand, a boat that performs well, is properly rigged, and has a well-trained crew can sail into the wind with a triple-reefed main—and enjoy a much better chance of survival.

In all but very close quarters, your sails and rigging are your boat's primary and best sources of power. Unfortunately, few cruisers know much more than the bare essentials about their rigs. The number of accidents that can be laid at the doorstep of this ignorance is considerable. They are not all as serious as being driven on a lee shore against an adverse current in high winds, or accidental loss of stays, shrouds, or mast. Sometimes they involve merely a loss of comfort, convenience, or time. In any case, though, selecting the proper rig and understanding how its components work to drive your boat will increase your peace of mind and enjoyment of cruising.

Selecting the Proper Rig

A sail can be square, trapezoidal (gaft), or triangular (Marconi). I will ignore the first two kinds, and deal only with Marconi sails and rigs.

MARCONI SAILS

The triangular sails seen on most modern sailboats, Marconi sails, can be either masthead or fractional. The difference between is whether the jib halyard goes to the masthead or stops at some point on the mast. Fractional rigs were developed when mast strength and weight became problematic. Supporting the mast partway up has some structural advantages; however, today fractional rigs primarily benefit racing boats, whose mast flexibility, minimum weight, and cross-sectional area provide a premium in speed. In cruising this premium is not worth the potential problems that would result from failure of the minimum cross-section. Thus, my discussion will be limited to the masthead rig.

Figure 8.1 shows a vessel with the common masthead Marconi rig. This rig is efficient upwind, simple to operate, and cheap to maintain. It has totally replaced other rig systems except for historic-sailing buffs.

The Marconi sail's advantage lies in its leading edge. It turns out that the leading edge of any sail is what most contributes to upwind performance. Laboratory testing has shown that, upwind, the aft portion of a sail only adds drag and heeling forces. The result is that upwind, a tall, thin (or high-aspect-ratio), triangular shape performs best. Off the wind, the shape of the sail is not as important as its overall area—a larger area will outperform a smaller regardless of shape. Since the triangular main is shaped more for upwind performance, downwind the modern rigs must rely on large headsails (genoas or spinnakers). This is, in fact, one of the reasons cruisers prefer the masthead rig: The sail running to the top of the mast supplies more headsail area. Some cruisers prefer twin headsails for a downwind run.

The high-aspect-ratio main makes a more powerful sail easier to handle for a small crew. The long side of the main is secured by the mast; considerably less sail runs fore and aft to flog. Further, since the boom on a high-aspect-ratio sail is short, it does not enter the air space over the cockpit on a rear-cockpit vessel, eliminating the need to duck or the possibility of a serious blow to the head.

Downwind, where the headsail is used to drive the boat, the driving force is situated in front of the boat, much as in a front-wheel-drive automobile. Under these conditions the center of effort moves far forward—approximately one-third the length of the sail foot aft of the headstay. Not only does the center of effort stay forward of the center of resistance, but the lever arm between these centers is much larger as well, which in turn generates a much larger restoring couple. Since any variance from the intended course is opposed by this couple, the headsail-driven rig is easier to control downwind and much less likely to broach.

The center of effort of the main is approximately one-third the length of the sail foot aft of the mast. Therefore, rigs with longer booms or low-aspect-ratio sails will move the center of effort farther aft than will high-aspect rigs and tend to create greater lateral instability.

GENERAL CONSIDERATIONS

Back when humans were hairy beasts squatting around their fires, someone said, "You know, the perfect rig for cruising is the ketch rig." From that day hence, Neanderthals blindly followed that advice—and promptly became extinct. It follows, then, that to avoid becoming extinct, you should avoid mindlessly selecting the ketch. It is better to consider what you are trying to accomplish and the advantages and disadvantages of all the various rigs.

Be aware that the rigs on many cruising boats today are too small for proper performance or even convenience (Beiser, *Proper Yacht*). The proper way to select a rig is to consider the shape of the sails, the type and size of the hull, the number and strength of the crew, and the winds in the area where you intend to cruise. In the late 1960s, Hal Roth gave a good definition of what to look for: "People who talk about reduced rigs for ocean cruising are simply uninformed. The ideal rig is one that can hold up clouds of sails when the going is light and be shortened down easily when the wind increases" (Roth, *After 50,000 Miles*).

WINDS

Most people underestimate the amount of time it is necessary to fly "clouds of sails." They unfortunately focus their attention on strong winds. On the average 30-day passage between 40 degrees north and 40 degrees south, however, there will be 15 days with winds of between 11 and 17 knots; 11 days with winds of less than 11 knots; 2 calm days; and only 2 days with winds of above 22 knots. With winds between 11 and 17 knots, most sailboats will operate efficiently. But notice the amount of time you can expect winds of less than 11 knots; poor-performance boats do not operate well in such winds. This means that the traditional underpowered cruising rig will operate efficiently only about half the time.

HULL TYPE

Your hull type is important because it determines amount of wetted surface; for proper light-air performance, you'll then need a sail area of between 2.2 and 2.6 times that wetted surface area. The higher number is for multiple-mast rigs. A full-keeled hull with a large wetted surface will need a much larger rig to move it adequately than a modified-fin-keeled boat, with its smaller wetted surface.

The wetted surface area is not an easy value to obtain. It cannot be calculated by water-line length times beam or draft; it is dependent on the actual hull shape. A circular shape has the minimum perimeter for a given area. Therefore, the closer the hull cross-section is to circular, the less wetted area. Deep V, wineglass-shaped, and full keels all add wetted surface and require more power.

HULL SIZE

Once you know the general size of your hull you can determine your optimum rig—reducing the number of alternate rigs you'll need. The size of the hull is related to the optimum rig by a factor I discussed in chapter 7, the sail area:displacement (S_a:D) ratio. Of this ratio, Beiser, in *The Proper Yacht,* said that "anything under 16 misses the point of having a sailboat, except in some exceptionally windy parts of the world." I agree, but much depends on the aspect ratio of the sails and the type of keel. I feel the S_a:D ratio should be between 15.5 and 18. Rigs over 18 should be approached with caution and with full understanding of the consequences of that much power. Research has shown that one large sail provides more drive than two small sails having the same total area. Therefore, ketches and schooners need a higher S_a:D ratio than sloops and cutters to provide the power necessary for good performance.

When in doubt, go higher. For example, the *Bird of Time* has a sail area:displacement ratio of 18.6 and handles very well in the high winds normally found around Hawaii. Our standard set for interisland sailing is similar to the sails used by our friends with smaller rigs.

Because displacement can be roughly correlated with overall size, some general rules of thumb can be stated. To keep performance adequate, boats under 40 feet should be sloops or cutters; boats between 40 and 50 feet, cutters or yawls; boats above 50 feet, schooners or ketches. The relationship can be pushed upward if the crew is in good physical condition, but it should not be pushed down. It is more efficient relative to cost and effort to keep the individual sails as large as you and your crew can manage.

CREW

There is obviously a limit to the size of sail that an individual can handle. However, no one seems to agree on what that limit is. Sizes have been quoted from 300 square feet to 650 square feet. Eric Hiscock put the upper limit at 400 square feet. My own mainsail is just slightly less than 400 square feet, and this sail is easily handled by the 115-pound crew. However, one reason for this is the sail's configuration: The aspect ratio of the *Bird*'s main is 3.59. I suspect Hiscock's experience was with sails with aspect ratios closer to 2.0.

Once the sail becomes too large to handle, the standard solutions have been to sail a smaller boat, or to divide the sail area into many smaller units by using a multiple-mast rig. There is, however, another solution—go to a lighter, more easily driven hull. You can see from the discussion of S_a:D ratio earlier that to keep performance up and sail area down, you simply decrease the displacement. A high-aspect-ratio, light-displacement sloop can get away with a much lower sail area:displacement ratio than a low-aspect, heavy-displacement ketch. Therein lies the wisdom of the lighter boat over the split rig when sails become too large. With this solution you avoid being cramped by a smaller boat, but maintain performance and safety.

With these general concepts in mind let's examine individual rigs—sloop, cutter, yawl, schooner, and the ever-present ketch—to determine their strengths and weaknesses.

SLOOP

The Marconi masthead sloop is the most sensible rig for small cruising vessels and the most common for ocean racing. It has the advantage of minimum standing and running rigging (especially if the masthead rig is used, which avoids the running backs required on fractional rigs). Also, it has only two sails to handle, can sail closer to the wind, and is more aerodynamically efficient than other rigs. For sailing ability on all points and for simplicity, the sloop is probably still your best choice.

The ability to sail close to the wind is a function of how many sails the boat has set in the fore-and-aft direction. When the foremost sail is set at an optimum angle to the wind, the wind coming off it affects the next sail aft. The interaction of these sails requires that either the aft sail set farther to windward, or the foresail farther off the wind. Since the aft sail can be set only so close to the wind before stalling or providing negative drive, however, it is the foresail that must be set farther off the wind. The more sails you have, the farther off the wind you must set the forward sail. The sloop, with only two sails, can sail relatively closer to the wind than the other types of rigs.

Further, with its single mast and minimum rigging, the sloop is generally a more stable rig than others. Even though its mast is taller and the rigging larger, the sloop's total weight aloft is less, because it's a single-mast rig (unless the multiple-mast rigs are vastly underpowered). The simplicity of the rig also reduces the cost and effort involved in maintenance.

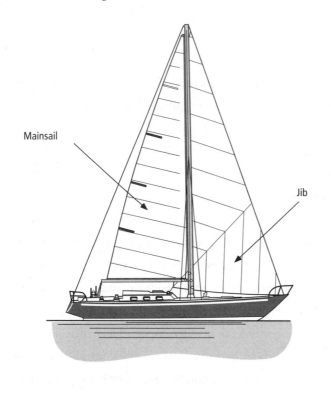

Figure 8.1   Typical Sloop Rig

The only disadvantage of the sloop is the need to change the size of its headsails to maintain sail balance when the wind velocity changes and the main needs to be reefed. (Contrary to popular belief, the wind is always changing at sea.) Changing the size of the main causes the center of effort to move and unbalance the boat. On the wind this can require considerable helm to restore the balance. If the helm needs to be held hard over to keep the boat on course, the rudder is in fact acting as a brake. Not only is this tiring, but the boat is not sailing as fast as it could. To balance the boat and regain this efficiency, the jib must be changed.

Roth complained of 61 headsail changes in a 19-day passage (Roth, *After 50,000 Miles*). I can see all the roller-furling advocates rubbing their hands together, but roller-furling headsails are not necessarily the answer. (See "Roller Furling," later in this chapter.) They certainly weren't Roth's answer. To reduce the number of headsail changes he re-rigged his boat to a double-headsail sloop—not the same thing as a cutter, but almost.

CUTTER

The cutter has a single mast and, forward of it, two sails: the jib and a staysail. The true cutter is different from the double-headsail sloop in that the mast is stepped farther aft. This places it more nearly amidships, where the wider beam allows better placement of the shrouds. The placement of the mast aft requires a shorter boom on the main. Fifty years ago this was seen as a serious defect in the cutter. However, with modern high-aspect-ratio mainsails, the boom is already considerably shorter, so it's now a nonproblem.

One advantage of the cutter over the sloop is that the inner forestay provides additional support for the mast. If the headstay fails, the boat can be sailed using the staysail and the jib halyard as a forestay. The standing and running rigging are simpler than those of a multiple-mast rig, yet the cutter's flexible sail plan allows the boat to be balanced under a wide variety of wind conditions.

The first headsail change is a simple dropping of the staysail. In most cases the sail is easily blanketed and will drop right on the deck; you do not even have to go forward. This sail can just as easily be pulled back up when it's time to change the jib. The advantage of this flexibility is that when you make headsail changes, the fore triangle area is not completely bare. The boat keeps driving, and the foredeck is easier to work when the boat is under control and moving. Because the staysail stay is closer to the center of effort, in extreme heavy weather the boat can be sailed under staysail alone, or even with the storm jib rigged on the staysail stay.

The advantages of the cutter rig for boats between 35 and 45 feet are being recognized by the cruising community. In a recent survey, 48 percent named the cutter as their preferred rig. Also, 19 percent of the sloop owners would abandon that rig in favor of the more

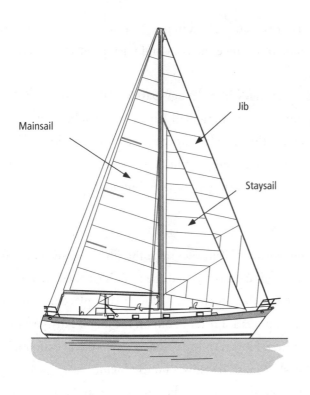

Mainsail

Jib

Staysail

Figure 8.2   *Typical Cutter Rig*

flexible cutter; but, more surprisingly, 10 percent of the ketch owners would opt for the more efficient cutter rig. Eighty percent of the boat owners involved in this survey had vessels between 35 and 45 feet long (Cornell, *World Cruising Survey*).

It is not uncommon for people to consider the sails on a cutter or sloop of this size to be unmanageable and opt for a multiple-mast rig. In my opinion, boats smaller than 45 feet with multiple-mast rigs are little more than cute motorboats. If you need to reduce the size of your rig, I still urge you to consider first a lighter, more efficiently driven hull. However, as hull size increases and boat length reaches the upper 40s or lower 50s, the mainsail on a single-mast rig can become too large for most cruisers to handle. At this length, it's time you consider a multiple-mast rig.

YAWL

A yawl is a double-masted rig with the smaller or mizzenmast aft. A true yawl has its mizzenmast aft of the rudder post. The mizzen therefore is very far aft, and both the mast and sail are small. (The mizzen sail generally makes up about 10 to 15 percent of the total working sail area.) The main on a yawl is considerably larger than the main on a ketch or schooner of similar length. Because of this large main, the yawl is almost as weatherly as the cutter; in fact, many refer to it as a cutter with an undersize rig. The rig can have a single or double headsail.

The aft location of the mizzenmast makes it difficult to stay properly, and downdraft off the mizzen can affect wind-vane steering. The small mizzen of the yawl does have some advantages, however. It's small enough to easily be backed by hand, and can thereby act as a wind rudder controlling the direction of the boat even if the boat is not moving through the water. Yawls are quite often effectively sailed backward by backing the mizzen (Street, *Ocean Sailing Yacht*). Also, the small mizzen makes an excellent riding sail when at anchor, keeping the boat's head into the wind and reducing the roll in an uncomfortable anchorage.

The primary disadvantage of the yawl is that it has more complicated standing and running rigging than a single-mast rig. Consequently it is more costly, more complicated to operate, and more difficult to maintain. Nonetheless, it's a better selection than a ketch.

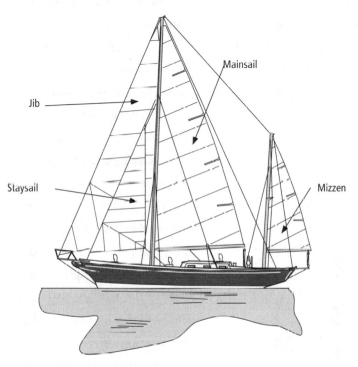

Figure 8.3   Typical Yawl Rig

There may be many reasons why the yawl isn't seen often today. A major one is that the rudder post is so far aft on modern yachts that it's impossible to get much of a mizzen aft of it. Thus, those hulls with small aft mizzens are no longer yawls; they're ketches with undersize mizzens. It seems to me that if you are going to consider a ketch, consider first one with an undersize mizzen.

KETCH

A ketch is a double-masted rig with the smaller or mizzenmast aft of the main mast but forward of the rudder post. Because the ketch commonly has a larger mizzen than the yawl, its mizzenmast needs to be farther forward where the boat is wider, so that it can be properly stayed. The mizzen on a ketch commonly contains 20 or 30 percent of the total sail area, but since it is a larger sail than the yawl's, the downdraft off it can still affect the wind vane. In the aft-cockpit ketch, the mizzenmast always seems to be in the line of sight of the helmsperson.

The single benefit of the mizzen comes during that 1 percent of your cruise when storm conditions occur; the boat can then be balanced with just the mizzen and a small jib flying. I have already discussed the folly of selecting a boat on the basis of its being a storm attack vessel. However, such is the state of anxiety in nouveau cruisers that they often fear storms above all else and succumb to the misery of a ketch rig in hope they will survive. The truth is that they will survive quite satisfactorily with other, more efficient rigs as well.

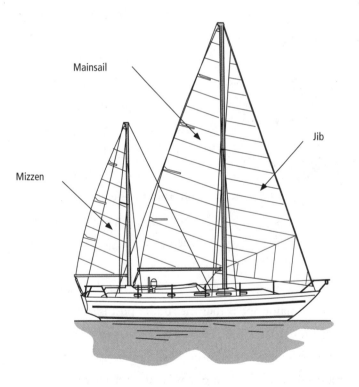

Figure 8.4   Typical Ketch Rig

Reaching with the wind on the beam is the only point of sail on which the ketch rig operates effectively. It is not a weatherly rig; everything goes to windward better than the ketch. If the mizzen is set when the boat is pointing high on the wind, it must be set so far to windward that it acts as a brake. If it is set properly, then the main and jib must be set too far to leeward, and the boat does not point very close to the wind.

Setting up the boat so that a mere 30 percent of the sail is drawing properly is, of course, not the best way to make progress. Your alternative is to set the main and jib and douse the mizzen when on the wind, thus operating at 70 percent efficiency, at best: The main and jib are not sufficient to drive the hull effectively. Downwind, the large mizzen of the ketch will blanket either the main or the jib, depending on how the sails are set. So upwind or down, the mizzen is usually unused, and the ever-popular ketch performs poorly (Wareham, "Voyage of a Lifetime").

If I had to pick the worst-possible boat to go cruising in, it would be a double-ended, heavy-displacement, full-keeled ketch with a bowsprit, a stern-hung rudder, and a footwell for a cockpit. Interestingly, most beginning cruisers consider this the ideal boat. The survey I mentioned earlier, however, shows that this attitude is changing; at least 65 percent of respondents had done some homework and selected a better rig.

Anyone thinking seriously of cruising with a ketch smaller than 55 feet should charter one for a few weeks first. One month's charter experience on a 41-foot ketch changed my choice from a ketch to a cutter. The boat would not sail anywhere, and putting the mizzen up or down had no effect on its speed.

This experience is not unique. Once while I was discussing an upcoming passage with a friend who owns a 32-foot ketch, he expressed amazement at the speed we were hoping to make. I was just as amazed when he told me that his top speed rarely exceeded 3½ knots. We made the passage in 17 days; he and his crew required almost 40. With a proper staysail sloop he could have made the trip in half the time. He sold his ketch on returning and took up land cruising.

Three good things can be said about a ketch: The mizzen does provide a nice support for the sun awning and a handy place to hang the radar antenna or laundry; and it does look very nautical. The picture of a ketch cruising by under full sail with its bowsprit stabbing into the setting sun brings salty feelings to most people, even to me. Just don't be fooled by the imagery.

I should add that much of what is wrong with a ketch goes away in a boat over 55 feet in length. In this size vessel, the mainsail—even on a light-displacement sloop or cutter—is just too large for a small crew to handle effectively. The ketch provides a flexible sail plan, however, with smaller sails more easily handled by the average cruising couple and a foredeck long enough to contain an adequate jib without a bowsprit. If your dream is of a boat over 55 feet, the ketch could be for you; the other rig that shows potential at this length is the schooner.

SCHOONER

The schooner rig was very popular in the early part of this century, before aerodynamic research revealed the advantage of high-aspect-ratio sails. You would not have to go far to hear it said that not even the ketch is as beautiful as a schooner under full canvas. I have always had a secret desire to stand on the deck of a schooner and shout to the crew, "Up with the golliwobbler!" This rig has the taller mast stepped aft of its mizzen, thus relying more on the aerodynamics of the main than on its jibs. Off the wind, the large, low-aspect-ratio main can spread acres of canvas to the wind, and the rig performs well as long as the course is not dead downwind. Upwind the performance is dismal, maybe even worse than a ketch's, because the small mast forward reduces the size of the sails forward; this forces the larger sails aft to be less efficient when sailing to windward, because the large main must be set farther off the wind.

The modern staysail schooner was thus developed to improve the efficiency of the traditional schooner rig upwind. It relies on the more efficient shape of staysails (Parker, *Ocean Voyaging*). The staysail schooner sails better to windward and off the wind than the ketch, but not as well into the wind as a yawl. This rig can set a cloud of sail in light air or with the wind on the beam, where it is a reaching fool, outrunning almost any other boat. In heavy weather, it has enough flexibility that you can balance the rig in all conditions and set a small staysail amidships in even the ultimate storm.

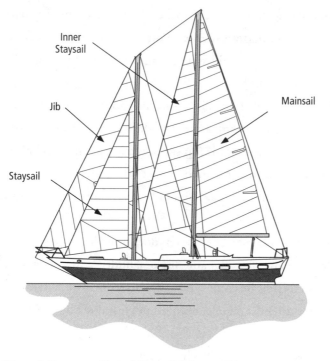

Inner Staysail

Jib

Staysail

Mainsail

Figure 8.5   *Typical Staysail Schooner Rig*

Like all the multiple-mast rigs, this one has large amounts of standing rigging to maintain, probably more than any other rig. The complex running rigging also has more strings than any other rig, and probably much more than the average shorthanded cruising couple enjoys pulling daily.

The modern staysail schooner is a fast and weatherly two-masted alternative to the yawl for a boat over 55 feet. It will require a larger crew to operate effectively, but those who contemplate a boat of this length are usually also contemplating a crew. If you're going cruising with your two hefty teenage sons, this may be the rig for you.

Rigging Components

The rig is composed of a compression post called a mast, wires that prevent the mast from falling over sideways called shrouds, wires that keep the mast from falling forward or backward called stays, and other minor fittings. The stays, shrouds, and mast work together to transfer the wind loads from the sails into forward motion of the boat. Let's examine each of the major components, and many of the minor fittings.

MASTS

The long, almost straight, skinny stick called a mast would by any other name be uninteresting. However, if you are to choose the perfect rig, you need to learn something about the mast. It should be light, be strong enough to take the loads imposed by heavy weather and slatting sails, and have low windage. Windage or drag is related to the mast's size and shape, and is important because even under the best conditions the mast reduces the driving power of the main by 20 percent (Baader, *Sailing Yacht*).

WOOD

Wood was historically the first material used for masts. The abundant forests of the New England colonies were of more than just passing interest to His Majesty's Royal Navy. All those armadas sailing about splintering each other's masts with chain shot used up a lot of wooden masts. Even though we no longer use chain shot, you can still find wooden masts today. Generally, however, they are hollow, laminated, and made from Sitka spruce.

They are hollow to reduce their weight, since analysis shows that bending strength is the critical strength for a mast, even though it is essentially a compression post. Most of this bending strength is contained in the outer fibers; the interior wood adds only deadweight. The lamination process increases the strength of wooden masts because weak spots can be removed, and the resulting small pieces of quality wood glued together make a large piece of sound wood. You may recall from our discussion of hull materials that the strength-to-weight ratio of wood is similar to that of steel. However, this still leaves wood too heavy for a good mast material.

Since most masts these days are laminated, the choice of glue is an important consideration. Glues made from casein should be avoided because they deteriorate very rapidly, especially in the Tropics. (Of course, everything deteriorates rapidly in the Tropics.) Resorcinol glues are structurally adequate but seldom used, because they are black and are unattractive on a varnished mast. Most builders today use epoxy glues, which are superior in strength and colorless. You are likely to have maintenance problems with a mast put together with other kinds of glue.

Sitka spruce is light, flexible, and easy to work; however, it does have a tendency to rot. Douglas fir is also commonly used for spars; it is less susceptible to rot, but heavier. Regardless of species, any timber used in a spar should be well seasoned and dry. To retard deterioration the mast should be continually protected by either paint or varnish.

For this, paint is a better choice, because it is opaque—although any rot present remains hidden for the same reason. Because varnish looks better and most boaters hate surprises, almost all masts are thus varnished. If you're headed for the Tropics, however, consider painting your wooden masts white. The paint will last longer than varnish and reflect more of the heat. Again, though, varnishing or painting a mast is a continual requirement for boats with wooden spars.

There are no sound reasons to select wood as a mast material. Wooden masts are heavy and weak and require more stays and maintenance than other materials. The reasons for using wood seem to be more emotional than rational.

ALUMINUM

All the qualities that make aluminum a fine hull material make it just as desirable for a mast. Unlike hulls, though, aluminum masts can be made from extruded or rolled shapes, and the costs of such masts are competitive with if not less than those of other materials. For these reasons, the extruded aluminum mast is almost universally used in modern yachts.

The best alloy is 6061-T6; fasteners and fittings should be aluminum or the proper kind of stainless steel insulated from the aluminum. Unlike wood, aluminum is difficult to taper, and most aluminum masts are of a nearly constant section with only a slight, uniform taper.

Aluminum masts require less maintenance and are far more durable than those made from other materials. The aluminum mast should always be anodized to protect it inside and outside from electrolysis and corrosion. Its base should allow for proper drainage; seawater in the bottom portion of a mast can cause serious corrosion and electrolysis problems.

The electrolysis that can occur between stainless-steel fittings and an aluminum mast can be minimized by using a polysulfide sealant to insulate the fittings completely from the mast before attaching them. Wooden pads should not be used at the base of the mast or as winch pads, because the acid in the wood affects the mast even if a proper gasket is supplied.

Holes in the mast should be kept to a minimum, because stress concentrations occur around all mast openings. Any holes should be staggered down the length of the mast to prevent overstressing a single area, which can lead to mast failure.

Maintenance of an aluminum mast includes periodic washing with fresh water and inspection for corrosion or electrolysis. Where you find corrosion, sand down the metal to a clean, fresh surface; prime with the proper primer; and paint with a good two-part epoxy paint.

STEEL AND FIBERGLASS

A few steel spars were used by L. Frances Herreshoff at the turn of the century. Since that time their use has been all but discontinued because of the adverse strength-to-weight ratio of a steel mast. Such a mast simply puts too much weight high above the center of buoyancy, raising the center of gravity to a dangerous position.

Fiberglass offers promise as spar material, especially if carbon fiber is used as the reinforcing material in place of glass. These spars are lighter, stiffer, and stronger than aluminum. Since the stress in a mast is approximately axial, the glass can be laid up with the majority of the fiber reinforcing strands in the axial direction, a configuration that improves the strength-to-weight ratio. A fiberglass mast might be as much as 50 percent lighter than an equivalent aluminum mast (Warren, "The Carbon Alternative"). And even if the weight of a cruising mast is increased by about 15 percent—to decrease the probability of failure—the weight saved by a fiberglass mast over an aluminum one is still weight aloft, where every pound is worth 10 pounds of ballast. On a typical cruising boat it is possible to save 120 pounds or more aloft, thus improving the boat's motion, safety, and performance by increasing its ability to stand to its sails. Replacing an aluminum mast with a carbon mast is like adding 1,200 pounds of ballast except that there is no extra weight to slow your boat.

Carbon-fiber masts do not corrode or suffer electrolysis; they hold paint well and do not need constant refinishing. Their only problem, in fact, is their cost. Presently they are all hand laid by specialists, because small mistakes can produce major consequences and potential failure. When these problems are resolved and the masts can be mass-produced, they will become the mast of preference.

RIGIDITY

Most masts on cruising boats are rigid; however, I have noticed a few flexible ones. Changing the shape of such a mast can improve the performance of a sail made from Dacron or other modern sail materials. Although the equipment necessary to use a flexible mast is complex, it is generally simpler than the average roller-furling gear. Unlike the case of roller furling, however, effective use of this equipment requires sailing skills generally not found in the average cruiser. If you do possess the requisite skills, the flexible mast has just as much a place on your boat as a rigid one and will certainly improve the boat's overall performance.

STEPPING THE MAST

The material of the mast is not the only factor involved in its performance; how it is attached to the boat, or stepped, is also significant. As I said earlier, the loads on a mast are compressional, or column, loads basically aligned axially with the long axis of the mast. This gives masts, which are really long columns, a tendency to bend under a load—reducing their load-bearing capabilities considerably and presenting a complex analysis problem.

The bending is dependent on the unsupported length, the manner in which the ends of the column are fastened, and the eccentricity of loading. By experimenting with axially loaded soda straws of different lengths you can quickly see that a relationship between strength and unsupported length exists. This relationship is almost inversely linear, in that a column twice as long has half the strength. Therefore it is important to keep the unsupported length as short as possible.

The end of a column can be restrained in essentially two ways—by pinning it in place, which allows it to rotate freely, or by rigidly restraining it and allowing no rotation. The first method is simpler; the second, stronger. Preventing rotation from occurring at the bottom of the column can reduce that column's effective length by a factor of two. Both methods are used in boating. The deck-stepped mast is normally pinned; the keel-stepped mast uses a combination of the two methods.

KEEL-STEPPED MASTS

The keel-stepped mast, which is the more common, is used because it passes all the load directly to the keel. If the mast is then blocked at the deck in a manner that restrains all rotation at the cabin top, then the mast's effective column length is reduced first by its length below the cabin top and second by half its remaining length. As you have seen above, reducing the effective length by half doubles the axial load the column can withstand before failure.

This additional strength, however, requires the mast to be perfectly rigid at the deck level. A keel-stepped mast obtains this rigidity at the deck by being tightly wedged into the cabin top. The normal practice of using removable wedges allows the mast to be easily removed from the boat when you wish, but leaves some doubt about the effectiveness of this joint in preventing mast rotation at the deck level.

Proper blocking will prevent the mast from moving fore and aft, but any tendency to rotate would have to be resisted by the cabin top. The capacity to completely resist this rotation would require structural reinforcement to a degree not found in the average cabin top. The slight rotation caused by imperfect blocking and a flexible cabin top increases the unsupported length and likewise decreases the mast's real load-carrying capabilities. It is possible that a keel-stepped mast, even if braced properly at the deck, is only 10 to 30 percent stronger than a deck-stepped mast that is just pinned on the deck.

Further difficulty arises because many times these wedges are not set properly. A seaway will constantly work the mast, and rough weather can loosen or remove the wedges entirely. If this occurs, considerable mast column strength is lost because the unsupported length has increased. This strength loss most often occurs during rough weather, which is assuredly a very inopportune time.

The result could be that the whole mess goes over the side; the good news, however, is that the keel-stepped mast is supposedly less likely to do so during dismasting: It generally breaks somewhere in the middle. If you can free the bent, flailing appendage from the rest of the ship before it beats a hole in the boat, a stump is generally left for jury-rigging to help assist your safe return to port.

DECK-STEPPED MASTS

The deck-stepped mast is generally just pinned on the cabin top and left free to rotate. This method of attachment decreases the unsupported length of the mast by the height of the cabin but requires a stronger section, because the unsupported length is now the full length of the mast. The larger cross-section needed to increase the strength also increases the windage and reduces performance, but the possibility of mast failure is reduced, since you are no longer relying on wedges for support.

There are other advantages to a deck-stepped mast, not the least of which is the banishment of the unsavory hole in the cabin top that the keel-stepped mast must pass through to reach the keel. This hole can be a never-ending source of water and irritation to all who reside beneath it. The numerous electrical wires that normally run up the mast can be passed through the cabin top by means of hermetically sealed plugs. I estimate a 24-pin plug to be adequate in most situations.

Another advantage of a deck-stepped mast is that it takes up less room in the living area. Although a strut may still be required to pass the high compressive loads to the keel, it will be a separate and shorter structural element, and therefore can be made from a smaller-diameter stainless-steel pipe with a thick wall for strength. A 3-inch-diameter stainless-steel thick-walled pipe, for example, could easily transfer the loads produced by a 14-inch-diameter mast to the keel.

Deck-stepped masts are also easier to step and unstep and are therefore an advantage if you are cruising inland waters such as canals and rivers with low bridges. If you lose a deck-stepped mast overboard, it will sustain very little actual damage. With a little luck you can retrieve it, haul it home, and restep it (albeit jury-rigging for the trip home may be more of a challenge).

Further, you can have your deck step and rigidity, too. It is certainly possible to fix the end of a deck-stepped mast in as rigid a manner as the cabin-top-wedged joint of a keel-stepped mast. With this accomplished, you have all the virtues of the deck-stepped mast plus the strength and lighter section of the keel-stepped mast. Such a mast may even be better, since it has no wedges to work loose.

This technique requires a sturdy deck plate that keeps the base of the mast from rotating, spreads the loads over the cabin top, and transfers the bending loads to the keel. Figure 8.6 shows a detail of a typical cabin brace that would ensure better rigidity for the mast step on the cabin top.

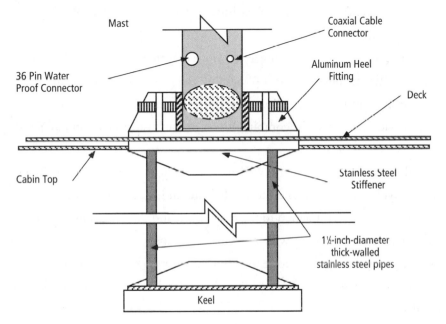

Figure 8.6   Deck-Stepped Mast Detail

GETTING TO THE TOP OF THE MAST

Before we leave the subject of masts, a few words about getting to the top of the stick. Like it or not, someone will have to go up there to inspect the mast and fittings, do maintenance work, or make repairs.

If two people are available, one can use a halyard and winch or an anchor windlass to raise the other in a bosun's chair. Those who want or need to get to the top by themselves can use ratlines or mast steps, a handybilly and a bosun's chair, the Prussian climbing knot or some variation thereof, or a collapsible ladder that attaches to the main halyard.

Maintenance is easier atop the mast if you can use both hands. If the task requires considerable time, sitting is a more comfortable position than standing, especially standing on the narrow rungs of most mast steps. For these kinds of operations, the bosun's chair is probably best.

One disadvantage of the team method is the effort required to get the person to the top of the mast. For most people, this means five minutes or more of serious grinding on a halyard winch. Those who have a power anchor windlass can take a few turns of the halyard around the cathead and step on the power button. Some boats use a combination of team and individual methods to ease the effort of the winch grinder.

Another disadvantage of working as a team is that there's not much for the deck crew member to do after the physical effort of hauling the person aloft except to reposition the mast person every half hour or so. Boredom easily sets in. One way to avoid this is to use one of the individual methods in combination with the bosun's chair and a locking device on the halyard.

I find that a handybilly, or a simple three- or four-part block and tackle, is a good system. The handybilly can be attached to the halyard and raised above the desired working height. The bosun's chair is attached to the handybilly, and the person in the chair can then raise or lower him- or herself at will. No more shouting to the winch operator when it becomes necessary to change positions. Two hundred feet of $\frac{7}{16}$ line is sufficient to reach the top of most cruising rigs with a four-part line. A smaller diameter would take the loads, but it is uncomfortable to operate.

Certainly the top of the mast provides a good vantage point from which to con your way through an uncharted reef. However, since getting there is far more than half the battle, few people really ever go up there for that purpose. Ratlines or their modern cousin, mast steps, are easier to use, but again, they are only comfortable for short periods. As for the view, it's not that much better than from the bow at deck level. The advantage of additional height is somewhat offset by the greater distance from the bow and the water.

The trouble with ratlines and mast steps is that they add windage and weight aloft, which increases anchor loads, makes the boat harder to maneuver in a windy marina, increases overturning moment, and reduces overall boat performance. In heavy weather, too, this additional windage cannot be reefed. For those who still feel they need surveillance capability, the windage and weight can be minimized if the steps go only to the first spreader.

SHROUDS AND STAYS

The shrouds and stays are the wires that keep the mast upright. The shrouds run athwartships and keep the mast from falling over sideways. They are generally lightly loaded; except when under sail, the windward shroud carries the entire wind load.

The purpose of the stays—the wires that run fore and aft—is to keep the mast from falling over forward or backward. The load on the stays is considerably higher than that on the shrouds, because the headsails are attached to the forestay, and to keep the proper sail shape that stay must not sag. More about this later when I discuss tuning the rig.

At various times the stays and shrouds carry considerable loads. To get the most out of your rig it is helpful to understand these loads under different conditions.

Newtonian physics tells us that if a body is not moving, all the forces on it must be balanced. Since the top of the mast is not moving relative to the stays, then, all the forces acting on it must be balanced. More specifically, the forces in every possible plane through the masthead must be balanced.

To begin to understand these forces let's look at a simple condition without wind loads in the athwartships direction. Because the mast is always on the centerline of the boat, the shroud angles (ß) will always be equal (see figure 8.7). This simplifies the relationships between the stresses in the shrouds and mast.

Without wind loads, the compressional forces (BD) in the mast acting vertically upward are opposed by the tensile forces in the shrouds acting at angle ß (see figure 8.7). Because Newton tells us that all the forces are in balance, we know that all the forces in the vertical direction must be equal—that is, all the forces acting up must equal those acting down. Since the mast is vertical, all the force in the mast is thus in the vertical direction.

However, because the shrouds are at an angle to the vertical, not all the tensile forces in the shrouds (BA and BC) act totally in the vertical direction. Only part of the shroud forces act to oppose the upward force in the mast. The portion of the force that acts downward in the shroud is called a component of the force and is related to the angle the shroud makes with the mast and the force in the mast (BD), as shown by equation 8.1:

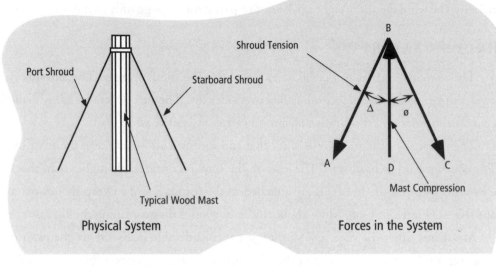

Figure 8.7   *Typical Shroud Components at the Masthead*

$$BD = (BA + BC)\cos ß \qquad\qquad \textit{Equation 8.1}$$

Newton's law also applies to the horizontal direction. Because the mast can carry only vertical load, there is no mast force in the horizontal direction. In this situation, the only forces in the horizontal direction are those caused by the shrouds themselves. Equation 8.2 shows the horizontal component of stress in the shrouds:

$$BA\sin ß = BC\sin ß \qquad\qquad \textit{Equation 8.2}$$

Several things are apparent in these equations. First, equation 8.2 states that without wind loads, the stress in the shrouds is equal. Second, equation 8.1 states that the stress in the mast is dependent on the stress in the shrouds. The more tension in the shrouds, the more compression in the mast. Third, the total stress in the shrouds and the mast depends on the angle ß. As ß gets smaller, the cosine gets larger, and more of the shroud tension is transferred to load in the mast. Fourth, because sinß gets smaller as ß gets smaller, the smaller the angle, the larger the shroud tension when wind loads are added. Most cruising boats today have a mast-height-to-beam-width relationship that would result in a shroud angle of about 6.5 to 7 degrees. This small angle is unacceptable, because it results in extremely high loads in both the shrouds and the mast. You can increase this angle by putting in a compression strut partway up the mast. Called a spreader (see figure 8.8), this strut generally increases the shroud angle to about 20 degrees, which reduces the loads in the mast by about 15 percent.

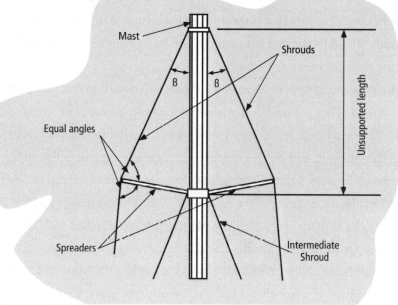

Figure 8.8   *A Typical Spreader*

The unassuming little spreader pays another dividend: It stiffens the mast in the athwartships direction. Remember, the strength of the mast is dependent on its unsupported length. The spreader breaks up this length by providing athwartships support of the mast at the spreader base. The spreader is so useful, in fact, that many masts have more than one.

There is a small premium to pay for the installation of a spreader, however. Recall that when the boat is sailing, the lee shroud is without load; it follows that the lee spreader is also without load, so the windward spreader is forcing the mast to bend to leeward. Also remember that in a compression member, such as the mast, the load-bearing capacity is reduced by bending. The problem is solved by the introduction of the intermediate shroud (as shown in figure 8.8). This shroud is attached at the base of each spreader and applies the necessary force to keep the mast from wandering off to leeward. Of course, the new spreader introduces the shroud-angle problem again, so you introduce another spreader, and so on. The process can't go on forever; windage and weight aloft place a practical limit on the number and extent of spreaders. Most boats have one or two.

Spreaders are such a good idea that sometimes they are run fore and aft as well, from just above the staysail stay. Such spreaders are called jumper struts. The staysail stay performs somewhat the same function as the intermediate shrouds to keep the loads in the mast in static equilibrium. The jumper strut stiffens the mast, reduces the unsupported length, and lessens the need for running backstays.

The spreaders and jumper struts are generally angled upward so that they bisect the angle made by the shroud. They are held in this angle by the mast fitting or by seizing the spreader to the shroud. The equal angle is necessary so that when the windward shroud becomes loaded, the forces on the outboard end of the spreader are in equilibrium and will keep the outboard end of the spreader in place. On the leeward side there are no forces to keep the outboard end of the spreader in place; the seizing or the mast fitting keeps the outboard end from collapsing.

Eventually the shrouds reach the deck, where they are attached with fittings suitable for the loads they are required to handle. The above discussion of the angles (ß) would indicate that the most beneficial location of the deck fitting is as far outboard as the hull will allow. Unfortunately, that is not always the case, because the placement of the shroud deck fitting also controls the sheeting angle, and the sheeting angle controls upwind performance.

SHEETING ANGLE

This is the angle between the boat's longitudinal axis and the clew of the headsail in the horizontal plane. It is controlled by the location of the jib sheet lead block and the athwartships location of the shroud deck fittings (see figure 8.9). The sheeting angle is measured from the clew of the sail, not from the jib sheet lead block, which in most instances will be farther inboard than the sail clew.

The tighter the headsail can be sheeted in, the closer to the wind the boat can sail, especially in winds of less than about 12 knots (Marchaj, *Aero-Hydrodynamics*). Obviously the sail can only be sheeted in until it contacts the shrouds. When it does so depends on the sail's curvature, how high its foot is off the deck (since the shrouds angle inboard as they rise), and the position of the shroud chainplate. The first two items are variable, but the position of the chainplate is fixed and therefore will determine how close to the wind the boat can be sailed in light air.

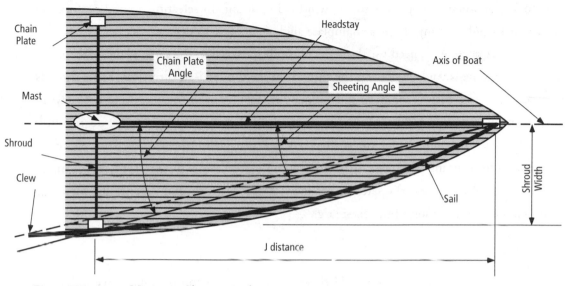

Figure 8.9   *Minimum Sheeting Angle*

The size of this angle gives a good indication of a boat's windward performance. By dividing the distance from the mast to the outermost shroud chainplate (shroud width) by the distance from the jib stay to the mast (J distance), you obtain the tangent of the chainplate angle. By using a table of tangents or the arctan function on your handy calculator, you can obtain the angle that corresponds to this tangent. This is not the minimum sheeting angle, but it is a good angle for comparative purposes. The minimum sheeting angle is always 4 or 5 degrees less than the chainplate angle (see figure 8.9).

Racing yachts shave the minimum sheeting angle to 9 or 10 degrees to get good windward performance in light winds. A good deal has been said about the need for a 10-degree sheeting angle. In *Skene's Elements of Yacht Design*, for example, Francis Kinney recommends a 10-degree sheeting angle, but his actual example shows the spreader chainplate at an angle of approximately 19 degrees off the boat's longitudinal axis. This angle appears to be too large to be able to set the average jib with a sheeting angle of 10 degrees. I suspect his sample yacht would in reality have a minimum sheeting angle of about 15 degrees unless the sheets are brought inside the shrouds. If the jib has no overlap, it is possible to run another sheet inside the shrouds, but this requires considerably more fussing than most cruisers care to do. Still, if you have a wide shroud angle, keep this suggestion in mind, in case you get into a spot where sailing close to the wind is important. In selecting a good-performing cruiser I would opt myself for a chainplate angle of around 15 degrees.

Since there is no need for the lower shrouds to attach in the same plane as the mast, you have some latitude in placing the shrouds in the fore-and-aft direction. These shrouds can easily be led forward or aft of the mast and thereby assist the headstay and backstays in supporting the mast. Further, if the intermediate shrouds are led aft 10 or 12 degrees they can be used as aft support for the staysail stay and, along with the jumper strut, eliminate the need for running backstays. Although the complexity of the system increases the maintenance, it also increases the safety, since the loss of a single shroud is generally not severe enough to cause the loss of the entire rig.

STAYS

The stays are more complex. Their situation without wind is similar, except that the angles between the mast and the stays are not equal. Figure 8.10 shows the relationship of those forces through a plane fore and aft, where Δ and ϕ are the angles between the masts and the fore- and backstays, respectively.

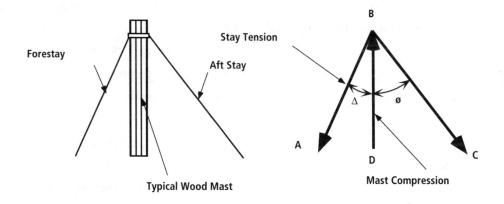

Figure 8.10   Forces in the Fore-and-Aft Plane at the Masthead

The downward portion, or component, of the backstay tension BE is equal to the tension in BE multiplied by the cosine of the angle ϕ (BEcosϕ). The downward component of the force in the headstay is BFcosΔ. Given these two facts, the components of the forces in the downward direction in the stays can be related to the upward force in the mast caused by the tension in the stays as follows:

$$BD = BF\cos\Delta + BE\cos\emptyset \qquad\qquad\qquad \textit{Equation 8.3}$$

From this relationship you can see that a portion of the compression force in the mast (BD) is also dependent on the stay tension (BF and BE). As with the shrouds, the force in the mast has no component of force in the fore-and-aft direction, so the fore and aft components of the tension in the stays have to balance one another. The fore and aft components can be found by multiplying the tension in the stay by the sine of the angle. This balance of fore and aft forces can be written as follows:

$$BF\sin\Delta = BE\sin\emptyset \qquad\qquad\qquad \textit{Equation 8.4}$$

Because the angle Δ is not equal to the angle ø, the sines of the angles are not equal; therefore, the tensions BF and BE cannot be equal. In our example, the tension in the headstay is greater than the tension in the backstay because the angle the headstay makes with the vertical, or the mast, is smaller; recall that the smaller the angle, the smaller its sine.

If $\sin\Delta$ is smaller than sinø, BF must be larger than BE to make the equation balance. This difference in stay angles holds true for most modern rigs except the schooner. It may be one reason why headstays fail more often than backstays, and why the upwind performance of a schooner is so poor.

Upwind performance is dependent on headstay sag. The less sag, the better the performance. Sag, in turn, is dependent on headstay tension: The more tension the less sag. The problem is that as the wind increases, the mast moves forward, and the tension in the headstay decreases. The amount of this forward movement depends on the diameter of the backstay. The cost of reducing this sag and improving performance is an increase in the ever-present windage and weight aloft. For example, doubling the diameter of the backstay decreases the stretch by a factor of four, doubles the wind resistance of the backstay, and quadruples the stay's contribution to the weight aloft. As intriguing as the idea is, a larger-diameter backstay is not often found on sailboats. Another way to increase backstay stiffness, however, is to use two backstays.

DOUBLE STAYS

Two backstays would reduce the forward movement of the mast by half, while doubling the weight aloft and the wind resistance. With less movement forward, there is less headstay sag; thus, windward performance is improved.

Double headstays are used on a few cruising rigs to allow two poled-out jibs to be flown wing and wing without going through the protracted process of interweaving the two headsails' hanks on the same stay. Another advantage to twin headstays is that the two sails are independent, making headsail changes vastly simpler. The trip to the foredeck is reduced to changing the jib halyard and sheets from one jib to the next, and securing the downed sail to the lifelines with bungee cord.

All of this sounds so good I have come to the verge of making the change to a double headstay rig myself several times. What has always kept me from doing so is the veiled threat I hear from riggers that I'd lose windward performance, because each headstay would have only half the tension. Although this seems true intuitively, it may not be true practically. A properly designed and tuned double-stayed rig would not necessarily double the loads in the mast or produce unacceptable sag. The result very well could be only a small loss of windward performance due to the added weight and windage aloft.

NO STAYS

The complexity of proper stay and shroud tension has made a few people yearn for an unstayed mast. The earliest masts were, of course, unstayed. However, they were also made of wood and very heavy. It was found that lighter and longer masts could be stepped through the use of rigging; and so stays were born. These days, because of the strength and weight of modern materials, unstayed masts are returning.

Such rigs are simple to operate and maintain. The most efficient rig for this type of mast is the cat rig, which has only one sail per mast—the main. Since there are no shrouds or stays, nothing impedes the set of the sail, and the boom can be set at any desired angle. Since the main requires minimum tending once it is up, sailing becomes 90 percent steering. With good self-steering gear, sailing becomes 90 percent happy hour.

However, all is not perfect in the land of unstayed Oz. First, the main on a cruising-size catboat can get quite large; enter the cat-ketch. Some of the bad things about the ketch go away in the cat-ketch because, like the sloop, it has only two sails to set. You may recall that the fewer the sails set in a row, the better the windward performance. The bad news is that whereas a normal mast reduces the efficiency of the main by 20 percent, the larger, unstayed mast reduces the efficiency even further. There is nothing like the jib out there in clean air to pull you along effectively—providing, of course, that the leading edge does not sag too far to leeward.

The efficiency of headsails has forced some designers to add a headstay to this rig, turning it into a sloop rig. But without the backstay to oppose the jibstay loads, the jibstay sags a long way to leeward, thereby bending the mast forward; the result is poorly set sails both before and aft the mast. Well, that is simple to fix. Add a back-stay. . . .

To take full advantage of an unstayed vessel you must stay away from the sloop rig. Your best bet may be to select the untraditional-looking (and ugly, in my opinion) cat-ketch rig. You'll lose a small amount of performance, but gain ease of handling.

The other drawback to unstayed masts in cruising boats is that there's nothing to prevent pumping from the kind of dynamic loads you might encounter in a seaway or during calms with a sea running. The solution is to make the mast section very large—or, then again, how about adding shrouds?

RIGGING WIRE

The standing rigging on most modern boats is generally 1 x 19 stainless wire. Any other material signals caution. The owner and/or builder who failed to use this wire was probably uninformed or under severe budget restrictions. Either case bodes ill for the rest of the boat. True, many traditional cruising vessels satisfactorily use other materials, but this book is concerned only with optimum cruising vessels.*

The 1 x 19 stainless wire is composed of 19 single strands. It is constructed with a core of 1 wire; 7 strands wound counterclockwise around that core; and an outside layer of 11 strands wound clockwise. Count the strands to tell if you have the proper wire. This construction results in a stiff wire with very little stretch under stress. Because of its stiff-

---

*If you're interested in an excellent discussion of all types of rigging wire and their uses and abuses, see Street, *The Ocean Sailing Yacht,* pages 137–49.

ness and lay, it is difficult to splice; you need commercial end terminals to attach it to your boat.*

TERMINALS

There are several methods for putting on end terminals: poured sockets, swage fittings, mechanical fittings, crimp fittings, and epoxy fittings. The poured socket fitting is the oldest method in use, but it has largely been replaced by simpler and more effective methods and I will not discuss it further. Crimp fittings are for smaller-diameter, more flexible wire than is normally used for standing rigging. I'll discuss them briefly under "Running Rigging."

Swage terminals, generally installed by professionals with a special machine, are the fitting most commonly found on modern yachts. The fitting is a hollow stainless-steel tube that is cold-rolled onto the wire at tremendous pressures. If the terminal has been installed properly, failure is mostly due to seawater getting inside it and causing corrosion. Sealing the end with wax or epoxy can extend the life of the swaged fittings, especially for boats in the Tropics.

Because stainless steel fractures easily if it is cold-worked excessively, these fittings should not be run through the pressing die more than once. A common fault in the installation procedure produces a fitting that has a slight curve. This curve causes stress concentrations in the wire where it exits the terminal, and can lead to wire failure there. Since the fitting cannot be removed without cutting, the whole stay is lost unless it can be reused for a shorter stay. If the bend is not too severe it is better to use the fitting bent than try to straighten it by rerolling.

Because it is practically impossible to tell how many times a fitting has been pressed, and because improper fitting installation is the most common cause of fitting failure, you must deal with only reputable installers. You also need to inspect the fittings regularly for hairline cracks or excessive corrosion. The presence of the former indicates imminent failure.

Recently, mechanical terminals have gained popularity, because they can be installed by anyone using common sense and readily available tools. If properly installed these fittings are reputed to distribute the stress to the individual wire strands more evenly than

---

*I should mention for the sake of completeness that there is another popular stainless-steel wire. This is laid with seven strands made up of seven wires each, a core wire, and six wires wrapped clockwise around the core. It is not as strong as 1 x 19 but it has more stretch, is considerably more flexible, and can be spliced, a tedious and onerous task usually reserved for elitist masochists. The ability to do your own splicing is not an adequate reason to choose this as your stay wire, however.

swage fittings. The products on the market generally consist of some sort of wedge-and-sleeve system that uses the stress in the cable to set and hold the fitting in place; the more stress, the better the fitting grips. They are generally slightly more expensive than swage fittings, but they can sometimes be reused; they can also be replaced at sea or some remote port if necessary.

Epoxy fittings are similar to mechanical fittings but use epoxy to fill the cone portion. The epoxy is sensitive to the presence of any oil or grease on the wire and has a short shelf life. If you carry these fittings as spares, be sure to check the expiration date, and remember that epoxy shelf life is temperature dependent—a real problem in the Tropics.

ROD RIGGING

Rod rigging has the advantage of less stretch and lighter weight and windage. The terminals are fastened to the rod by cold-formed pressure. The result is a terminal as strong as the rod and one that cannot retain moisture. The disadvantages of rod rigging are the expense and the difficulty of obtaining spares in remote locations. Rod rigging also seems to be plagued with a fatigue-type failure from impact loading, probably because of its low stretch.

With wire rigging, one or more strands fail before the entire stay does; on inspection, you can spot these failed strands and replace the cable. Since rod rigging has only one strand, however, you have little warning before failure. The result is that you'll replace it much earlier than you would cable rigging. This high level of maintenance and replacement makes rod rigging impractical for current cruising yachts.

RUNNING RIGGING

Running rigging is the term for the group of lines used to operate the boat. The running rigging on a modern cruiser should consist of most of the following lines: halyards, sheets, reefing lines, preventers, topping lifts, vangs, cunninghams, handybillies, and pendants. All of these lines are used to control the sails and spars, and their proper use is necessary for a safe and pleasant cruise.

HALYARDS

Halyards are used to raise and lower sails and control the tension in the leading edge of the sail. By controlling this tension, you control the location of maximum draft—the distance the sail is to windward of the sail chord (see figure 8.11). The location of this maximum draft is also the approximate lateral location of the heeling and driving force.

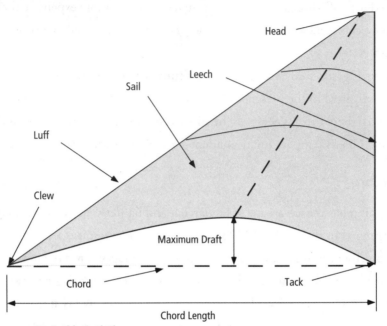

Figure 8.11   *Desirable Sail Shape*

For most conditions the maximum draft should be somewhere forward of the middle of the sail. Getting the draft this far aft in light air requires an extremely loose halyard, even to the point of forming definite wrinkles at the luff. In moderate to fresh winds more luff tension is required to hold the draft at the center of the sail (Marshal, "Shaping up the Main"). Moving the location of the draft not only improves the performance of the boat, but is also important in balancing the sails for more efficient use of self-steering gear. Obviously, a boat that is properly balanced will require less power from an autopilot.

Maintaining the proper halyard tension is easier if the stretch in the halyard is minimized. Nylon should never be used for halyards because of its great elasticity. Even regular Dacron line will stretch 7 to 10 percent when loaded to 30 percent of its breaking strength. A low-stretch all-Dacron halyard stretches 3 percent under similar loading conditions; some of the new lines with Kevlar strands reduce the elongation to about 1.5 percent. Stainless-steel wire, which elongates about 1 percent under these loading conditions, stretches least.

Pulling on a small-diameter wire with your hands requires palms of leather. Since most people can't stand the pain, all-wire halyards should be worked with a reel-type winch. These winches are very dangerous; if your hand should slip off the handle while the sail is partway up, the handle will spin violently, breaking whatever gets in its way—heads and arms, for instance. They have no place on cruising boats.

To avoid this problem most halyards combine wire and rope such that the wire portion just reaches the winch when the sail is fully raised. Human hands and normal winches can handle such a halyard; only the last couple of wraps on the winch are steel. (If the winch has an aluminum drum, stop the wire just short of the winch.) When the sail is in use, the load is taken by the wire portion; the soft line portion is used only while the sail is being raised. Table 8.1 lists the recommended wire halyard diameters for various boat sizes.

TABLE 8.1

Wire Diameter

Boat Length	Main Halyard	Jib Halyard	Topping Lift
25–35 feet	5/32 inch	3/16 inch	1/8 inch
36–45 feet	3/16 inch	7/32 inch	5/32 inch
46–55 feet	7/32 inch	1/4 inch	3/16 inch

The fiber portion of the halyard is generally made of Dacron or Kevlar. These manmade materials are stronger and more rot resistant than natural materials. Kevlar, however, while having very low stretch, is presently very expensive; it also requires larger-than-normal-diameter sheaves because of its stiffness (see table 8.2), and special end fittings because it loses a great deal of strength when knotted. This leaves Dacron as the most popular choice.

TABLE 8.2

Sheave Diameter

Material	Sheave Diameter
Dacron	6 times line diameter
Kevlar	16 times line diameter
7 x 19 stainless wire	20 times wire diameter

Although Dacron resists rot, it is still susceptible to deterioration when exposed to sunlight. Dacron line comes in several different weaves, each with different handling and stretching properties. For halyards, which are not handled as often as sheets, it makes sense to opt for minimum stretch over maximum handling comfort. When selecting line diameter, remember that any lines less than ⅜ inch in diameter are hard on the hands. Table 8.3 can be used as a guide for selecting the rope portion of halyards.

TABLE 8.3

Dacron Halyard Line Diameter			
Boat Length	**Main Halyard**	**Jib Halyard**	**Topping Lift**
25–35 feet	⅜ inch	⅜ inch	⅜ inch
36–45 feet	⁷⁄₁₆ inch	⁷⁄₁₆ inch	⅜ inch
46–55 feet	½ inch	½ inch	⁷⁄₁₆ inch

Halyards can be rigged on the mast externally or internally. External halyards, commonly found on wooden masts, present considerable windage and twice the slating problems while the boat is moored. Halyards can be led down the inside or the outside of aluminum masts. Most modern boats have internal halyards; the only credible argument I know of against this practice is that these are more difficult to replace if they fail.

Figure 8.12   *A Better Forward Halyard Winch Position*

Halyard winches seem to be situated in one of two spots: on the mast or on the aft cabin top near the cockpit. Leading the halyards aft to the cockpit makes sense: While you are exposed when you go forward to attach the halyard to the sail, you can return immediately to the cockpit. Halyard winches on the mast reduce the effort of hoisting sails because the halyard goes through fewer turning blocks, but the crew member who has gone forward to hook up the halyard must remain in this exposed position, high on the cabin top, while the sail is hoisted. To improve safety, some cruisers have constructed stainless-steel baffles at the mast (see figure 8.12).

Working the jib halyard commonly requires more time on the foredeck, because you must often handle the sail itself. In this instance it makes more sense to leave the jib halyard winch forward. However, I still recommend removing the winch from the mast and installing it in the more protected position shown in figure 8.13. From this position a single crew member can raise or douse the jib with a much lower center of gravity. If conditions are really rough, the crew member can operate the winch while sitting or kneeling. The placement on the cabin top also allows you to use a larger winch than you could normally place on the mast. A large winch forward has other applications on the foredeck.

Figure 8.13   The Best Forward Halyard Winch Position

SHEETS

Sheets are the lines used to control the camber of the sail. Camber (C) is the amount of draft; it is equal to the draft (D) divided by the cord length (L_c) (see figure 8.11).

$$C = D \div L_c \hspace{4cm} \textit{Equation 8.5}$$

Camber is adjusted by the sheet tension; the more wind, the less camber, and the greater the sheet tension needed for proper performance. Because you adjust sheets continually as you sail, they should be easy on your hands. A soft woven Dacron material is the best; nylon stretches too much, as do twisted lines (which are hard on the hands to boot). A Dacron-core line with nylon cover is also a good choice. Table 8.4 lists the recommended sizes for sheets relative to boat size. The 7/16-inch-diameter line is the minimum size the average crew member can grip and haul on with any power.

TABLE 8.4

Dacron Sheet Line Diameter				
Boat Length	**Main Sheet**	**Jib Sheet**	**Mizzen or Staysail Sheet**	**Spinnaker Sheet**
25–35 feet	7/16 inch	7/16 inch	7/16 inch	7/16 inch
36–45 feet	1/2 inch	5/8 inch	7/16 inch	5/8 inch
46–55 feet	5/8 inch	3/4 inch	1/2 inch	3/4 inch

Sheets for the main and mizzen sails are attached semipermanently to the booms using multipart block arrangement. The mainsheet should be attached to the boat by an athwartships track called a traveler. The traveler greatly improves boat performance by allowing better control over the shape of the sail and its angle of attack on the wind. The mizzen is not a performance sail and need not be attached to the boat at all.

The jib and staysail sheets are generally attached directly to the clew of the sail using a bowline. This knot is simple to tie and, more important, simple to untie even after it has taken large loads. The bowline is physically large, however, and can get caught on shrouds and stays during tacking; this slows the process of trimming the sail and increases the work involved in tacking. When the knot does not get snagged, you can hand adjust the jib sheet very close to its final trim position before the sail is filled completely by the wind. If the knot does get snagged on the stay, it generally stays there until the wind power in the sail is sufficient to free it. The delay requires that all the slack in the line—from the snag to proper trim—be retrieved with the sail under full wind load.

Snap shackles can reduce the physical size of the attachment; however, they can also cause severe injury if a crew member is struck by one when trying to smother a flogging jib. Another way to reduce the size of the attachment is to use a single line: Pass a loop made in the middle of the sheet through the clew eye, then pass the two ends of the sheet through the loop in the line. This makes a much smaller mass at the attachment point, but the knot is difficult to untie after the sheets have been loaded; normally the process will require a marlin spike. To avoid untying this type of knot when changing headsails, most people use separate sheets for each headsail. Using permanently attached sheets slows down the headsail-changing process somewhat, because the sheets need to be rerouted through deck leads, turning blocks, and winches.

In addition to changing sails, some cruisers like to change jib sheets to match wind conditions. In light air the weight of the standard sheet can be enough to collapse the sail; changing to light sheets can keep the sails working longer, and with a better shape.

CUNNINGHAMS, OUTHAULS, AND TOPPING LIFTS

These three minor lines affect the shape of the sails. Cunninghams are attached to the lower part of the luff of the main or jib. They are used to stretch and pull down the luff, changing the shape of the sail and moving the maximum draft fore or aft.

Outhauls control the tension in the foot of sails attached to a boom. In a good breeze the outhaul tension should be at a maximum. In light air, ease the outhaul so that you can work the excess cloth at the foot of the sail up into the sail for maximum draft.

Topping lifts are attached to spars to help control the shape of the sail, and to prevent the spar from falling when the halyards are eased. They can also be used to change the fullness of the sail by changing the leach tension. In light winds, when a full sail is desirable, you can lift the boom with the topping lift and still tension the main sheet to pull the boom amidships without removing the belly from the sail.

HANDYBILLIES

Technically, a handybilly is a specific tackle with a double block on one end and a single block on the other rigged to provide four-to-one purchase. However, the term has been bastardized into referring to any block and tackle—most commonly a four-part line with a snap shackle on one end, and a jamb cleat and snap shackle on the other. As such, handybillies are handy for anything you need to pull, lift, or hold in place. They can be rigged to the end of the boom and used to lift heavy loads aboard. They can also be rigged as preventers: Attach the end with the jamb cleat to a padeye on deck near the gunwale, and the other end to the boom somewhere aft of the midpoint. Such a configuration prevents an accidental jibe. The farther aft the attachment on the boom, the less the stress in the tackle, and the less chance of breaking a boom if the boat rolls and dips the end of one in the water. You must rerig preventers on each jibe unless you use two, one on each side.

The handybilly can also be rigged to the clew of a jib and used to pull it inboard, thus narrowing the slot or improving the trim angle.

A specific handybilly called a vang is used to control the lift of the boom. The vang generally runs from the base of the boom to a bail one-quarter to one-third of the boom length aft of the mast; when set, it prevents the boom from lifting when the sheets are eased. This adjustment allows you much better control over the shape of the sail, and improves the performance of the mainsail. Unlike preventers, vangs do not need to be moved when jibing. Recently hydraulic and mechanical vangs have begun to appear. These have the additional advantage of being able to support the boom when the sail is not up, which does away with the topping lift and its windage and weight aloft.

Vangs can add considerable loads to the boom and gooseneck, and they take up some prime storage space for dinghies and life rafts under the boom. Still, these are minor objections.

PENDANTS

Pendants are short pieces of cable with a loop on either end used to attach the clew of headsails to the boat. They're attached to the tack of the sail and to the stemhead fitting on the bow. You can use pendants of different length to position the jib at different heights above the deck along the forestay. For example, I use a 5-foot pendant to shackle my spitfire jib over the downed regular jib.

Pendants are easily made from small-diameter 7 x 19 stainless-steel wire and Nicropress fittings. The 7 x 19 wire is more flexible than 1 x 19. The Nicropress tools and fittings have other uses aboard; they're especially handy for jury-rigging.

SAILS

Your inventory of sails for cruising needs to be well thought out. Conditions both asea and in port will be varied; space for sail storage, like all space, will always be at a premium. Sail storage is a particular problem, though, because sails are bulky yet must be relatively accessible. You don't want to be rummaging in the bowels of your boat for storm sails when the weather is kicking up.

Because folded sails take up considerably less room, sails that are to be stored for several months should be stored folded rather than flaked.

On-deck storage of working sails is a blessing. Here is where the ketch has a distinct advantage over the sloop. Most of the ketch's sails can remain hanked on while you're cruising; you simply hoist one or drop another as wind conditions change. The sloop requires that extra sails be taken off and stored somewhere. My own cutter rig has sailed for weeks on passages with one jib up and two more lashed to the lifelines, one on each side. This saves some labor working the foredeck, but it is hard on the sails and looks a little messy.

Real sailors would bag those sails every time they were dropped; however, there seems to be a common tendency to do the minimum amount of bagging on passage. In fair weather and changeable winds, bagging sails always seems like too much work for most of the cruisers I know. This is, of course, a fair-weather solution; if the weather really kicks up, those sails have to come off the foredeck before the working conditions become too difficult.

Cruising sails need to be strong and well built. They need to be made from heavier cloth and have more reinforcement than average sails at the head, tack, clew, and reef points, along with extra chafe protection and triple stitching. They are going to take more of a beating from flogging; suffer greater exposure to sunlight, salt water, and high winds; and, if damaged, be subjected to less skilled repairs.

Fair-weather sails, such as a large genoa or spinnaker, are extremely bulky. On my first passage I took along my 170 genoa, which in protected waters pulled us along in 1 or 2 knots of wind. With my trusty 170, I felt ready to sail right out of the North Pacific High. I forgot to consider the seas.

In protected waters with 2 knots of wind the seas are calm; outside, though, you can still have a 6-foot sea running. Light winds do not have enough pressure to keep the sails full during a roll caused by even a 2-foot sea. Anyone who has sailed in calm waters in light winds and had a powerboat pass knows what happens. Sailing outside is just like bobbing around in an endless parade of powerboats: The large sail constantly flogs and shivers the boat's timbers without mercy.

As it turned out, my large genoa took up entirely too much room for the one or two days of use I got out of it. My spinnaker, however, was a different story. Since it is flown like a kite, it was not as affected by the roll of the seas and rarely collapsed or flogged. It pulled us through many a light-air pocket. We used a full spinnaker with a spinnaker sally. It may have taken the two of us a half hour to get it rigged, but we flew it on many occasions for several days at a time.

MAINSAIL

On a modern cruiser the mainsail's main job is to get you to windward—and I've already expressed my opinion on the cruising boat's need for good upwind performance. One way to get this performance is to use a no-nonsense, high-aspect-ratio main. While some of the tricks used by racing sailors are simply rule beaters and should be avoided, the tall stick and short boom provide a definitely superior airfoil into the wind. If you use this configuration, your headsails will play a more important role in performance on the other points of sail. For example, dead downwind we often dropped the main entirely.

Most modern Bermudan-rigged sailboats have an aspect ratio of between 2.2 and 3. For cruising I would consider a ratio of between 3 and 4 to be high aspect. My own boat has a 3.6 aspect ratio. I suffered no ill effects from this tall stick, 60-plus feet off the water, and short boom. Such high rigs increase the heeling force, however, and should be accompanied by a high ballast ratio. A minor but still positive effect of this configuration is that it keeps the boom out of the cockpit area in boats with a rear cockpit.

Another way to get good performance is to use a fully battened main. Mains come with full, partial, or no battens; most are partially battened to comply with racing rules. Some cruisers believe that a main with no battens is best because the battens are a bother. There are also people who believe the earth is flat. In this no-nonsense world where nature eats cruisers who are ill prepared, I believe the only main to consider is a fully battened main.

Such a main holds its shape better, thereby giving you better performance, especially off the wind. This increase recaptures some of the downwind performance lost by high-aspect-ratio mainsails. A fully battened main does not rattle as much in the wind when luffing or flogging. It also drops more quickly because of its added weight, and with the use of lazy jacks is almost self-flaking—a point that ought even appeal to the traditional cruiser's distaste for bother.

The mainsail should have triple reef points. Before I ventured forth to do battle with the open ocean I read the books on heavy weather written by the traditional cruisers. Dutifully I went about rigging my boat for a storm tri-sail. After many hours of research and phone calls, though, I could find no one on the Pacific Coast who had ever flown such a sail. Many of these experts said that they had used a triple-reefed main, but never a tri-sail. Nevertheless, coward that I am, I still rigged the boat with an extra track on the mast so my trusty tri-sail could be raised in an instant. The trusty tri-sail became the rusty tri-sail, because it stayed rigged and bagged through the whole three years of our cruise. We triple-reefed a few times but never changed our course because of high winds.

Granted, many sailors have seen higher winds than we did. Some would credit that to luck; I prefer modestly to credit it to intelligence. I finally removed the tri-sail and stowed it in the bilge. Maybe the next time I will save space and leave it ashore. For my money, a triple-reefed main on a proper boat will take you through close to 50-knot winds before you have to alter course.

JIBS AND GENOAS

The windward-efficient, high-aspect-ratio main must relegate downwind power to the headsails. This division of labor is not necessarily traditional, but it does make good sense. As with front-wheel drive, pulling the boat downwind from its front tends to keep it on a more stable course. As so often happens in sailboat design, many features interact: A large mainsail produces a need for a full keel in the traditional boat, but reducing the size of the main and letting the jibs pull the boat eliminates at least this particular reason for having a long keel.

Controlling the shape of the headsails is accomplished by controlling the tension on the luff, foot, and leach of the sail. As with the mainsail, the luff tension controls the fore-and-aft location of the maximum draft. The foot tension controls the amount of draft; the leach tension controls the draft at various heights. Unlike the main, however, whose foot tension is controlled by the outhaul and leach tension by the topping lift, the headsail's foot and leach tension are both controlled by the placement of the sheet lead on deck. Tracks on each side of the boat allow you to change the position of this sheet lead. Moving it forward reduces the tension on the foot of the sail but increases the tension on the leach. Both of these changes increase the draft of the sail. Moving the sheet lead aft has the opposite effect, increasing foot tension and decreasing leach. This flattens the lower portion of the sail and increases the twist, both of which reduce the sail's draft. In light winds the lead should normally be forward; in heavy air, aft.

The location of the lead also affects where luffing begins. If the sheet is too far forward, the sail will begin to luff at the bottom first; too far aft and it will begin to luff at the top first. To get the best performance out of the jib, the sheet lead should be placed such that the sail luffs evenly from head to foot. The optimum location will change with the velocity of the wind, however, so you must find it for several different wind speeds, a process best done by trial and error.

The draft cannot be positioned in the jib the way it would be in the main because the luff of the jib is not vertical like the luff of the main. When the halyard is tightened the sail moves up and aft; this movement changes both the tension on and lead angle of the sheet, because the head of the sail is a long way from the clew. Although using a Cunningham on the jib tightens the luff by lowering the tack, it does not materially affect the sheet lead or tension, because the tack of the sail is close to the clew.

In any reasonably sized cruising boat—say, above about 35 feet—you should consider adding reef points to the jib as a way to fill a hole in your sail inventory and reduce the effort and time you'll spend changing headsails. Only one row of reef points that reduces the sail area by about 20 percent is reasonable in a headsail; any further shortening of sail needs requires changing sails. A reefable headsail allows cruising sailors to carry one sail rather than two for two different wind conditions.

Whether to reef or to change headsails depends on whether it requires more effort to remove the hanks of one sail and attach the hanks of the other, or to tie in the reef. Reefing the jib, like changing headsails, still requires the sheets to be removed and reattached to the new clew position, as well as attaching the new tack position to the stem.

Sail area can be added to a jib in two ways: by increasing the length of the sail foot or by increasing the length of the luff. Increasing the foot increases the overlap and affects the slot between the main and the jib. Much has been made of the slot effect of the jib and its effect on the driving force when sailing upwind. It turns out, however, that for a given area of sail, the sail that has the longer luff gives the best upwind performance. So if you want to increase windward performance by adding a larger headsail, first add area to the luff, then increase the overlap.

Downwind the driving force of the sail depends primarily on its area. Where you add this area doesn't matter. On a reach across the wind, heeling force is added by any extra sail area, but this force can be minimized if you add the area low or along the foot of the sail rather than on the luff or leach.

SPINNAKERS

My experience with spinnakers while cruising has always been positive. Two of us have set and operated a spinnaker for days at a time on all points of sail, from reaching to running. Our spinnaker was strictly a light-air sail and came down when the true wind was over 10 knots. Running downwind required a little more attention to the wind indicator to ensure that we doused the sail before conditions overpowered it.

For the cruiser, the major problem with spinnakers is getting the right one. The racing sailor can carry different spinnakers for different conditions, but you must settle for just one. There are spinnakers for running and for reaching in light, average, and heavy air. All are different. In light air a huge sail won't stay full unless it's made from very light cloth. In heavy air a large sail will overpower the boat. A full cut produces a more stable sail when running, whereas a flatter cut is better for reaching, because it reduces the heeling forces.

Most spinnakers are racing sails, and you should be aware that many were designed to fit rules that do not apply to cruising sailors. My choice is a light-air spinnaker designed for running, because normal sails give the poorest performance in that situation. Even if you need to reach, in light winds the heeling forces of the running spinnaker are not large enough to overpower the boat; and when the wind gets above 10 knots, the working sails will move your boat adequately.

Poleless cruising spinnakers or gennakers are cut more like reaching spinnakers, and reaching is not normally where a cruiser needs light-air assistance. The only real advantage of these sails is that you don't have to handle a heavy pole. However, handling the pole is a nonissue as far as I am concerned, because it only becomes a problem when the winds are above 10 knots—at which point my spinnaker is already doused.

A spinnaker dowser or spinnaker sally is useful when you're sailing shorthanded. This device is essentially a large sock that slides over the spinnaker by means of a couple of lines and a pulley (see figure 8.14).

Figure 8.14   Spinnaker Sally

The sail can be raised and fully rigged even when collapsed inside the sally, where it is easier to control and the loads are much lighter. When everything is ready and the crew is in position, one crew member raises the sally while the other trims the sheet.

Getting the spinnaker set is, of course, not the only problem to be solved. Because this sail is free-flying—that is, attached only at the three corners, to three different lines—controlling the shape of the sail is different from (but not much more complex than) controlling normal sails. You use the three lines to move the sail forward or aft, windward or leeward, higher or lower, toward or away from the boat.

Like the rest of the sails, the leading edge of the spinnaker must be at the correct angle of attack. If it is overtrimmed it stalls; if undertrimmed it will luff or collapse. To find the correct angle, rotate the spinnaker horizontally by manipulating the lines attached to the tack (the pole corner) and the clew. The leading edge should always be attached to the pole. The leading edge is at the correct angle of attack when the upper part of the sail is on the verge of curling. To find this point, overtrim until the sail curls, then back off slightly.

If the spinnaker starts to break or collapse low, the pole is set too low. A low break will generally cause the whole sail to collapse. In light air the spinnaker should be flown as high as possible, and the pole and halyard raised to their full height. As the wind picks up you can ease the halyard somewhat, because the wind strength will support the entire weight of the sail. Easing the halyard allows the sail to move away from the boat into cleaner air.

Trimming the sail in unstable conditions is best done by turning the boat off the wind with the helm rather than the sheet or guy. If you have to move a line, moving the guy is easier and quicker.

You control the draft of the sail by tensioning the sail's foot or leach. Tensioning the foot and easing the leach removes draft from the spinnaker; easing the foot and tensioning the leach adds draft. You can control the tension in the foot by moving the tack and clew farther apart or closer together. This draft control is almost automatic. On a run, where you want the most fullness, the tack and clew should be separated by half the beam of the boat plus the pole length. On a reach, where you want a flat sail, the tack and clew can be separated by almost the full length of the boat if desired.

You can adjust the tension on the leach by changing the load on the sheet and the position of the sheet lead. The spinnaker sheet lead must be situated to balance the tensions on the leach and foot. Moving the lead forward increases the leach tension. If the lead is too far forward, the trailing edge of the sail will curve inward and add too much fullness to the sail aloft; if it's too far aft, the foot will be overtensioned, and the spinnaker will be too flat and low.

Setting the pole height is done last and is very simple. The pole should almost always be set perpendicular to the mast and so that the tack matches the clew height. This is true for all normal cruising conditions. The only exceptions occur with star-cut spinnakers—not generally found on cruisers—and in very light air. In the latter case the luff may sag below the pole level, making it hard to fill the sail; lowering the pole will usually add enough tension to the luff to keep the sail full. In light air you can also angle the pole to shorten the distance between the tack and the mast, thereby allowing the luff to develop a more vertical position.

ROLLER FURLING

I am often asked what I think about roller furling. My first response is to point out that it is called roller *furling,* not roller *reefing.* A furling system is an all-or-nothing device. Compared to halyard operation, it is an easier means of setting or furling sails; it requires less brute strength and less time exposed on the foredeck. If I had to sail a boat with a bowsprit, I would insist on roller furling.

However, the labor-saving advantage of roller furling is a two-edged sword. In normal conditions it allows you to operate a vessel larger than you could without it. This is, of course, great—until you hit conditions that are not normal. Then your dependence on roller furling places you in a life-threatening situation that you may not have the strength or endurance to overcome. Roller furling, in other words, allows less skilled individuals to place themselves in more threatening situations; its use should be considered living on borrowed time, and you'd be wisest not to get too far from help.

As with any multiple-use gimmick, using roller furling as a reefing device is a compromise. Although it permits easy furling, it is not as safe or flexible a reefing method as setting a drifter or storm jib. Reefing reduces the stress on the boat by diminishing the sail area and lowering the center of effort. When used to shorten sail, the furling device rolls the sail up on the stay, reducing the sail area, but during this process the tack of the sail rises. And as that tack rises so does the center of effort—just the opposite of what you are trying to do when reefing.

Further, the rolling mechanism is a drum operated only at the bottom of the sail. So as heavy loads are placed on a partially furled sail, its upper portion will tend to unwind (Ross, *Sail Power*). In wind conditions requiring a storm-jib-size sail, the sail area is high on the stay and the forces are too severe for the roller mechanism, so the sail needs to be completely furled.

Setting a normal storm jib would require removing the roller-furling gear, which is not practical under these conditions, so the fore triangle remains empty—or, in reality, worse than empty, because the furled sail and gear add weight and windage aloft. The more conventionally reefed rig can remain under power longer, and therefore retains control over its situation longer.

As for the sail itself, it must be designed to handle a multitude of wind conditions. This means that in really light airs the sail cloth will be too heavy to fill properly, and in very heavy winds it will be too light and will stretch or tear.

The furling equipment needs to be strong and bulky. It must operate in the bow of the boat—the worst location for mechanical equipment, because it is constantly doused with salt water there. Consequently, it requires considerable maintenance and repairs, which are only available in large population areas. As a result, the roller-furling gear on a bluewater cruiser is often inoperable.

Much is made of the safety of roller furling because the sail can be doused quickly from the cockpit. This is indeed true; however, in judging the safety of any system it is necessary to consider all conditions of exposure. Figure 8.15 compares the relative safety of roller furling and hanked sails when wind velocity increases: The safety of hanked-on sails initially drops, whereas that of roller furling rises. But as the wind continues to intensify this trend changes because of the loss of control over sail shape. In high winds roller furling rapidly becomes less safe, especially if you've been seduced into buying a boat with sails larger than you are physically capable of handling and the system fails.

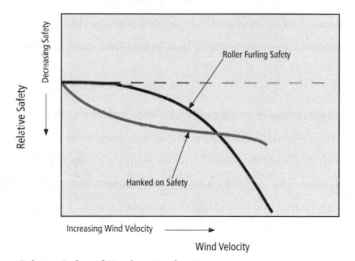

Figure 8.15   Relative Safety of Headstay Reefing System

Recently a storm hit a marina in the Northwest with 50-knot winds and blew out 30 or 40 roller-furling gear systems. A live-aboard friend moored in the marina lost both his roller-furling jib and staysail. Even though he was on board and in a relatively protected spot, he was unable to save his sails, which were ripped to shreds. Consider the consequences of the same failure at sea with a violently pitching boat and waves washing your foredeck.

Rigging Failure

Rigging failure—whether in the sails, running rigging, or standing rigging—is most common during passages, and generally when the rig is stressed by high winds or choppy seas. Quite often fixing something properly at sea is impossible because the correct replacement parts, tools, or even enough space to work is not available. If you're close to a port, your first choice may be to try to reach it under engine power. In many instances, however, you'll find you are too far offshore with too little fuel—thus forcing a repair at sea.

This isn't easy. In the most serious cases you will have lost the stabilizing effect of some or all of your sails, and your boat may be moving violently. Patching together something that will get you to the next port is one thing, but in many parts of the world the next port may not have the proper replacement parts or tools. You'll then have to beef up your jury-rig in port sufficiently to allow your voyage to continue until you can make proper repairs. I know of several people who sailed many months and thousands of miles using jury-rigged headstays. Almost anybody who plans to cruise for a considerable time or into remote places will need to put to sea on occasion with a boat in less-than-perfect condition.

SAILS

Sail damage can occur if seams pull apart, the cloth tears, or the fittings fail. Repairs are easier if someone on board has experience in mending, even if it's just mending clothing. Unfortunately, in this throw-away world, mending is becoming a lost art. For example, we were called on the ham radio by a companion boat whose crew needed coaching in repairwork to a torn sail while on passage back from Hawaii. During this conversation it became apparent that they had little on board to effect the repair and lacked even a basic knowledge of stitching.

The basic tools for sail repair include several heavy needles, a sailmaker's palm, waxed Dacron or nylon thread, sticky-back Dacron cloth, a hot iron to melt synthetic fabrics, and extra slides and hooks. An awl for punching holes in heavy cloth, 2-inch or wider cloth tape, and pliers to pull the needle through are also useful. Four stitches are commonly used in sail repairs: flat, round, herringbone, and zigzag (see figure 8.16).

Mending a torn seam may be tedious, but it is the easiest of the sail repairs. Many times early seam repair can prevent major seam failure (hence the saying, "A stitch in time saves nine"). If the tear is long, holding the two panels together while mending may be difficult; you can do it with pins, but it's better done with cloth tape. Two-sided sticky tape is even easier: Secure the cloth panels together with the tape, then sew diagonally across the

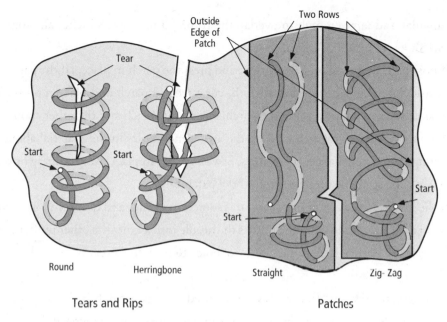

Outside Edge of Patch

Two Rows

Tear

Start

Start

Start

Start

Round   Herringbone   Straight   Zig- Zag

Tears and Rips   Patches

Figure 8.16   Stitches Commonly Used in Sail Repair

warp of the sailcloth with a flat or zigzag stitch. In many instances the seam failed because the old thread failed (rotted or wore through, for instance). The existing cloth may be perfectly sound, and you can sew the new thread through the old thread holes.

Repairing a failure in the cloth itself can be a more complicated task, depending on the location and size of the tear. Mend small tears by first treating their edges to stop fraying, and then sewing them up with a round or herringbone stitch. The herringbone is more difficult but leaves a smoother patch, because it does not pucker the cloth.

The amount of pucker depends to some extent on how far from the tear you can start sewing. If the sailcloth is synthetic and you can fuse the frayed fibers next to the tear with a hot iron, you can begin your repair within ¼ inch. If the cloth is natural fiber you may need to start the repair as much as ½ inch from the tear to gain enough bulk of fiber to anchor your thread.

A large tear will require a patch. It may be necessary to trim the tear first by cutting away the torn fabric; once again, seal the edges with a hot iron. Next, select a sticky-back Dacron patch to match the weight of the sailcloth you are repairing; too heavy a patch will put excessive strain on the original sail adjacent to the repair. Cut the patch so that its warp (or weave) coincides with the warp in the sailcloth, and heat-seal its edges. The patch should be rectangular and large enough to overlap the trimmed tear by 1½ inches all around (see figure 8.18).

If possible, lay the sail on a flat surface and press the patch in place. (If the patch material is considerably lighter than the sailcloth, cut a second patch and place it on the other side.) Make two pencil lines around the patch, one about ½ inch and the other about 1 inch from the outside edge of the patch. With the awl, punch holes in the material about every ½ inch along these lines. Stagger these holes. Sew the patch in place using a zigzag or straight stitch. (With the straight stitch, go around the patch twice.)

If the hole is in the center of the sail, it is sometimes easier and quicker to use two people, one on each side of the sail. One pushes the needle into a hole, the other pulls it through with pliers then pushes it through the next hole. Repeat the process until the patch is secured.

In an emergency, rust-free staples can be used to affix a patch if the tear is near the edge of the sail. Such tears may otherwise be difficult for the inexperienced, because there may not be enough material between the tear and the sail edge to properly anchor the repair. Try wrapping the patch around the bolt rope or edge tape so that it extends 1½ inches beyond the tear (see figure 8.17).

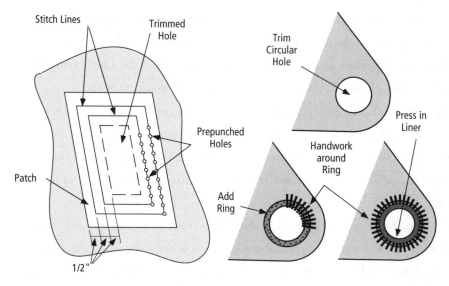

Figure 8.17   Patches and Handworked Holes

Tears along batten pockets may require you to remove the pocket before beginning repairs, to prevent sewing the pocket closed. Finish by restitching the batten pocket into place.

Probably the most difficult repair is one in at the tack or clew of the sail. The loss of a corner hole requires handworking a ring into the hole and inserting a metal liner (see figure 8.17). Several sizes of rings and liners should be kept on board for emergency repairs.

RUNNING RIGGING

Sheet failure is the easiest to repair. Drop the sail and attach a new sheet, or repair the old sheet temporarily with a knot or splice, preferably an end-to-end splice. Sometimes the sheet attachment points will fail; this takes a little more ingenuity to repair, depending on the failure and the spare parts and tools you have available.

For example, the ⅜-inch stainless-steel bail holding the mainsheet to the boom let go on the *Bird of Time* during a passage in the North Pacific. A couple of handybillies attached to the end of the boom acted as temporary sheets until conditions abated several hours later. When I went to get my hand drill, however, I discovered that the motion of the storm had dislodged a tool in the tool drawer—which jammed the drawer shut.

Between attacks on the drawer I recalled that my electric drill was available. The 10 amps required to start it through my 1,200-watt inverter probably sucked the top of my batteries down, but everything held together long enough for me to drill out the offending rivets and reposition the replacement part, a scavenged, unused, boom vang attachment.

Halyard failure is a little more difficult to repair, especially if the halyards are internal (as most are today). Since the process often requires you to ascend the mast, it is best to postpone it until you reach port if possible; the top of a mast in a seaway would be on everybody's list of the top 10 places to avoid. Some cruisers have extra halyards rigged and use the spares until they get to port. If you have no extra jib halyard, you can use your spinnaker halyard to raise the jib in a pinch.

The recommended procedure for replacing an internal halyard is to first tighten and secure all remaining halyards. Then heel the boat to the side on which the new halyard will be coming down the mast, and feed an electrician's snake or weighted messenger down from the top of the mast. Snag the messenger at the exit point with a loop of stiff wire, then attach the new halyard to the messenger and pull it into place.

STANDING RIGGING

Failure of intermediate shrouds or the headstay is the least serious of rigging failures. Even if these wires fail, the mast will probably stay in the boat. In contrast, failure of the backstay or upper shroud is almost always accompanied by loss of the mast. Repairing a broken shroud or stay is a bit difficult, because you can't knot or splice wire. You will need to replace the failed wire with a spare wire, halyard, or tackle.

An extra jib halyard is often used as a spare headstay. Stainless-steel-wire rope clamps can be used to clamp two ropes together, or swages and a swaging tool can be used for ropes up to ¼ inch in diameter (see figure 8.18). A spare wire rope that is, say, ³⁄₁₆ inch in diameter and longer than the longest stay can be stowed more easily than several spare stays. This wire will suffice as a jury-rig under a reduced sail in place of a larger-diameter stay.

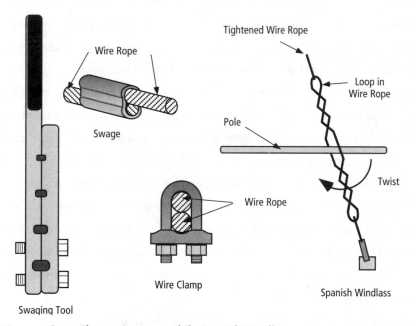

| Wire Rope |
| Swage |
| Wire Rope |
| Wire Clamp |
| Swaging Tool |

Tightened Wire Rope
Loop in Wire Rope
Pole
Twist
Spanish Windlass

Figure 8.18   *Rope Clamps, Swages, and the Spanish Windlass*

It is always best to patch a shroud so that you can use the existing turnbuckles to tension the wires. If this cannot be done, your only alternative is to rig a Spanish windlass—a rope loop with a bar placed through it. Rotating the bar twists the loop and tightens the rope. Then you lash the bar to the rope to keep it from unwinding.

DISMASTING AND JURY-RIGGING

The exact jury-rigging process after a dismasting depends on whether your boat had multiple masts, whether these masts were deck or keel stepped, and which mast went over. (On a multiple-mast rig, for example, you may be able to sail in on your remaining mast with very little effort.) Nevertheless, the general steps are similar: Recover the usable parts, repair broken stays, restep the mast, and, finally, modify the sails.

RECOVERY OF USABLE PARTS

When a mast fails your first task is clearing the wreckage and salvaging usable parts. The good news is that the mast isn't going anywhere, because it's still attached to your boat by its shrouds and stays. The bad news is exactly the same. Because the mast remains attached to your boat, the sea can turn it into a battering ram. The first step is to frustrate the sea in this endeavor by padding your mast and hull, and securing the former firmly to the latter. It is no simple task now to untangle this ball of cloth, wire, and poles—even in the best of sea conditions. Since masts do not generally fail in the best of conditions, your task is likely to be complicated by high winds, steep seas, and a wildly pitching boat that has lost the steadying effect of the sails.

If the mast cannot be lashed securely alongside, it will have to be cut loose—but not entirely loose. This is a job for cable cutters and hacksaw. How much to cut depends on the situation. If possible, get the sails free and back aboard, then attach a long, stout line to the mast so that when it is cut free it will either sink beneath the boat or float sufficiently aft to remain clear of the hull. Do not trust the stays to keep the mast attached to the boat. Many stays are not attached to the mast permanently; the constant motion of the seas will eventually work them loose.

Once conditions settle down enough that you can work the mast safely, recover the stays and shrouds, then remove the boom and any spinnaker poles, spreaders, jumper struts, antennas, and miscellaneous fittings to lighten the mast and make it easier to handle. Then wait until the sea subsides further. While you wait, survey the situation and plan your recovery. Many times there will be nothing left above deck; or you may have a stump of a mast or the mizzen still standing. Having something above deck level is a real plus. Still, even then getting the mast back on board in anything other than a small chop is next to impossible (Knox-Johnston, *Seamanship*).

When sea conditions are calm, move the mast alongside and position it horizontally, with its center of gravity in the center of the boat. Next, remove the lifelines and attach the main boom or spinnaker pole securely to the gunwale and cabin top aft, and the other spar forward. Attach two lines to the free end of each spar, to act as guys. Reposition the mast so that it rests on these two spars and they will act as a ramp (see figure 8.19). Then attach several 20- to 25-foot lines at regular intervals (say, at the center and each end) along the gunwale. Pass these lines under the mast and lead them back on deck to form several Spanish parbuckles.

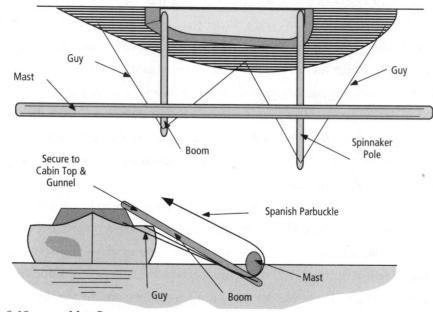

Figure 8.19   *Mast Recovery*

With the ramp in position, work along the row of parbuckles using a block and tackle or deck winches to pull the mast a foot or so at a time up the ramp until it rolls onto the deck. Move the recovered mast near amidships and secure it firmly in place while you plan your jury-rigging. At this point much depends on the nature of the accident—whether the mast was deck stepped and went over the side as a result of a backstay failure, for example, or whether it was keel stepped and is broken in the middle.

If your mast is intact you need only replace or repair the broken stay (as discussed above) and restep the rig. If the mast is bent or broken, you must decide which section to use for your jury-rig. The longest section would allow more sail to be set; the top section has all the halyard sheaves and rigging attachment points; the shortest section will be the easiest to step.

If you select any but the top section, consider the stay and shroud attachment points. A good place to attach these wires is just above a spreader, even if the spreader is not at the top of the mast section. If no spreader exists on the section you must attach something to the mast to keep the stays from slipping down it.

The traditional fix is a jury mast knot backed up with a turk's head underneath to prevent slipping (see figure 8.20). However, a spike, dowel, or rod through the mast works just as well. You'll also need to attach blocks to the top of the mast so you can hoist the sails. Be careful to protect against chafing if you use line. Finally, in this planning process give some thought to what kind of sails will be flown and how they will be sheeted.

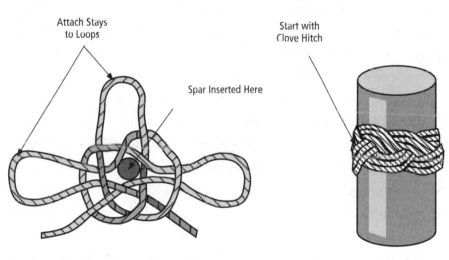

Attach Stays to Loops

Spar Inserted Here

Start with Clove Hitch

Jury Knot

Turk's Head

Figure 8.20   Jury-Rig and Turk's Head

RESTEPPING A MAST

First, position the mast along the deck with its bottom near the mast step and its top running forward or aft, whichever keeps as much of it on deck as possible. Secure the foot of the mast so that it cannot move sideways, forward, or back but can pivot upward. Attach all halyards, shrouds, and stays, leaving only a small amount of slack in the shrouds.

Now you must find some form of leverage above deck level—the farther, the better. The reason for this involves trigonometry: The upward component of force in the lifting line is the force that actually lifts the mast. It's similar to the loading on shrouds or stays: The greater the angle between the mast and the lifting line, the greater the lifting component.

There are many ways to maximize this situation, depending on the circumstances on your boat. These come down to essentially two methods: One uses a single-strut rig, the other, a double-strut. The double-strut method requires you to lash together two poles at their tops, using the shear lashing shown in figure 8.22. Then separate the poles, forming a set of shear legs (see figure 8.21). The basic advantage of this method is that it is easier to set up and brace the strut. The disadvantage is that the lifting point is lower than with a single strut.

The closer the legs are to the free end (the end being lifted) of the mast, the greater the angle between the lifting line and the mast. As the lift proceeds, the angle between the lifting line and the mast constantly changes; the lifting load may become larger than can be applied by the line. This means one of two things: either the legs must be moved before the angle gets too small, or the initial setup must be beyond the end of the mast, minimizing the lifting angle. Moving the legs requires blocking the mast in position during the move. If four spars are available you may be able to make two shear legs and leapfrog them as the lift progresses. If this is not possible it may be best to look at a single-strut lifting method.

The single-strut method raises the lifting point farther off the deck, since it uses the longest pole set up generally either vertical or perpendicular to the mast. The difficulty is bracing the pole in place. Once the pole is set up, the lifting process is similar to that of using shear legs, explained above.

Setting the pole up perpendicular to the mast requires that the pole be lashed and guyed to the mast such that it remains perpendicular to the mast throughout the lifting process. It is all right to have the line running from the pole to the deck lift free of the pole, provided that the leverage is sufficient to continue the lift. If it's not, you must rig a secondary lifting line, as shown in figure 8.21. This is probably the best way to raise an undamaged deck-stepped mast.

Select the longest spar and lash it firmly to the mast with a square lashing, as shown in Figure 8.22. Again, the position of the strut that produces the greatest angle between the

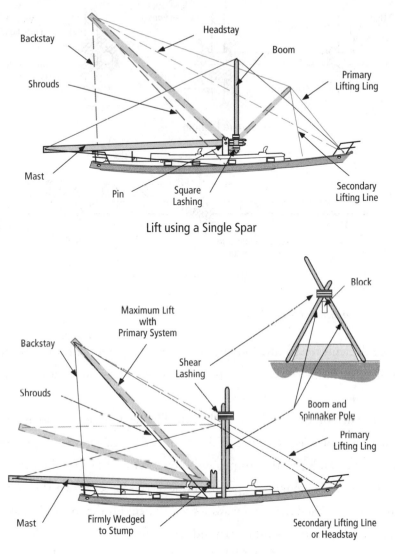

Lift using a Single Spar

Lift using Two Spars

Figure 8.21   Some Possible Lifting-Strut Arrangements

lifting line and the mast is nearest the lifting end of the mast. However, in this method the strut becomes essentially a single spreader. You may recall from our earlier discussion that spreaders impart considerable bending load to the mast.

In this case this bending load is acting downward and is transferred to the ends of the mast, one of which is supposed to be lifted. Obviously, the more downward load on that

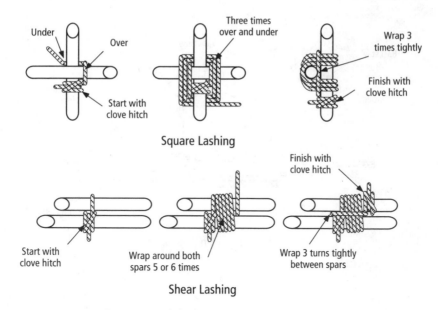

Figure 8.22   *Square and Shear Lashings*

end, the more difficult it is to lift. Moving the strut away from the lifting end reduces this load—as well as the lifting angle. Still, it is best to mount the strut as close to the pivot end as possible.

Sometimes this process can be carried a little further. Consider a case in which a 5- or 6-foot stump of a mast is left standing. If the pivot end of the mast is positioned such that 5 feet of the mast extends past the stump, and then is raised 5 feet up the mast and pinned to it so that it will pivot around this point, the strut can be set up on the extreme end (5 feet beyond the stump) and the downward force will help lift the top end, making the lifting process easier than with any other method (see figure 8.21).

Regardless of whether you select the vertical or shear-leg method, attach a couple of blocks containing the lifting lines to the top of the lift structure, and guy both the tops and bottoms of the framework in at least three directions each, to keep the system in place during the lift.

Using multiple lift lines allows you to begin with a line attached to the top of the mast, and then switch to the other line attached at a point farther down the mast when the lift is partially completed and the angle between the upper line and the mast gets too small. In fact, a third line can be used that does not go through the blocks but runs directly from the top of the mast to the deck forward. This line can be used as the mast nears vertical. If there are enough winches to go around it may be prudent to pull on two or all three lines simultaneously.

SAIL PLANS

All that remains now is to set as much sail as your weakened rig will stand. With luck, the main—suitably reefed—may be set. In many instances, however, sprit, lanteen, lug, or even square rigs will be necessary.

The sprit rig sets a squarish sail with the spar attached diagonally, as shown in figure 8.23; the sail is normally set with a loose foot. The lanteen sail is trapezoidal with a definite peak. It has a spar along its bottom, as well as one that runs from the forward end of the boom to its peak. It is raised like a scissors (see figure 8.23).

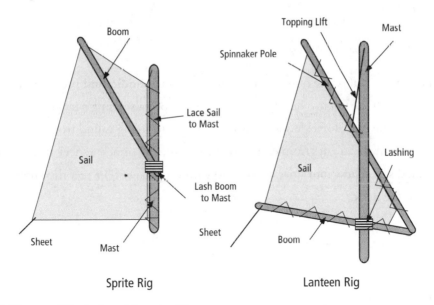

Figure 8.23   The Sprit and Lanteen Rigs

The lug sail's leading edge is not attached to the mast and can be set in a number of different ways: as a balanced lug with a spar on the bottom and top, as a standing lug, or as a dipping lug. The latter two are both free footed but have two blocks to control the upper spar (see figure 8.24).

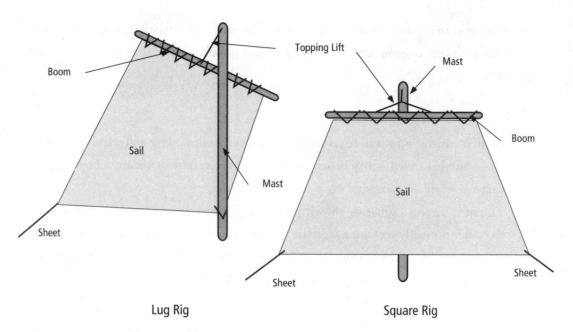

Figure 8.24   *The Lug and Square Rigs*

The square sail is one of the simplest to make and handle, and provides an easier run downwind. Lash the sail to a horizontal yard, which you raise using a tackle on the fore side of the mast. The play in tackle should allow the yard to swing round from athwartships to near fore and aft. Lead guys from each end of the yard, and attach a sheet at each end of the loose-footed sail. These four lines are used to trim the sail. Furl or reef the sail by lowering the yard to the deck.

9

Interior Space

Interior space is the neglected child of cruising. A 35-foot boat has about as much living space as a small bedroom. Lynn Williams compares it to a large shoreside bathroom (Rousmaniere, *Offshore Yachts*). The layout, arrangement, and amenities of this space, then, are very important to the health and happiness of the occupants.

Remember that on a sailboat, as elsewhere, no two things can occupy the same space at the same time. If you find a 35-footer with the apparent living space of a 40-footer, you've found a boat with very little room for storage; you simply can't have one without losing the other. Whereas living space hits you in the eye, assessing proper storage requires a good mental picture of the quantity of appurtenances, trappings, personal effects, and chattel necessary for cruising, and the fortitude to rummage about in the bowels of the boat to see if the space is available.

Do not underestimate the need for adequate storage; a great deal of parts and paraphernalia are necessary for successful cruising. If you select a boat with maximum living space and inadequate storage, you will tour the world while living in a very cluttered closet. Also bear in mind that the smaller the boat, the easier it is to clutter.

Remember that the sum of the parts may equal the whole, but the whole sure looks bigger. Avoid chopping up a boat into many separate cubicles. A 40-foot boat has room for only two or three separate living areas. I know of a 56-foot boat whose main salon is smaller than that of many 25-foot boats, because the interior is chopped into too many small living areas.

To get the maximum appearance of space, choose a boat with clean and simple lines, and without intricate or ornate detail. And keep the living spaces free of obstructions. Anything that stops the eye from seeing across and through the space will break it up and make it look smaller. To make a small space appear larger, you can add light and mirrors.

Sleeping Areas

Often the first question asked about a boat is, "How many does she sleep?" I've always wanted to answer, "Thirty-five: 17 on deck, 12 in the cockpit, and 6 on the floor of the main cabin." A better question is, "How many does it need to sleep?" The layout of the interior will change depending on the answer to that question. Additional questions are, "How many guests? How often, and for how long?" Living with someone sleeping in the main cabin is like camping; it's fun for a while, but the competition for the prime cabin space results in either the guest or the host becoming irritable after about three days.

My own boat is designed for two people full time, four people for two weeks off and on, and six people for a rare weekend. When we have guests we are always twice glad: glad to see them come and glad to see them go. If you plan on long-term guests, then sleeping areas should include some space to dress or change clothing. Infrequent weekend guests, however, can put up with more discomfort and less privacy.

Privacy is at a premium on a small boat. The bunks should be situated to maximize it. Fortunately, this is commonly done by default—one cabin forward, the other aft. However, I recall the maiden voyage of the *Bird of Time,* with six aboard. My daughter and her husband were sleeping in the main cabin with their heads not far from the forward cabin where a lady friend and I slept. On the first night out my friend whispered to me, "Your daughter tells me that everything can be heard aboard a boat."

"That's right," answered my daughter from the next cabin.

Needless to say, all noisemaking activities were curtailed in the forward cabin for the rest of the voyage.

Comfort should also be considered. A common interior layout for boats is a cabin forward with V-berths, followed by the head and the main cabin. The second sleeping cabin runs aft under the cockpit. Is there a law somewhere that says a sailor must get into bed from the top? The recent trend toward side-loading berths is to be applauded. This is generally accomplished in two ways: moving the forward berths slightly aft to get them out of the forepeak, or running the aft berths athwartships.

Moving the forward berths slightly aft and placing the head in the forepeak makes sense. You will spend more time in bed than in the head, so the bunks should get the prime midhull area. Add some strong grab rails in the head, though, in case it needs to be used during rough sea conditions.

The placement of sailboat bunks to run fore and aft is based on sleeping while under way. Inasmuch as passage making is only about 10 percent of cruising, there's no reason not to have a bunk that runs athwartships. Regardless of the bunk layout, though, sleeping at sea is different from sleeping in port. On passage you will be sleeping less (or at least for shorter stretches at a time), because you have to periodically stand watch. When you do sleep, you'll commonly slip into the bunk just vacated by your replacement coming on watch. These sea bunks need to be of minimum width and confined on five sides so that you don't fall out during rough conditions. They are most often the main cabin settees outfitted with bunk boards—which are not necessarily boards, but more commonly and comfortably trapezoidal pieces of stout canvas long and high enough to keep you from falling off the settee (see figure 9.1). This canvas is permanently attached to the settee beneath the cushion. A line is fed through grommets along the upper edge of the bunk board so that it can be fastened securely to the overhead. If bunk boards are added to both the port and starboard settees, there will always be a leeward bunk. In port it is pleasant to have a little more room to move about. For this and other reasons, double berths are preferred in port.

> But a double berth is, after all, something that most cruising couples nowadays would expect to have installed aboard their yacht, and even the single-hander will, with any luck, before many islands are left behind, meet up with many compelling and attractive reasons for wanting to have one, too (Cloughley, *World to the West*).

All bunks are not created equal. Many production models come with a standard 4-inch-thick foam pad. If you take my word for nothing other than this, know that 4 inches of foam just doesn't cut it. Replace those cushions with at least 6 inches of firm, good-quality

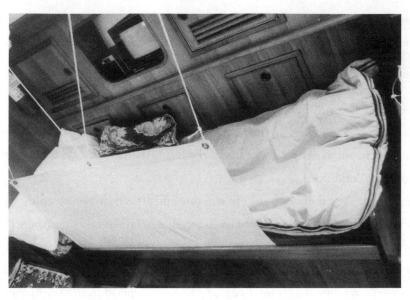

Figure 9.1   Settee Equipped with Bunk Boards

foam. You may even want to replace 6-inch cushions, because the standard boat-cushion foam was not designed for the constant use of cruising. Most large cities have wholesale foam rubber outlets where you can buy something suitable.

If your cruising grounds include any temperate climates where outside temperatures can get nippy, a peculiar malady develops under the foam cushion. Moisture gathers, and the bottom of cushion can get quite wet. This is caused by the migration of warm, moist air from the top of the bunk through the foam to the cold bulkhead below, where it condenses.

Since the source of the moist air is a warm body, one solution is to place a moisture barrier between the warm body and the foam pad. This barrier will block the flow of moisture and keep the bottom of the foam pad dry. We found that placing a plastic liner around the foam pad and underneath the normal cushion cover is a good way to provide the moisture barrier.

Every berth should have its own ventilation, either a hatch or opening port—or preferably both, so that some cross-ventilation occurs. Dorades often do not provide enough air to be comfortable, and they provide no light. Falling to sleep with a view of the stars greatly improves the quality of dreams.

Heads

The term *head* can be used in the specific sense of "toilet" or in the general sense of "the room containing the toilet." The American way—"If one is good, two are better"—breaks down when it comes to marine heads. The need for two complete heads on a cruising vessel of 40 feet or less is quite beyond my comprehension. The root of this lunacy is anybody's guess; my own is that it lies with boat manufacturers capitalizing on the bareboat-charter industry. If you are using a boat for two weeks with another couple, the convenience and privacy of the second head can outweigh the loss of living space. But on a real working, cruising home, let me reemphasize that space is at a premium. A single head in the general sense is adequate—although there is some value in a second head in the specific sense. On our own boat we have a second toilet installed in the forward cabin under a settee, just in case that somewhat balky device in the main head plugs up. This arrangement is a whole lot better than the alternative—inelegant bucket method. The second head also allows us to avoid stumbling aft in the middle of the night on those occasions when guests are aboard. The elimination of a separate compartment for the second head provides extra space that can be used for many more important things—a separate shower stall, for instance.

Using the head compartment itself for a shower is not necessarily a good idea. Taking a shower in the head area requires removing the toilet paper, towels, and so on, from the compartment before showering; wiping down the mirrors, toilet, and so on, after you're finished; and finally replacing all the bits and pieces you removed earlier—quite a daily hassle.

A separate shower is high on many cruisers' want list. It should be large enough to contain the active scrubbing and buffing maneuvers of the largest body aboard without banging knees, elbows, or anything else on bulkheads. However, there is no need to have a standing shower. Aboard the *Bird of Time* we have a sitting model. It is quite comfortable—particularly so on a boat. It is much easier to wash your feet while you're sitting, for example, and the position is also much more stable if the boat's motion becomes erratic.

While on the subject of showers, a few words about shore facilities. We put together a duffel bag for shore showers. It contains a rubber suction mat for inside the shower, a bath mat to stand on outside the shower, a soap dish on a rope, shampoo, and extra quarters—lots of extra quarters. Thus no matter what the condition of the shoreside showers we always had our own island of sanitation, and sufficient money to rinse the soap out of our eyes.

Although plastic, solar-heated hot-water bottles are not a workable, long-term solution to the shower problem, they do have valuable uses. They are easily modified and improved by adding a better nozzle and a longer hose (see figure 9.2). With these changes they can be stowed high up on the mast in the tropical sunlight, with the longer hose run aft to the cockpit. This keeps them out of the way, yet provides ample pressure to rinse the salt water off your body quickly after a dip. We also used this contraption to rinse dishes: We ran the hose down the hatch over the sink and rinsed the soapy water off a sink full of dishes with just a few cups of hot fresh water. The nozzle upgrade provides much better control over water flow than the old nozzle, a foot pump, or the sink tap.

Hot water is a function of cost and convenience. The Moellers insist that they never felt a need for it (Moeller, *Living Aboard*). Adding hot water to a boat is not that complex, however, and if you consider that it also adds an additional 5 to 10 gallons of water storage in case of emergency, it can also be justified for safety's sake. When all other tanks are pumped dry, you can still access the water in the hot-water tank with just a little extra effort by draining the tank.

Hot-water tanks are generally heated by electricity when the boat is attached to shore power, or by a heat exchanger attached to the engine when the motor is running. Often when we were coastal cruising, just running the engine to get into our anchorage would heat enough water for an evening cleanup. I persuaded a dockside friend to install a water heater aboard his boat after several years without one. It may have been a coincidence, but his wife returned from their summer sail proclaiming it the best trip ever.

The alternative to the hot-water heater is heating water on the stove. We have done this on occasion and developed what we call the three-bucket shower: a bucket for hot, a bucket for cold, and a bucket for mixing. This system is most often used for a saltwater shower. It is, however, somewhat inefficient and inconvenient.

Installation of a propane flash hot-water heater reduced our use of the bucket system considerably and extended the luxury of taking hot showers beyond populated ports. Since we already cook with propane, the addition of the water heater—about the size of a large dishpan—was relatively simple. We now have quick, hot fresh water even under sail or on passages.

The addition of a hot-water system to a cruising boat does require the addition of a hot-water *circulation* system to conserve fresh water; this system allows the hot-water tap to be opened without wasting any unheated fresh water. A simple system to install, it consists of a couple of pipe tees and a valve. The tees are installed to allow a bypass line with a valve to be run from the high-pressure side of the hot-water line to the low-pressure side of the pump. The bypass line must be farther from the pump than the last hot-water tap. When the valve is open, hot water flows from the upper end of the system to the pump and is circulated without waste until it reaches the desired tap and the valve is closed.

So far I've been talking about water supply; now let's turn to disposal. Because of pressure from environmentalists, politicians in many parts of the world have enacted laws requiring that small cruising vessels use holding tanks. In my opinion, most of these regulations are ill considered. The culprit here is not the discharge of human waste into the sea, but the overharvesting of clams, crabs, oysters, and fish from the sea and the concentration of human waste resulting from modern collection systems. I have personally observed the feeding frenzies that accompany the pumping of human waste overboard in areas of adequate sea life. These swarms of fish let no morsel reach the bottom. In every area where human waste is a pollution problem, though, you will find that the native waters have also been overfished for decades, if not centuries. A well-flushed body of water with adequate sea life can easily safely and naturally dispose of the amount of waste generated by a marina full of boats while at the same time providing food for a diverse amount of sea life. Rather than stopping the pumping of waste overboard, stop overfishing, stop poisoning the food supply with disinfectants, and let nature take care of the problem the way it has for hundreds of millions of years.

Galley

It is often said that the galley should be close to amidships, where the motion at sea is more comfortable. Let's face it, there is no place on a cruising vessel where motion at sea is comfortable—and most cooking is not done at sea, anyway. The galley should rather be in an area that is open, airy, light, and easy to get out of in case of fire. It should be convenient to the cockpit for snacks and drinks, and convenient to the dining area so the cook can be a part of the conversation while the meal is being prepared. Since very few galleys are in the bow or stern of the boat, most are where they belong, between the dining area and the companionway. A poor location for the galley on boats with center cockpits is in the passageway between the fore and aft cabins. This is generally dark, cramped, and remote from the boat's activities.

The galley should take up only the floor space necessary to supply maximum counter space, and should be shaped to contain the cook as much as possible. Many boats are rigged so that the cook is literally strapped to the stove in rough weather. Would you like to be strapped to something that might burst into flame or toss boiling hot food onto you? Even ignoring such humanitarian concerns, this rig also requires the cooking area to be compact enough that everything needed can be reached from the strapped position.

There are better ways of containing and bracing the cook. For example, a small U-shaped galley can provide balance without restraint. A short, erratic motion in most directions will bring a soft body part in contact with a balance-restoring rigid bulkhead. And by bracing feet and buttocks against opposing counters, the cook can work in almost any attitude the boat can assume. No matter the shape of the galley, however, burns from spilled foods are too common, especially in the Tropics where attire is minimal. It is therefore a good idea for the cook to wear a plastic apron while cooking in a seaway.

Many boats have covers that fit over the stove or sink to add counter space. You can do little cooking without using the stove or the sink, though, and I personally found such covers to be so inconvenient I ceased to use them. I am also not a great believer in fiddles, but a galley without them is impossible to cook in while at sea. Galley fiddles should be at least 3 inches high so they can contain sliding pots and dishes, not just trip them as they pass.

REFRIGERATION

Any refrigeration unit should be as far away as possible from the oven, the engine, and anything else that generates large quantities of heat. It should be well insulated with at least 4 inches of good urethane foam. Front-opening doors, while convenient, waste energy; doors should be top opening and well insulated. We found in the Tropics that our refrigerator seemed to be running more than necessary. We also found that its lid was always cold to the touch. With a giant leap of intuition, we connected the two and fashioned a secondary cover of foam rubber and part of a space blanket. This cover, when placed under the lid, returned the refrigerator to its normal cycle, and we lived happily ever after.

If you opt to return to the Dark Ages and use an icebox, it should not drain into the bilge. This water contains small food particles and spilled refrigerator ingredients. Since the bilge does not drain immediately, it begins to smell bad—and as the bilge smells, so smells the boat. There is no need nowadays to rely on ice. We have a small Adler Barber refrigerator that operated continuously for seven years before its first failure—which only required a fan to be replaced. The new fan turned out to be quieter and more efficient than the original.

There are essentially two kinds of refrigeration systems: cold plates driven directly by the engine, and normal refrigeration driven by an electric compressor off the battery. The argument for cold plates is one of efficiency: If you have to run the engine to charge the battery to run the refrigerator it is more efficient to skip the internal linkage, where energy is lost at each transfer point, and go directly to cold plates. The argument against cold plates is that the engine must be run every day whether you are at sea or the dock. In my mind the arrival of efficient solar panels makes the battery-run refrigerator by far the better selection. Three 3-watt, fixed solar panels kept the refrigerator on our boat running with power to spare from latitude 0 to 59 degrees—with no engine noise, no heat, and no fuel loss.

STOVES

The cooking stove should be gimbaled and placed so that it performs properly on either tack. If space permits, it should have three burners and an oven. Whether you use diesel, alcohol, kerosene, electric, propane, compressed natural gas (CNG), or a solid fuel depends on your needs along with such factors as cost, availability, safety, and ease of cooking.

Solid fuels are cheap, but they are rarely used because they require large volumes of precious shipboard space for fuel storage. In addition, the stoves are generally large, heavy, and not gimbaled, and they produce a lot of heat. They also take a long time to heat up to, and cool down from, cooking temperatures.

CNG is convenient and safe and provides a hot flame for cooking, although not as hot as propane. Someday it may be the preferred fuel for cooking; presently, it is too expensive and unavailable in remote—and some not-so-remote—places around the world.

Propane is convenient, hot, economical, and readily available, but it also can explode if allowed to gather in bilges. The mental picture of their boat exploding like those in James Bond movies is enough to keep many people from using an excellent fuel. Here is Hal Roth's opinion on the matter, from his book *After 50,000 Miles*: "Many people use butane or propane stoves, but after having personally watched two vessels get blown into a million pieces—including their owners, who were carried past *Whisper* on bloody stretchers—I refuse to have bottled gas on board."

If propane is used with good sense, however, it is safe. As Donald Street says in *Ocean Sailing Yacht*,

> *Propane, butane, Butta gas, or whatever—gas is in my view by far the best fuel for cooking on a boat. To be sure, one can blow oneself up with a gas stove. But a good stove, properly installed, and used with normal safety precautions and common sense, will not explode. In any event, I would rather risk getting blown up by a gas stove than die a slow tortuous death fighting with an alcohol or kerosene stove.*

Another advantage of propane cooking is the ease with which you can add other propane appliances, such as the water heater I mentioned above. Although convenient, I do not recommend the propane barbecue, because it does not produce the intense heat of the conventional charcoal unit.

Safe use of propane requires it be stored in a separate, sealed locker that is vented overboard. The propane bottle needs to be fitted with a solenoid valve that can be actuated from a panel in the cooking area. Most books on cruising advise leaving the installation of the propane system to professionals. We did, and they installed copper lines to carry the fuel. We found out later that this was a mistake, because propane can contain contaminants that react badly when exposed to copper. The combination of salt water and these contaminants quickly turn the copper tube into a green gunge. Figure 9.2 shows several sections of copper tubing removed from our boat; all the deterioration occurred within a few weeks. You can imagine, from the size of these leaks, the amount of propane that escaped into our boat during the weeks before we found the source. I repeat, copper tubing should never, never be used for propane lines. If you have professionals install the system, insist that the propane lines be either stainless steel or high-pressure, thermoplastic hose specifically designed to carry propane.*

---

*A couple of interesting things happened during the deterioration of the copper tubing on our boat. First, although the leak was detectable by the human nose, we couldn't find the source when we looked. The odor was more noticeable high in the cabin than near the cabin sole. The bilge never filled with propane, and we didn't blow up even though we had several major leaks and an open flame for half an hour at a time while cooking. It is possible that we were just lucky, but our experience does indicate that not all propane leaks are fatal, and that it takes considerable effort to blow yourself to bits.

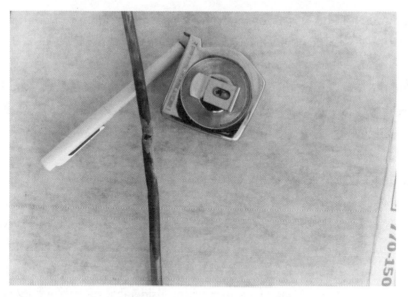

Figure 9.2   *Deterioration of Copper Propane Lines*

Propane requires the use of at least two bottles, one hooked to the system and a full spare to attach in case the tank empties in the middle of cooking Thanksgiving dinner for 75 people. The size of the tanks depends on available storage and your arm strength. Remember, you may have to carry the tanks a great distance in some remote spot to get them refilled.

Refilling the propane bottles in foreign countries, in fact, may require a pigtail attachment with an American fitting on one end, a metric on the other (though hosing and clamps may suffice). We have three 2½-gallon tanks; each will last from three weeks to a month, depending primarily on the amount of baking we do.

Many people select kerosene because it is supposedly available in far-flung ports where propane is not. This may have been the case several years ago, but I found that where kerosene was available, propane was. The reverse, however, was not always true.

I have used kerosene and alcohol—their availability and cost are about the same—but do not recommend them. Before the burner on an alcohol or kerosene stove will function, it must be primed—that is, you must preheat it by burning a small amount of alcohol in a cup surrounding it. The burner needs to be hot enough to vaporize liquid fuel. If it isn't, the liquid produces a large flame that will readily ignite any nearby flammable material.

The number of shipboard fires caused by alcohol and kerosene is significantly greater than those caused by other fuels. In fact, I suspect that more boats have been destroyed by kerosene than propane. Even if the fire is contained without flame damage, save a little loss of arm hair, the smoke from the inefficient burning of the fuel produces a soot that covers most of the overhead and walls—a troublesome cleaning task. In addition, both alcohol and kerosene smell strong enough to induce seasickness in those who are borderline at the time of exposure.

Alcohol is considered safer than kerosene because the fires it produces can be put out with water, whereas kerosene fires require a special extinguisher. On the other hand, alcohol can be considered less safe because its flame is not readily visible; it's entirely possible for you to place flammable material or your hand unknowingly into an open flame. In the case of your hand, the warning is instantaneous and painful. In the case of flammable material, it may not come until the material is burning with considerable vigor. Nor does alcohol supply much heat. Alcohol ovens are almost useless, because the fuel does not keep the oven at a cooking temperature.

There are more problems: Even without flare-ups, kerosene produces a gray film on the overhead above the stove after a few months' use. In addition, kerosene burners require pricking to keep them clean and functioning properly. And alcohol, when burned, produces water. In higher latitudes, where boats are often kept closed in the winter months, this can produce rain indoors.

The Moellers ran a test on cooking fuels, which if not rigorous was at least scientifically reported so the data can be evaluated (Moeller, *Living Aboard*). They compared the heating efficiency of various fuels; figure 9.3 shows the results. Alcohol is the least-efficient fuel; propane, the most efficient, boils water two-and-a-half times faster than alcohol.

The advantages of diesel fuel are that it is already aboard most cruising boats, it's available everywhere, and it's relatively inexpensive. Diesel stoves are especially popular in the upper latitudes, where cabin heat is needed most of the time. Diesel has some of the same drawbacks as solid fuels: The stoves are inconvenient, they generate considerable heat in the cabin, and there are presently no gimbaled stoves that burn diesel available on the market. Cooking with diesel also imparts a strong diesel smell to the boat.

Although electric stoves don't provide the instant heat that gaseous fuels do, electric cooking is convenient, safe, and available as long as the generator has fuel. Their drawback

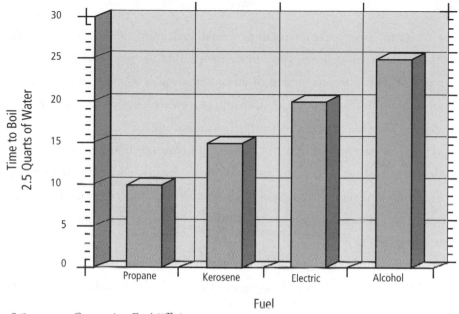

Figure 9.3   *Comparing Fuel Efficiency*

is, of course, the need for a generator and the loss of space that entails. Still, electric cooking eliminates the need for a second fuel-storage system, since the generator can run on the same fuel as the engine. It also opens the door for you to add many other appliances normally considered too power hungry for boats without generators.

Introducing a generator large enough to provide electric cooking is a major decision. There are many reasons that most cruising boats do not have generators of this size; space and budget are the two most common. However, because it is so convenient, electricity is still commonly used dockside on many boats with fuels other than propane or CNG. These boats carry a small two-burner portable electric stove for use in port.

Regardless of what fuel you use, be sure that adequate fire protection is easily accessible. This includes both a quick-acting fuel shut-off valve and fire extinguishers rated for fires caused by the cooking fuel you're using. A fire on the stove should not prevent the cook from access to the shut-off valve, fire-protection devices, or the galley exit. Curtains or other flammable material should not hang over the stove where a sudden flare-up could ignite them. Last—and maybe least—ventilation should be provided to remove smoke and odors from the cooking area. On our boat the dorade vent immediately over the stove has been equipped with a small 2-amp fan that greatly improves its efficiency as a galley vent.

SINKS

Don't try to "save" space by installing a small galley sink. It should be a stainless-steel double model, large enough that you can submerge a dinner plate and all but your largest cooking pot or pan. The sink should drain on either tack, which in most cases means it should be on your boat's centerline. A deep and narrow sink is preferable to a shallow, wide one, because it's less likely to spill when the boat is heeling.

Even if you have pressurized fresh water (hot, cold, or both), you should have foot pumps for fresh and salt water. The saltwater pump greatly reduces the demand for fresh water, since much of your cleaning can be done with salt water. At sea and in areas where fresh water is at a premium, we always wash the dishes in salt water and finish with a hot freshwater rinse.

The spouts on the sinks should be high enough to allow a large pot to be filled. Next to the sink a counter that slopes slightly toward the sink will provide an area to drain and air-dry dishes when you're at rest in a harbor.

The only simpler method is the Bahamian wash, a method generally used after eating in the cockpit. You simply stack the dishes and casually drop them over the side. Remember, this only works in the Bahamas, where you typically anchor in crystal-clear water only 6 to 8 feet deep. The next morning you don mask and snorkel and retrieve the dishes, which have been picked clean by the hungry, happy ocean scavengers. Give them a quick rinse in hot fresh water and leave them to dry on the sloping drainboard; this is dishwashing at its simplest, with no harsh chemicals introduced into the environment.

STOWAGE

Stowage in the galley is not a whole lot different from storage in a kitchen, except that there's less room, and the "kitchen" moves. Items with special uses or rarely used must be left at home. A single utensil has to fill a variety of applications. What you used *most* on shore is probably what you should take on board.

A waffle iron seems an odd contraption to be controversial, but I have seen one mentioned in two different books.

> *Not helpful: anything that takes up space and is not used often; for example, a waffle iron* (Rousmaniere, *The Sailing Lifestyle*).

One of our favorite items is a cast iron waffle maker that fits over one burner on
any stove. We wouldn't change it. The waffles it makes are superior to any we have ever
had (Moeller, *Living Aboard*).

Let me throw in with Jan and Bill Moeller; we also have a cast-iron waffle maker that
fits on the burner. It makes little heart-shaped waffles. Anybody against heart-shaped waffles should be kept under close surveillance.

We also heard many tales of the need for a pressure cooker while cruising. Dutifully
we purchased one and stowed it aboard. We used it once, maybe twice; most of the time it
just corroded quietly in its locker, taking up valuable space we could have used for other
things. A 4- or 5-gallon pot *should* find its way aboard, however. A pot of this size is necessary for cooking up a batch of crabs, lobsters, or other large delicacies. Most people store
this pot in the aft lazarette or similar spot, filling it with coiled line until needed.

Galley lockers need to be subdivided. Not only do large, cavernous lockers require you
to shift their contents to get at what's in the bottom or back, but any items stowed in these
large open areas tend to shift while under way, too. This shifting can produce annoying rat-
tles or, worse, breakage when a sea is running. All lockers, especially galley lockers, require
doors and shelves with large fiddles, to keep items from flying across the cabin when the
locker door is opened on the wrong tack.

There are many handy little racks made for dishes and cups, but I am not one for hanging cups or utensils in a boat—too much swinging. Most sailors end up with plastic din-
nerware and glassware, but I loathe drinking wine from a plastic goblet. We toasted the
sundown in many a remote tropical paradise with margaritas and mai-tais served over ice
tinkling in a real glass. I will admit that the glass stowage on board our boat took a little
more space and some ingenuity, but it was quite secure. We simply lined the shelf with a
piece of 4-inch-thick foam rubber with cutouts or slots for each glass (see figure 9.4); we
found we broke no more glasses on board than we did on shore.

Cooking knives also require special stowage. Good-quality knives are generally stowed
in a wall-mounted wooden rack—leaving me to imagine the ship taking a healthy roll and
the knives a not-so-healthy flight around the cabin. Figure 9.5 shows one solution for the
knife-stowage problem: They are stowed in a block safely in a drawer.

Food stowage is primarily common sense. Keep the dry foods dry, the canned foods
from rusting, the fresh food from spoiling, and the cockroaches at bay. Cardboard and paper

Figure 9.4   Glassware Stowage

absorb moisture and are breeding grounds for cockroach eggs. All cardboard should be removed from food items before stowage. Debby didn't corner the market on Tupperware, but she did force the company to put on an extra shift before our cruise. Other than that,

Figure 9.5   In-Drawer Knife Stowage

everybody who has cruised has her or his own special, clever ideas for stowing things. Here is one of ours.

Before each passage we remove the ice cubes from the freezer compartment in our refrigerator and pack the small space with boil-a-bag freezer meals. You can get a surprising number of these into a small space if you remove them from their boxes. The meals are reasonably palatable, and during those first few days when we're getting our sea legs, we can prepare tasty food with a minimum of effort below.

Don't forget garbage stowage. Indiscriminate tossing of garbage overboard is not, and maybe never was, a thing that can be tolerated. Not only do we have plastic-littered beaches, we have a plastic-littered ocean as well. In one 12-hour period on a passage we recorded each item of floating garbage we spotted *larger* than a football. Although we were 1,500 miles off the nearest shore, our sightings came every five minutes or less.

Proper garbage management means that all plastic, paper, and other burnable garbage should be stowed on board for future disposal ashore. I am not a proponent of onboard garbage compactors for cruising sail-boats; if you have one, use it only for burnables. On board our boat we have a 13-gallon bag next to the companionway stairs (see figure 9.6). When this bag is filled it is transferred to a 33-gallon plastic bag and stowed in the aft lazarette. In this manner we can carry three to four weeks worth of garbage. Nobody should be at sea longer than four weeks, but if you plan to be, plan for more storage space as well.

Food and edible items should be separated from the burnables and thrown over the side, where they can be eaten and returned to the food chain. Cans and bottles are processed differently, depending on the space available and your

Figure 9.6   *Intermediate Garbage Stowage*

proximity to shore. I think that all commercial and large cruising boats should bring every-thing back from the sea. Because there are only a few small sailing ships in remote deep waters, however, sinking these bottles and cans is still acceptable. Either fill them completely with salt water before tossing them overboard, or open both ends of each can and break any bottles. Aluminum cans are a problem because they are so light: They must be torn com-pletely in two or they may not sink properly.

How you finally dispose of stored garbage will depend at least in part on where your passage concludes. Many places you visit will not have proper solid waste disposal systems; some that do may not want your garbage. In other areas, disposal is not considered a prob-lem. For example, on reaching a remote Pacific island after a two-week passage I went ashore with my garbage and asked where I should dispose of it. The official was quite pleasant when he said, "Throw it in the bushes." I am sure that the islander who found me digging a large hole in the sand in a remote spot and burning my store of garbage thought I was crazy. I spent several hours reducing the garbage to the smallest ash, then covering the whole mess with several feet of sand. I consider the effort required to dispose of garbage properly a cruis-ing cost, and urge others to do likewise.

Dining Areas

Have you ever noticed that almost all human endeavor other than making war or love has to do with ingesting food or drink? Christmas has its dinner, the Fourth of July its pic-nic, even baseball its hot dog. It is therefore not surprising to find that much of the pleasure of cruising revolves around enjoyable dining. We all know that it is possible to eat in almost any situation. However, a real sense of security can come from eating a good meal in com-fort. Those who understand cruising ask not "How many does it sleep?" but "How many does it feed?"

Gracious dining revolves around the table. It should be large enough to serve at least four, with room for serving dishes and the necessary accoutrements as well. I personally pre-fer room to serve six. The table can be fixed or gimbaled. A gimbaled table is designed to make eating under way comfortable. Figure 9.7 shows a typical gimbaled table at a 30-degree heel; obviously, at this heel your table will be on your knees or directly under your chin. Neither position is conducive to elegant dining.

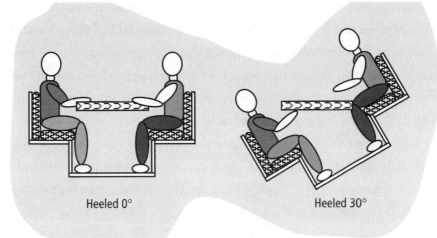

Heeled 0°   Heeled 30°

Figure 9.7   *Gimbaled Table in Use*

In truth, though, elegant dining is not usually part of passage making. We ate very few meals at the table during passages. Most of the time everybody ate with a bowl 2 inches from their chin, a cup between their knees, their back against a bulkhead, and one foot wedged against the mast or other stable fixture to keep them in place. Since the gimbaled table is useful only on passages, and then only at a few select times, I judge it unnecessary.

I have met many cruisers who say the same for the hallowed fiddles on dining tables. They have tables without these traditional fiddles and seem to be well fed and none the worse for any missed meals.

The dining table is generally close to amidships, either along the centerline or offset to one side. Placing it on the centerline—generally seen in smaller, narrower vessels—has always seemed to me some naval architect's cruel hoax of maximum use of space. This location does allow the folded-up table to be used more easily as a cocktail table—because access to the settees is easier—but gracious dining is a different matter. Half the party is on one side of the boat, half on the other; each side is perched on the edge of the settee, with the edge of the table just out of reach. Besides this inconvenience, the mast is generally in the way, making conversation, if nothing else, difficult.

Needless to say, I like a dining area with the table off the centerline. This frees up the main fore-and-aft passageway for traffic; it makes access to the settee around the table more difficult, however, like entering a booth in a restaurant. Most people can tolerate that for meals, but remember that the main cabin is not used only for dining; thus it's useful for this table to have drop leaves and an adjustable height, to allow easier access to the settees. The drop leaves also allow the table to be folded, lowered, and used for cocktails. A benchmark to shoot for is a U-shaped settee with space for six to eat in close comfort, and four to dine in splendor. Eighteen to 20 linear inches of table length is necessary for each diner.

The main cabin is not the only dining area on a cruising yacht. Eating in the cockpit is an enjoyable break and pleasant in the Tropics or on warm evenings in higher latitudes. You can dine or entertain in the cockpit without a table: Serve the meal buffet style, as long as each person has a comfortable place to sit.

Eating while under way in the big, bumpy water is a little more difficult. Plates, bowls, and cups with nonskid bottoms are less likely to slide out of reach; a gimbaled drink holder is also useful.

Cabin Heating and Ventilation

VENTILATION

Cabin ventilation is another area in which designers follow the mistaken idea that cruising sailboats are used mostly at sea. Thomas Young, who presents a detailed and informative chapter on ventilation in *Offshore Yachts,* cites Rod Stephens, the inventor of the dorade air vent, as recommending the following formula to determine the air volume needed to keep a yacht properly ventilated:

$$A_i = B \times LWL \quad \text{where:} \qquad\qquad Equation\ 9.1$$

A_i is the total intake area in square inches,

B is the beam in feet, and

LWL is the waterline length in feet.

This formula yields 400 to 500 square inches of inlet area for the average cruising boat, which is equivalent to three or four 4-inch vents and one 8-inch vent or large hatch in 16 knots of wind. That's not much fresh air. It may be adequate for heavy weather, when safety is at stake, but for the other 99 percent of cruising this amount of ventilation is woefully inadequate.

The answer is hatches, hatches, and hatches; the more hatches, the more air below. Get as many opening hatches as you can without compromising the safety of your vessel. Hatches can be left open when under way in settled weather as long as they are dogged down the minute things change. Water down open hatches is responsible for the sinking of many ships.

I have almost 2,600 square inches of opening hatches and ports, not counting five small dorades. I consider this amount of ventilation adequate in the Tropics. Most cruising yachts have only about a third as much. It is one thing to choose to sit in the cockpit, and another to be forced out of the cabin because it is too hot and stuffy.

When considering ventilation, consider that many islands in the Tropics are not in the trades. The wind does not blow 16 knots all the time in these harbors; much of the time it doesn't blow at all. In such calm, hot, humid spots, happiness is an oscillating fan—even a nonoscillating fan.

In the battle for a cool interior, deck color helps. Dark-colored decks absorb heat and radiate it below. The difference even between white and gray is astonishing and can be felt quite easily with bare feet. White, however, produces a lot more glare than gray, and this can be more annoying than gray's increased heat.

In tropical harbors, the heat produced by the sun's radiation on the deck and cabin top can be controlled by an awning. It should shade the entire cabin and as much of the cockpit and deck as possible. A secondary benefit is that it will shield open hatches and ports from tropical showers.

Remember that although any opening hatch or port should have adequate screening to keep out the little biting varmints, this same screening will restrict about 50 percent of your airflow; plan your number of hatches accordingly. If you choose to go without screens consider that when the number of these biting critters becomes intolerable, you will have to close the ports, thereby really degrading ventilation. There are, of course, a few warm areas where bugs are not a problem, so if possible your screens should be easily removable to take advantage of maximum airflow.

The main hatch is a little different, because it opens in two planes, vertical and horizontal. A screen that slips into the main hatchboard slots is a neat way to screen the vertical opening. The horizontal opening can be covered by a screen put up with Velcro. Another trick for odd-shaped openings is to use a piece of screening material with a chain sewn into its hem. The weight of the chain will hold the screen in place on any horizontal or nearly horizontal surface, regardless of the shape of the opening.

The forgotten weapon against heat in the Tropics is hull insulation. No boat that people intend to live on should be built without this. (The insulation in our own boat nullified the effects of the sun on the black hull in the Tropics.) In higher latitudes insulation not only keeps the boat warmer with less heat, but also keeps the hull from sweating.

HEATING

If high-latitude cruising is part of your plan, you need to consider heating as well. Your choice of heater will depend on your choice of fuel, and you have a narrower range to pick from than for cooking. The most common heating fuels are diesel, propane, solid fuels, and electricity.

For short stays and when you're in a slip that has power, small electrical heaters are probably the most convenient. These come in various sizes, and most have a thermostat. Even if you have to replace a cheap heater every two or three years, it's still probably the most economical choice.

A common problem on board, however, is that the electric outlet circuit is often a 10-amp. This limits the size of your heater to less than 1,200 watts. Taking into account the normal dockside service, and to give your circuits a break, I recommend a heater of about 1,000 watts. These small-wattage units are harder to find, but they are less bulky (therefore easier to stow), they cost less, and you can use multiple units to spread the heat around the boat more efficiently. You can get either a modern ceramic disk heater (about $180) or an old-fashioned wire-resistance-type heater (about $15).

Other heating methods need to be considered for when you're swinging on the hook or under way. Solid fuels can be used in a fireplace. Boat fireplaces come in several models, ranging from plain to fancy. They generally burn wood, charcoal, or coal and, of course, must be vented to the outside with a flue. A fireplace gives a warm, romantic, cozy atmosphere to a cabin. The flickering light of the flame captures the attention and casts shadows on a dimly lit cabin, providing a special ambience to quiet evening conversation.

The Moellers warn that if you use coal it should be the hard variety, because the soft kind produces large quantities of soot both inside and out (Moeller, *Living Aboard*). The quantity of solid fuel needed for a cruising boat can be a limiting factor, because on-board stowage is limited. Nonetheless, many people go from port to port buying whatever is available—Presto logs, charcoal, coke, and so on.

The advantage of propane as a heat source is its simplicity, especially if the fuel is already aboard for cooking. Propane heaters—like propane water heaters—require thermocouples to provide instant fuel shutoff if the flame is extinguished, and an oxygen-depletion device to shut off the gas if the oxygen level in the cabin drops too low.

Because propane combustion is clean—that is, it does not produce smoke—some propane heaters are not vented to the outside. This is a mistake. All heaters should be vented to the outside. Combustion always produces carbon dioxide and carbon monoxide—colorless, odorless gases that are deadly to air-breathing mammals. Carbon monoxide poisoning kills many people every year on and off boats.

The vent to the outside for propane heaters does not need to be as large as the flue for heaters that burn solid fuels, but it does need to be there. The vent also will get rid of another of propane's bothersome by-products, H_2O.

The major advantage of diesel as a heating fuel is that it minimizes the number of fuels on board. When you consider that it has neither of the major disadvantages of the other two fuels—that is, solid fuel's bulk and propane's tendency to explode—diesel becomes a compelling choice. Most diesel stoves feature a glass door so that you can watch the flickering flames and enjoy much of the same atmosphere that solid fuels provide.

There are several kinds of diesel heaters or furnaces. The furnaces generally use forced air or hot water and have thermostat regulation. These units operate almost unnoticed, provide a more uniform cabin temperature with fewer hot spots than heaters, and do not take up living space on the boat. Normally, they are tucked away in some secluded locker. These benefits are not without cost: Furnace units have higher power demands to keep the fan, pump, and glow plug operating, and since they have more moving parts and are so complex, they require more maintenance. Furnaces also produce a penetrating roar—or what seems like one in a secluded anchorage. It is not too noticeable inside the cabin, but it can be annoying to those outside. And there have been reports of the hot gases escaping from the vent melting fenders.

A heater is a simpler piece of machinery. You will, however, need a pump to keep it supplied with fuel (either a continuous-demand pump, or one to fill a small gravity-fed day tank from the normal fuel tanks), and a fan to circulate the heat throughout the cabin so that the warm air doesn't simply sit at the top of the cabin.

Heater flames can be blown out if gusts of air are forced down the flue. When this occurs the fuel flowing into the heater does not immediately burn. If you are present and quick, you can shut off the fuel. If not, two things can happen: Clouds of noxious gas can be emitted from the heater; then, when the heater does reignite, it is generally with an unnerving if not damaging explosion. The solution is to add an extra fan to provide a forced draft up the flue when necessary. This will keep the heater flame from being blown out (but it does draw a bit more power).

Using a small gravity-fed day tank along with external fans gives you flexibility. You can turn off the fans if your battery power is low, and the stove will still produce enough heat to prevent hypothermia, if not provide comfort. The day tank is also of value for those people who don't like things to go bump in the night. While the heater burns at night, the demand pumps have an annoying little habit of going off periodically, and they sound amazingly like a dinghy bumping your boat.

Heaters need to be situated away from combustible walls or insulated with metal reflecting shields. They also need to be placed where you won't accidentally bump into them or their flues. Furnaces and heaters both require a minimum length of stovepipe to produce enough draft to make the things work properly. Getting that length, finding available floor or wall space, and avoiding locations where downdrafts from sails and waves might extinguish the fire must be considered when you install the unit.

The stack itself can become very hot and can produce an instantaneous second-degree burn with the slightest contact—and any motion of the boat increases the probability of such contact. You can prevent this by surrounding the stack with a stainless-steel sleeve, which never gets hot enough to burn. I often seek it out when I return below from an extra-cold watch and grip it like a hot cup to warm my numb hands quickly. The sleeve also helps radiate heat from the stack into the cabin.

A major advantage of heaters is the drying that results from heating. This drying occurs because hot air can hold more moisture than can cold. However, to get less moisture, the hot moist air must be removed from the cabin and replaced with cold dry air. Otherwise the evaporated moisture simply recondenses when the air cools. In cold damp climates it is necessary to vent hot air to dry the cabin.

Cabin Lighting and Decoration

All captains have a list of things to do before cruising. Very few of those lists say, "Decorate the cabin." Even real sailors, however, can cruise in pleasant surroundings. Psychology has shown that color and light strongly affect temperament and disposition. So if you're feeling surly, you should closely read and apply what you learn from this section.

Lighting and decorating a cabin, if not simple, is at least straightforward. The trick is to make a small space comfortable and to make it appear both pleasant and larger. Dim light and dark colors are depressing. Because most boats lack light and many have lots of dark varnished wood inside, the average boater starts from a losing position.

NATURAL LIGHT SOURCES

Every cabin should have the maximum sources of daylight consistent with boat safety. With the arrival of Lexan, light sources can be safely added to most boats in a number of ways. Replace solid hatch covers with transparent Lexan covers. Replace the wooden slides in the main companionway hatches with Lexan slides. If the main companionway hatch has doors, replace the wooden panels with Lexan.

Another way to add light to a cabin is to increase the size of existing ports or to add more—but only in areas with minimum exposure, where additional ports will not compromise safety. Once you find a safe location, consider the effect the port will have on the looks of the boat.

Additional ports can usually be installed in the aft cabin, in the wall surface that opens into the cockpit. Jan and Bill Moeller suggest placing a port on the forward part of the cabin trunk (Moeller, *Living Aboard*). This location sounds inviting, since it would allow you to look forward without going on deck and would certainly add more light to the forward cabin. An opening port in this location would be exposed to the wind and an excellent source of fresh air; however, safety considerations make me hesitant to recommend it.

The forward bulkhead of the cabin trunk can take considerable battering from breaking seas during a blow. If I did install such a port, though, I would certainly carry a heavy plywood gusset to cover the opening in case of failure.

Deadlights can be installed in overheads to get natural light into small compartments such as the head. The best deadlights are made from prisms. These are more expensive, but they gather considerably more light. Remember that since deadlights are always set flush with the deck, they will be walked on, and are a potential source of leaks.

Mirrors are not only functional, but can also make an area appear larger and lighter. The obvious place for mirrors is in the head. Another small space is the sleeping cabins; try a full-length mirror on the back of the door. Even the main cabin can be improved by the addition of a mirror or two. I recall one boat where an entire athwartships bulkhead on the forward end of the main cabin was a mirror. The cabin looked light, bright, and enormous. I have often wondered why more people don't make similar uses of mirrors.

ARTIFICIAL LIGHT SOURCES

So far I have talked only about natural light, but proper use of artificial illumination is necessary as well. Regardless of what you have read, the sun does not always shine on cruisers. Some days are dark and dreary. For those days, and at night, you'll need artificial light. Also, you have more control over the use and placement of artificial than natural light. It can be used for concentrated light in work areas, as general background illumination, or to highlight specific spaces.

Fluorescent fixtures give off much more light for less power than incandescent bulbs and should be used to provide high levels of illumination in work areas such as the galley. Strategically placing fluorescent bulbs throughout the cabin can also provide good light for working. Aboard the *Bird of Time* we have three double fluorescent lights, which light the entire cabin if necessary. Several single fluorescent tubes under the galley cabinets brightly illuminate the countertop.

Overhead fluorescent lighting should be mixed with normal incandescent lights. The correct location of incandescent bulbs can change the tone of the cabin from bright for work to warm for entertaining or relaxing. Wall-mounted lamps can be used for reading or for accent. These lamps are generally on swivels that allow the light to be directed as desired. We find that directing one or two onto the overhead provides just the right amount of additional background light for a romantic candlelight dinner.

Many cruisers claim that you can't go cruising without kerosene lamps. Come on, get into the 20th century before it's over. Kerosene lamps should go the way of the candle snuffer. With the arrival of solar, wind, and water generators, there is always sufficient power to use electric lighting. Kerosene lamps might seem romantic, but they are dirty and smelly, and if you don't trim the wick properly, they give off black soot that will layer the overhead. Even when they are burning correctly, soot still builds up, unnoticed until you happen to wipe a spot; then the entire overhead needs to be cleaned. Kerosene lamps also pose a significant hazard aboard a boat. If they tip over, break, or spill, you have the Chicago fire in your cabin. Think how easy it is to tip things over in a boat that itself tips over, and how many fires have been started in cowboy movies by the breaking of a kerosene lamp. If that's not enough, think of how hot they get, and of how the exhaust from the chimney can burn wood, fiberglass, or personal parts placed carelessly in the way.

I once chartered a boat with a huge swinging kerosene lamp in the galley that was the pride of the owner's wife. It was large enough to illuminate an entire messhall at the Running "K" Ranch. Fortunately, the lamp was removable, but the owner's wife was unable to comprehend my insistence that she take her lamp off the boat while I was aboard.

I had two small kerosene lamps aboard our boat at one point, but after numerous cleanings of the overhead and a few burns, I finally relegated them to lighting the cockpit during late-summer-night cockpit parties. Even there the damn things performed improperly, getting forever blown out. Fortunately, with the discovery of two cheap and South Pacific–looking flashlights (see figure 9.8), I retired the kerosene lamps completely.

Figure 9.8   *Sensible Cockpit Lighting*

COLOR

If you have exhausted all your options for adding light to the interior of the boat, turn to color. Much can be done through its prudent use. Light colors make things look larger; dark colors make them appear smaller. Since your space is already small and may be filled with dark wood, every spot available to decorate should be given light colors. White overheads and countertops add space and light. Colors also add the illusion of temperature to space. Warm colors are yellows, oranges, reds, and browns; cool are greens, turquoises, and blues. Since most boating is done in warm climates, the cooler colors might be a good choice for a color scheme. Regardless of your choice, it is always good to have a little of the opposite color family as an accent. The warm brown wood colors automatically provide that for cool-color schemes.

Because too much detail in a small space adds clutter and makes the space appear smaller, don't use busy patterns and plaids. If you must use some bold patterns, use them sparingly. Reduce the clutter of the cabin itself. A cabin filled with many small objects looks small and crowded.

Openness adds to the livability of the cabin. It is true that open space reduces the boat's stiffness, because of the loss of bulkheads, and that storage space may be lost; still, an unbroken line of sight gives a feeling of spaciousness. The right mix of storage space and open area is a personal matter, of course, but too many people add cute, clever little storage places until their boat looks like the inside of a Gemini space capsule. Why do you think they call them *capsules*?

FLOOR COVERINGS

The floor coverings most commonly found in boats are carpet and wooden floors. (I have never seen a tile floor in a boat, although I don't know why it wouldn't work.) Carpet is a less expensive floor treatment than wood. A light-colored carpet adds light to the cabin, but it may be difficult to keep clean. A tweed or variegated pattern will show less dirt than a solid color. A very fine nap is soft but tends to hold onto lint, string, hair, and the like, especially under the attack of boat vacuum cleaners, which do not have the power of their shoreside cousins. For the same reason shag carpet, with its long nap, is also difficult to keep clean on a boat.

Nylon or polyester are preferable to natural fibers or rayon for carpets. These synthetics wear much longer, are unaffected by wetness or prolonged dampness, and dry more quickly when accidentally soaked. Rubber-backed carpets should be made of closed-cell sponge rubber, which doesn't hold moisture.

Many boats have beautiful teak- and holly-wood floors—which are also dark and tend to get dents and dings if something heavy is dropped on them. They can be cold on the feet in high latitudes, too, but it is a shame to cover this beauty with a carpet. We solved this conflict aboard our own boat by using some small scatter rugs. The rugs added color to the floor, were easily removed for cleaning or washing, and, in place, allowed us to cross the cabin without once touching the cold wooden floors. The rugs had a closed-cell rubber backing that kept them stationary no matter what the angle of heel or who was standing on them.

WINDOW COVERINGS

Window coverings for boats tend toward the boring, especially if you settle for those that come with your craft. If you go for something a little more original, be careful of patterns. Go easy on the floral and nautical motifs; remember, the area you are decorating is small.

There are many devices for attaching or hanging curtains on boats, all intended to keep the curtain from swinging while the boat is under way. Most involve rods on the top *and* bottom. When I added curtains to my cabin I fussed for months, because to me all these standard solutions were singularly unattractive.

The problem vexed me until I realized that the curtains would only swing when the boat was under way—and that we only needed curtains when the boat was not under way. So we hung our curtains on normal curtain hardware and held them in place while asea with tie-backs and Velcro (see figure 9.9).

Although hanging pictures aboard a tippy boat can be problematic, a few pictures can add that final touch that makes a boat a home. The Moellers drilled small holes in the center of the top and bottom of each picture frame to nail it to the wall (Moeller, *Living Aboard*). Bulkheads are often thinner than shoreside walls, so take care that nails don't go clear through them. We preferred self-adhesive Velcro tape. Use plenty of it.

Figure 9.9   *Sensible Window Coverings*

Stowage

If you are a typical cruiser, from the time you buy your boat in "sail-away" condition—which, by the way, means that it floats—until you are ready to cruise, you will place in the neighborhood of 8 tons of crap aboard. Let me deal with the logistics of this maneuver.

Debby and I spent 18 months getting the boat ready before we left. When the final Friday night came we had already disposed of or stored most of our possessions. We loaded all those that remained aboard our pickup and headed for the marina. The truck looked like something out of *Grapes of Wrath:* The wheels were squat, and various paraphernalia hung out on all sides. The only reason that all this junk made it to the marina was the copious amounts of rope we used to lash the agglomeration together.

We arrived at the marina after midnight. Now, the marina was in a part of the city where, had we left our equipment in the pickup overnight, none of it would have been there to unload the next morning—a tempting solution, since the boat was moored on the visitor's dock a full quarter mile from the marina gate. However, we spent the next few hours hauling these possessions to the foredeck of the boat, which by luck or good planning was spacious.

The cold, gray light of morning revealed a monstrous pile on the foredeck that we then needed to stow below—and as we'd already spent 18 months stowing necessary items aboard I saw no available room or solution. In my usual captain's manner, I busied myself with something important to do on deck and relegated the chore to Debby. By midafternoon she not only had everything below but also out of sight and cataloged. Moral: *Boats have an amazing amount of storage space; Debby does impossible tasks; both the above.*

Before attempting to stow anything, go through your entire boat and catalog the available storage space. (This process uncovered three spaces on our boat with no access.) Note the location of each space and its approximate size. Then plan a general layout to help you put the right item in the right place. Heavy items need to go low and in the center of the boat, if possible. Breakable items need to be protected against impact, and those items that can be damaged by water need a dry location. Items that are used constantly need to be handy.

Storage space is divided into drawers, shelves, hanging lockers, areas under and behind things, and bilge areas. Each of these spaces has unique features.

Drawers are handy for small items or items that need extra protection from the damp. Drawers on boats should be designed so that they don't open during rough weather and heeling. A common design features a notch cut out of the base, so that when the drawer is closed you must lift it before you can open it. A problem with drawers is that they do not make maximum use of the space. There is always wasted space around and in back of a drawer. If too much space has been left behind one of yours, you can regain some of it by lengthening the drawer. We rebuilt eight of the drawers aboard the *Bird of Time* in this manner.

Shelves are better than drawers for making optimum use of space. Most shelf space should be closed, with a door to keep the items in place. Open shelves can be used for books—but must have not only a fiddle but also a guardrail about 6 inches above the shelf to hold the books during rough weather. Shelf sizes should be varied. You need large ones to store large objects, but too many large shelves waste space. Items that you need often are relatively easy to reach in shelf storage.

Hanging lockers are a little like shoreside closets: They are very convenient and keep clothes in good shape, but waste considerable space. Nevertheless, you need some hanging locker space for bulky clothing. One of those lockers should be reserved for hanging wet clothes. It should be well ventilated, heated if possible to assist in drying, close to the companionway, and drained, so water doesn't pool in its bottom. Aboard our boat the separate shower compartment fits all of these requirements and therefore doubles as a wet locker. We installed a removable clothes rod for storing wet clothing on hangers when we're not using the compartment as a shower.

The space "under and behind things" is all those odd-shaped nooks and crannies under and behind settees, bunks, and so on. The odd shapes of these spaces make stowage awkward. And because of their location, access is inconvenient, and the stored objects are subjected to considerable dampness and occasional free water.

Bilge stowage is found below the floorboards of the boat. Modern round-bottomed boats have less of this space than the traditional wineglass-shaped hulls. This space is good for those items that are heavy and impervious to salt water. We found out, however, that aluminum beverage cans are *not* impervious to salt water: The aluminum is thin and corrodes quickly. Two weeks in a bilge and the beverages once contained in the cans will become part of the bilge liquid.

Items that need to be stored aboard can be divided into several basic categories: food, clothing, books, charts, hazardous materials, small parts, and bulky objects. Each of these items has different storage requirements. (I discussed food storage earlier in this chapter under "Galley.")

The battle for clothing storage on board is a losing one. Everybody takes too many clothes. Instead, though, your cruising destination should dictate how much and what type of clothing you take. Limit your wardrobe; mold and mildew will get to clothes jammed into a hanging locker filled with little-used garments. Also, try to make your clothing serve more than one use. A wardrobe of clothing that can be layered is the most flexible. Off-season clothing can be stowed in giant self-locking plastic bags along with a little dehumidifier, and put in a less accessible locker. Many items of clothing take up less room when rolled rather than folded. And knitted clothing that is rolled is virtually wrinkle-free when taken out of storage.

Space for books is always at a premium. There are books on sailing and navigation; cruising guides; books on weather and nature; general reference books like dictionaries and atlases; and books for enjoyment. We had close to 10 linear feet of book space on board our boat and found that to be insufficient. Whatever space you do have should be safely away from water. Salt water will turn your favorite books into mush in a few hours. We lost several treasured volumes to an undiscovered leak.

Chart storage is always a problem unless you intend to sail around the world using a couple of *National Geographic* world maps. I may be a little fanatical, but I have a stack of charts over 5 inches thick and growing. Charts are darn expensive these days, but I figure the best boat insurance is to know where you are and where you are going. It used to be that you could pick up old charts from commercial boaters who found it less expensive to buy new ones than to take the time to update the old ones. No more; the price of charts today causes even the big boats to keep updating.

Because of their importance and expense, then, charts require special storage areas. Rolling them up in tubes is hard on them, hard on the user, and just not feasible for a large number of charts. Storing them under the bunk pad is all right for short summer cruises, but the number you need for any reasonable bluewater trip will make for mighty bumpy sleeping. Some chart tables feature storage under the tabletop—if the charts are folded in half. The ideal space is a storage area large enough to store them flat and unfolded. There are only two possible spaces for this on most boats—over or under a double bunk. We store about 150 charts under the forward bunk (see figure 9.10); Jan and Bill Moeller store theirs over the bunk (Moeller, *Living Aboard*).

Hazardous material such as fuel and paint needs dedicated storage areas. Many cruisers start out a passage with extra containers of fuel lashed to every available square foot of deck space. This keeps any spilled fuel out of the bilge, but it also greatly increases the risk of moving about the deck. And it leaves the problem of storing these containers when they are

Figure 9.10   Sensible Chart Storage

empty—since they take up the same space empty as full. In the stupid old days, cruisers used disposable containers and threw them overboard when they were empty. I hope we have gained some intelligence since then. The best place for fuel is in a permanent tank. If you must take extra containers along, the next best place is in deck lockers that have overboard venting.

Most stowage spaces on a boat are small; a few items, however, require large spaces. Bulky items—sails, dinghy, life raft, outboard motor, and bikes, for example—are often stored above deck at least part of the time. Although our own outboard, bikes, and dinghy go below when we make a passage, while we're in port or coastal cruising they are on deck. We place the dinghy beneath the boom and hang the outboard on the aft rail—standard procedure. However, what is not standard is storing the bikes over the side on an automobile bike rack and holding them in place with bungees (see figure 9.11). This procedure works well provided the port rail doesn't go too far under. Once, crossing between Oahu and Molokai at about 7½ knots, we did drag a couple of wheels. I was pleasantly surprised and relieved that the whole thing remained attached to the boat.

Figure 9.11   *Sensible Bike Storage*

Special space is required for long items such as sail battens, poles for the sun awning, and fishing rods. Quite often these are lashed to the cabin-top handrails, where they are exposed to the weather. A better solution is to first put them into a length of 3- or 4-inch-diameter PVC pipe with end caps. They will be protected from the elements and the eyes of anyone who might covet them—and it looks neater, too.

On a boat, as ashore, small items are stored in various small containers. The little chest of drawers you used at home will be all right on your boat if it doesn't corrode and you can keep its drawers from flying out during rough weather. Figure 9.12 shows one solution to storage-chest problems, a box of drawers built into the boat. Notice that the successful storage of the items inside depends not only on the built-in storage space, but also on the use of a secondary container.

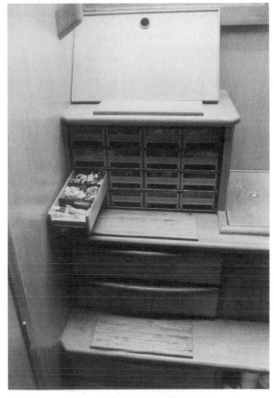

Figure 9.12   Sensible Small-Item Storage

Another method is to stow a commercially available chest in a larger drawer, with the chest drawers facing the side of the larger drawer to prevent spilling.

Secondary containers can help solve other storage problems aboard as well. Many people use small net hammocks to hold fresh fruit and vegetables, along with a variety of other items such as books or clothing. The hammock is generally strung up across the corner of the cabin most convenient to the items' use.

Canvas bags with drawstrings can be quickly made to hold many awkward items. We have separate bags for short pieces of line, bungee cords, electric cords, and water hoses, all of which have a way of becoming entangled with the rest of the contents of any locker if they are stowed sans bag. Another use for bags is to group often-used items together. A sewing or a bosun bag, for instance, can keep all the gear needed for splicing and whipping together.

Plastic boxes with sealable lids are a godsend to cruisers. The plastic doesn't rot, no moisture gets in once the box is sealed, and the small items inside don't move around in the locker. Grouping items into families and putting each into a separate box makes sorting through that locker to get to the gear on the bottom much simpler.

Entertainment

You might think that discussing the rather mundane entertainment available on board a small cruising vessel would be good subject matter for a TV program called *Lifestyles of the Poor and Stupid*. However, books, musical instruments, stereo, TV, games, wine, liquor, dining, and hobbies can provide good entertainment.

Books will range from the practical to the purely enjoyable, such as good fiction or poetry. Rarely do I read poetry ashore, but late at night in a cabin lit only by the glow from a single lamp and the flicker flame of the heater, we often read poetry aloud. It is best read aloud anyway, and the intimate space of the cabin lends a special ambience not found elsewhere.

Many musical instruments are small enough to be taken sailing. Harmonicas have long been a favorite of sailors. They can be carried in a buttoned-down pocket ready for use at the first idle moment. Debby and I both used the isolation of the foredeck to learn to play the harmonica, albeit not very well.

Small accordions, also a traditional favorite of ancient sailors, are a little beyond my skill level. A modern and much more versatile counterpart is an electronic keyboard. The small one we have on board has provided many hours of entertainment. These instruments come with myriad voices and other features—even headsets, so that the plunking of the unskilled doesn't offend the ears of anyone but the plunker. The appearance of a guitar in the cockpit seems to spawn sing-alongs and attracts many new friends. A guitar does take considerable room, but the smaller ukulele will work almost as well in attracting a singing group.

Many models of car stereos are battery driven and small enough to install in the boat. Some are even sold at marine stores and touted as sealed against the rigors of the marine environment. This "sealing" comes at a great increase in cost. With a little ingenuity, you can seal one of the cheaper car models as well. We have two speakers in the cabin and two excellent waterproof speakers in the cockpit. The latter have taken many doses of salt water and direct hosing downs and still produce beautiful sound. Good music can lift the spirits and improve the environment considerably. Nothing seems quite as wonderfully decadent as cruising along in the middle of the blue ocean with the white trade-wind clouds scudding along overhead, listening to a 50-piece orchestra play your favorite melody.

Another way to get music aboard is with a portable stereo. These units are cheaper, can be stowed easily, and can be used on deck or below, wherever the party is. Another advantage is that portables can be taken ashore to provide music for picnics on the beach.

There are also many small DC or AC/DC television sets available. As grim as it may sound, most cruising boats now have a TV. We claimed that we used ours as a monitor so we could show the natives along our route what they looked like on video. However, in the spirit of honesty I will admit that once, when we were moored in a large population area, I watched a football game. The Moellers claim that their set is useful for weather reports, and they give some excellent ideas for portable antennas (Moeller, *Living Aboard*). If run up the mast with a halyard, for instance, these antennas can greatly extend your viewing range. The question is whether or not you want to disclose to the rest of the marina that you are a settee potato by hoisting an antenna up your mast.

If you're a game player ashore you will be aboard as well. The best games are compact—cards, dominoes, chess, and small board games. Having a few decks of cards offers the most versatility. They can be used to entertain one individual playing solitaire or groups of six or eight. It is certainly worthwhile to learn several solitaire games—and cribbage. Many cruisers consider cribbage the best two-handed card game ever invented.

I remember cruising with a friend in sheltered waters on an unseasonably warm winter afternoon. We had just enough wind to keep the sails full as long as we headed in whatever direction it dictated. Since we had no particular place to go and the purpose of our cruise was just to unwind, we let the boat steer itself and played cribbage in the cockpit for hours. By the time the sun drew near the horizon, we had logged about 3 miles and 30 games of cribbage—10 games a mile. We kicked on the engine and an hour later were snug at anchor; mission accomplished.

Chess is also a good two-handed game, and the electronic boards make it a good solitary entertainment as well. We had one of the inexpensive Radio Shack models on board. We also had dice and dice cups on the *Bird* for games of liar's dice. Board games can be popular even with the natives. When we were in Kiribati (Gilbert Islands), the islanders were captivated with the old standby Sorry. We witnessed several heated games on homemade boards—one in which the patriarch of the family refused to let any player send him back to start. With a stream of what we imagined to be island profanity, he would remove the offending player's piece, throwing it and the card back at the player. We also fancied his win-loss record was admirable.

A few words about the number-one form of entertainment on board cruising boats—booze. That might be too strong a statement, but we surely consumed more booze on board than we did ashore. How does this happen? Somehow a cocktail at sundown just feels right; and when anybody comes aboard for a chat, wine, beer, or some strange rum drink seems only neighborly. In any marina or anchorage, the stream of people coming aboard or inviting you aboard for chats is endless. Then, of course, what is dinner without a little wine for thy stomach's sake? The result is the consumption of large quantities of alcohol. I suppose one of the advantages of drinking on the dock is that you generally must negotiate only a few feet of dock to get home, not drive a car or boat.

Storage of large quantities of booze on board requires some thought to prevent breakage, leakage, and customs charges. Breakage can be handled by buying your hard liquor in plastic bottles and by careful storage. Debby made small bags or socks of heavy material that slipped over the lower three-quarters of a wine bottle. We never lost a bottle.

Passing through customs with a large supply of liquor can be costly, however, because most countries require you to pay a duty on it. If you choose not to pay it, you can avoid it by clever smuggling tactics, outright perjury, bribery, or having a locker that can be sealed in bond. We have successfully used all of the above methods except bribery.

Dining aboard can provide enjoyment thrice over. With the proper equipment you can enjoy the preparation, the serving, and the eating of a fine meal. I've discussed some of the logistical requirements already; what you need for dining as enjoyment, though, are a few small special pieces of gear such as cloth napkins, candleholders, serving dishes, proper tableware—whatever will make the table presentable to you. We have spent many an enjoyable hour with good friends on our own floating restaurant.

10

Water and Power Systems

Water Systems

The quantity of fresh water you carry on your cruising yacht will be a compromise between your desire and your available space. A cubic foot of space holds only about 7½ gallons. Most boats designed for cruising carry at least 100 gallons (Cornell, *World Cruising Survey*). This is another place where those cruising on small or slow boats lose out. A smaller boat travels slower than a large boat on passage, so it's at sea longer. This, of course, requires more water—but the smaller boat has less space to store it. Those who need to lash water jugs to the decks before every passage probably should not be going on the passage. The fact that it can be, and is, done continually doesn't make it a good practice. A proper cruising boat should be designed to operate without Band-Aid solutions.

WATER TANKS

The usual recommended allowance of fresh water on a passage is 1 gallon per person per day (Campbell, *Passage Making*). This allows reasonable amounts for drinking, cooking, and cleaning. Cleaning, which generally uses the most water, can be drastically curtailed in an emergency. An experienced crew can wash the dinner dishes using only a couple of cups of fresh water by washing and rinsing the dishes in salt water, then using the fresh only for a final hot rinse, catching the runoff for reuse.

Every skipper should monitor closely the quantity and condition of the water supply during a passage. If the reserve drops below the point where it will provide the recommended 1 gallon per person per predicted remaining days, enforce a water-rationing system. You do not have to jeopardize your health to get by on ½ gallon of water per day, but you do have to make considerable efforts to prevent waste. A person can live only a few days without water, but life can be sustained for a considerable period on 1 cup a day (although some permanent health damage may occur).

Overconsumption is not the only problem that can affect your water supply during a crossing; contamination or leakage can also waste large quantities. The best defense against these is multiple tanks. If you have two or three tanks, the accident will affect only one-half or one-third of your water supply. With luck the accident will not affect your last tank of water.

If you have the misfortune to run out of water, remember that in most modern cruisers there are still two places more can be found. While most tanks cannot be drained or pumped dry, you can open their access ports and sponge up the remaining water. The real water mine, however, is your water heater. Six to 10 gallons of usable water are locked away in this device and can be retrieved by draining the tank.

As a last resort, turn to your emergency sources. Every boat at sea should have a 5-gallon portable container in a locker above deck for emergency use in case the vessel must be abandoned. Most life rafts have a small amount of emergency water in sealed tins inside. Once all emergency water is gone, you are left with only what you can catch or make.

WATER CATCHER

No cruising boat should be without a water catcher. A bucket is simple but inefficient. The next simplest method is to use the mainsail; make this system more efficient by adding belly to the mainsail by taking up on the topping lift and easing off on the halyard. The rain will soon wash the mainsail free of salt, and you can catch the water cascading off the forward end of the boom in a bucket, carrying it to your tanks. Some cruisers simply catch the water running along the deck by damming the deck just downstream of the deck-fill plate. I would try this only in an emergency and with a tank that was already empty, because this water can be contaminated easily. For example, in most boats the deck can get washed unexpectedly by a good dollop of sea water, thereby ruining any water already in the tank.

Almost all boats in the Tropics already have a sun awning or bimini top. It is a simple matter to alter this canvas so that you can rig it for use as a water catcher. On the *Bird of Time* we use the bimini top, which is designed to stay in place in heavy winds. It is normally held up in the center by a topping lift to the aft stay. When we use it as a water catcher, we slack this line so that the top hangs down and forms a pocket. A hose bib has been sewn into the center of this pocket (see figure 10.1); we attach to it a hose that leads to whichever tank we choose to fill.

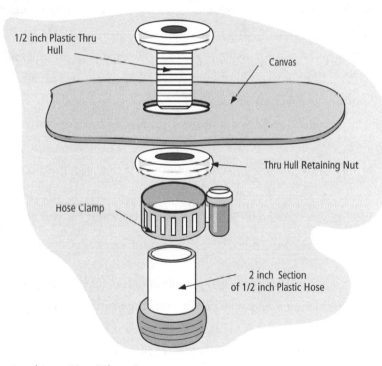

Figure 10.1   Attaching a Hose Bib to Canvas

An amazing amount of fresh water can be trapped in a short time in a good tropical rain squall. You may at times need to turn off course to keep your boat on an even keel during this process.

Other water catchers can be made by stretching a canvas pocket between the lifelines and the cabin-top handrail (Roth, *After 50,000 Miles*). Almost anything will work. The larger the canvas, the more water it will catch, but the more difficult it becomes to rig. Also, the farther the canvas is rigged above the sea, the less chance of contamination.

WATERMAKERS

Watermakers have been improved to the point that they are showing up aboard more and more cruising yachts. They presently come in several sizes and produce from about 1-½ to almost 7 gallons per hour. These units filter out all organic pollutants, such as bacteria and cysts, but not all chemical pollutants.

The smaller models can be hand operated for life rafts, or powered with an electric motor that draws about 4 amps. One hour of use per day per crew member will provide ample water for a passage. With a couple of solar panels for power, you'll have an infinite supply of fresh water; if you're using your engine, figure that a gallon of diesel fuel can produce 20 to 25 gallons of water (Rousmaniere, *Offshore Yachts*). The small units weigh only about 20 pounds and take up about a cubic foot of space.

The large models require 8 amps but supply copious amounts of water in return. Three gallons of water per hour may not seem like much until you try drinking it. The larger units are more efficient, producing 0.4 gallon per amp hour compared to 0.35 for the smaller units. To get this extra efficiency, though, you lose the portability and pay a higher initial price. If you plan to cruise with more than a two-person crew, a larger unit may be feasible.

Life is not free of all worry and trouble with these units: They must be kept clean and free of contamination. They come with membrane cleaners, prefilter cartridges, and biocide inhibitors, all subtle warnings of the care and feeding required to keep them performing satisfactorily on a day-to-day basis. They were designed originally for emergency use by shipwrecked crews. Therefore, they are intended to be used in clean salt water only—the kind you normally find in the middle of the sea, not in a typical coastal harbor, with its pollution and silt. A little oil in the ceramic membrane and your unit will malfunction.

Even if you are in clean, clear water, however, I should point out that the water intake for these devices is generally close to the toxic bottom paint on your vessel. Within a few millimeters of the boat bottom the concentration of the chemicals in the paint—lead, mercury, copper—is high enough to kill marine organisms. Small amounts of these toxic chemicals will be drawn into the watermaker during operation. Even though you are not a marine organism, taking in large quantities of these chemicals is not conducive to good health. The U.S. Health Bureau requires public water supplies to contain less than 0.05 part per million of lead. The watermaker filters out only about 99.9 percent of this metal; that means it passes through about 1 part per 1,000—which is 1,000 parts per million.

Since the difference between 1,000 and 0.05 is considerable, why isn't everyone who uses watermakers dead? Certainly the concentrations of the poisons in the intake water are low. How low is the important question, and is presently unknown. Given this uncertainty—and given that many of these chemicals are of the type that can accumulate in the body—it may be prudent to refrain from routinely drinking the water from these units. Like smoking, poisoning from heavy metals is slow and debilitating rather than quick and clean; the change is gradual and imperceptible until the damage is serious and irreversible, causing severe illness or even death. To be on the safe side, use these devices as they were intended—as emergency systems.

In a harbor it may be safer to haul your water in 5-gallon jugs and purify it with iodine. Do not rely on chlorine and halazone tablets to purify water. These chemicals kill germs and bacteria but not cysts and parasites. The cysts, including *Giardia,* are spread by animals defecating in a water source. In North America, giardiasis is sometimes called "beaver fever" and produces diarrhea, stomach cramps, nausea, fever, gas, and headaches within 7 to 10 days. To protect against such organic pollutants boil your water, filter it through a 1-micron filter, or use the iodine water purification tablets developed by Harvard University. These contain tetraglycine hydroperiodide as the active ingredient and are marketed under the name Globaline. They are effective against all the common waterborne bacteria; cysts of *Endamoeba histolytica* and *Giardia;* and the parasite cercaria of schistosomiasis (flatworms) (Whelen and Angier, *On Your Own in the Wilderness*). They can be found at your local pharmacy. The tablets are more effective if the water is warmer than 68 degrees and allowed to stand for at least 20 minutes before drinking.

FILTERS

Even in the United States and Canada, shoreside water may contain silt, be discolored, and taste bad (Moeller, *Living Aboard*). In the Bahamas we developed the habit of smelling the water before drinking. The small water filters that are normally installed under the sink counter can help when taking on water in these problem areas. The only modification required is a 2- or 3-foot hose with female couplings on both ends. Attach this to the hose bib on the dock, and the fill hose to the other end of the filter, as shown in figure 10.2.

Figure 10.2 Hose Filter for Shoreside Water

FRESHWATER PUMPS

Pressure water systems are an ever-increasing part of the cruising scene. Hand pumping is being relegated to use in emergencies or on passages that require a tight control of water. A pressure water system consists of a pump, a pressure-sensitive switch to tell when the water is turned on and off, and, in some instances, a small pressure tank to reduce cycling. The pump should be of the variety that can be run dry for a considerable time without damage. On more than one occasion I have turned off the engine or returned to the boat to find my water pump running furiously, drawing on an empty tank. Certainly failures can and do occur, but installing a spare water pump takes about the same time as reefing the mainsail. One in the boat, one as a spare, and one in the shop getting repaired is a system I have been living with for 10 years. I suspect I average about one pump change a year—not bad, considering the convenience of pressure water.

Despite my fondness for pressure systems, however, I do think that there should be two foot pumps in every galley, one for cold fresh water, the other for raw water. This convenient access to the water that your boat is sitting in can save you a considerable amount of your freshwater supply.

Many manufacturers of pressure water pumps recommend adding a surge tank to the system to eliminate unnecessary pump cycling, to reduce the water hammer effects on the system, and to prolong pump life. On the surface these seem like valid reasons for installing a surge tank—so valid that I installed one on my own boat.

The pump cycled as much with the surge tank in place as without it. Unless the tank is very large, the only difference is that when the water is turned on, the pump doesn't come on immediately; it waits a few seconds before it starts, and then runs for several seconds after the water is turned off. This would save you a pump cycle only if you were using less than a few cups. I was also unable to perceive any increase in pump life due to decreased water hammer. There is generally enough flexibility in the plastic piping found on boats to absorb any shock resulting from starting and stopping the pump.

However, I did have a problem with the surge tank's delayed reaction to a pressure drop in the line: It gave me a system that could waste several cups of water before I was aware of it. Without the surge tank, only a few drops from a leaking faucet would start the pump and sound an alert that water was being wasted. In the end I removed my surge tank to conserve water.

Most boats are plumbed with vinyl hose, a very flexible, inexpensive, easy-to-install, and FDA-approved piping. Regardless of all these features, however, vinyl hose should be avoided as piping material on a cruising boat because it outgases for years—that is, chemicals evaporate from the plastic and go into the water.

Granted, these amounts are small, but remember that water is the universal solvent and occasionally it may sit in a pipe for weeks or months before it is used, allowing these outgassing chemicals to build up. Once again many of these chemicals are of the kind that do not pass through the human system but build up until toxic levels are reached. The polybutylene pipe used almost exclusively in the recreational vehicle industry is much safer.

BILGE PUMPS

The freshwater system is not the only fluid-handling system on your boat. There are also systems to handle bilge water, sewage discharge, shower sumps, galley salt water, fuel pumps, and deck washing—to mention but a few. Of these systems, the most common and important is probably the bilge-water system. This should have at least two pumps, one hand operated, and another electrically operated and automatic.

On occasion the very squeamish choose to have a third large-capacity standby pump, but its value is psychological only. It is impractical to carry a pump large enough to bail the water produced from major hull damage. Remember that a 3-inch hole 4 feet below the surface will admit 350 gallons of water per minute into the boat. Compare this volume to the capacity of the largest bilge pumps commercially available—about 65 gallons a minute, while drawing 20 amps of power. It should be clear that bilge pumps are not meant for damage control; they are a convenience for packing gland leakage and small spills.

Most bilge pumps come with built-in strainers to keep debris from plugging the pump intake. These screens need to be cleaned regularly, especially when the boat is new. I have found that most of the debris that reaches my bilge was deposited by careless craftsmen during construction. With a little care, unwanted material can be kept from the bilge. Labels from food tins are famous for plugging pump screens. If you clean up your debris from boat alterations and think about what you store in the bilge, your pump screen will perform adequately.

There has been some discussion in the literature about the proper location for the pump discharge—does it belong above or below the waterline? The argument that discharging above the waterline increases the capacity of the pump because the discharge will not have to work against the back pressure of the water outside the boat is false (Moeller, *Living Aboard*). The discharge of a pump is dependent on the total pressure head the pump must work against. When the discharge is into the atmosphere, this pressure is dependent on the total vertical distance the water needs to be lifted from the suction end to the discharge end of the line. Extra energy is required to raise the water above the waterline, which is then lost in its fall back to the surface. When the discharge is at or below the surface of the water, the total pressure head is the vertical distance between the suction end of the line and the *surface* of the water. The latter distance is obviously the shorter, and therefore the pump discharge in this configuration is the greater.

Electric Equipment

The most startling difference between a cruiser of the 1970s or 1980s and those that will leave in the 21st century is the amount of electronic and electrical equipment on board.

We all long for the simple life, but most of us only want it if it comes with the comforts of modern life. When the choice comes down to simple or comfortable, put your money on comfortable. Comfort is what allows all those annoying tasks to be done easily. These days, electricity provides the energy for those annoying tasks that we used to get the Phoenicians, Slavs, or members of other vanquished nations to perform.* So like it or not, electricity is an integral part of any modern cruiser.

The primary power on a cruising boat is a direct current (DC) system. There are some 24-volt DC systems, but the most common is the 12-volt. The 24-volt systems allow you to use smaller-size wire, which makes real sense if you have an electric windlass, but electric shock danger is also greater and more destructive with a 24-volt system—and most DC equipment is designed for 12-volt power anyway.

Regardless of the voltage, the system consists of something to make power, something to use power, and something to store power. Each of these subsystems must balance out if the total system is to operate. The size of the total system depends ultimately on how much power you need or desire.

Individuals have different wants and needs. How yours translate to power requirements is important in the overall design of your electrical system. To find the total power requirements you will need, you must know the power requirements of all the major electric devices on board your boat, and the estimated time per day that they will be operating. (Any time period could be chosen, but a day is a convenient period for most applications; we are dealing with round numbers here, not precise figures.) Once you select your voltage, you need only determine your total amperage draw to obtain your total power draw. Power (P) is equal to the amperage (I) multiplied by the volts (E):

P = IE   *Equation 10.1*

Table 10.1 lists some representative values for various pieces of equipment found on board most boats. Its numbers are, of course, only average values, and you may not have all the equipment shown on the table. You should thus customize the table for your own boat by listing all the electrical equipment on board, listing the amperage draw found on the nameplate of the equipment or in the specifications, and then estimating the time that the equipment will be in use. It is better to err on the high side here.

---

*In fact, the word *slave* is derived from the Roman practice of using Slavs as slaves.

The sailing instruments figure is based on the usual package: depth sounder, knot meter, log, and wind velocity and direction indicator. On passage the depth sounder can be shut off, but you'll be saving only a couple of amps per day.

TABLE 10.1

Values of Resistance for Common Electrical Gear

Item	Amperage	Daily Use in Amp-Hrs	Passage	Coastal	Dockside
Sailing instruments	0.5	12	5		
Autopilot	4	50	20		
Refrigerator	4	50	50	50	
Freezer	9	100	100	100	
VHF radio	0.5		5		
Ham radio	20	12			
Weather fax	2	2			
Stereo	3		10	15	
Cabin lights	2	4	22	50	
Running lights	6		12		
Spreader light	3	2	2	2	
Spotlight	9		5		
Anchor light	1		12		
Bilge pump	12	3	3	3	
Water pump	6		1	1	
Watermaker	4	5			
Fan	1		3	6	
Furnace	3.5		80	80	
Starter	900		90		
Radar	4	9	12		
LORAN	0.7		7		
GPS	1	24	10		
Approximate Total		280	460	310	

The autopilot numbers can vary widely from boat to boat; those in this table are based on the heavier units designed for bluewater work. These units are capable of producing 10,000 to 15,000 inch-pounds of torque. The small, cheaper units produce only about 700 to 1,000 inch-pounds and—regardless of any claims you may hear along the dock—are not really made for open ocean work.

The current draw for the autopilot shown in the table is a good average value to be used for sizing your own power system, but in practice this current demand can be reduced. Here is where good sailing skills can pay high dividends. On a boat whose sails are set correctly, the loads on the helm are light. In this position the boat almost sails itself with the autopilot working less than 5 percent of the time. The autopilot will thus kick in only now and then—whenever a wave momentarily knocks the boat beyond the preset error bands.

Remember to figure in the extra power the autopilot will draw during heavy weather, when it must work harder. Although it is true that the pilot can be turned off and the boat hand steered during these conditions, it is also true that at these times steering is exhausting and uncomfortable; the autopilot can provide needed rest. Exhausted crew members make bad decisions, and bad decisions in heavy weather can lead to disaster.

The refrigerator numbers depend on the size of your box, how cold it must be kept, the amount of insulation, and the ambient temperature. In moving from a temperate to a tropical climate there will be a noticeable increase in how much the refrigerator compressor runs. Some cruisers reduce the current demand on passage by turning off their refrigerators and freezers. We preferred to keep our refrigerator running as long as the battery power remained normal. Setting our refrigerator thermostat so that the ice just remained frozen minimized the current draw and kept the freezer portion of the refrigerator essentially frost-free. (Some frost occurred when the unit was on, but it melted completely when the unit was off.) This low setting required about 24 hours to freeze a tray of ice—a small inconvenience offset somewhat by the fact that ice frozen this slowly is crystal clear and much more aesthetically pleasing.

The option of turning off our refrigerator was always available. The effect of doing so midpassage is not as severe as that of turning off a freezer, especially near the end of the passage, when nothing is generally left in the refrigerator to spoil. Since the freezer is designed to carry more food, however, there is generally something left, and everything spoils if it needs to be shut down.

The radio numbers listed in this table are relatively representative unless you are extremely talkative. The cabin light numbers, however, have a certain amount of flexibility. Obviously, you can limit usage, but considerable power can also be saved by using more efficient bulbs. Incandescent lights use a lot more power than fluorescent. Table 10.2 shows the power requirements and candlepower of various bulbs.

TABLE 10.2

Power Required to Produce Light

Bulb	Amperage	Lumens
Incandescent		
15-watt	1.25	145
25-watt	2	230
Fluorescent		
8-watt	0.65	400
13-watt	1.05	820
22-watt	1.8	1300
Halogen		
10-watt	0.8	125
20-watt	1.5	260

Although using fluorescent light in the cabin can conserve considerable power, I still recommend a blend of incandescent and fluorescent for two reasons: cabin ambience and the instability in electronic units that some fluorescent lights cause. I always got better reception on my ham radio with the fluorescent lights off, and they certainly play havoc with the reception of LORAN signals.

Halogen lights have not made large inroads into the marine industry; spreaders are the only fixture on which they are presently commercially available. A regular automotive headlight can be rigged as a spreader light. Personally I'd like to see a 100-lumen anchor light that would draw about ½ amp.

Starters and inverters are huge power hogs. Usually the starter is used for only seconds at a time. The power output from the inverter depends on what equipment you're running off it. To estimate either of these power loads, take the power rating of the equipment and divide it by 11—or the 120-volt current draw, multiplied by 11—to get the current draw from the batteries. (I use 11 instead of 12 and 10 because inverters are not 100 percent efficient. They range from 80 to 95 percent efficiency, depending on the manufacturer and the amount of power being drawn; the more power, the less efficient.)

The selection of an inverter is not a trivial matter; there are a number of factors to consider. Their power output varies with time, so inverters are rated for continuous power and various load durations, such as one hour, 15 minutes, and so on. Alternating current (AC) is not as simple as direct current (DC), because AC current has a wave form, which affects the operation of electrical equipment.

The output wave form of inverters ranges from a square wave (the cheapest) to a modified sine wave (the best). Also, things like dynamic impulse phase correction may be necessary, so you can see why it pays to get expert advice on equipment selection! The expert will need to know what kinds of loads you intend to power off the inverter. And remember, if you're asking dealers or manufacturers for this advice, consider their motives along with their advice.

The power drain for navigational equipment such as radar and positioning equipment depends on how long you leave it on. It is my experience that the positioning units, though they can be turned off and on, are always left on. Radar, on the other hand, is a considerable draw if left on, and most people only do so during foggy weather or for short periods at night when other boat traffic is in the area. Even when on, the better units have a power-saving setting whereby they can be kept in standby condition with little power drain, flipped on for a quick look around, then put back on standby.

The last figure in table 10.1 is the total power consumption per day for each of the three situations: passage making, coastal cruising, and dockside. Dockside assumes the constant availability of shore power. Coastal cruising assumes the almost daily use of the engine for at least a couple of hours, and the occasional availability of shore power—say, every week to 10 days—to top off the batteries. Passage making assumes no shore power and only occasional engine use—every three to five days for a few hours, for instance.

Now that you have some realistic values for load, you must decide how to get the power into your batteries before you can make a final decision on how much reserve capacity you need in your battery bank.

CHARGING

I feel that to have reliable power, you must have multiple ways of generating that power. Sometimes the fuel tank is empty, shore power is not available, the sun doesn't shine, and the wind doesn't blow—but it's rare that all these happen at once. For example, I have been limited to one source of power only once—in Radio Bay, where there's no shore power. While basking in beautiful, cloudy, windless downtown Hilo, I had to rely on diesel power to boost my batteries.

You'll need the total dockside power value from table 10.1 to size your 110-volt battery charger. These chargers are rated at maximum output amperage and range from trickle chargers to about 50 amps. Table 10.1 shows that a constant current flow of about 13 amps (310 amp-hours ÷ 24 hours) is required just to keep even with the stated dockside power drain.

There are two additional factors to consider: any future increase in power demand and how rapidly the power has to be returned to the battery banks. A few additional amps should satisfy increased demands—say 5 amps if you don't use much power, 10 if you use moderate amounts, 15 or 20 if you use large amounts and have large-capacity batteries. The second factor requires selecting some minimum time in which the used power must be returned to the batteries.

That "used power" is, of course, the power you used while dockside, plus some allowance for regaining power used when not attached to a power source. For example, a suitable battery charger for the boat in table 10.1 would be about 35 amps and would provide an overnight charge of about 420 amps, which would return the day's usage plus a deficit of another 110 amps.

The engine alternator is the next most common source of power for the batteries. Almost all engines come with alternators. The bad news is that they were designed for truck or automobile use. Trucks and automobiles have rapid-draw-down, high-power-output batteries; therefore, their alternators and generators are designed to put back that kind of power, by supplying a large current load for only a short time and then substantially reducing the current output. This is a good idea for the average car battery but a poor one for boat batteries. If you have one of these alternators it should be modified to bypass this regulator system, or replaced with a good marine alternator.

A good marine alternator provides power at low RPM and has a multiple-stage regulator. The latter allows 100 percent of the alternator's current output to be sent to the batteries until the voltage rises to above 14 volts. Then the regulator adjusts the current, keeping the voltage constant, until the battery is fully charged; at this point the regulator again adjusts to a float position in which the voltage is maintained between 13.5 and 13.7 volts. The reduced current input will reduce water usage in the batteries.

Alternators come in various sizes, from 50 to 150 amps. The size you need will depend on how often and how long you operate your engine, your daily power demand, the presence of other power-generating equipment on board, and the reserve capacity of your batteries. Selecting the proper size of alternator can be somewhat of a trial-and-error proposition, especially if other power-supply systems are present on your boat.

SOLAR POWER

Solar power is a viable option for cruisers. It's marketed in two basic configurations: flexible and rigid panels. The flexible panels are less efficient and a little more prone to failure, but they can be attached to curved and flexible surfaces such as dodgers or bimini tops—a good use of space. These panels produce about 0.25 amp per square foot in direct, perpendicular sunlight. The rigid panels require dedicated deck space but are much more efficient, producing as much as 0.70 amp per square foot in direct, perpendicular sunlight.

The total charge provided by solar panels depends on the intensity of the sunlight, the angle at which it strikes the panels, the panel temperature, and the length of time the panels are exposed to the light. Not much can be done about the intensity of sunlight, because that is controlled by the weather, but ideally the panels should be placed perpendicular to the sunlight in locations with good ventilation for cooling and without shade. Now, on board a moving boat exposed to a moving sun, achieving such optimum placement would require a full-time technician to monitor and regulate the panels. Installations that allow for adjustment are more costly and certainly more time consuming. As time goes on the bother of moving the panels tends to override the need for the few extra amps, and the movable panels slowly become operated as fixed ones.

One of the significant features of solar panels—at least fixed ones—is that they are effortless. They just sit there quietly day after day pumping power into the batteries. I consider the three aboard my own boat the smartest cruising purchase I ever made. Instead of trying for the optimum position, I chose to install enough panels to provide the necessary power under average conditions. They are permanently, horizontally mounted on the cabin top, and at least two are relatively shade-free at any given time regardless of the point of sail or how the boat swings on its anchor. The cabin top gets very little traffic, but the units are still mounted so that they can be stepped on with no damage. On passages one unit sometimes has equipment stored over it. At first I thought that this was a waste of the unit, but it functions normally when we are not on passage, which is the majority of the time. Also, if we do need extra power on passage, we can temporarily shift the equipment. The output of the panels is difficult to predict, because the variables are difficult to control and are constantly changing. The angle of the sun, for instance, changes not only during the day but throughout the year and north and south of the equator. In Alaska the panels are subjected to 18-hour summer days, compared to 6-hour Alaska winter days or the 12-hour days of the Tropics. Clouds and shrouds cast ever-moving shadows that also affect the output.

There are different methods of rating the panels to determine total output. Most are based on maximum output and some guessed-at fudge factor. The best way to determine output, though, is just to monitor it over time and find an average value. Over the years my three panels have produced about 60 amps per day. They are ARCO M65 rated at 3.25 amps. That works out to about 20 amp-hours per panel per day.

The flexible panels come regulated; the solid panels, either regulated or unregulated. While an unregulated panel is theoretically capable of producing a little more power, the actual gain may be negligible. The regulated panels require a minimum size of battery bank to operate effectively. The flexible panels require about 70 amp-hours each, whereas the solid require about 130. The panels should be equipped with internal bypass diodes to bypass the shaded areas of a unit in partial shade. These will improve the unit's efficiency.

WIND GENERATORS

Wind-generator systems are designed to be permanently or temporarily mounted. The permanent systems by their very nature must be quite small. The power generated by wind systems is dependent on the size of the blades. I would not consider cluttering up my boat with less than 36-inch blades. Even these produce only about 2 amps in a 10-knot wind. Unless the boat is anchored exposed to the trades, the wind never blows hard enough to generate much power.

The temporary models are generally strung up over the foredeck. These units have much larger propellers and can generate some serious amounts of power. In a 10-knot wind my 72-inch prop generates about 5 amps, and when anchored in a lagoon in the trades the unit generates about 12 to 14 amps consistently. This, coupled with my three solar panels, produced about 400 amp-hours per day during our cruise. I considered selling my excess power to the natives to light their village. The noise of the unit was barely noticeable inside the boat, although outside an occasional strong wind gust made us sound like a Cessna moving into position for takeoff.

The best of the wind generators also can be dismantled and turned into trolling generators. These are mounted as a unit on the aft rail and attached to a 150-foot line with an outboard motor prop on a short stainless-steel shaft. Use a stiff woven halyard type of line, such as Sta-Set. This line transfers more of its twist into torque at the generator, and its low stretch minimizes the energy it stores during speed surges. At higher speeds the prop tends to get pulled out of the water. When this occurs, the elasticity of the rope and the lower drag of the air cause the prop to spin faster than the rope, which knots the line. The knotted line causes a drop in the power output and the speed of the boat.

We found that after a few hours in high winds and large seas, the trolling line on our unit had to be retrieved and untwisted—not an easy task at 7 knots. The easiest way to retrieve it was to shield the prop from the water so that it would not turn. Our practice was to use a large plastic funnel split down the side so it could be placed over the line when needed. We then taped the funnel closed with the ever-present duct tape. The funnel was forced down the line by the water pressure until it reached the prop. Then the prop stopped spinning and could be hauled to the boat. The amount of effort we spent in recovery depended on the speed of our boat. In some instances we had to slow the boat to retrieve the unit.

The drag of the unit is considerable and did slow the boat when it was over the side. I did not measure this speed loss, but estimate it was about 1 knot at boat speeds above 6 knots. In exchange, the generator turned out about 3 to 12 amps (depending on vessel speed) and generally supplied about 150 amp-hours per day. This unit and the solar panels provided us with ample power without using the engine.

STAND-ALONE GENERATORS

The feasibility of installing a stand-alone generator depends on the size of your boat. Generally boats below 45 feet in length do not have enough room for even a modest-size model. Many boats above 45 feet install these units, though, because they also have a considerable AC demand. A unit of 2,500 to 3,500 watts can provide considerable AC power; that it can also produce auxiliary DC power is a secondary consideration.

Those with smaller boats seldom have room for the luxuries allowed by an abundance of AC power, let alone room for the generator. However, there are some small, portable generators available for both gasoline and diesel. The gasoline models are considerably cheaper because of their wider market. They take up about 1 to 1½ cubic feet of space, weigh between 45 and 55 pounds, and can produce about 10 amps DC or 4 to 7 amps AC. Depending on output, they run about six to eight hours on a gallon of gas. Four amps AC, however, will not run very many appliances or power tools, so such a unit's only real use is as an auxiliary battery charger.

The small diesel units provide DC power alone. They are probably best suited for augmenting battery power. All units require additional fuel and maintenance, as well as producing noise.

BATTERIES

Now that you know what's going out and what's coming in, you need something to store your extra power when too much is coming in and feed it out when the demand is high. This item is called a battery or, more realistically, a battery bank, since more than one battery is generally needed.

Batteries are made up of lead and acid enclosed in a plastic case. The amount of power one supplies is very closely dependent on the amount of lead in the battery. The plastic case takes up very little room. Getting one very large battery in place of several smaller ones thus saves very little space and requires a very strong back. I recommend leaving those monster batteries in the industrial vehicles.

Batteries used in boats are called deep-cycle batteries and should not be confused with their common look-alike, the car battery. The deep-cycle battery is designed internally to provide a low but long-term power output, while the car battery is designed for a rapid, high-power output. The major difference is in the plate design. Car batteries have many thin plates; boat batteries, a few thick ones.

Deep-cycle batteries are rated by reserve capacity. A standard 25-amp load is attached to a fully charged battery and the time required to draw the battery down to 10.5 volts is measured. The result—generally expressed in terms of amp-hours—is found by multiplying the time in hours by the 25-amp load. It is well worth remembering that there is very little useful power left in a battery at 10.5 volts. Most of the usable power is gone when the battery reaches 11.5 volts, and it should not be discharged further. Figure 10.3 is a typical battery voltage discharge curve showing the percentage of usable power left at any given voltage.

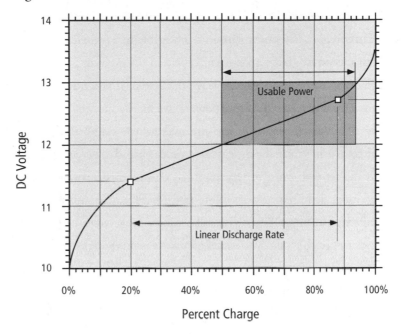

Figure 10.3   *Battery Voltage Compared to Percent Charge*

From this figure it can be seen that when a battery reaches 11.5 volts, 80 percent of its storage capacity has been withdrawn. At this point the discharge rate accelerates until the battery is completely discharged. It is very difficult to recharge a battery that has been drawn down much below 11.5 volts. Therefore, the maximum usable power is commonly considered to be only 80 percent of the reserve capacity rating.

Unfortunately for battery users, most DC equipment is designed to operate more efficiently when the voltage is above 12. Figure 10.3 shows that this point is reached when the battery is only 50 percent discharged. This figure also shows that a rapid discharge occurs above about 13 volts—or about 95 percent charge. Most systems therefore are designed to operate at between 50 and 95 percent charge; in other words, only about 45 percent of their rated amp-hours are really usable on a day-to-day basis.

Now we move into the twilight zone. Most boats come with too little battery capacity, especially for cruising. A survey of transatlantic racing and cruising boats showed the average boat to have about 300 amp-hours of capacity (Cornell, *World Cruising Survey*). Complicating this issue, there are no fixed rules to guide you in selecting battery capacity.

For example, it is possible to get by on almost no battery capacity; just turn off all power equipment and leave the engine running while you swing on the hook. That may seem a little extreme, but my point is that it *is* possible to juggle load, generating capacity, and storage capacity to balance any system.

But such questions as how long to leave the system unattended, how long to run the engine, and how often to return to shore power have highly personal answers. Taking a carte blanche recommendation from someone else makes little sense. If you don't agree, I recommend your total amp-hours be at least five times your daily coastal cruising usage. This is considerably higher than most other experts recommend (Rousmaniere, *Offshore Yachts*). The present trend is definitely toward more power equipment, and most of the problems common to this equipment go away with an adequate power supply. If you still don't agree, the following example will take you through the reasoning steps necessary to arrive at a usable battery capacity.

Let's assume that your boat uses about 125 amp-hours per day when coastal cruising, and that its engine is run about an hour and a half per day to enter and leave a harbor. If the boat has a 50-amp alternator on the engine and three solar panels, then while leapfrogging from harbor to harbor every day, the system puts in 60 amp-hours from the panels and 75 from the externally regulated alternator. The total amperage input is thus more than is taken out—if the sun is shining.

On days the boat does not travel it has a net deficit of 65 amp-hours. Therefore it can lay over about one in every six days (on the days it moves it gains about 10 amp-hours) and still have full batteries at the end of the period. If you'd like a longer layover, you have two choices: Draw the batteries down further or put up a wind generator. We'll assume that you want the boat to be able to sustain itself for four days using only solar power. The total reserve power you'll need will be:

4 days x 65 amp-hours/day = 260 amp-hours   *Equation 10.2*

To allow for irregularities, we'll increase this reserve power to 300 amp-hours. The battery capacity necessary to supply 300 hours is the reserve power required divided by the usable power factor of 0.45:

300 amp-hours ÷ 0.45 = 666 amp-hours   *Equation 10.3*

Therefore your boat will require about 660 amp-hours of storage. For longer periods at anchor your wind generator needs to operate or your engine be used for generation. With an adequate-size generator the wind must blow at only 10 knots for half the time your boat is stationary to return your battery capacity to full.

At this point it is necessary to see how this capacity will perform during passage-making conditions. Let's assume that your boat, while on passage, consumes about 150 amp-hours. The daily deficit is then about 90 amps, which must be made up from reserve power by the trolling generator or starting the engine. The reserve power of approximately 300 amps supplied by the 660-amp battery bank will allow your boat to cruise a little over three days before you must take other action.

It is highly probable that during those three days you will encounter one or several calm periods. Powering for six hours, using a 50-amp alternator, during a calm will top off a three-day deficit. If no calms occur, my experience shows that at normal boat speeds, trolling for 24 hours will generally supply about 150 amps. Ninety of these go to make up your daily deficit, leaving 60 to go into your batteries. Trolling the generator for about five days would also top off the batteries. These constraints seem to be reasonable; therefore your 660 amp-hour battery bank is adequate.

Whatever battery capacity you select, if you have self-regulated solar panels on board you must provide at least 130 amp-hours of battery capacity for each solid panel, and 70 amp-hours for each flexible. The 660 amp-hours calculated above meets these requirements and provides a deep reservoir difficult for any charging system to overpower.

The need for two banks of batteries—one for house use, the other for starting the engine—is often stressed in boating literature, and most new boats come with a double bank and switching gear already installed. In my opinion this double-bank system is of value only if the capacity of your house batteries is too small and multiple power-generating systems are not available. A small house-battery bank will often get run down below the level necessary to start the engines, hence the need for a reserve bank. If an adequate bank of batteries is installed and alternative power-generating systems are available, the system will very seldom get drawn down that low. If "seldom" happens, though, then your wind-, water-, or solar-generating capacity will provide the power to start your engines—given a little time.

On my own boat, I have only one 660-amp-hour battery bank, and in more than 15 years of cruising I have never lacked the power to start my engines (but then, I have many alternative ways to generate power, and I monitor the power in and out of my system).

MONITORING USAGE

With all this power going in and out it is helpful to know what is really going on in your system. There are myriad instruments that will help you with this task, including voltmeters, ammeters, and amp-hour meters. Some are of more value than others.

VOLTMETERS

Voltmeters measure the DC voltage in the batteries or the AC voltage entering the boat. Most of the time the latter falls into the "hmm, that's interesting" category. Sometimes dockside circuits are not the best, and the voltage they supply is considerably below the 120 volts intended. The AC voltmeter lets you monitor dockside power levels. This is especially important if your boat contains voltage-sensitive AC equipment, such as electronic gear, that may not operate properly or may be damaged if the incoming power is outside the suggested range. The specifications that accompany the equipment will provide the necessary information on power supply.

DC voltmeters come in several models. The inexpensive, expanded-scale analog meter can be purchased with one of two faces. The first reads from about 8 to 16 volts and is calibrated in increments of 0.2 volt; the second reads from 0 to 100 percent charge. The insides of both meters are essentially identical; only the face of the latter changed to reflect the values of charge, not voltage (see figure 10.3). For this service you can expect to pay an additional $5 to $8—the price of stupidity. The basic problem with both of these meters is that they are too insensitive to be of much value.

There are several DC digital voltmeters available, which provide the voltage to the nearest 0.1 volt. This is still too inaccurate to be of much use. Combination instruments are complex to install and cost about $150 more than analog meters. The price of stupidity goes up.

A less expensive and more accurate way to measure voltage is to use a digital multimeter. These units are portable and are designed to troubleshoot electronic or electrical circuitry. They have a wide market so their price is low—about $70, or twice the cost of the analog voltmeter. Every modern cruiser should have a good multimeter aboard anyhow; all you need to turn it into a very accurate voltmeter is an extra set of test cables with banana plugs on each end. Install a couple of female banana plugs in line with your DC power input and the multimeter will read voltage to the nearest 0.01 volt. Now you have a unit that is cheaper and more accurate than the standard meters, and has more uses. What more could you ask?

To measure accurately the power available in your batteries you must read the curve in figure 10.3 using the *no-load voltage*. This is read from your voltmeter when no power is flowing *out of or into* the system. This means that everything is off, including the solar panels. Realize that this state does not occur very often. Nighttime—using a flashlight to read the meter—may be the only time. If the in- or outflow of current is small, the voltage reading will be close. Outflow provides a lower voltage; and inflow a higher-than-normal reading. Once you have a voltage reading, read the percentage discharge from the bottom of the graph. If you prefer, the following equation gives the values for the straight-line portion of the graph:

$C = 54.3 \, V – 601.6$ where: *Equation 10.4*

      C is the percentage of charge, and

      V is the voltage.

For a really fancy system, a table similar to table 10.3 can be generated and used in its place. To customize this table for your own boat, the value in the first row of the amp-hour available column is the total amp-hour capacity of your battery bank multiplied by 0.45. This is the usable power available in your batteries, which by definition will be all gone when the voltage reaches 12 volts. This total usable power value divided by 10 is the difference in the amp-hour value between each adjacent row in the column. The values below 12 volts are shown in the contingency column, because the power is there if needed (and it should be used *only* if needed). The table ends at 11.5 volts because that is the end of the linear portion of the discharge curve, and damage to the batteries can occur below this voltage.

For a more accurate table the voltage can be broken down in any increment you wish. For example, every 0.05 volt the amp-hours would drop 5 percent, or 0.05 of the total usable power. In table 10.3 that would amount to 15 amp-hours a step.

TABLE 10.3

Battery Reserve Power

Voltage	Amp-Hours Available	Contingency Amp-Hours
13	300	
12.9	270	
12.8	240	
12.6	180	
12.5	150	
12.4	120	
12.3	90	
12.2	60	
12.1	30	
12.0	0	
11.9		150
11.8		120
11.7		90
11.6		60
11.5		30

AMMETERS

Ammeters measure current flow. Any good battery store carries suitable analog meters for about $20. The problem with reading current on them is that it can vary from 500 milliamps to 900 amps. This means that the meter must be multiple ranged or that you must use more than one meter. It is possible to use banana plugs and the multimeter to read amperage as well.

The values of total DC current output, except for the starter, are of interest. (The starter current, while large, is of little interest because it lasts for only a few seconds.) The normal daily DC current output is generally less than 30 amps, except for the current to the inverter, and can be monitored quite nicely with a single 30-amp-capacity meter. The inverter current output can be very large and as such should be monitored on its own separate meter.

The DC current input is also of interest—but unfortunately comes in different bulk quantities. The engine alternator supplies 50 to 150 amps, whereas the battery charger may supply 20 to 50 amps. Wind and water generators supply about 10 to 20 amps, and the solar panels supply 1 to 10. Trying to read the solar-panel input on an ammeter capable of reading the alternator input is foolish. It is true that total input is all that is important, but it is also true that much of the time the total input will be too small to be read accurately on a large-capacity meter.

I like to have a better handle on my incoming power. Since the meters are so cheap, I divide the incoming power into four of them: a 10-amp-capacity meter for the solar panels, a 20-amp-capacity for the wind and water generator, a 50-amp-capacity for the battery charger, and a 100-amp-capacity for the engine alternator.

AMP-HOUR METERS

Several specialty houses are marketing amp-hour meters, which monitor the total amp-hours to be used or supplied to the battery. As yet the market for this device is quite small, so it is expensive ($300 to $600). The information this gauge supplies is no more accurate than that of the voltmeter. It does give the actual input and output of amp-hours more precisely, but not the total amount available, which is referenced to some arbitrary number.

The sole purpose of the amp-hour meter is to indicate when the batteries need charging. Since the whole battery system is so fraught with inaccuracies, though, it seems to me that the precision and cost of this instrument is overkill. The DC voltage is a basic parameter that is always needed, and after a few weeks the no-load voltage will provide the same information. Unlike the ammeters, amp-hour meters provide little information on the health of your charging system or load system. The amp-hour meter is a good marketing ploy aimed at those who worry a lot, but in my opinion it's comparable to shooting cockroaches with a 155 howitzer.

SHORE POWER

The capacity of the shore-power circuit depends on two factors: the 120-volt equipment used aboard your boat and the outlets available in the marina. A few remote marinas provide only 15-amp circuits, but 90 percent provide at least 20-amp. About half of the marinas can handle 30 amps, but only the most modern are equipped to handle 50. So even if you size your boat for 50 amps, you may not be able to acquire that much power from the dock without multiple circuits. It is also worthwhile to mention here that not all marinas have been wired by experts. Therefore, an AC polarity indicator provides an important safeguard for any AC system.

Calculating your boat's 120-volt power needs are simpler than calculating its 12-volt power requirements, because the duration of use is unimportant and there are likely to be only a few items aboard that require 120-volt power. Table 10.4 lists a few of the more common ones. Most boats come with 30-amp circuits and, because of the marina situation, you may not wish to mess with upgrading.

TABLE 10.4

Resistance for Common 120-Volt Electrical Gear

Item	Amperage
Battery charger	3
Water heater	13
Electric heater	13
Blow dryer	13
Vacuum cleaner	6
Power tools	10
TV	3
Computer	3
Total	64

If you do wish to upgrade, determining the current draw of AC equipment is similar to the DC method except that you use 110 as the conversion factor instead of 11. Obviously, not all of this equipment will be operating at the same time. Still, it can be seen from this table that a 20-amp circuit is barely adequate; for a 30-amp circuit, some things will have to be turned off if others are being used. Aboard my own boat the hair dryer seems to be the biggest circuit blower. A blown circuit is not particularly annoying unless someone is working on the computer and has not saved recently; then some rather strong feelings are generated. Josh Slocum never had to deal with these kinds of problems.

ELECTRICAL APPLIANCES

All sorts of electrical appliances are finding their way onto boats, especially live-aboard boats, and since many live-aboards end up cruising, all of this equipment goes along. Now, it is true that equipment such as bread makers, mini microwave ovens, air conditioners, and apartment-size washers and dryers make shoreside living more enjoyable, and cruising is a lot of shoreside living. Nevertheless, your use of this equipment will be limited by the size of your boat, and to facilities where ample dockside power is available. If you intend to spend 70 to 80 percent of your time in these locations, then take it along. Otherwise leave it home; space is, again, always at a premium on board a cruising boat, and improperly stored equipment can become airborne at sea. The AC equipment aboard a cruising yacht should be limited to those items that use very little power and that take up very little space— small fans, power tools, small TV sets. Until Acme Fusion produces a pocket-size nuclear reactor, cruising boats will always be power poor.

Electronics

It is fitting to end this book with a section on electronics, for it is electronic technology that is responsible for the greatest change in cruising in the last five years—and will certainly continue to be responsible for large changes in the future. All the old guard still cry, "Keep it simple," meaning stay away from electronics; but tell me, which is simpler, shooting and reducing a sun shot or reading your position from a global-positioning system? If your GPS fails, turn on your backup GPS.

Electronic devices are here to stay, and generally speaking they are a lot more reliable than any mechanical device. As for the complexity of repairs, that is a myth. In most instances these days, all you need to do is plug in a new circuit board.

I am often asked what is the first piece of electronic equipment I would buy. The answer, for the average shorthanded cruiser, is simple: an autopilot. A day without your autopilot is like a day without sunshine.

AUTOPILOTS

Traditional cruisers use wind vanes rather than autopilots. The major differences between the two are that wind vanes use no electric power, and autopilots steer better downwind. A minor difference is that if the wind changes, a wind vane will continue to sail the boat—but off the desired course. An autopilot will steer the course you want regardless of wind changes. Such changes will, however, affect the set of the sail. Most of the time this alters the sound or motion of the boat, which in turn alerts the crew. Finally, autopilots can be used in confined and congested waters where wind vanes cannot.

Autopilots come in a variety of sizes. This is not a place to save a few bucks; get the best and strongest autopilot you can afford. The unit should have a stall torque rating above 25,000 inch-pounds. The cheaper and lighter units are okay for sheltered waters but not for open ocean work.

The units also come with a variety of features; at a minimum get one with a multiple loop processor and dead-band control. The former senses changes in helm response to current, leeway, and wave action; processes this information; and steers the boat on a better course using less power. The dead-band control allows you to adjust the sensitivity of the pilot. The larger the dead band, the farther your boat can stray off course before the pilot will correct it.

Waves often push your boat off course first in one direction, then the other. The result is that the boat makes a slight S-motion through the water—but its resulting course is straight. Opening up the dead band on the pilot stops it from making unnecessary course corrections. Other times—for example, in a following sea—it is necessary for the autopilot to sense motion changes in the boat quickly and respond at once, to keep the boat from broaching. My autopilot sensed these motions much more quickly than a human pilot would have and steered very well in following seas with the dead band shut down tight.

Wind sensors for autopilots sound useful, but in practice they turn out to be of little value. First, the sensor must be in clean air; the downwash from the sails is not what you want to steer by. Second, my experience with this attachment showed that the autopilot and the wind sensor are too sensitive to work well together. The sensor, of course, detects apparent wind direction, which changes with variation in the speed and direction of either the wind or the boat. And for me, one of these four variables seemed always to be changing. The little wind sensor dutifully followed the changes, and the autopilot obligingly sent our boat wandering all over the sea.

GLOBAL-POSITIONING SYSTEM

It is amazing how much navigation has changed in the last few years. It is also amazing how little experienced cruisers have sensed these changes. A book on passage making published in 1988 devoted almost 20 percent of its pages to celestial navigation. Nobody does that anymore. Well, almost nobody. About as many people still use celestial navigation as carry board pikes. Certainly you can do it if you feel a need to practice ancient rituals, but there is no need for it today, and I've met many successful cruisers who don't know which end of the sextant to look through.

Electronic navigation is faster, more accurate, and less bother. Most of the boats leaving the dock in the 1990s that are adequately funded will have a GPS aboard, and rightly so—if for no other reason than that GPS has an overboard button. When pushed, this records the boat's position, allowing you to return to within a few tens of feet of where a person was lost overboard.

The GPS will locate a boat anytime, anywhere, regardless of atmospheric conditions, to within the goalposts on a football field, or about 350 feet. That sort of accuracy is sufficient for almost any conceivable need, especially when compared to the 15,000-foot accuracy of the average celestial sight. GPS units also provide continuous over-the-bottom speed and course data and a wealth of other information not so important to cruisers. One incidental bit of information that is useful, however, is the very accurate time provided by the satellite.

These units are small and use little power. The bigger the display and the more bells and whistles, the more power, and since the unit may be left on 24 hours a day, a few tenths of an amp are important. Changing from 0.8 amp to 0.5 amp can save about 7 amps per day. For cruising, a portable unit should have a 12-volt power cord rather than just a battery charger, even if it is a 12-volt battery charger. There is a considerable loss of power going through a battery charger.

SAILING INSTRUMENTS

Good information is crucial to good decisions. A good set of sailing instruments provides the basic parameters you need to sail efficiently and safely. The package should contain at least one depth sounder, a boat-speed and distance-through-the-water indicator, and an apparent- and true-wind-speed and -direction indicator. Many feel that only racing enthusiasts need to know the true wind direction and speed, but getting the maximum from the boat's primary source of power is just as important to cruisers. Some of these units now have a module that will read engine data, such as temperature and oil pressure, as well. I find this a welcome trend.

The best units come with multiple modules that can provide this information at more than one location on the boat. I prefer to mount the unit designed for the navigation station in the captain's quarters, where I can check any strange noise or motion at night against the instrument data without moving from my bunk.

The forward end of the cockpit is also a handy place for depth and wind instruments, providing everyone seated there with vital information. I find it particularly handy because much of the time no one is at the helm; the autopilot is steering.

RADIOS

The VHF is commonly the first radio brought aboard a boat, probably because it is cheap and easy to use, but it does not get heavy use on board an ocean cruising boat. I do find it handy for avoiding collisions. Most large ships leave their VHF on while at sea. Any boat you can see you can call and, with a few sentences, assure yourself that it knows where you are and in what direction you're bound. (Incidentally, I've noticed that passing ships are much more inclined to answer a female voice on the radio than a male voice.)

I strongly recommend a ham radio for any cruiser. It will take you a little effort to get your license, but the radio is considerably more useful at sea. The marine mobile nets keep track of boats on passage, provide emergency assistance and weather information, and allows scheduled personal communication.

A great deal of the enjoyment of cruising comes from meeting people, and the ham radio gives you the opportunity to do so both over the airwaves and in person. And while one of the most difficult parts of cruising is leaving new friends, the radio lets you keep in contact with them and arrange rendezvous as your paths crisscross. Finally, good information about the ever-changing conditions of various cruising grounds can be relayed over the radio, allowing for a more enjoyable stay when you reach your destination.

The emergency position indicator radio beacons (EPIRBs) transmit on two internationally recognized frequencies to aircraft, satellites, and U.S. Coast Guard vessels. The signals and frequencies are designated for emergency use only, so when they are received a rescue operation gets under way immediately—*provided the unit has been registered*. A satellite can fix the position of the EPIRB within about 12 miles.

EPIRBs come in class A, class B, and 406 mhz. The 406-mhz EPIRB is the most expensive, but it's also the most likely to be monitored in the open ocean. These units are also more accurate, with an ability to locate a vessel within 2 to 3 miles. We can only hope that the international community will settle their differences and the class A and B will come to be monitored as well—and maybe the 406 units will come down in price, as the market enlarges.

RADAR

Now we've come to the not-necessary-but-pleasant-to-have category. The first such instrument is the radar. At first blush this seems to be an important piece of gear, but as your seamanship skills improve you will find less and less use for it. Certainly the all-seeing eye of radar is pleasant to have when you're approaching land at night or in the fog. Unfortunately, the all-seeing eye presently sees rather indistinctly. In critical situations, you need considerable concentration to determine the correct course of action.

If you decide you do need radar and your boat is small, evaluate a system on how close it can see, not how far. The heavy antennas and power draws of the larger and more powerful radar are not necessary for cruisers. Most power-poor cruisers use their radar only in critical situations. The most common is when getting into an anchorage or harbor under conditions of poor visibility, where radar's ½-mile range really pays off.

WEATHER FAX

Weather-fax information is sometimes pleasant to have, but it's only as good as the person interpreting the charts. I find weather faxes most useful when traveling from a bad-weather area into a good, because predicting the weather more than a few days in advance is difficult. For example, if you're leaving the Straits of Juan de Fuca for Hawaii, waiting in port for a favorable weather pattern will generally give you two or three days in which to sail 300 miles and duck considerable bad weather. However, leaving Hawaii for the Straits, the bad weather is two weeks away and impossible to predict with or without weather fax; you just have to take what comes.

There are a couple of types on the market. One is a stand-alone unit that receives and prints the charts automatically; the other is a modular unit that works off the ham radio. The latter consists of a radio modem that can unscramble fax transmissions, a computer, and a printer. Obviously this is not an economical or viable machine unless a ham radio, computer, and printer are already aboard; then the modem will provide you weather fax and other communication for a couple of hundred dollars.

STEREO AND TV

Certainly a stereo and TV are not necessary for cruising. However, they can increase your enjoyment—especially the stereo, since you can use tapes or CDs to provide music.

The car stereo business has provided a wide variety of 12-volt DC models from which to choose. The power requirements depend on the power of your speakers and the volume setting. Play quietly and conserve power, especially if you have outside speakers. Jensen makes an excellent outside speaker that can take considerable salt water and still keep functioning. We have had no trouble with our electronics—but considerable trouble with our tapes. Even though we kept them in a special storage container, they seem to have a very short life.

You might think that a TV would have little use on a small tropical island. Au contraire, mon capitaine; you can purchase copies of your favorite movies or, with a video camera on board, show your own personal videos. Once we spent an exciting afternoon surrounded by humpback whales; that evening while swinging on the hook, we fired up the inverter and watched the whole show over again while sipping good wine.

COMPUTERS

I am amazed at the number of computers I have found aboard cruising yachts, both full size and small laptops. The majority are used as word processors. Both Debby and I are computer literate and used ours continually. We kept our itinerary on a spreadsheet that allowed infinite variations and immediate updates. We also made use of some graphic and database applications. One database not suitable for the computer, however, is the boat's stores: We found that the location and quantity of food changed so rapidly that the pencil-based system works better than firing up the computer, booting the program, and opening the database just to eat a can of soup.

The locations of our boat parts and equipment was in our computer, though, and changed seldom enough that locating fan belts through the computer proved useful. Also, a data file on friends helped us keep track of who belonged to what boat.

If you are going to buy a computer, remember that you are buying it to use it. A cheap computer that doesn't get used is not really cheap.

What all this amounts to is that times change. Cruising today is done in a different world by different people than Eric and Susan Hiscock, Hal and Margaret Roth, or even

Lin and Larry Pardey. Those folks were surely the fastest guns in their day, but like the Old West, their day is gone forever. Those who don't recognize that fact are in for disappointment.

Appendix A: Ship's Articles

Or, How to Avoid Keel Hauling, Walking the Plank and other Traditions of the Sea.

Welcome aboard!

We are pleased you accepted our invitation to visit aboard the *Bird of Time*. Boats, at least our boat, are very small homes. There are, however, some distinct differences in customs and procedures that have developed between boat and house living. These differences, most of which seem to stem from the limited space on a boat, require a certain amount of adaptability, whether permanent or temporary. We will try to briefly cover some of the more important differences and the resulting ship policies in order to answer your questions and make your stay safer and more enjoyable. If you have further questions after reading these notes, please feel free to ask.

ARTICLE I: ENTERING

Stepping on board a yacht is much like entering someone's home. Just as you would not enter someone's home without knocking and waiting for permission to enter, neither should you step on board any yacht without permission to do so. It does not always have to be a formal request, but it is nice; you can still hear people in marinas rap on hulls to ask, "Permission to come aboard?"

ARTICLE II: SHOES

When given permission, be careful of what you wear as you step aboard. If you are just coming aboard for a social visit and do not have the proper shoes, remove the shoes you are wearing and step aboard in your stocking feet. Much of the deck surface on boats is a highly polished, varnished surface similar to a gymnasium floor. These surfaces are high maintenance and are easily damaged by steel insoles, nails, and high-heeled shoes. If you intend to do some sailing, then you must be well-prepared. Sailboats underway often have wet decks, which are often at odd angles to the horizontal. The sole of the deck shoe is designed to prevent you from becoming parallel to the odd deck angle and bruising some of your more tender body parts or, worse yet, immersing your entire body in liquids whose temperature is around 10 degrees centigrade. Unpleasant at best, fatal at worst.

Here is a list of acceptable shoes in order of preference: deck shoes, tennis shoes, basketball shoes, running shoes. One more thing before leaving footwear: If you have been walking along the beach or wharf where oil, grease, tar, and other such materials are present, please check the soles of your deck shoes so you do not track those substances aboard.

ARTICLE III: SMOKING

Because the captain and the significant crew are non-smokers, the "smoking lamp" will not be lit and we request that all smoking be done ashore.

ARTICLE IV: MARINE TOILETS

Now that you are aboard and have had a few beers or cocktails, you will need to familiarize yourself with one of the more diabolical devices ever devised by man: the marine toilet or, nautically speaking, "the head." It comes with various design nuances to frustrate and embarrass almost everyone. Please do not try to use one unless you are accompanied by a card-carrying crew member, have taken 20 minutes of intense instruction providing hands-on experience, and are willing to disassemble, unclog, and reassemble the entire apparatus if it malfunctions due to your malpractice. Remember, you can put anything into a marine toilet as long as you eat it first—with the exception of a very small amount of clinically approved toilet paper.

ARTICLE V: DUTY

Those of you who, by now, have decided that anything more than a few hours' stay is tantamount to admitting mental retardation need not read on. Those of you who are intent on spending 24 hours or more here can continue to read—that is, if you have the mental ability to do so.

Up to this point, there are three distinct social classes found on board: captain, guests, and crew. As a mere human, you have no chance of being classified in the former category.

The second group ceases to exist aboard this vessel once the mooring lines are cast off. That means that, at this point, you fall into the "crew" category. On the evolutionary scale, this species falls just below the cockroach but above the elementary flatworms. As a crew member, you have to do only what the captain, affectionately called the skipper, tells you to do. It is the skipper's kind belief that you will enjoy the trip more if you share the sailing of the boat as much as your limited skill allows, and that he will enjoy the trip more if you do your share of cleaning and cooking. The duty roster will be posted; please consult it frequently for what the skipper considers to be your fair share and report for duty on time. Duties will not be assigned according to gender. Mutiny is dealt with on this vessel as severely as maritime law allows. There are no maids or mommies on board; crew members are expected to be able to tell when they are thirsty, remember the location of the beer locker and get it themselves, and restock if they take the last one from the storage locker.

ARTICLE VI: PRIVACY

While cruising on board you will find four items to be in short supply: privacy, space, water, and electric power. The very confined space and thin walls allow very little privacy and a minimum of solitude. However, the foredeck, especially underway, effectively shuts out the rest of the world. One of the sleeping cabins can offer some isolation when the weather is bad and, in port, a stroll along the beach can get you away from people for a while. The main social areas on board are the cockpit and the main cabin. As the main cabin is sometimes also a sleeping area for crew members, a certain compromise is expected to be reached during those occasions. That is, those who sleep in the cabin cannot expect to go to bed early, and those who do not sleep in the cabin cannot expect to socialize until the wee hours. The very confined space is also a problem because of the aforementioned lack of mommies and maids. The small space and multiple bodies using the same space require a dedication to neatness not commonly found in most situations. The confusion of a sloppy cabin mixed with a choppy sea and a 40-degree angle of heel can quickly become not only hopeless squalor but also a downright dangerous critical mass of sliding and flying equipment. Besides all of that, the skipper has a distinct aversion to being up to his armpits in other people's cast-off clothing and equipment. If you take it out or off—put it away when you're finished! If you can't handle this, consider how long you can tread water.

ARTICLE VII: WATER

There is a maximum of 180 gallons of fresh water aboard. Running out of water can be very serious or even fatal. Water usage may require strict regulation but, generally, there is enough to provide for all you want to drink and cook with and all you need to wash. Need varies and is defined by the captain. That need is based upon the amount of water and the sweetness of the cabin atmosphere, but is generally the minimum necessary to get wet, turn the spout off, soap up, scrub, turn the water back on, and rinse. Hair washing is a luxury allowed only with direct permission of the captain, unless done with salt water. Complete showers happen only when you are capable of rising on the third day after your death, ascending to heaven 40 days later. Dishes are best washed and rinsed with salt water. A final, hot, freshwater rinse is allowed to scald the dishes. A saltwater foot pump is found at the kitchen "galley" sink. No limit is imposed on the amount of salt water you wish to use for washing.

ARTICLE VIII: ELECTRICITY

Electric power comes from shipboard batteries that are charged by various and mystical means at random and odd times. There is generally enough power to operate critical equipment and lights for cooking, cleaning, reading, or writing. However, please turn off all lights and equipment when not in use, as power is limited. If the battery power gets too low, critical equipment will not function and we will be without power until we can get one of the mystical methods to work and recharge the batteries, which may take several days.

ARTICLE IX: EQUIPMENT

The following discussion will outline the minimum equipment needed for the trip; the maximum is not a whole lot more as storage space is limited. The equipment should be packed in soft luggage such as a duffel bag, as rigid luggage takes up more storage space. Most commonly, shorts and T-shirts or jeans and sweaters/sweatshirts are the uniform of the day. Layered clothing is best, as the weather is changeable; even during constant weather, the temperature on board may change depending on the point of sail. Running with the wind from behind can effect bikini weather on board, while suddenly beating upwind will result in down-jacket weather. If there is an all-night sail, it can get very cold standing watch at 4:00 A.M. Heavy wool socks, long wool underwear, wool sweaters, hooded down jackets, warm gloves, and wool stocking caps are a good idea. Rain gear and boots, if necessary, will be provided by the boat. Getting a good fit, however, is not guaranteed. On occasion, moderately formal dress may be required for a decent meal ashore. You will also need a sleeping bag, a couple of sets of towels and washcloths, toiletries, two pairs of deck shoes, and sufficient socks and underwear to last between clothes washings—which may be done by hand in a bucket of seawater. Sunglasses are a necessity. A swimsuit, a camera, and a good book or two fall into the "nice to have" category. Please choose the non-oily variety of suntan lotion or sunblock and take care not to stain the woodwork or upholstered portions of the boat. Please get permission in advance from the captain to bring aboard any bulky equipment such as a guitar, diving gear, or fishing gear.

ARTICLE X: FISHING

A few words about fishing: Fishing aboard a sailboat is not all it might seem. The speed of the boat is controlled by the wind, which generally does not stay at proper trolling speed for more than a few minutes at a time. In addition, the boat's course is usually not through the best fishing waters. However, you are welcome to go for it underway whenever you believe conditions are right; of course unlimited jigging from the anchored boat is always available. Finally, if you do catch something, be aware that you can keep only what the crew can eat as there are no refrigeration facilities for preserving the catch.

ARTICLE XI: SEASICKNESS

For all those concerned about *mal de mer*, better known as seasickness, it is most often caused by the unaccustomed motion of the boat, which affects the inner ear and stomach. The risk of being adversely affected is greater if you are cold, apprehensive, or hungry. Keep something in your stomach, if possible, and keep warm. Lack of apprehension comes from confidence that the boat—and consequently you—are in no danger, especially in rough weather. Until you get the experience necessary to feel safe, you will have to rely on the captain's judgment. Watch him: If he appears calm, try to remain calm. If he appears panicked, then you can puke. If you find yourself getting queasy, get above deck, fix your eyes on the forward horizon, get the wind in your face, find the most comfortable position, and eat Saltines. Sometimes, sitting on deck just forward of the mast, where motion is minimal, or laying down in the cockpit works best. There are several drugs available that are worn on the wrist or behind the ear and supposedly are quite effective. I have no personal experience with their results, but I understand that they are better than Dramamine. Generally, if you start the trip using drugs, you have to stay on them. You will enjoy the trip more if you can avoid them altogether.

Signed this day _____

The honorable and lovable Donny Dodds, Captain _____

Lowlife Trainee Guest _____

Appendix B:
Work Breakdown Structure

This is a complete look at the work breakdown structure as referred to in chapter 4.

1. Preparation
    1.1 Planning
        1.1.1 Goals
        1.1.2 Strategy
        1.1.3 Work breakdown structure
        1.1.4 Schedule
        1.1.5 Budget
        1.1.6 Itinerary
    1.2 Training
        1.2.1 Basic Sailing Skills
        1.2.2 Advance Sailing Skills
        1.2.3 Seamanship Skills
        1.2.4 Bare Boat Chartering
        1.2.5 Ham Radio Training
        1.2.6 Maintenance and Repair
        1.2.7 Foreign Languages
    1.3 Shakedown Cruise
        1.3.1 Itinerary
        1.3.2 Outfit
        1.3.3 Modifications
    1.4 Final Preparation
        1.4.1 Close Down Shoreside Living
        1.4.2 Arrange Storage
        1.4.3 Arrange for Mail
        1.4.4 Arrange Finances and Banking
        1.4.5 Arrange Communications Links
        1.4.6 Dispose of Car
        1.4.7 Arrange Send-off Celebration
2. Equipment
    2.1 Boat
        2.1.1 Determine Whether to Build or Buy
        2.1.2 Determine Kind of Boat

2.1.2.1 Assess Comfort Requirements
    2.1.2.1.1 Seakindliness
    2.1.2.1.2 Living Space
    2.1.2.1.3 Storage Space
    2.1.2.1.4 Light and Air
    2.1.2.1.5 Performance
2.1.2.2 Assess Safety Requirements
    2.1.2.2.1 Seaworthiness
    2.1.2.2.2 Stability
    2.1.2.2.3 Strength of Hull
    2.1.2.2.4 Cockpit and Deck Layout
    2.1.2.2.5 Performance
2.1.2.3 Assess Cost Requirements
    2.1.2.3.1 Initial Cost
    2.1.2.3.2 Maintenance Cost
    2.1.2.3.3 Fitting Out Cost
    2.1.2.3.4 Modifications Cost
2.1.2.4 Assess Individual Needs
    2.1.2.4.1 Physical Fitness
    2.1.2.4.2 Itinerary
    2.1.2.4.3 Patience
    2.1.2.4.4 Space
2.1.3 Acquire Boat
  2.1.3.1 New
    2.1.3.1.1 One Off
      2.1.3.1.1.1 Select Designer
      2.1.3.1.1.2 Approve Preliminary Design
      2.1.3.1.1.3 Select Builder
        2.1.3.1.1.3.1 Foreign
        2.1.3.1.1.3.2 Domestic
      2.1.3.1.1.4 Approve Final Design
      2.1.3.1.1.5 Inspect Construction
      2.1.3.1.1.6 Approve Change Orders
      2.1.3.1.1.7 Prepare Punch List
      2.1.3.1.1.8 Accept Boat
      2.1.3.1.1.9 Launch Boat
    2.1.3.1.2 Production
      2.1.3.1.2.1 Select Suitable Models
      2.1.3.1.2.2 Inspect Construction

2.1.3.1.2.3 Approve Change Orders

2.1.3.1.2.4 Prepare Punch List

2.1.3.1.2.5 Accept Boat

2.1.3.1.2.6 Launch Boat

2.1.3.2 Used

    2.1.3.2.1 Research Buying Areas

        2.1.3.2.1.1 Local

        2.1.3.2.1.2 Distant

    2.1.3.2.2 Select Suitable Models

    2.1.3.2.3 Inspect Candidate Boats

        2.1.3.2.3.1 One Off

            2.1.3.2.3.1.1 Research Designer

            2.1.3.2.3.1.2 Research Builder

            2.1.3.2.3.1.3 Get Boat Specs

            2.1.3.2.3.1.4 Marine Survey

        2.1.3.2.3.2 Production

            2.1.3.2.3.2.1 Get Boat Specs

            2.1.3.2.3.2.2 Marine Survey

    2.1.3.2.4 List Boats in Order of Preference

    2.1.3.2.5 Negotiate With Sellers

    2.1.3.2.6 Take Possession

2.2 Outfit

  2.2.1 Internal Equipment

    2.2.1.1 Mechanical

        2.2.1.1.1 Engine

        2.2.1.1.2 Generator

        2.2.1.1.3 Windlass

    2.2.1.2 Electrical

        2.2.1.2.1 Direct Current

            2.2.1.2.1.1 Refrigeration

            2.2.1.2.1.2 Bilge Pumps

            2.2.1.2.1.3 Water Pump

            2.2.1.2.1.4 Generation

                2.2.1.2.1.4.1 Solar Panels

                2.2.1.2.1.4.2 Wind Generator

                2.2.1.2.1.4.3 Water Generator

                2.2.1.2.1.4.4 Engine Generator

                2.2.1.2.1.4.5 Stand-alone Generator

    2.2.1.2.2 Alternating Current

2.2.4 Sails
     2.2.4.1 Genoa
     2.2.4.2 Storm Sails
     2.2.4.3 Spinnaker
2.2.5 Deck Layout
     2.2.5.1 Winches
     2.2.5.2 Sheet Stoppers
     2.2.5.3 Tackle
     2.2.5.4 Anchors
3. Financing
  3.1 Savings Plan
  3.2 Cash Flow Projections

Works Cited

Anderson, Romola and R. C. *The Sailing Ship: Six Thousand Years of History.* New York: Bonanza, 1963.

Baader, Juan. *The Sailing Yacht.* New York: W. W. Norton, 1974.

Beiser, Arthur. *The Proper Yacht.* Camden, Maine: International Marine, 1978.

Bowditch, Nathaniel. *American Practical Navigation.* Washington, D.C.: Defense Mapping Agency, 1984.

Brewer, Ted. *Ted Brewer Explains Sailboat Design.* Camden, Maine: International Marine, 1985.

Briggs, Jeffrey. "Cruisers Talk Cruising," *48 North,* January 1994.

Bruce, Errol. *This Is Rough Weather Cruising.* Boston: Sail Books, 1980.

Campbell, Stafford. *Passage Making.* New York: Dodd, Mead, 1988.

Carkhuff, Vicki. "Seeing New Places but Always at Home," *Sail,* January 1984.

Carleton, Michael. Introduction to *The Ocean Sailing Yacht,* by Donald Street, vol. 1. New York: W. W. Norton, 1973.

Casey, Don and Lew Hackler. *Sensible Cruising: The Thoreau Approach.* Camden, Maine: International Marine, 1986.

Chapman, Charles F. *Piloting, Seamanship, and Small Boat Handling.* New York: Hearst, 1991.

Clarendon, Joanne. "The Cost of Cruising," *Yachting,* April 1983.

Claughton, A. and P. Handley. "An Investigation into the Stability of Sailing Yachts in Large Breaking Waves," *Southampton University Report,* January 1984.

Cloughley, Maurice. *A World to the West.* New York: David McKay, 1979.

Coles, Adlard K. *Heavy Weather Sailing.* Tuckahoe, N.Y.: John de Graff, 1979.

Cornell, Jimmy. *World Cruising Survey.* Camden, Maine: International Marine, 1989.

De Roos, Willy. *Northwest Passage.* Camden, Maine: International Marine, 1979.

Dodds, Don. *Modern Seamanship.* New York: Lyons and Burford, 1995.

Dvorak, Ed. Untitled editorial, *Practical Sailor,* October 1980.

Francis, Clare. *Woman Alone.* New York: David McKay, 1977.

Griffith, Bob. *Blue Water.* Unity, Maine: North Press, 1979.

Gufstafson, Charles. *How to Buy the Best Sailboat.* New York: Hearst Marine Books, 1985.

Haggard, E. A. *Isolation and Personality.* London: Worchel & Byrne, 1964.

Hamburg, D. A. *Society, Stress and Disease.* New York: Oxford, 1971.

Haythron, W. A. "Program of Isolation and Confinement," *Naval Research Reviews:* 1–8 December 1967.

Hollander, Neil and Harold Mertes. "The Successful Castaways," *Nautical Quarterly,* Summer 1988.

Kinney, Francis S. *Skene's Elements of Yacht Design,* 4th ed. New York: Dodd, Mead, 1973.

Kissling, Mark. *Writers Market.* Cincinnati, Ohio: Writers Digest Books, 1992.

Knox-Johnston, Robin. *Seamanship.* New York: W. W. Norton, 1987.

Lane, Carl D. *The Boatman's Manual.* New York: W. W. Norton, 1979.

Lapworth, William C. *Offshore Yachts.* New York: W. W. Norton, 1987.

Lawick-Goodall, J. V. "My Friends the Wild Chimpanzees," *National Geographic,* August 1967.

"Living Aboard in the Northwest," *Northwest Sailor,* October 1987.

Marchaj, C. A. *Aero-Hydrodynamics of Sailing.* New York: Dodd, Mead, 1980.

———. *Sailing Theory and Practice.* New York: Dodd, Mead, 1964.

———. *Seaworthiness: The Forgotten Factor.* Camden, Maine: International Marine, 1986.

Markov, Walter and Heinz Helmert. *Battles of World History.* New York: Hippocrene Books, 1979.

Marshal, John. "Shaping up the Main," *The Best of Sail Trim.* Boston: Sail Books, 1975.

Moeller, Jan and Bill. *Living Aboard.* Camden, Maine: International Marine, 1977.

Moesly, Sue. "Tips for Long-Range Cruising," *Yachting,* September 1982.

Pardey, Lin and Larry. *The Capable Cruiser,* New York: W. W. Norton, 1987.

———. "The Ultimate Gear Test," *Sail,* June 1983.

Parker, David M. *Ocean Voyaging.* Tuckahoe, N.Y.: John de Graff, 1975.

Payson, Herb. *Blown Away.* Boston: Sail Books, 1980.

———. "Guns on Yachts: Peril, Placebo, or Panacea," *Sail,* July 1984.

Phillips-Britt, Douglas. Sailing Yacht Design, Santa Rosa, Calif.: Adlard Coles, 1976.

Rasmuessen, John E. *Man in Isolation and Confinement.* Hawthorne, N.Y.: Aldine Publishing Co., 1973.

Ross, Wallace. *Sail Power.* New York: Knopf, 1975.

Roth, Charles. *The Sky Observer's Guidebook*. New York: Prentice-Hall, 1986.

Roth, Hal. "After 25,000 Miles. Part XXI: What Does It Cost?" *Yachting*, April 1973.

————. *After 50,000 Miles*. New York: W. W. Norton, 1977.

Rousmaniere, John, ed. *Offshore Yachts*. New York: W. W. Norton, 1987.

Rousmaniere, John. *The Sailing Lifestyle*. New York: Simon and Schuster, 1988.

Rubin, Steve. "Myths that Go Bump in the Night," *Sail*, September 1982.

Russell, Bill and Alma. "What It Costs to Cruise Away," *Sail*, March 1982.

Schlaifer, Robert. *Analysis of Decisions under Uncertainty*. Melbourne, Fla.: Krieger, 1978.

Scott, Annis Pepion. "Chancing the 'Big One'," *Cruising World*, March 1986.

Slocum, Joshua. *Sailing Around the World Alone*. Mineola, N.Y.: Dover Books, 1956.

Smeeton, Miles. *Once Is Enough*. New York: Oxford, 1985.

Stadler, Michael. *Psychology of Sailing*. Camden, Maine: International Marine, 1987.

Street, Donald. *The Ocean Sailing Yacht*, vol. 1. New York: W. W. Norton, 1973.

Street, Donald, ed. *The Best of Sail Trim*. New York: W. W. Norton, 1975.

Tomalin, Nicholas and Ron Hall. *The Strange Last Voyage of Donald Crowhurst*. New York: Stein and Day, 1970.

U. S. Department of Transportation. "Federal Requirements and Safe Tips for Recreational Boaters," Washington, D.C.: U.S. Department of Transportation, 1992.

Van Doren, William G. *Oceanography and Seamanship*. New York: Dodd, Mead, 1974.

Vito, Dumas. *Alone through the Roaring Forties*. Santa Rosa, Calif.: Adlard Coles, 1960.

Vogt, Richard J. *Altering Course*. Camden, Maine: Sail Books, 1978.

Ward, Ted. *Living Overseas*. New York: Free Press, 1984.

Wareham, L. "Voyage of a Lifetime," *Yachting*, August 1992.

Warren, Quentin. "The Carbon Alternative," *Cruising World*, June 1992.

Whelen, Townsend and Bradford Angier. *On Your Own in the Wilderness*. Mechanicsburg, Pa.: Stackpole, 1963.

Zadig, Ernest A. *The Complete Book of Boating*. New York: Prentice Hall, 1972.

Zuckerman et al. "Sensory Deprivation versus Sensory Variation," *Journal of Abnormal Psychology*, 1970.

Index